Latifundium

LATIFUNDIUM
Moral Economy and Material Life in a European Periphery

Marta Petrusewicz

Translated by Judith C. Green

Ann Arbor
THE UNIVERSITY OF MICHIGAN PRESS

Originally published as *Latifondo*
Copyright © 1989 Marsilio Editori, Venice

English translation copyright © by the University of Michigan 1996
All rights reserved
Published in the United States of America by
The University of Michigan Press
· Manufactured in the United States of America
♾ Printed on acid-free paper

1999   1998   1997   1996   4   3   2   1

A CIP catalog record for this book is available from the British Library.

Library of Congress Cataloging-in-Publication Data

Petrusewicz, Marta, 1948–
  [Latifondo. English]
  Latifundium : moral economy and material life in a European
periphery / Marta Petrusewicz ; translated by Judith C. Green.
      p.   cm.
  Includes bibliographical references and index.
  ISBN 0-472-10342-3 (hardcover : alk. paper)
  1. Latifundio—Italy—Calabria—History—19th century.   I. Title.
HD1329.I8P4813   1996
306'.0945'709034—dc20   95-52357
                                                                    CIP

To Witold Kula

Contents

Tables

Figures

Archives and Statistical Sources (not always cited specifically)

Annuario della Stampa Italiana, Milan, 1895.

Annuario Statistico Italiano.

Atti della Giunta per la inchiesta agraria e sulle condizioni della classe agricola (Jacini report), Rome, 1883.

Bollettino delle leggi del Regno di Napoli, Naples, 1807–15.

Bollettino of the Lower Calabria Economic Society.

Bollettino of the Upper Calabria Economic Society, or Royal Society of Economics, Province of Cosenza.

Collezione celerifera delle leggi, decreti, circolari e manifesti, Turin, 1822–70.

Collezione delle leggi ed atti del governo del Regno d'Italia, Naples, 1861 et seq.

Collezione delle leggi e decreti reali del Regno delle Due Sicilie, Naples, 1815–60.

Dizionario delle leggi del Regno di Napoli.

Dizionario universale economico-rustico, 15 vols., Milan, 1776.

Inchiesta parlamentare sulle condizioni dei contadini nelle provincie meridionali e nella Sicilia (Nitti investigation), Rome, 1909.

Proceedings of the Chamber of Deputies of the Kingdom of Italy.

Proceedings of the Royal Institute for Promotion.

Proceedings of the Senate of the Kingdom of Italy.

Sommario di statistiche storiche dell'Italia, 1861–1965, Rome, Central Institute of Statistics (ISTAT), 1968.

Sommario di statistiche storiche italiane, 1861–1955, Rome, ISTAT, 1958.

State Archives, Catanzaro (SACZ): notary records, property register, Grand Criminal Court records.

State Archives, Cosenza (SACS): Sila collection, notary records, Upper Calabria Civil Court records.

Statistiche sul Mezzogiorno d'Italia 1861–1953, Rome, Agency for the Development of Southern Italy, 1954.

Weights and Measures

Grain: 1 *tomolo* = 1.43/1.83 bushels (= 2 *mezzette* = 4 *quarte* = 24 *misure*); 1 cart = 3,960 pounds; 1 *cantajo* = 2.2 *tomoli*.

Olive oil: 1 *salma* = 319/330 pounds (= 16 *staja* = 160 *rotoli*); 1 *rotolo* = .95 quarts; 1 *salma* = 38 gallons; 1 *militro* = 7.8 pounds.

Wine: 1 cask = 122.6/129.7 gallons (= 12 barrels = 720 decanters).

Cheese: 1 *cantajo* = 195.8 pounds (= 61 to 64 rounds).

Meat: 1 *cantajo* = 196/199.7 pounds (= 100 *rotoli*); 1 *libbra* = .7 pounds; 1 *salma* = 324 pounds.

Coins: 1 *ducat* = 4.24 *lire* (= 10 *carlini* = 100 *grani* = 1,200 *cavalli*); 1 *oncia* = 6 *ducats* = 30 *tari*.

Yarn: 1 *pisa* = 8.8 pounds (= 5 *rotoli*).

Length: 1 *canna* = 6.9/8.5 feet.

Area: 1 *tomolata* = .84 acres (1.013 in the Sila region) (= 58,800 square *palmi*); 1 *versura* = 3 *tomolate;* 1 *moggio/a* = .82/.96 acres.

Acknowledgments

I have been working on this study for many—perhaps too many—years; it has traveled with me to numerous academic institutions in various countries, and it has indebted me to a great many people. Space does not permit me to thank all of them here, but I am most grateful to everyone who helped and supported me.

I must thank Maurizio and Mirella Barracco first of all, not only for allowing me to use their splendid archives but for the friendship they showed me over the years. I am beholden to Gustavo Valente for first bringing to my attention the copious Barracco Archives in Isola di Capo Rizzuto. The Luigi Einaudi Foundation, the Italian National Research Council, the American Council for Learned Societies, the Mellon Foundation, the National Humanities Center, Princeton University, and the University of Calabria offered me precious financial and logistical support without which this work could not have been completed. I am most obliged to the staffs of the Cosenza City Library, the Widener Library in Cambridge, Princeton's Firestone Library, the National Humanities Center's library service, and the State Archives in Naples, Catanzaro, and Cosenza, particularly to the late director of the Cosenza Archives, Dr. Michelangelo Baldassare, for their expert and patient help. Marla Stone, Giuliano Caldo, and especially Mark Laurenzi assisted me with the research and processing of quantitative data. I am most grateful to Carlo Poni, David Landes, and Immanuel Wallerstein for their guidance, support, and criticism. Claudio Rotelli has been a faithful friend as well as teacher. Marina Beer, Adrian Lyttelton, Augusto Placanica, and Louise Tilly were the first to read my manuscript, and I hope they recognize the impact of their criticism and suggestions in the final version. I also hope that Franco Piperno recognizes his own imprint in it. The inadequacies of this study are my own responsibility.

I must also thank Piero Moretti, Maurice Aymard, Arno Mayer, Giovanni Arrighi, Giovanni Sole, Piero Gagliardo, Rodolfo Ajello, and Agostino Tarsitano, friends and colleagues who gave me the benefit of their expertise and critical spirit. Lastly, thanks to Ornella Mastrobuoni, Jan Opdyke, and Nancy

Vlahakis for their intelligent editing, respectively, of the Italian and the American version.

This work is dedicated to Witold Kula, my first, and unforgettable, teacher.

Latifundium

Fig. 1. The Barracco latifondo

Introduction

Latifundia Italiam perdidere. Held to express the irrefutable verdict of history, and in currency since the time of the decline of the Roman Empire, this dictum became emblematic of Italy's "Southern Question" toward the end of the nineteenth century. The phenomenon of *latifondismo* came then to be identified with the social, economic, and cultural backwardness of the South—the breeding ground for reactionary forces, "contemporary barbarian Italy," in the words of Alfredo Niceforo.[1] In a 1902 article significantly entitled "War against the Latifondo," Gaetano Salvemini wrote that "inherent in the problem of the latifondo is . . . the whole Southern problem, . . . [and] all of the factors that . . . could lead to a great resurgence of reactionary forces."[2] The areas "infested by the latifondo," he continued, were ipso facto afflicted by all conceivable ills.[3] The latifondo in all of its aspects stood indicted. As a form of land tenure, latifondismo was "pathological." Held responsible for environmental devastation, desertification, and malaria, the latifondo was described as "a vast expanse of virgin lands belonging to a single individual who, by virtue of indolence, leaves them untilled."[4] As an agricultural system, latifondismo was

---

1. Niceforo maintained that Italy was anthropologically divided into two peoples with different cultures, social lives, and moralities: the modern Italy of the North and the socially backward Italy of the South. See *Italia barbara contemporanea* (Palermo, 1898), particularly 9–11. According to O. Dito, the latifondo came to dominate Calabria's agrarian structure in the tenth century due to the decline of agriculture following the increase in swampland and the scarcity of labor ("La Calabria nel passato," *La Giovane Calabria,* June 12, 1917).

2. In *Avanti!* December 13, 1902; reprinted in G. Salvemini, *Movimento socialista e questione meridionale,* ed. G. Arfé (Milan, 1963), 237.

3. Regions infested "by malaria and by the arrogance of the barons and the knights" (G. Salvemini, "La questione meridionale," *Educazione politica,* December 25, 1898; reprinted in *Movimento socialista . . . ,* 73 and passim).

4. F. Chessa, *La produzione agraria e le forme di gestione della proprietà fondiaria* (Turin, 1940–48) 195–99. A century earlier, Sismondo de Sismondi spoke of the latifondo as a collection of immense vacant lands "not cheered by the presence of a house, or of a dweller born and bred

deemed by Salvemini "unvaried and regressive," inefficient and monocultural. As a social system, it was identified with the most mindless and reactionary injustices, with "customs and privileges inherited from the distant past," and with the solitude, poverty, and ignorance of the peasantry. The *latifondisti* were judged greedy, violent, arrogant, and absentee landowners—heirs to and standard bearers of a feudal past. Culturally and structurally hostile to innovation of any kind, they were interested only in perpetuating their unbridled dominion, or at least a decisive political influence. The latifondo and latifondismo were thought to be at once the cause and the most dire symptom of the malady of the South.

The ethical-political origins of the "war against the latifondo" are readily identifiable. Southern agriculture had been particularly violently affected by the general crisis at the end of the nineteenth century, which caused its decline and resulted in several decades of emigration. Latifondism had reacted to the crisis by reorganizing along the lines of predatory capitalism, which resulted in social polarization and class antagonism, the exploitation and policing of hired farm labor, specialization tending toward monoculture, under-use of productive capacity, and the effective impoverishment of the physical and social environment. Nevertheless, the historical judgment passed by partisans of the "war against the latifondo" ultimately condemned to oblivion those original characteristics of southern latifondismo that were in evidence in the period from the decade of Napoleonic monarchy to the Great Depression. This omission is likewise felt throughout the historiography of Southern Italy. To date, few structural analyses of the great estates have been put forth that emphasize their internal coherence, stable economic performance, penetration of the world market, or their capacity to survive well into the twentieth century.[5] Indeed, the numerous existing monographs timidly refrain from generalization.[6] Moreover,

---

there, or of any sign of people's love for their native soil; in short, not gladdened by man's works" (*Studi intorno all'economia politica* [Capolago, 1840], pt. 2, 374). Leopoldo Franchetti, too, spoke of the "cheerless aspect" of the immense *latifondi* and the terrible state to which they had reduced agriculture (*Condizioni economiche ed amministrative delle province napoletane* [Florence, 1875], 72–78). For Domenico Demarco, the latifondo, though indispensable, was the main obstacle to progress ("La borghesia fondiaria del Regno di Napoli nel secolo XIX: le origini, i problemi," *Rassegna Storica del Risorgimento,* 38 [1951]; and *Il crollo del Regno delle Due Sicilie* [Naples, 1960]).

5. Cf. M. Aymard, "L'Europe moderne: féodalité ou féodalités," *Annales E.S.C.* 36, no. 3 (1981): 426–35; Aymard, "Strutture delle aziende e studio della produzione e della produttività agricola in Italia meridionale nell'età moderna: prospettive di ricerca," in *Problemi di storia delle campagne meridionali nell'età moderna e contemporanea,* ed. A. Massafra (Bari, 1981), 17–24; and J. Kochanowicz, "Historia wsi włoskiego południa," *Przegląd Historyczny* 75, no. 1 (1984): 119–25.

6. Agrarian historiography has so far preferred to study large estates (partly because more source material is available on them), even at the expense of the study of the peasant economy. See, for example, G. Pescosolido, *Terra e nobiltà: I Borghese (secoli XVIII e XIX)* (Rome, 1979) but

in keeping with the inclination, dear to Italian historiography, to posit 1860 as the great divide for all aspects of Italian civil life, the history of latifondismo has been neatly divided into two periods, the first confined to a feudal past and the second to a bastard capitalism generated by the "historical bloc."

Throughout the period from the French Revolution to the Great Depression, however, the great land properties and the complex of social systems adherent to them (like latifondismo, the plantations, *folwark,* and *ciftlik*) were at the crux of the so-called agrarian question. Nearly all of the agricultural products for the world market were, in fact, provided by the great estates— usually under direct management, often specialized in their output, and capable of accommodating profit and market logic.[7] Peasant economy was marginalized everywhere except in the hinterlands of the large industrial cities. The physiocratic notion that held that the wealth of nations depended on communities of yeoman farmers (although both Turgot and Quesnay had already emphasized the economic advantages of large-scale capitalist agriculture) had triumphed in the French Revolution (as well as in the American) although it was, at the same time, undone. The political and judicial conditions, created by the French Revolution and by the market opportunities that opened up with the economic expansionism that was spread throughout Europe by the "passive revolutions" and Napoleon's armies, were more favorable to the great agrarian concentrations than to the physiocratic farmstead. Considered a modern and rational form of agricultural enterprise, the great land estate reigned supreme.

It is not surprising, therefore, that nineteenth-century politicians, economists, and sociologists focused their attention on the great estates. The conviction that small-scale farming was uneconomic, wasteful, and destined to fade

---

also the fine studies by A. Sinisi ("Le aziende calabresi dei principi Serra di Gerace nella prima metà del XIX secolo") and M. L. Storchi on an estate belonging to the Doria d'Angri ("Un'azienda agricola della piana del Sele tra il 1842 ed il 1855"), both in Massafra, *Problemi di storia,* 91–116, and 117–39; and R. Ago, *Feudo esemplare: Immobilismo padronale e astuzia contadina nel Lazio del '700* (Fasano, 1988). M. A. Visceglia's study, "L'azienda signorile in Terra d'Otranto nell'età moderna" (ibid., 41–72), is exceptional among recent works for its breadth of generalization. Not that all the limitations of research can be explained by the "war against the latifondo." Piero Bevilacqua rightly attributes them to a sort of theoretical and historiographic "bloc" (despite the more than thirty years in which Braudel's liberating influence has been at work) as well as to the failure of Italian institutions to sponsor long-term research projects ("Agricoltura e storia delle campagne nel Mezzogiorno d'Italia," *Studi Storici* 23, no. 3 [July-September 1982]: 671–82).

7. The modes of labor control used on these large estates varied according to their location within the world system. In peripheral regions such as Russia, the American South, and southern Italy, they usually practiced extensive agriculture based on the cheap labor of slaves, serfs, or semiproletarian peasants. See I. Wallerstein, *The Modern World-System: Capitalist Agriculture and the Origins of the European World-Economy in the Sixteenth Century* (New York and London, 1974); and I. Wallerstein, *The Modern World-System II: Mercantilism and the Consolidation of the European World-Economy, 1600–1750,* (New York, 1980).

away, and that the peasants would soon transform themselves either into capitalists or, more likely, into wage laborers ran deep.[8] It was only after the crisis of the 1880s and 1890s had exposed the structural weakness of large-scale European agriculture, both noble and bourgeois, that scholars—as well as legislators and governments—began to reconsider the relative merits of the peasant economy, and question the rationality of a large-scale agrarian economy.[9] Even then, however, the notion of capitalist agriculture, rational by virtue of its scale, was by no means discarded. The line of reasoning that culminated in the perceptive defense of the rationality of the peasant model in Chayanov's *Theory of the Peasant Economy* prospered alongside that which was embodied in Kautsky's argument in favor of the great modern latifondi.[10]

In this context, the work at hand, which examines nineteenth-century latifondismo in Southern Italy as a rational and efficient system of production and a stable and livable form of social organization, is hardly isolated.[11] This

---

8. As Karl Marx put it, the "peasant who produces with his own means of production will either gradually be transformed into a small capitalist . . . or he will suffer the loss of his means of production . . . and be transformed into a wage-worker. This is the tendency in the form of society in which the capitalist mode of production predominates" (*Theories of Surplus Value* [London, 1951], 193–94).

9. In Russia, for example, this debate involved populists, revolutionary Marxists, and populist Marxists. In *The Development of Capitalism in Russia*, published in 1899 (the same year as Karl Kautsky's *The Agrarian Question*), Lenin argued that capitalist peasants—that is, owners of lands too large to be farmed by one family alone and therefore requiring the use of hired labor—were already a majority in Russia. On the debate Kautsky's book provoked in Germany and Western Europe, see A. Gerschenkron, *Bread and Democracy in Germany* (Berkeley, 1943). On the other hand, A. V. Chayanov's fundamental *The Theory of Peasant Economy* (Homewood, Ill., 1966; originally published in German in 1923, then in Russian in 1925) built on the fine work of a group of late-nineteenth-century Russian scholars who attempted to formulate a theory of the peasant economy, basing their studies on that outstanding source that consisted of the *zemstvo* statistics (it will be remembered that Marx learned Russian primarily in order to read these statistics). Most noteworthy among these scholars were the statistician A. I. Chuprov, who in 1904 gave a series of lectures in Paris at the Ecole Supérieure Russe des Sciences Sociales on the advantages of small-scale production (*Mel'koe zemledelie i ego osnovnye nuzhdy* [St. Petersburg, 1907]) and especially the economist V. A. Kosinskii, who worked in much greater depth on the theoretical problem of distinguishing the peasant and the capitalist economies (*K agrarnomu voprosu* [Odessa, 1906]). See also D. Thorner, *Chayanov's Concept of Peasant Economy* (Madison, 1986), XI-XXIII.

10. In *The Accumulation of Capital*, published in Berlin in 1913, Rosa Luxemburg speaks differently from Lenin of the economic peculiarity of the peasantry; neither capitalist entrepreneurs nor wage-earning proletarians, they were engaged in producing commodities but not in capitalist production.

11. Other scholars have already studied the effectiveness of such systems in peripheral areas of the world economy, especially outside Europe. See, for example, on the slave economy in the United States, R. W. Fogel and S. Engerman, *Time on the Cross* (Boston, 1974); on Spain, A. M. Bernal and J. F. de la Péna, "Formación de una gran propriedad agricola del siglo XIX," in *Agricultura, comercio colonial y crecimiento económico en la España contemporánea,* ed.

study attempts to bring to light the internal dynamics of a single large latifondo, that of the Barracco barons in Calabria. The resulting picture differs so vastly from that painted by Salvemini that it enables us to unveil nearly all of the commonplaces of the "war against the latifondo"—accusations of rigidity, uniformity, monocultural practices, and so forth—as prejudices. My analysis demonstrates, to the contrary, that the latifondo enterprise enjoyed a remarkable flexibility, which is manifested in the plurality of contractual associations, the variety of judicial institutions, a remarkable degree of crop diversification, and the coexistence and interdependence of production for direct consumption and for the market.[12] Far from being an indiscriminate agglomeration of underexploited lands, the latifondo was an organic and rational structure, the stability of which was guaranteed by two fundamental qualities: economic efficiency and social assuredness. Its golden age, during which it dominated Calabrian agricultural existence, preceded the birth of the "Southern Question" altogether. Indeed, the latter arose at precisely the time of the structural decline of the latifondo. What this study brings to light, in fact, is not the latifondo as such but the latifondist system that characterized southern agriculture when it still differed from—but was not necessarily inferior to—agriculture in the North.[13]

In what follows, no attempt has been made to construct a general model of latifondismo insofar as it is not possible, however strong the temptation may be, to draw general conclusions from a single case study.[14] This study consists of a reconstruction, by means of an analysis of a single actual latifondo, of the economic and social mechanisms that propelled latifondismo at the periphery

---

J. Nadal and G. Tortella (Barcelona, 1974), and P. Carrión, *Los latifundios en España: su importancia, origen, consecuencias y solución* (Barcelona, 1975); on Russia, S. Bensidou, "L'évolution des grands domaines en Russie de 1861 à 1902," *Revue du Nord* 54 (1972): 173–84; on Latin America, F. Chevalier, *La formation des grands domaines au Mexique* (Paris, 1952), W. Dean, "Latifundia and Land Policy in 19th Century Brazil," *Hispanic American Historical Review* 51, no. 4 (1971): 606–25, C. H. Harris, *The Sánchez-Navarros: A Socio-Economic Study of a Coahuilan Latifundio, 1846–1853* (Chicago, 1964), C. Wagley, "Plantation America: A Culture Sphere," in *Caribbean Studies: A Symposium,* ed. V. Rubin (Seattle, 1960), A. J. Bauer, "Chilean Rural Labor in the 19th Century," *American Historical Review* 76, no. 4 (1971): 1059–84, and M. Carmagnani, *Meccanismi della vita economica in una società coloniale: Il Cile 1680–1830;* and, with reference to various parts of the world, R. Dumont, *Economie agricole dans le monde* (Paris, 1954).

12. According to Maurice Aymard, it was precisely this variety of contractual arrangements and the plurality of modes of controlling labor that gave the southern agrarian system a notable degree of flexibility and adaptability. Cf. "L'Europe moderne," op. cit., 431; and "La transizione dal feudalismo al capitalismo," in *Storia d'Italia: Annali* (Turin, 1978), 1:1135–92, esp. 1187–92.

13. Cf. R. S. Eckhaus, "Il divario Nord-Sud nei primi decenni dell'Unità," in *La formazione dell'Italia industriale,* ed. A. Caracciolo (Bari, 1963); and the bibliography, 7ff.

14. As Edoardo Grendi rightly points out in "Sulla 'Teoria economica del sistema feudale' di Witold Kula," *Quaderni Storici* (Sept.-Dec. 1972): 753–54.

of the European capitalistic system—a heuristic representation of latifondismo as a specific system.

The Barracco estate cannot be taken as an average example of agricultural entrepreneurship in the South, or of latifondismo. As a matter of fact, not many landlords had the same characteristics as the Barraccos; their practice of direct management, to take just one instance, was by no means the rule on other great estates.[15] Nonetheless, their story is emblematic of that whole period. In the first place, there is the route traveled by the family itself: its ascent to the pinnacles of agrarian wealth, to marriage with the highest nobility of the realm, and to important political positions first at the provincial level, then at the Bourbon court, and later in the Italian Parliament. Second, their family history was part and parcel of the general history of southern Italian lands in the nineteenth century: the French conquest and the war in Calabria, the failed revolutions of the 1820s and 1840s, Italian unification and "grand brigandage," and finally the economic subordination of the South to the North after the 1887 protectionist turn. There is a quantitative consideration, too: the Barracco estate was the largest in Calabria; its social territorial influence stretched from the mountains to the hills and the coastal plain, encompassing cities and villages, and thus incorporated a host of ecological and cultural universes, different histories and traditions. The enterprise itself was exemplary— complex and diversified in both production and administration, with a whole mosaic of tenancy forms, a multiple-crop system, industrial production, and a great variety of farming techniques ranging from the archaic to the most modern and sophisticated, as well as a complex web of markets. The latifondo also constituted an all-inclusive but nonrepressive social universe, which incorporated preexistent relationships, customs, networks, and hierarchies of authority, and thereby succeeded in preserving social peace and perpetuating a peasant world converted to the wage system but not proletarianized. In addition, it vaunted a modern, ramified, efficient, and conscientious adminstration whose records offer the historian a uniquely rich and complete source comprising ledgers and demographic data; accounts of fairs and markets, lawsuits and trials; and business, political, and personal correspondence.

The Barracco case therefore allows for a remarkable opportunity to reconstruct the latifondo experience in its historical context and trace the development, through interaction, of its various aspects. Three questions are especially

---

15. In fact, the Sicilian latifondisti generally preferred to rent their lands to agents (*gabellotti*). The Apulians used both forms, while those of the Roman countryside, gradually moving to the city, were becoming the champions of absentee administration. On Apulia, see A. Lepre, *Feudi e masserie: Problemi della società meridionale nel '600 e nel '700* (Naples, 1974); and, more recently, F. M. Snowden, *Violence and Great Estates in the South of Italy: Apulia, 1900–1922* (Cambridge, 1988). On the Roman *Agro,* see the itinerary followed by the Borghese family in G. Pescosolido, *Terra e nobiltà,* op. cit.

worth exploring: the relationship between this system and its feudal and capitalist counterparts, its place in the transition from feudalism to capitalism, and, finally, the moral bases of its functioning.

As to the first question, it should be clear that latifondismo was not a feudal system in the sense in which that term is used with reference to medieval Europe. It was not a seignorial system or a "feudal society" such as that described by Marc Bloch: the laws passed in 1806 had abolished feudalism in the kingdom, depriving the barons of their judicial powers and their administrative and political prerogatives over persons and land. Nor does the latifondo embody the feudal mode of production described by Guy Bois, for it was not dominated by small-scale family production subject to seignorial obligations.[16] Its mode of production was not feudal in the Marxist sense either; although land was the principal means of production, labor relations were not based on extraeconomic constraints.[17] It does not fit the "Polish model," for it lacked corvées, servitude, and other obstacles to the geographical and social mobility of the workforce.[18] Nor was it manorialism, for its production was market- and profit-oriented.[19] Lastly, latifondismo differed from its own southern feudal predecessor in that the nobility no longer held jurisdiction and thus territorial control over the land, and the peasants were no longer tied to it.[20]

---

16. M. Bloch, *La société féodale* (Paris, 1939); G. Bois, *Crise du féodalisme* (Paris, 1976), 352–55; See also R. Coulborn, ed., *Feudalism in History* (Princeton, 1956).

17. See the discussion on the various interpretations of the term *feudalism* in M. Dobb, *Studies in the Development of Capitalism* (New York, 1947); and in Eric Hobsbawm's introduction to K. Marx, *Pre-capitalist Economic Formations* (New York, 1964).

18. W. Kula, *An Economic Theory of the Feudal System,* trans. L. Garner (London, 1976; originally published as *Teoria ekonomiczna ustroju feudalnego* [Warsaw, 1962]).

19. Witold Kula's model, characterized by the preeminence of large landed properties, the output of which was directed almost exclusively to the western markets, has proved extremely useful in analyzing the agrarian economy of southern Italy. See, for example, *Istituzioni, cultura e società in Italia e in Polonia,* ed. C. D. Fonseca (Lecce, 1979); and A. Lepre, "Discutendo di 'Sistema feudale': Feudi e masserie nel Seicento," *Quaderni Storici* (1972). J. Kochanowicz gives an excellent summary of the debate on Kula's theory in "Teoria ekonomiczna . . . W oczach krytykòw," in W. Kula, op. cit., 2d rev. ed. (Warsaw, 1983), 247–70.

20. Feudalism in southern Italy had always incorporated some unusual "nonfeudal" features, due to its relatively late cónsolidation in the thirteenth to fifteenth centuries. Maurice Aymard proposes a model of "southern" feudalism that is by and large valid for Sicily, parts of southern mainland Italy (especially Apulia), and western Andalusia. Market-oriented, diversified in its output, managed directly, and worked with wage labor, the great feudal estate benefitted precisely from its coexistence with a world of small sharecroppers who lacked any (or almost any) rights to their land and offered a practically unlimited supply of labor; hence, it had the advantage of both the mixed farming system and the absence of institutional barriers to the mobility of labor. ("Amministrazione feudale e trasformazioni strutturali tra '500 e '700," *Archivio Storico per la Sicilia Orientale* 81, no. 1 [1975]: 17–42; "L'Europe moderne," op. cit., particularly 432). In the eighteenth century, a combination of factors created strong pressure to reform this older mode of land tenure: the increase in population, the new market opportunities for high-priced commodities,

As to the second question, the rise of latifondismo was not equivalent to the transition from feudalism to capitalism.[21] A number of conditions—among them the abolition of feudal jurisdiction and the freeing (and commodification) of land—were prerequisite to the transformation of the feudal lords into great commercial landowners and of their fiefs into latifondi. These conditions were created only by the antifeudal legislation enacted by the French conquerors in 1806. Notwithstanding the limitations proper to any passive revolution, the law struck the death knell of feudalism in southern Italy and created conditions that would foster the process of original accumulation in agriculture and of its potential capitalistic development. These were the conditions in which the new latifondo grew. The Barraccos, attracted by the new markets that were opening up for farm produce and by the new opportunities for purchasing land, threw themselves into a formidable project of land concentration.[22] In four decades of feverish accumulation, they assembled their enormous estate by buying cheaply vast fiefs from debt-ridden ex-feudal landowners, immense tracts of expropriated Church lands, peasants' allotments, and mortgaged properties, and by encroaching on and enclosing common and state-owned lands.

Through this rapacious process of land concentration (i.e., privatization) and modernization, the Barraccos fulfilled the prerequisites for transition to the capitalist economy. There is no evidence, however, that these preconditions necessarily determined a further development in the direction of capitalism or that the people who achieved them were aiming at this kind of evolution. The end of feudalism did not signify an automatic transition to capitalism. In fact, the transformation of an agricultural society into a capitalist one—Karl Pol-

---

the decline in feudal rents, the growing difficulty of enforcing direct and indirect rights over persons, and the Bourbons' various attempts at reform (for instance, the Cassa Sacra).

21. See the classic controversy on this issue between M. Dobb and P. Sweezy, published in the 1950s with contributions from C. Hill, R. H. Hilton, H. K. Takahashi and others, in *Science and Society* 14, no. 2 (Spring 1950). This debate focused on the contraposition between the city and the country. In the 1970s, the argument was renewed with E. Laclau's article on "Feudalism and Capitalism in Latin America," *New Left Review* 67 (May-June 1971); and especially I. Wallerstein's publication in 1974 of *The Modern World-System*. See also R. Brenner, "Agrarian Class Structure and Economic Development in Pre-industrial Europe," *Past and Present* 70 (Feb. 1976); and the subsequent debate in the same journal, with comments by G. Bois, R. H. Hilton, E. Le Roy Ladurie, and M. M. Postan.

22. It will be recalled that these opportunities originated with the 1806 law abolishing feudalism, which freed former feudal, ecclesiastical, and state-owned lands and made them available for sale. With the decline of feudal rents and the difficulties of collecting them, the old landowning system's inability to take advantage of the new economic opportunities, and the Bourbons' attempts at reforms such as the Cassa Sacra, the conditions for a change of this kind had already ripened, but the fact that the break with tradition was imposed from the outside had a marked influence on the nature of land accumulation in the South. These are precisely the terms in which H. Donid put the matter in 1876 in his comparison of the abolition of feudalism in France, England, Germany, Spain, and Italy (*La révolution française et la feodalité* [Paris, 1876]).

anyi's "great transformation"—implies a whole series of further profound changes in economy and society. There must be a change in the motive of action on the part of society's members: the motive of gain must be substituted for that of subsistence. All transactions must be turned into money transactions, and the medium of exchange must be introduced into every articulation. All the factors of production (land, money, and above all labor) must be not only freed but transformed into commodities so that their societal being is completely severed from their natural and historical context and subordinated to the laws of the marketplace. As Polanyi observes, "normally the economic order is merely a function of the social, in which it is contained," but with the great transformation, "instead of economy being embedded in social relations, general social relations become embedded in the economic system."[23] Only a society thus transformed can be deemed truly capitalist.

As the history of the Barracco latifondo confirms, no such great transformation took place in southern Italy in the nineteenth century. The end of the fief made way for the new latifondo but did not imprint upon it a capitalist character. Landowners did not become bourgeois; their laborers did not become proletarians. The motive of gain remained subordinate to the pursuit of security and the preservation of status, titles, and "social capital"; though land, money, and labor were bought and sold on the market, they never became mere commodities but continued to perform a number of functions within the system, often without any market mediation. In other words, although latifondismo participated fully in the world market, its original features made it a specific system in its own right.[24]

In the first place, the latifondisti—the very agents of this agrarian entrepreneurship—were by origin and mentality neither feudal lords nor bourgeois. The fact that they built their fortunes in the first decades of the nineteenth century by buying disentailed land did not automatically transform them into bourgeois; still less did it bestow upon the bourgeoisie a "position of hegemony."[25] In Calabria, the middle classes had neither the opportunity nor

---

23. K. Polanyi, *The Great Transformation: The Political and Economic Origins of Our Time* (Boston, 1968), 71; K. Marx, *Capital,* vol. 1, chap. 26.

24. But, according to Immanuel Wallerstein, after the modern world system was consolidated, the "feudatories" of the periphery should be seen simply as heads of enterprises, acting perfectly legitimately within the dominant capitalist mode of production (*The Modern World System,* op. cit., passim). See also A. Gunder Frank, *Capitalism and Underdevelopment in Latin America,* op. cit. On the other hand, J. R. Mandle, though taking sides with Dobb and Laclau rather than Sweezy and Frank (and, presumably, Wallerstein) in the debate on the transition, believes that the socioeconomic periphery he himself studied—the plantation economy in the Western Hemisphere—cannot be classified as either feudal or capitalist and hence needs its own conceptualization. See "The Plantation Economy: An Essay in Definition," *Science and Society* 35, no. 1. (1972): 49–72.

25. The Calabrian bourgeoisie is often said to have conquered "a position of hegemony at a

the cultural capacity to conquer heqemony. The bourgeoisie had undergone, not fought, a revolution; the abolition of feudalism—a gift bestowed by a foreign conqueror—merely enabled it to strengthen its ownership of land. The people the French appointed to fill the political and administrative vacuum created by the withdrawal or removal of the highest-ranking Bourbon aristocrats came from the intermediate echelons of the nobility and the patrician class of the ancien régime, not from the middle classes.[26] In a region so little accustomed to institutional politics, they were the only ones with any experience of power at the municipal and provincial levels—levels important enough to make their co-optation desirable for the French but not so important as to make it dangerous. This ambitious and rather unscrupulous social stratum helped King Joachim Murat consolidate his power and endorsed his reforms, receiving in exchange the go-ahead for land acquisition; with the Restoration, it reverted its allegiance to the Bourbons and strengthened its social position still further. The Barraccos were almost an ideal-typical example of this class.[27] A patrician family of ancient origin but with a modern structure,

---

time when the feudal class was on the wane and ready to merge with the landed bourgeoisie" (A. Placanica, *Alle origini dell'egemonia borghese in Calabria* (Salerno and Catanzaro, 1979) 10. Many historians date this supposed triumph of the Calabrian bourgeoisie from the French reign and the economic ruin and decline of the baronage. "In Calabria, the bourgeoisie was the main, if not the only, protagonist in the purchases of disentailed land" (G. Brasacchio, *Storia economica della Calabria* [Chiaravalle, 1986], 3:103, but other scholars share this opinion). This dominion over the land after the abolition of feudalism is supposed to have given the bourgeoisie a position of hegemony in Calabrian society. Yet the figure of 268 bourgeois purchasers of disentailed land cited by both Placanica (op. cit.) and P. Villani (*La vendita dei beni dello stato nel Regno di Napoli, 1806–1815* [Milan, 1964]) is hardly impressive. Curiously enough, these same scholars reproach this bourgeoisie for its subservience to the old feudal and semifeudal conventions during the Risorgimento period and for its inability to achieve cultural hegemony (see Placanica, op. cit., passim; D. Demarco, *Il crollo*, op. cit., 5 and passim; U. Caldora, *Calabria Napoleonica, 1806–1815,* (Naples, 1960), 210–13 and passim; and F. P. Cerase, *Sotto il dominio dei borghesi* [Assisi and Rome, 1975]). To the contrary, Pasquale Villani rightly points out that the southern bourgeoisie, which was born and bred in the shadow of the fiefs and had the benefit of the feudal heritage without having had to fight for it, was prevented by its very origin from becoming a truly hegemonic class (*Feudalità, riforme, capitalismo agrario* [Bari, 1968], 135–48). The fundamental study of the way the passive revolution affected class initiative remains V. Cuoco's *Saggio storico sulla Rivoluzione Napoletana del 1799* (Bari, 1929). See also E. Sereni, *Capitalismo e mercato nazionale* (Rome, 1974), esp. 119–48.

26. In this case, class boundaries inevitably remain fluid, but the new notables' earlier history and social position do not justify including them generically in a "third estate," as does F. Assante, for one, in her generally excellent comparative study of Calabrian landownership before and after the Napoleonic era (*Proprietà fondiaria e classi rurali in un comune della Calabria, 1740–1886* [Naples, 1964]).

27. A similar example is that of Giuseppe Compagna, another great latifondista whom Caldora considers "the most interesting case of bourgeois fortune in the first thirty years of the 19th century" (*Calabria Napoleonica,* op. cit., 210–13), and Raul Merzario presents as an example of a Calabrian *gabellotto* (*Signori e contadini di Calabria: Corigliano Calabro dal XVI al XIX secolo*

urbanized but with ever-keen agrarian ambitions, educated and accustomed to political roles and administrative functions, the Barraccos were ideal allies for the Napoleonic regime. The immense fortune they so rapidly amassed by virtue of their services to the French was managed according to a modern mentality and the principles of political economy. In their social behavior, however, the Barraccos still followed a traditional pattern, seeking to construct for themselves an aristocratic identity by means of specific marriage strategies and the acquisition of titles and positions at court. This conjunction between modernity in economic matters and traditionalism in social matters was precisely the Barraccos' *differentia specifica*.

The latifondo inserted itself in the preexisting social territory by preserving and incorporating practically all of the preexisting economic, social, and cultural structure.[28] In effect, this was a highly rational choice, as it avoided the heavy social and financial costs that any thoroughgoing attempt at transformation would have entailed and capitalized on the existing social organization and know-how. Unlike the plantation economy that developed on the so-called empty lands, the Calabrian latifondo penetrated a territory that already had a fairly dense population and its own traditions, know-how, and social relations.[29] The latifondo was therefore superimposed on the territory as a principle of *reorganization,* not organization, and became a predominant presence. Its owner was the region's greatest proprietor, the major, if not the sole, employer, the person to turn to for needs and requests not strictly pertaining to the employment relationship, the holder of an effective monopoly of force, the political reference point, and the center of the cliental network. This variegated and all-encompassing presence enabled the latifondo to modify the very structure of its territory by constructing new lines of aggregation and interlinkage between the mountains and the coast, between the towns and villages, thereby creating a new socialization. To be sure, this form of socialization cannot be compared to that of the modern factory, which recomposes social relations after they have been deeply fractured and thoroughly atomized; to the contrary, the latifondo incorporated relations without fracturing. The characteristics of the earlier reality—often inefficient, impoverished, and oppressive, with its antiquated methods of production, its patriarchy, and its isolation, which pre-

---

[Milan, 1975]). The Compagnas, too, were an old patrician family; they had moved from Messina to Longobucco in the seventeenth century, and after aspiring for centuries to the status of land-owners they behaved just like the Barraccos when they finally attained it (see, for example, *Atti della Società Economica di Calabria Citra* [Cosenza, 1836], 27).

28. As we have seen, the "changing of the guard" and the privatization of land were not sufficient in themselves to impose a radical transformation of the social territory.

29. An "empty" territory is one whose ecological and social equilibria are simply ignored during the process of transformation. See P. C. Emmer, D. H. A. Kolff, and R. J. Ross, "The Expansion of Europe and the Transformation of Third World Agriculture," paper read at the Eighth International Congress of Economic History, Budapest, August 1982.

vented the population from taking advantage of the few benefits the state could offer such as education or medical care—were not automatically carried over into the latifondo system. Rather, the latifondo proved in a certain sense efficient enough to exploit the preexisting historical and social infrastructure so as to create a highly profitable enterprise.

The term *enterprise* gives a better idea than the more reductive *farm* of the complexity of this economic entity with its highly diversified production and marketing and its ability to organize and manage all three of the factors of production: land, capital, and labor. The latifondo economy was by no means primitive and monotonous; it vaunted a large spectrum of crops and products, a true multiculture. If a large part of its resources was devoted to a combination of raising cereals and sheep, this was because such use of land was simple but functional: the available land was cultivated in "an admirable cycle that linked the mountains and the plains, summer and winter, in harmony with the climate and nature's own cycle of fertility."[30] In addition, the enterprise grew specialty crops, especially olives and oranges, and attached great importance to its industrial products, such as silk thread and licorice, not to mention the host of products grown to meet the demands of the local market and of subsistence needs.

Each activity had its own type of organization and method of production. For example, sheep raising proceeded according to the traditional techniques, which involved no capital investments, but sophisticated machinery was installed to spin silk and process licorice. Grain farming followed the age-old extensive cycles, while specialized agronomists were employed to grow bergamot and produce olive oil.

The latifondo enterprise was self-sufficient to a high degree. Diversification enabled it to produce practically everything needed for the subsistence of masters and laborers and raw materials, fodder, and maintenance materials. In addition, the enterprise was self-sufficient with regard to almost all of the services it required, from transportation (at least until the advent of the railroad) to construction. Although this self-sufficiency in no way partook of the "natural economy," it did give the latifondo a considerable degree of autonomy with respect to the market and its fluctuations. Since both production and consumption depended very little on outside purchases, rising and falling prices created little more than an accounting problem. The latifondo economy had a dual relationship with the market (or markets) similar to the one Kula has shown to have operated on Polish feudal estates: "richer" output produced for

---

30. In Manlio Rossi Doria's words, though he considered it "an agriculture of the absurd" (see "Struttura e problemi dell'agricoltura meridionale," in *Riforma Agraria e Azione Meridionalista* [Bologna, 1956], 10–11).

distant markets was exported whatever the current prices, while "poor" products served for auto-consumption and their surplus was sold in local markets.[31]

In addition, the organization's flexibility allowed easy and painless transformation of capital from one form to another. Given production could be increased in response to changes in the terms of trade—to counterbalance lower prices or take advantage of higher prices. In practice, as we shall see, since the owners were more interested in maintaining their status and standard of living than in maximizing their monetary gains, their decisions to increase production were most often made in response to negative rather than positive market incentives. But the originality of the relationship between the latifondo and the market lay in the fact that—contrary to modern economists' belief that multiple market relations lessen the risks an enterprise faces[32]—its *limited* nature was precisely what enabled the latifondo to prosper even in times of market depression. Of course, there were structural limits—physical, social, and technological—to the flexibility of the enterprise's response to market incentives, but within these limits it could, and often did, make full use of all the factors of production to operate at maximum capacity.[33] Then, too, its highly integrated organization enabled the enterprise to dispense with middlemen. Sales were handled by its own employees, both locally and in Naples; products were shipped directly to Naples in chartered vessels and stored in the latifondo's own warehouses. Lastly, the enterprise was characterized by an extensive administrative structure, simple but efficient, decentralized but with a central accounting system. This ensured that ledgers and inventories were kept properly and regular reports submitted, even by illiterate overseers.

One of the most surprising and least known features of the latifondo system was its variety of modes of labor control. Contrary to what is generally believed, the simple owner–field-hands dichotomy was by no means predominant. Each kind of production commanded a specific labor relationship, so that it can be observed (to paraphrase a well-known saying) that sheep raising gave rise to participatory arrangements, grain farming to day labor, and licorice manufacture to wage labor. Often labor contracts were also contracts for land use—sometimes partial and sometimes for a single crop.[34] Although the wage

---

31. For the distinction between "rich" and "poor" products and their different relations with the markets, see *I prezzi in Europa dal XIII secolo a oggi,* ed. R. Romano (Turin, 1967).

32. See, for example, J. J. Liebowitz, "Tenants, Sharecroppers, and the French Agricultural Depression of the Late Nineteenth Century," *Journal of Interdisciplinary History* 19, no. 3 (Winter 1989): 429–45.

33. This thesis was put forward many decades ago by Ghino Valenti, who spoke of the rationality and functionality of the latifondo organization and of the possibility of full utilization of resources within its economy ("L'Italia agricola dal 1861 al 1911," in *Cinquanta anni di storia italiana* [Rome, 1911], 2:104–5). Obviously, this was also Kautsky's idea in *The Agrarian Question.*

34. Recently this kind of blurring of the lines between the two was perceptively noted by J.

relationship predominated in the ledgers regarding permanent employees, it was more apparent than real; in fact, workers were paid only partly in cash, the rest of their remuneration taking the form of commodities, land use, and sharecropping. The monetary portion of the retribution tended to be a standard amount, creating the impression of wage egalitarianism; it was the second portion that represented the real wage differential and gave access to "invisible wages." Only day laborers (the *braccianti*) were actually recruited and paid solely in cash; significantly, their names were never recorded in the ledgers. In fact, the anonymous day laborers of the nineteenth-century latifondo belonged to that world of petty subsistence peasants who rounded out their own tendential self-sufficiency with occasional wage work.[35] The great estate coexisted with this social class and used it as a reservoir of labor.[36] Generally speaking, occasional employment on the latifondo—and not only on its particular form known as the "peasant latifondo"[37]—far from turning farmhands into proletarians, enabled them to perpetuate in some way their peasant condition. It was this aspect, and not any form of extra-economic coercion, which induced them to accept the low pay and seasonal employment.[38]

Kochanowicz ("Historia wsi włoskiego południa," op. cit., 124), but it had already been pointed out by Franchetti (*Condizioni economiche,* op. cit., 78–79, 87). At any rate, the practice of remunerating farm labor in whole or in part with assignments of small plots of land for partial-use tenancies was widespread during the nineteenth century on both the latifondi and the great commercial estates in Scandinavia, Germany, Egypt, South Africa, Ecuador, Peru, Chile, and northeastern Brazil. See M. Mörner, "A Comparative Study of Tenant Labor in Parts of Europe, Africa and Latin America, 1700–1900," *Latin American Research Review,* 2, no. 2 (Summer 1970): 3–15; and E. Feder, "'Latifundia' and Agricultural Labour in Latin America," in *Peasants and Peasant Societies,* ed. T. Shanin (London, 1976), 83–97.

35. Cf. M. Aymard, "Autoconsommation et marchés: Chayanov, Labrousse ou Le Roy Ladurie?" *Annales E.S.C.* 33, no. 6 (November-December 1983): 1392–1411.

36. Maurice Aymard considers the coexistence of *la grande exploitation* with sharecropping and the world of precarious peasant land tenancy an important feature of the "southern" model. Cf. "L'Europe moderne," op. cit., 431–32. See also M. Petrusewicz, "Wage-Earners but Not Proletarians," *Review* 10, no. 3 (Winter 1987): 471–503. On the other hand, it has been pointed out more than once that the growth of the capitalist world market can lead to the generation or reproduction of archaic forms of class domination on the periphery of the world system. Cf. E. J. Hobsbawm, "A Case of Neo-Feudalism: La Convencion," *Journal of Latin American Studies* 1, no. 1 (1969): 31–49.

37. Following Rossi Doria's work, G. Arrighi and F. Piselli (in "Capitalist Development in the Hostile Environment," *Review* 10, no. 4 [Spring 1987]: 649–751) put forward the idea of the peasant latifondo as a transitory form between the eighteenth-century fief and the capitalist latifondo of the second half of the nineteenth century. However, the concept of such a stepping-stone does not appear to be justified by the results of research.

38. M. Aymard emphasizes that the absence of "extra-economic coercion" (serfdom and corvées) in the southern economy is one of the features that most differentiates it from Kula's model ("Amministrazione feudale," op. cit, 17–42). Several studies have demonstrated that extra-economic coercion is unnecessary when labor is relatively abundant (with a high person/land ratio) because population pressure plays the same role. See, for example, L. Masella, "Appunti per una

This socioeconomic configuration sui generis was characterized by a remarkable degree of stability, which rested on a set of "moral" premises articulated in what is called here a "guarantee system." In reconstructing these premises, we must naturally take into account the specific historical nature of latifondism. When E. P. Thompson defines the moral economy of the eighteenth-century crowd as a "consistent traditional view of social norms and obligations of the proper economic functions of several parties within the community,"[39] he is referring to a society with centuries of effective tradition behind it. But modern latifondism—engendered by defeudalization and the market—had no tradition of its own. Its "community" was a newly invented aggregation that had no "consistent traditional view" of reciprocal rights and duties. In effect, its tradition had to be built from scratch with new combinations of the notions of justice, rights, duties, and reciprocity that belonged partly to the peasants' cultural heritage and partly to that of the new elite—a rather delicate tissue of older social norms combined with new needs and demands. It was too new to justify confidence in a unity of moral judgments between masters and peasants of the kind that Thompson saw prevailing between the crowd and the paternalistic authorities in eighteenth-century England. Rather than the expression of a common morality, the guarantee system was the meeting point between masters' and workers' shared notions about the legitimacy or illegitimacy of certain practices, needs, and expectations, hence about reciprocal rights and duties. In short, it was a form of consensus as to what ought to be considered an "equal" exchange of protection for service.

The masters expected this exchange to ensure the stability of their enterprise and their social status; the workers sought security for their subsistence and their own status.[40] The shared moral basis of the guarantee system not only

storia dei contratti agrari in Terra di Bari," in his *Economia e classi sociali nella Puglia moderna* (Naples, 1974), 113–45; M. Aymard, "Féodalité," op. cit., 433; and S. Anselmi, *Mezzadri e terre nelle Marche: Studi e ricerche di storia dell'agricoltura fra Quattrocento e Novecento* (Bologna, 1978), 11–21. My own explanation is intended to be complementary, not alternative, to the demographic one.

39. E. P. Thompson, "The Moral Economy of the English Crowd in the 18th Century," *Past and Present* 50 (1971): 79.

40. Recent American historical and anthropological studies demonstrate that market exchanges that did not involve a commercialization of all exchange (that is, which placed the pursuit of stability and collective security above the individual's interest in growing rich) characterized even the American farmers' economy, thought to be the most capitalist of nineteenth-century agrarian structures. Cf. M. Merrill, "Cash is Good to Eat: Self-Sufficiency and Exchange in the Rural Economy of the United States," *Radical History Review* 3 (Winter 1977): 42–71; C. Clark, "Household Economy, Market Exchange, and the Rise of Capitalism in the Connecticut Valley, 1800–1860," *Journal of Social History* 13 (Winter 1979): 169–89; S. Hahn, *The Roots of Southern Populism: Yeoman Farmers and the Transformation of the Georgia Upcountry* (New York, 1983); and M. Bernstein and S. Wilentz, "Marketing, Commerce, and Capitalism in Rural Massachu-

recognized the social legitimacy of the pursuit of stability and security, as in many rural societies, but also viewed security essentially in social rather than economic terms.[41]

---

setts," *Journal of Economic History* 44, no. 1 (March 1984): 171–73. For the opposite point of view, see W. B. Rothenberg, "The Market and Massachusetts Farmers, 1750–1855," *Journal of Economic History* 41 (June 1981): 283–314.

41. Cf. Chayanov, *Organizatsia,* op. cit. "The Socio-Economic Nature of Peasant Farm Economy," in *A Systematic Source Book in Rural Sociology,* ed. P. A. Sorokin, C. C. Zimmerman, and C. J. Galpin (Minneapolis, 1931). Karl Polanyi writes in this connection: "There is the equally mistaken doctrine of the essentially economic nature of class interests. Though human society is naturally conditioned by economic factors, the motives of human individuals are only exceptionally determined by the needs of material want-satisfaction. . . . Purely economic matters such as affect want-satisfaction are incomparably less relevant to class behavior than questions of social recognition. Want-satisfaction may be, of course, the result of such recognition, especially as its outward sign or prize. But the interests of a class most directly refer to standing and rank, to status and security, that is, they are primarily not economic but social" (*The Great Transformation,* op. cit., 153). See also K. Polanyi, C. Arensberg, and H. Pearson, *Trade and Market in the Early Empires* (Glencoe, 1957). Gunnar Myrdal mentions, by way of example, the great landowners of South Asia who "often managed to enjoy the prerogatives of a capitalist landlord without giving up the privileges of a feudal chief," though at the same time they "avoided nearly all the obligations of both" (*Asian Drama* [New York, 1968], 2:1039). Not all scholars accept the essentially social nature of a "social pact" such as the "guarantee" system, especially as regards the masters' side. In her discussion of Thompson's interpretation, for example, E. Fox Genovese ascribes the generosity of the paternalists to their own self-interest ("The Many Faces of Moral Economy," *Past and Present* 58 [1973]: 167). J. Scott, too, explains the behavior of the elites by economic necessity: "Where land was abundant and labor scarce, subsistence insurance was virtually the only way to attach a labor force; where the means of coercion at the disposal of elites and the state was sharply limited, it was prudent to show some respect for the needs of the subordinate population" (*The Moral Economy of the Peasant: Rebellion and Subsistence in Southeast Asia* [New Haven, 1976], 6). The quest for stability, moral motivations, and the fulfillment of ceremonial and social needs are more easily recognized as a part of culturally defined subsistence when they are referred to the peasant world. Most scholars, and not only anthropologists, admit that the peasant judges the world according to some notion of equality, crude though it may be (see B. Moore, *Social Origins of Dictatorship and Democracy* [Boston, 1966], 497–98; J. Scott, *Moral Economy,* op. cit., 4–14 and passim; and K. Polanyi, *The Great Transformation,* op. cit., 163–64). Some even idealize "the world we have lost." Others also attribute to the peasant a behavior that is essentially economic, hence rational: the peasant seeks above all to avoid risk and uses various risk-avoidance economic strategies to this end ("an optimizing peasant seeks survival algorithms, not maximizing ones," writes M. Lipton in "The Theory of the Optimizing Peasant," *Journal of Development Studies* 4, no. 3 [1968]: 331). In the last analysis, however, this idea of the peasant who puts "safety first" does not really differ from the idea of the peasant who is conservative "by nature," for it, too, tends to explain all peasant practices in terms of risk avoidance. See Lipton, *Theory of the Optimizing Peasant,* op. cit., 327–51; and D. N. McCloskey, "English Open Fields as Behavior Towards Risk," in *Research in Economic History,* ed. P. Uselding (Greenwich, 1976)1:124–70. James Scott rightly uses both explanations, on the one hand stressing the moral content of the subsistence ethic and on the other viewing the patterns of reciprocity, generosity, and communality of land and work as strategies worked out by the peasants in order to spread out the threats to subsistence (*Moral Economy,* op. cit., 3 and passim.)

In practice, the guarantee pact—quite open and easily accessible—operated through networks and codes of behavior in terms that were simple and familiar even if never formalized. Loyalty to the latifondo—the real prerequisite for access—did not imply servile or competitive behavior. Nor did it detract from the collective character of the social pact: as it involved no evaluation of the individual worker's productivity, it did not undermine his solidarity. It was precisely this characteristic that distinguished the guarantism of the latifondo system from the paternalism of the American slave system, as described by Eugene Genovese, in which the relationship between master and slave was essentially personal, and links of control and subordination led from the individuals within one class to individuals within another.[42] It is not surprising, therefore, that an atmosphere of consensus reigned in the social territory of the latifondo: there was a low level of conflict in general and a virtual absence of social struggles.[43]

Latifondism remained in equilibrium for over half a century. What began in the 1860s to disrupt the balance, weaken the system, and evidence its limits was the trend toward modernization. The latifondo enterprise per se never posited an antithesis to technological progress; to the contrary, it was perfectly capable, technology permitting, of introducing up-to-date farm machinery and methods. The propensity to modernize was hardly limited to the Barraccos; it was the vogue in the liberal and laissez-faire circles they frequented in Naples and became more pronounced during the 1860s when landowners were forced to come to grips with the fact that their traditional sources of income no longer sufficed to meet the greater costs of social display and new political expenses, while the usual methods of increasing income were becoming more difficult to pursue because taxes had risen and the reserve of available land was running out. The Barraccos began to modernize the organization of their enterprise by dissolving joint operations with workers, abolishing participatory labor ar-

---

42. This personalized relationship was often successful in undermining solidarity among the slaves, notwithstanding the fact that paternalistic domination clearly had a class, as well as racial, character. See E. Genovese, *Roll, Jordan, Roll* (New York, 1974), passim. In the latifondo system, to the contrary, loyal workers were not alienated from the village community. The instances cited by G. Arrighi and F. Piselli ("Parentela, clientela e comunità," in *La Calabria*, ed. P. Bevilacqua and A. Placanica [Turin, 1985], esp. 405–14) of latifondisti using their guards to suppress labor struggles are all from the period of the reconstructed latifondo of the twentieth century; such cases were extremely rare in the nineteenth. On the other hand, Piselli herself cites cases ("Circuiti politici mafiosi," *Meridiana* 2 [Jan. 1988]: esp. 147–60) of former latifondo guards becoming popular leaders in land struggles, which show how deeply rooted in the populace they remained.

43. Obviously this equilibrium cannot be ascribed solely to the consensus around the "guarantee pact," since the latifondo did have a strong armed defense at its disposal. Nonetheless, the potential use of force does not rule out the existence of consensus. See, in this connection, S. L. Barraclough and A. L. Domike, "Agrarian Structure in Seven Latin American Countries, *Land Economics* 42, no. 4 (Nov. 1966): 392.

rangements, and gradually eliminating grants of land use ("Calabrian share-cropping").[44] The next step was to modernize production by gradually intro-ducing quality crops and breeds while reducing the overall dimensions of the enterprise. These changes led to a reduction in the total workforce and an increase in the proportion of day laborers, which in turn imposed an increased incidence of supervisory personnel.

"Passive modernization," as Luciano Cafagna calls it, was not only in harmony with the landlords' mentality but also seemed the best way to solve their economic problems.[45] Nonetheless, it turned out to have a destabilizing effect. From an economic standpoint, it increased the latifondo enterprise's dependence on the market. While monetary revenues rose, cash outflow did too, due to the growth of capital investments and supervision costs and to the fact that the enterprise, having reduced its output of the "poor" products that were the staples of the laborers' diet, was compelled to raise their wages. From the social standpoint, as modernization undermined the guarantee system, it led to greater conflict and, for the first time, difficulty in recruiting a sufficient workforce. In short, as in any other instance of modernization, latifondism lost its self-sufficiency and became economically and socially vulnerable.

However, its new vulnerability did not mean that latifondism had broken down or that the whole system was on the way out. The signs of decline became evident and unequivocal only in the last two decades of the nineteenth century, clearly in conjunction with the situation on the world market. While it is difficult to say whether "internal" or "external" causes were more responsi-ble for the system's demise,[46] it is certain that both were working in the same

44. The advantages and drawbacks of "Calabrian sharecropping" were still being argued in the early twentieth century. D. Taruffi, L. De Nobili, and C. Lori, the young authors of an excellent study on the agrarian question and emigration in Calabria, praised its potential as compared to that of Tuscan sharecropping (*La questione agraria e l'emigrazione in Calabria* [Florence, 1908], 386–88), while E. Marenghi, author of the volume on Calabria in the Parliamentary inquiry, published in 1909, considered it a particularly pernicious phenomenon (*Inchiesta Parlamentare,* vol. 5: *Calabria* [Rome, 1909], 391).

45. The concept of modernization, as defined by Cyril E. Black (*The Dynamics of Modern-ization: A Study in Comparative History* [New York, Harper & Row, 1966]), remains ambiguous, especially if applied at the regional or subregional level. The term *passive modernization,* coined by L. Cafagna ("at the merely regional level . . . it seems . . . altogether appropriate to speak of "passive modernization," [238]), makes it possible to keep out of the discussion of the moderniza-tion process the otherwise necessary factor consisting of the intervention of political elites. At the same time, the term emphasizes by metonymy the subaltern character of such changes ("Moderni-zzazione attiva e modernizzazione passiva," *Meridiana* 2 [Jan. 1988]: 229–40.

46. The reference for the discussion on internal versus external causes of a decline of a system remains the above-mentioned debate between M. Dobb and P. Sweezy on the transition from feudalism to capitalism. This type of discussion always tends to stress the elements that herald the advent of the system-successor, and thus it tends to confer a sort of automatism on the whole process. In discussing Kula's book, J. Jedlicki rightly warns against building models that

direction. While internal modernization had made the southern latifondo more vulnerable to the influence of the outside world *tout court,* the new conditions of a national market forced it to face, unprotected, the challenge of the agrarian capitalism of the North in the very years when the whole of European agriculture was plunged into the great agrarian crisis. If, at the end, external factors hastened the crisis of the latifondo system, it was not (as Emilio Sereni maintained) because of its structural inferiority ultimately revealed after the advent of the national market. The real reason was the concomitance between the new state's policy choices and the general agrarian depression.

The crisis of latifondism was not caused by the competition of American wheat and the resulting fall in farm prices. It is true that a multitude of smallholders and leaseholders were hard hit, and consequently also the large absentee landowners whose income depended on rents. But the latifondism of mainland Italy—"presentee," owner-managed, flexible in its response to market fluctuations, and relatively insensitive to price fluctuations—was perhaps the only one in Europe, aside from the great Russian estates, the stucture of which enabled it to take advantage of the increase in aggregate demand generated by the drop in farm prices. In fact, the depression had little effect on the latifondo economy until the mid-1880s; the crisis began only after the enactment of protectionist legislation in 1887.

How the protectionist option was a determining factor in creating the gap between northern and southern Italy, in imposing the North's perpetual and growing economic domination on the South, and even in turning the South into a colonial market for the North's industrial products—all this has been amply discussed in the "meridionalist" literature.[47] The protectionist turn is usually considered the birth certificate of the so-called historical bloc, an alliance between northern industrialists and southern "feudataries" to push for protective tariffs supposedly beneficial to industrial development in the North and to preservation of the agrarian rents and economic power of the great southern

---

predict their own historical succession. See "W sprawie automatycznego krachu kapitalizmu," in *Między feudalizmem a kapitalizmem: Prace ofiarowane Witoldowi Kuli* (Wroclaw, Warsaw, Krakow and Gdansk, 1976), 243.

47. The literature on the southern question is too well known and too broad to summarize here. C. Barbagallo, *La questione meridionale* [Milan, 1948]); and B. Caizzi (*Nuova antologia della Questione Meridionale* [Milan, 1962]) remain good references. See also R. Ciasca, "Il problema del Mezzogiorno come fondamentale problema italiano," in Cassa per il Mezzogiorno, *Problemi dell'agricoltura meridionale* (Naples, 1953), 1–34. The concept of the North's perpetual hegemony was elaborated by Antonio Gramsci (*Quaderni dal carcere* [Turin, 1975], 1:131 and passim). It is interesting that it was a great landowner, A. De Viti De Marco, who referred to the 1887 tariff as an "attenuated form of the old colonial regime," which legitimates in response "a struggle for independence" (*La questione meridionale* [1903], reprinted in *Un trenntennio di lotte politiche, 1894–1922* [Rome, 1929], 36).

landowners.[48] But the assumption on which this interpretation rests—that the great landowners were interested in placing a protective tariff on wheat—is mistaken. In reality, they were less sensitive to prices than to market outlets, hence their interest lay in free trade. They rightly feared that, besides wiping out their competitive advantage by preventing a further drop in the price of wheat, the tariff would provoke foreign governments to retaliate by closing their markets to Italian specialty products (olive oil, citrus fruit, licorice) for which there were no alternative markets. In any event, the great landowners of the mainland were and remained free traders. Not only did they not vote for the 1887 tariff, but they opposed it as long as they could within the so-called agrarian party (within which they were actually a minority). Certainly the antitariff forces put up a weak opposition. During the crucial voting sessions in Parliament, for instance, the representatives of latifondo interests manifested their dissent by absenting themselves rather than casting nays, bartering this benevolent behavior toward the government for the latter's acceptance of their demands on other matters vital to latifondism.[49] Still, the weakness of the southern landowners' opposition testifies to their political inconsistency not to their supposed interest in the protective tariff.

Their fears were soon borne out. The subsequent crisis of the latifondo economy went deep, and there was no way of getting through it with the old system still intact. Many of the great estates succumbed in the process; those that survived, like the estate of the Barraccos, emerged with their very structures transformed. The whole "natural" and local sector of production had disappeared, production processes had been completely modernized, and relations of production were radically altered.

Thus ended the "guarantist" latifondo, a distinctive type of agrarian system that had dominated part of Calabria and influenced all of southern Italy for eighty years. Despite some affinities with its feudal predecessor and its capitalist successor, it was neither a direct derivative of the former nor a mere forerunner of the latter; it cannot be thought of as a system of transition in the deterministic sense of the term. Rather, it constituted one phase in the agrarian

---

48. An example uno pro toto is F. Barbagallo's opinion, stated in his otherwise excellent *Stato, Parlamento e lotte politico-sociali nel Mezzogiorno* (Naples, 1980): "The high import tariff on grain came at the right time to strengthen the economic and political power of the large landowners, who had been hard hit by falling grain prices" (2–3).

49. The argument that this docility was due to the fear of socialism spreading into the countryside, and a sign of the landowners' class solidarity and capacity for self-sacrifice in isolating the agrarian workers' movement, does not seem very convincing. It is true that the advocates of protectionism argued that the tariff, by offering a rescue to the small landowners, would have safeguarded them from the influence of socialism, but the same rhetoric was used by the laissez-fairists as well. Moreover, there was not a trace of socialism in Calabria. It is more likely that the group of latifondisti who were by then strongly progovernment found it difficult to vote with the opposition.

transformation of southern Italy—a phase bounded by two momentous episodes, the French decade and the Great Depression, corresponding to the two "watersheds" Hobsbawm identifies in the history of labor in the nineteenth century and to the two "agricultural revolutions" described by F. L. M. Thompson.[50] The phase of the guarantistic latifondo, when the rules of the game were being learned, ended with the agrarian crisis; its successor—where one did appear—was the capitalist latifondo.[51]

50. E. J. Hobsbawm, *Labouring Men* (New York, 1967), 405–35; F. M. L. Thompson, "The Second Agricultural Revolution, 1815–1880," *Economic History Review,* 2d ser., 21 (1968): 62–77; P. Bairoch, "Niveaux de développement économique de 1810 à 1910," *Annales E.S.C.* 6 (November-December 1965): 1091–1117. "Thus the first phase of the South's agrarian transformation," wrote M. Rossi Doria, "ended around 1880, at the time of the agrarian crisis. . . . The masses of laborers had by then acquired the appearance and the substance of braccianti and wage-earners" ("L'evoluzione delle campagne meridionali e i contratti agrari," *Nord e Sud,* April 5, 1955, 16).

51. In the 1940s and 1950s, the field workers' formidable struggle for land on the Croton plain, in the very heart of the Barraccos' restructured latifondo, forced Parliament to enact the agrarian reform law known as the Gullo Act. These struggles had a clear class character, being differentiated from those of the nineteenth century by the presence of nonlocal ideologies and political forces. At any rate, there was a huge difference between the two kinds of latifondo. See M. Alcaro and A. Paparazzo, *Lotte contadine in Calabria, 1943–1950* (Rome, 1976); A. Paparazzo, "Lotte per la terra in Calabria, 1943–1949," *Rivista di Storia Contemporanea* 3 (1975): 363–95; V. Barrese, *La scomparsa del latifondo* (Cosenza, 1981); F. Piselli, "Circuiti politici mafiosi," op. cit.; P. Pezzino, *La riforma agraria in Calabria* (Milan, 1977); and P. Bevilacqua, *Le campagne del Mezzogiorno fra fascismo e dopoguerra* (Turin, 1980).

PART 1

The Making of the Barracco Latifondo

CHAPTER 1

The Masters: Family History

When Chiara Lucifero Barracco died in 1873, after forty years of marriage to the Baron Luigi and twenty as his widow, she was over eighty and the mother of twelve: seven sons and five daughters.[1]

She was the last surviving member of the pioneering generation of latifondisti who, in the course of half a century, had made the Barracco family one of the wealthiest and highest ranking in the kingdom. The simultaneously austere and sumptuous character of Donna Chiara's generation was reflected in her personal effects. Her wardrobe, meticulously detailed in the postmortem inventory, was fairly small and sober (only one of her twelve blouses was new), and she had only 600 lire on hand, but her jewelry—earrings, brooches, rings, bracelets, pins, watches—was estimated to be worth 33,432 lire. The austere Chiara never wore this jewelry; it was simply the symbol of the social status her family had attained. Her daughter-in-law's godmother, Giulia Caracciolo, who lived with the family, was born an aristocrat; having no need to legitimate her rank in the public eye, she owned no jewelry at all. But Chiara was, after all, a *nouvelle arrivée* on the Neapolitan scene; the family's wealth had to be exhibited for the children's sake. Even her funeral reflected this need for display: the event cost eight thousand lire and was attended by *tout* Naples. First of all, there was the immediate family: Alfonso, Chiara's eldest son, and his wife, Emilia Carafa; her younger sons, Francesco, Stanislao, Giovanni, Guglielmo, Maurizio, and Roberto (four of whom never married as the primogeniture tradition demanded, while the other two married late); her daughters, Maria, Eleonora, Teresina, and Carolina, and their husbands, who bore such exalted family names as Lucifero, Pallavicini, Ruffo, and Pignatelli; Prince Enrico D'Aquino, widower of Chiara's daughter Emanuela; and all the grandchildren.

---

1. Except where otherwise indicated, the references in this chapter are to the Barracco Archives (hereafter BA), particularly Sec. E, vol. 14; Sec. F, vols. 1, 2, 3, 4, 5, and 8; and Sec. G, vol. 1.

"For the children's sake," certainly, but also for the logic of the story, Chiara, whose personal lack of pretention verged on the puritanical, died fast in the web of social conventions that governed the class she had joined.

1. The Pioneers: Unscrupulousness and Traditionalism

The social and economic rise of the Barracco family was surely one of the most spectacular in the southern kingdom in the nineteenth century. Everyone, from the great Jacini and the quidnunc De Cesare down to the peasants of Calabria, thought them the wealthiest family in the realm.[2]

The family was of patrician origin, hailing from Cosenza with a long-standing tradition of culture and political involvement, and had already played a certain role in regional affairs. Around the end of the fifteenth century and the early sixteenth, Giovanni Barracco was a man thought to be an "intimate" of the Aragonese; as such, he was dispatched by King Frederic to enlist Ferdinand of Spain's help against the French.[3] In 1646, thanks to another mission to Madrid undertaken by Giovanni's great-nephew and namesake, the Spanish king voided a sale to the grand duke of Tuscany of Cosenza's hamlets in the Sila mountains.

However, the Barraccos' aspirations had never been fully satisfied by their patrician rank. Imbued with agrarian ambitions, they had tried for centuries to build a landed property and become "feudal lords," but their repeated efforts had always met with failure. The land in Evoli with which Giovanni Barracco had been rewarded for his mission to Spain was lost during the "revolutions," that is, the anti-Spainish revolt. On that occasion the family also lost the baronial title conferred on Alfonso Barracco in 1564, along with the Lattarico fief to which it attached, situated north of Cosenza and east of the Crati River. The small Bruscano fief in the territory of Cerenzia, on the southeastern slopes of the Sila massif, had been lost in the great epidemic of 1528. The lands in Rocca Bernarda given in the seventeenth century to Captain Carlo Barracco as a reward for his services in defeating the Turks were too poor to insure the family aristocratic status. In 1765, Giovanni and Domenico Barracco and their uncle Tommaso were hard put to obtain even very small amounts of credit and had to mortgage their land to renew a loan from the Paolotti fathers

---

2. R. De Cesare, *La fine di un Regno* (Città di Castello, 1908–9), 1:145.

3. The correspondence on this mission is preserved in the Barracco Archives: letters from Luigi, cardinal of Aragon; from the infanta, Donna Julia of Aragon; from Carlo of Aragon; and one from Queen Isabella, dated March 1506, thanking Giovanni for his services (BA: G1 [1, 3, 6, 7, 8]). For other information on the family, see BA: Sec. F; and G. Valente, *Storia della Calabria nell'età moderna* (Chiaravalle, 1980), passim. On Calabria's landed aristocracy, see G. Galasso, *Economia e società nella Calabria del Cinquecento* (Naples, 1967), 80, 228; R. Colapietra, *Vita pubblica e classi politiche del viceregno napoletano, 1656–1734* (Rome, 1961); and D. Andreotti, *Storia dei Cosentini* (Naples, 1869–74).

in Spezzano Grande.[4] The first of the Barraccos to make the grade as a landed nobleman was Stanislao, landowner in Spezzano Grande and father of Alfonso. Upon his marriage in 1743 to Antonia, sole heiress of the marquises of Marano, Stanislao received the Manche forest in Marano, the Santa Chiara estate in Spezzano Piccolo, and part of the Camigliati enclosure in Sila Grande, which was to become the core of the Barraccos' future "Sila empire."

Despite the frustrations, the experience that the Barraccos gained over those centuries enabled this close-knit family to develop a certain modern patrician style. Well informed and active in public affairs, accustomed to forming and switching political alliances, and ranging easily between the Cosenza and Croton regions, the Barraccos were able to act with a mixture of unscrupulousness and traditionalism. By contrast, most of the South's lesser nobility stayed put on their provincial estates, "intent on defending their *rights* against assault from above and below."[5] The Barraccos' acquired style proved its usefulness and effectiveness when the crisis of the old regime, the revolution of 1799, and above all the "French decade" flung the gates of opportunity open to men of talent.

It was in those years that the Barracco "pioneers"—Stanislao's son Alfonso and Alfonso's son Luigi—quick to seize those opportunities, amassed the fortune that propelled the family onto the wider stage of the kingdom. At the outset of the troubles, when many noblemen were fleeing the kingdom, Alfonso, both unscrupulous and prudently traditionalist, decided to stay and play the new game. After this initial choice, others were dictated by rapidly changing circumstances. In those years Alfonso accepted, willingly or not, appointments and tasks that were at once perilous, difficult, and unrewarding. In 1798, when the Bourbon King Ferdinand was preparing his pathetic expedition to "save" Rome from the French, Alfonso Barracco was the royal recruitment commissioner (though as no volunteers stepped forth his job mostly consisted of rooting out draft dodgers town by town). A year later, he was the commissioner in charge of supplying army horses and mules, while he continued to lend a hand in hunting down draftees. When the political winds shifted later in 1799, he planted a liberty tree in Rocca di Neto, "using the same men-at-arms he commanded as tenent-in-chief of the former Carthusian fief."[6]

---

4. The mortgage encumbered the Arvicello holding in the township of Donnici. The cadet branch of the Barracco family never attained success; Uncle Tommaso's sons Giuseppe and Gaetano were compelled to borrow from their cousins Giovanni and Domenico, Alfonso's brothers, backing the debt with a further mortgage on the Arvicello holding. Years later, in 1814, Alfonso demanded that his cousins repay the debt with interest, threatening them with foreclosure.

5. A. Simioni, *Le origini del Risorgimento politico dell'Italia meridionale* (Messina, 1925), 29.

6. A. Placanica, *Alle origini dell'egemonia borghese in Calabria* (Salerno and Catanzaro, 1979), 380.

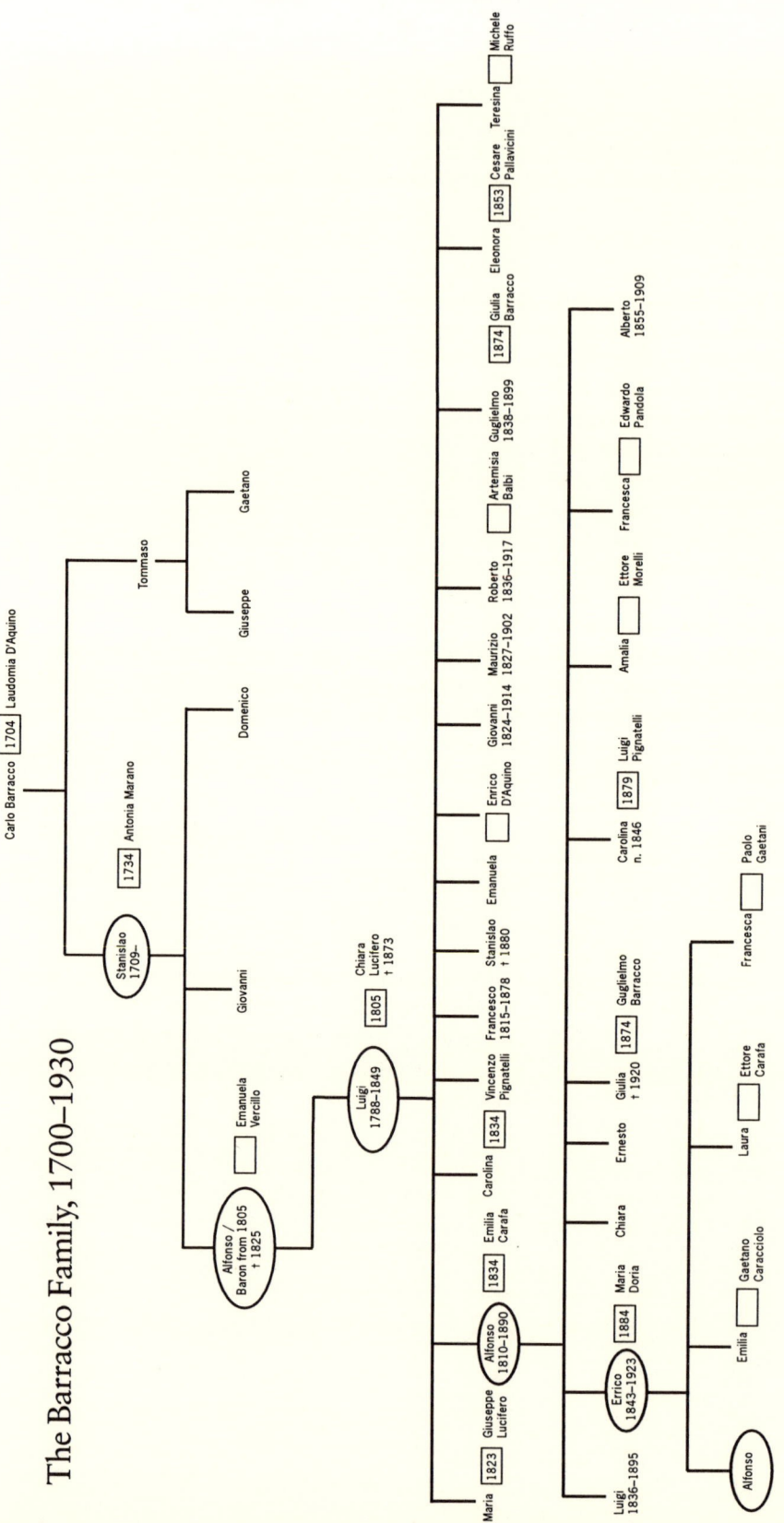

Fig.2. The Barracco Family

The year after, he promptly repudiated this gesture with the explanation that he had done it out of concern for the welfare of his fellow citizens.[7] During the war of 1806, Alfonso was appointed to oversee the distribution of food and forage, this time to the French army that had occupied Calabria.[8] That summer, after a few months of occupation, as the clouds were gathering for what turned out to be a five-year war against brigandage, Alfonso's various duties were expanded to include the repression of brigandage in his own district. He accepted the appointment unwillingly, but after being accused in public by the intendant Pierre Joseph Briot—who had preserved his hatred of the barons from his Jacobin past and railed against them in the Intendency Council[9]—Alfonso became a diligent liegeman of the French, earning praise even from the fearfully famous General Manhès.

All these appointments were highly remunerative in terms of power and prestige as well as money. The French, in particular, paid promptly and well (in cash and *assignats*) and cared naught for the methods of requisition. It is true that the central government prescribed respect for the lives and property of civilians, but—*à la guerre comme à la guerre*—a blind eye was turned in the provinces. Starting in May of 1806, Alfonso Barracco had been expressly authorized by General Verdier, the army commander in the Calabrias, to travel with a bodyguard of six armed men who also served as an "argument" to obtain prompt deliveries. The fifteen years of turbulence in Calabria earned the Barraccos a baronage and an immense fortune.[10]

With the Restoration, the Barraccos—once again loyal subjects of the Bourbons—stayed quietly for a while in Calabria. But as early as the 1820s

---

7. In 1800, Alfonso Barracco made "the authorities and private citizens of this City of Rocca di Neto and its clergy" write an open letter asserting that he had remained loyal to the Bourbons but had been forced to "embrace democracy" and plant "the infamous tree of Liberty" in order to "avoid endangering life and property" of the city, and that at any rate he had not been on the scene, "having gone hunting for pleasure in the country" (BA: G20 [7]).

8. He received this office from the French general in quite peremptory terms: "Any delay or resistance will be punished as a crime against the State. . . . You will be personally responsible to the French General, who in the event that you fail to meet this obligation, will send out a military force." See BA: G (letters relating to brigandage).

9. Intendency Council of Cosenza, April 20, 1809. P. J. Briot made it public "because it concerns you [Mr. Alfonzo Barracco] and others, who seem to form an isolated class of dubious repute in this Province." Briot denounced the greed and personal interest of Barracco, "whose immense wealth has suffered so little in the common misfortunes [and] . . . whose properties and day-to-day speculations are safeguarded and protected by our . . . fine Civil Guards." "Well, Sir," he exclaimed, "begin to take a strong and frank position against brigandage, and may it cease to be that the brigands respect your possessions more than everyone else's, and there find refuge and succor; at the same time . . . stop trying to accommodate the Police and the brigands" (Archives of Duke Serra di Cassano, Naples, folder 148). See also U. Caldora, *Calabria Napoleonica* (op. cit.), 43ff.

10. F. Bonazzi, *Elenco dei titoli di nobiltà concessi, legalmente riconosciuti nelle provincie meridionali d'Italia dal 1806 al 1891* (Naples, 1891).

Alfonso's son Luigi became president of Upper Calabria's provincial council, then a peer of the realm. In 1833 the king, stopping for a night in Croton during a visit to the distant provinces, "honored the home of Baron Barracco with his presence by deigning to dine and stay overnight"[11]—further proof that the Bourbons' policy, doubtless under the influence of Luigi de' Medici, was to forgive and forget, to avoid the error of vengeance committed in 1799.

It must be said that the Barraccos' political unscrupulousness, however opportunistic, was bound up with their inventiveness, courage, and a taste for risk—the very talents that induced Alfonso to dare to remain in "Calabria at war"[12] rather than follow the court into exile in Sicily as so many other noblemen did. But the Barraccos' soldier-of-fortune spirit went hand in hand with their prudence and traditionalism in social strategies and economic choices.

Alfonso invested the proceeds of his adventurous operations in buying land and climbing the social ladder. From 1800 to 1804, little by little, he bought the barony of Altilia with the attached title. In 1806, he bought the fief of Isola, on the coast, thereby adding winter pastures to his summer pastures up in the Sila mountains. This enabled him to set up a rational, large-scale, livestock operation, which brought him in turn further government contracts as well as praise in King Murat's 1811 statistical compendium.[13] During the decade of French rule, Alfonso took advantage of the priority accorded assignat-holders as creditors of the state and bought huge estates expropriated from the Church while continuing to purchase former feudal properties and peasants' allotments. This aggressive policy, which we shall examine in detail in the next chapter, allowed Alfonso to put together, in just a few years, a powerful latifondo extending through the provinces of Upper Calabria and Lower Calabria II, yielding sixty thousand ducats net a year (of which 75 percent was earned on directly managed operations) at his death in 1825.

Thus, the soldier of fortune was a traditionalist in the use he made of his fortune. Of course, all his confrères in Europe were doing the same in those years: hurrying to invest their new, perilously fluctuating capital in something traditionally solid and prestigious.[14] Or perhaps, as Pierre Vilar remarked, the urge to buy land is a constant in all the world's agricultural societies.[15] Be that

---

11. *Il Giornale del Regno delle Due Sicilie,* May 8, 1833.

12. See A. Mozzillo, *Cronache della Calabria in guerra,* 3 vols. (Naples, 1972).

13. U. Caldora, *La Statistica murattiana del Regno di Napoli: Le relazioni sulla Calabria* (Messina, 1960); S. Martuscelli, *La popolazione del Mezzogiorno nella statistica del Re Murat* (Naples, 1979).

14. In Germany, Poland, and Austria, the nouveaux riches behaved in exactly the same way. See J. Blum, *Noble Landowners and Agriculture in Austria, 1815–1848: A Study in the Origins of the Peasant Emancipation of 1848* (Baltimore, 1948), 44–65.

15. P. Vilar, "Discusión," in *Agricultura, comercio colonial y crecimiento económico en la España contemporánea,* ed. J. Nadal and G. Tortorella (Barcelona, 1974).

as it may, just as Barracco's economic traditionalism led him to think of land as a vehicle of wealth and security, so his social traditionalism impelled him to construct a noble status for his family by adding titles and a veneer of antiquity to his new wealth. Shrewd matrimonial strategies were the new baron's principal tools of social ascent.

2. Marriage Strategies and the Pursuit of Prestige

Alfonso consolidated his position as a Cosenza landowner and patrician by marrying Emanuela Vercillo, of the barons of San Vincenzo La Costa. In 1805, when their only son, Luigi, was seventeen, Alfonso arranged his marriage to Chiara, who was the daughter of Croton patrician Francesco Lucifero, the marquis of Apriglianello's eldest son. In this way a sheen of nobility was overlaid on Barracco's recently purchased lands in the Croton district.

Luigi and Chiara led the life of pioneering latifondisti. They normally stayed at Camigliati or in their Croton mansion, with frequent sojourns in Altilia, Isola, and Caccuri and only very rare visits to Naples. Luigi continued his father's work of enlarging and concentrating the latifondo and with the help of his growing sons and his administrators, he personally saw to the production and sale of grain, olive oil, cheese, licorice, and various kinds of livestock: hogs, goats, enormous herds of cattle and sheep, and a fine breed of horses.

Luigi went much farther than his father in the pursuit of status and prestige. His wealth and his eminent position in the region—in the 1820s he was twice president of the Upper Calabria Provincial Council and once president of the Croton District Council—helped him build a position in the kingdom as well. He was a peer of the realm, his hospitality was accepted by the king, and in 1843 he became one of His Majesty Ferdinand II's gentlemen of the chamber. But it was in his marriage strategies—in the tenacious and shrewd practice of hypergamy[16]—that Luigi showed himself most farsighted.

Luigi and Chiara had twelve children: five girls and seven boys. As family tradition dictated, all the boys except the eldest were destined for bachelorhood. For his five daughters, Luigi arranged marriages with the most sought-after names in the kingdom—names, not moneybags, it should be made clear, because the great Neapolitan aristocrats, decidedly impoverished by the wars and the French-era reforms, were quite happy to barter their noble luster on the marriage market in exchange for the dowries of the baron's daughters. This was an ideal condition for hypergamic practices. Maria, the eldest daughter, married Marquis Giuseppe Lucifero of Croton; Teresina married Michele Ruffo, count of Molino; Emanuela married the duke of Casole, Errico d'Aquino, eldest son of the prince of Caramanico; Carolina married the count of

---

16. *Hypergamy* is C. M. Arensberg's term for marriage above one's station (*The Irish Countryman* [London, 1937], 160–65).

Melissa, Vincenzo Pignatelli, eldest son of the prince of Strongoli; and little Eleonora married the Genoese marquis Cesare Pallavicini.

The price of these marriage alliances was quite high for the Barraccos. A reading of the marriage contracts shows how truly spectacular were the dowries Alfonso provided for his daughters, especially when we consider that in part they were paid promptly in gold coins—an extremely rare circumstance in times when aristocrats once again possessed many titles and mortgageable lands but very little cash.[17] Alfonso laid out (or should we say invested?) 260,000 ducats in the space of a few years. To get an idea of what these sums meant, we may compare Bianchini's figures for the revenues of the kingdom: 120,000 ducats yearly from the postal system, 56,000 from water rights, forests, state-owned property and hunting licenses.[18]

Of all the matrimonial transactions Luigi concluded, the one most significant for the family's social ascent and consolidation was the marriage of Alfonso, his eldest son, to Emilia Carafa in 1834, which brought the Barraccos the maximum amount of prestige, money, and land, as well as a new residence. The daughter of Prince Domenico of Colobrano, Emilia was then a twenty-two-year-old orphan who lived in Naples with her sister-in-law Giulia Caracciolo. Giulia, who was much older, childless, and had been separated for years from her husband, had "always been a mother to Emilia." She was the one who arranged a dowry of sixty thousand ducats for Emilia, and she undertook in the marriage contract to designate the son who would be born of the match as her universal heir. This was no mean inheritance: Giulia was the daughter and sole heir of Cataldo Caracciolo, marquis of Brienza and prince of Atena; her mother was Teresa Serra from the family of the dukes of Cassano. In addition, Giulia's marriage to Marzio Gaetano Carafa, Emilia's older brother, had brought her the titles of duchess of Alvito and princess of Colobrano. And so it was that the Barraccos came to be part of the crème de la crème of the Neapolitan aristocracy, by then fully reinstated in its ancient privileges and reverted to its traditions: truth to tell, the Bourbons had had little difficulty in forgetting the "republicanism" exhibited by the Carafas and the Colobranos in 1799.[19] Emilia's dowry also included precious status symbols—ancient family privileges such as the right to a private oratory, which Charles V had granted to Giangiacomo Trivulzio who passed it on, confirmed by popes Clement IX and

---

17. Maria's marriage contract, signed in 1823, assigned her a dowry of 20,000 ducats; Carolina's, in 1834, was for 60,000 (8,000 in cash upon signature of the contract, and the rest in the three years after the wedding). Teresina, Emanuela, and Eleonora were each assigned sixty thousand ducats (BA: F [various folders]).

18. L. Bianchini, *Della storia delle finanze del Regno di Napoli,* 2d ed. (Naples, 1859) 113.

19. As the good De Nicola complained, "Most of the noble families of Naples had been affected." See C. De Nicola, *Diario Napoletano: Dicembre 1798-dicembre 1800* (rpt.; Milan, 1963).

Benedict XIII, to the Colobranos. Though Marzio Gaetano Carafa was furious with his wife and her protégés, he could not prevent the irreparable transfer of wealth to the groom's family; he could only bar his wife and his sister from inheriting his personal property, which consisted mainly of debts.[20] As a matter of fact, Giulia Caracciolo was becoming more and more eccentric with age, and cohabitation in the sumptuous palace in Via Monte di Dio cannot have been easy for the Barraccos. She had taken the vow of poverty and given away all her jewelry; in her second will, written in 1868, she directed that only plain masses be said for her soul (". . . not wishing to be persecuted even after my death by music, the despair of my life") and that she should be remembered on her tombstone as "a victim of music and of the blackest ingratitude." Who knows what bizarre story was hidden behind these bitter words?[21] In any case, for young Alfonso and his father this match consolidated the family's role in Naples' high society, especially when the the the run of male children began: Luigi in 1836, Errico in 1843, followed by two more boys and five girls.

The difference between the marriages of this generation and those of the previous one is highly significant. In the early nineteenth century the family formed its alliances in a regional matrimonial market; now it was operating in the national market. The earlier matches were more or less endogamous alliances, the later ones were clearly hypergamic. Chiara Lucifero had a dowry of 4,000 ducats, payable in ten years; thirty years later, those of her daughters and her daughter-in-law amounted to 60,000 ducats each. By the same token, in 1805 Luigi's wife was granted 10 ducats a month as a personal allowance ("for pins and laces"), but three decades later the young *baroncino* Alfonso—or rather his father—was granting "to the future bride, by way of gift, according to the custom of the nobility," the sum of 2,000 ducats to form her trousseau. Luigi assigned his son 10,000 ducats a year, out of which Alfonso assigned his wife 60 month for "pins, laces and personal effects"—a 600 percent increase over what his mother had received—as well as the usufruct of a "counterdow-

---

20. Carafa, who died in 1861, bequeathed his few possessions to the children of his lawyer, one Del Preite, and in the event of their deaths, to the Jesuit fathers of the Sacro Monte dei Poveri Vergognosi. But, as we have seen, the prince had little to leave but debts. Though Giulia Caracciolo, by a secret will made in 1848, had disinherited him in favor of Emilia's children, because "she had already assumed too many of his debts that might otherwise have led to his arrest," she did assign him an income of 120 ducats per month so he could live "without being troubled." What the eccentric aristocrat seems to have valued most were his own writings and the well-stocked library of works listed in the index, for which he had received papal authorization and had left to the Jesuit father Giovanni Costa.

21. Marzio Gaetano and Emilia's brother was Michele Enrico Carafa di Colobrano (1787–1872), who had served as an officer in Napoleon's army and was a very prolific and internationally known opera composer in the 1820s and 1830s. See F. Clément, *Dictionnaire Lyrique ou Histoire des Opéras* (Paris, n.d. [1876]). See also H. Rosenthal and J. Warrack, *The Concise Oxford Dictionary of Opera,* 2d ed. (Oxford and New York, 1979), 81.

ry" of 9,000 ducats, which would yield her 450 ducats a year. This was a very different and much higher level of expenditure, a sign of the beginning of a different style of life.

3. Naples: The Life of Grandees

Despite this huge step up in the family's position, as long as Luigi was alive the Barracco life-style remained more or less the same as that of the pioneer generation residing on its Calabrian estates and managing its affairs in person. Luigi was a cultivated and ambitious man but also sober, practical, and thrifty. Besides the works of the ancient philosophers, and of Hume and Kant, and texts on arithmetic, geometry, differential calculus, and physics, his library contained numerous books on agronomy.[22] But after his death in February of 1849, the era of the pioneers drew to a close: his son Alfonso, the new head of the family, was clearly more interested in the life *more nobilium* and the family's social role than in its economic interests. Following what we might call the Buddenbrooks paradigm, the third-generation Alfonso "managed the family's assets more for the sake of luxury than for profit," as his brother Guglielmo bitterly recalled many years later.

To start with, Alfonso decided to move his family to Naples, near the court—an important choice, which, though not yet implying the absentee option, decisively changed the latifondisti's whole being. As early as April of 1849, he took out an eighteen-year lease on the upper *piano nobile* of Giulia Caracciolo's palace at 75 Strada Monte di Dio. Today this street lies in the heart of Naples' downtown popular district, but in the nineteenth century the area was home to the grandest of the grand. Alfonso's lease included fully equipped kitchens, stables, a carriage house, furniture, and silver services, but he was aiming at a standard of living much higher than Giulia's. In July of that year, while still in full mourning, he was already buying six carriages and cabriolets, six English saddles, a crystal service for eighteen, a set of colored English stoneware, tea and coffee services—all told, twenty-five thousand ducats' worth of pure luxury.[23]

Donna Chiara, Alfonso's widowed mother, joined his family in Naples with her younger offspring, of whom she had been appointed guardian: daughters Teresina and Eleonora, who would grow up and marry in the capital; Guglielmo, Roberto, and Maurizio, also still underage; and the twenty-year-old

---

22. See the catalogs of Luigi's and Giovanni's libraries (263 and 78 volumes, respectively) in BA: E,14 (3).

23. "One English gig . . . one French brougham . . . one Neapolitan brougham . . . one Neapolitan chaise, one foreign-made equipped for traveling, one coupé," six complete English saddles, a crystal service for eighteen, an English stoneware service for twelve, a tea service, and a coffee service: the whole costing twenty-five hundred ducats.

Giovanni, who was to become a well-known deputy, senator, and art collec-tor[24] and was already reading the constitutional histories of France, Belgium, and the United States as well as socialist writers, even Louis Blanc.

As mentioned above, while the move to Naples marked the beginning of a new phase in the family's history, it was not yet synonymous with absentee landlordship. The Barraccos continued to identify themselves, and to be identi-fied with, their holdings in Calabria. For instance, during King Ferdinand's visit to Croton in September of 1852, the city was represented by Alfonso and Maurizio Barracco, Marquis Lucifero, and Squire Albani, and the king very naturally honored "the good people of Croton" in the person of Baron Bar-racco.[25] What did change with the move to Naples was the family's life-style and the psychological motivation behind its activities. The era of the pioneers was over, and the family embarked on a new aristocratic way of life—luxurious, ostentatious, and costly.

4. Majorat and Primogeniture

Although the nucleus of the family, with its head and his mother, lived in the capital and saw to social affairs, the Barraccos' business in Calabria—farm production and marketing—was by no means neglected. The Baron's brothers Stanislao and Francesco, later joined by Guglielmo, managed the family enter-prise, insuring that absence did not become absenteeism. The key to this cooperation lay in the family's substantial as well as formal adhesion to the institution of *majorat*. The cadet brothers acted both as property owners and as vicars to their brother the baron. By preventing the partition of family property, majorat maintained the benefits of economies of scale and made use of younger sons to multiply the "owner's eyes."[26]

Yet all the eighteenth-century reformers—in the Two Sicilies and elsewhere—had inveighed against this ancient custom of the landed nobility.[27] Genovesi thought it had caused the disproportionate growth of the parasitical

---

24. Giovanni was an archaeologist and coin collector of some repute in his own day, and he was the founder of Rome's Barracco Museum (see F. Bruckmann, *La Collection Barracco* [Munich, 1892]). His political activities will be described in a later chapter.

25. In reality, these were "four cousins who represented the highest-ranking and wealthiest part of Croton's population," the Barraccos being the most authoritative members. The Duke of Calabria was astonished to find Maurizio Barracco, with whom he socialized in Naples, there in Calabria, and exclaimed in dialect, "Vui cca site? . . . Io vi credeva a Napoli" ("You're here? I thought you were in Naples"). See R. De Cesare, *La fine di un Regno,* op. cit., 2:27.

26. See V. Tafuri, *Della nobiltà e delle sue leggi nel Regno di Due Sicilie* (Naples, 1870).

27. In the same period, the abolition of majorats and fideicommissions was also the main goal of the Spanish reform movement and the battle cry of the "Amigos de el Pais" societies. The *Informe de ley agraria,* a clear and concrete proposal for abolishing the *mayorazgos* and *señorios* drawn up by Gaspar Melchor de Jovellanos for the Madrid Society (Madrid, 1784), became a sort of Bible for nineteenth-century liberals.

landowning class, thereby violating the law of the "least possible," a violation that could not fail to impoverish the class of the "mechanical arts"—the only class that created value, though not the only one necessary for the good working of society. The law of primogeniture and fideicommission "protects idleness or corruption [*poltroneria o il malcostume*]," he wrote, and as such "is by nature wrongful."[28] Filangieri, intuiting the relationship between land concentration and mass proletarianization, believed this "unjust and biased law" was "the reason for the exhorbitant wealth of the few, and the wretchedness of the many," and hence was an obstacle to population growth. In the first place, he explained, the concentration of property in the hands of the few prevented the many from acquiring it, thus depriving them of the subsistence necessary for their reproduction. In the second place, it hurt the nation's agriculture and general wealth because the great proprietors "sacrificed" their land for hunting preserves and for "all those proud and ostentatious villas" instead of farming it. Lastly, the exclusive privilege of primogeniture reduced the rate of reproduction in the landowning families themselves by sacrificing "many cadet sons to the first-born" and thereby condemning the same number of high-born girls to spinsterhood.[29] Even the moderate Palmieri, resolute defender of property for its social and economic usefulness, looked askance on the excessive engrossment caused by primogeniture and entail because "the desire to practice good farming only rarely coincides with the opportunity to do so"; he believed that "all land boundaries [should be] fixed in accordance with the possibility of cultivating them properly."[30] In short, the front of the enlightened reformers was one and united on the question of majorat and primogeniture. Consequently, all the proposals put forth for antifeudal legislation from 1799 to 1806 contemplated the problem; all sought to abolish escheat and entail, and at least to modify the rights of primogeniture. The law abolishing feudalism in the Kingdom of Naples, promulgated in 1806, maintained the hereditary nobility and the transmission of titles by order of birth (Art. 3), but the economic implications of primogeniture were modified by the adoption of the Italian version of the Code Napoléon, which established, as it had in France, equal

---

28. A. Genovesi, *Delle lezioni di commercio o sia d'economia civile,* pt. 1, chap. 11, reprinted in *Illuministi Italiani,* vol. 5: *Riformatori Napoletani,* ed. F. Venturi (Milan and Naples, 1962), 218.

29. G. Filangieri, *La scienza della legislazione* (Naples, 1788), pt. 2, chap. 4, 14–17.

30. G. Palmieri, "Riflessioni sulla pubblica felicità relativamente al Regno di Napoli," art. 8, and "Pensieri economici relativi al Regno di Napoli (Demani)," in *Illuministi Italiani,* op. cit., 1129, 1139, 1142. The grounds for John Stuart Mill's argument against primogeniture several decades later were quite different: modern farms ought to be run by people who have seriously studied the principles of scientific agriculture, while the large landowners never studied anything seriously (*Principles of Political Economy* [London, 1929], 231–32).

rights of succession for all offspring, firstborn and cadet, male and female alike.

Nonetheless, the class of new large landowners—spiritual children of the reformers—was the very one that defended the institution of majorat, though less for reasons of lineage than for economic motives. The same social and economic changes made during the "French decade," and the same world market situation that had led to the rise of this new class in southern Italy, also fostered the centralization and concentration of landed property for reasons of economic efficiency. After the Restoration, the class of latifondisti who wanted legal means to prevent property from being split found a powerful ally in Minister Luigi Medici, whose plan for economic reform benefitted large-scale enterprises. On August 5, 1818, a new law reinstated majorat, though it partly retained the spirit of the French-inspired legislation by reserving a portion of family inheritance to younger children.

In fact, it was primarily for economic reasons, and only secondarily the result of his desire to imitate the practices of the great, that by an act dated February 14, 1822, Alfonso Barracco instituted a majorat on some of his properties in Calabria for the benefit of his only son Luigi and Luigi's eldest son. These properties, located in ten different townships, amounted to about half of Alfonso's possessions and included various kinds of land ranging from arable fields to pastures, cottages, rural houses, palaces, gristmills, and stables, as well as the mansion in Altilia and the lodge at Camigliati.[31]

In the years following the majorat act, Alfonso and Luigi greatly engrossed the family latifondo, so that at Luigi's death, in 1849, the entailed properties amounted to only 18 percent of the total. But the Barraccos behaved as if the entire latifondo were entailed. As mentioned above, they adhered substantially as well as formally to the institution of primogeniture; they firmly believed that the family property should remain one and undivided—it should grow but never be parceled out—in the best interests of the family, of each and all of its members, of the family name, and even of the inhabitants of the territories concerned. For the patrimony to remain whole, no new heirs should raise claims against it; in fact, there should be no heirs other than those fathered by the eldest son.

For the younger sons, this goal was easy enough to achieve: they simply did not marry. While Alfonso II became the father of nine, his brothers had no children: Francesco, Stanislao, and Giovanni remained bachelors. Roberto and

---

31. The properties under the majorat were of various natures: arable fields, pastures, thickets, vineyards, olive groves, kitchen gardens, oak stands, uncultivated land, cottages, workshops, bakeries, gristmills, cowsheds and stables. They were located in the townships of Isola, Croton, Rocca Bernarda, Santa Severina, Altilia, Cotronei, Rocca di Neto, and Scandale, as well as Spezzano Grande and Celico in the Sila uplands (see BA: G and F).

Guglielmo married late, the latter in a rather unusual way, as we shall see. The younger sons never claimed the portions to which they were legally entitled. At once owners and nonowners, they continued to oversee the property in the family's interest. All of them appointed the titled brother's eldest son their universal heir, applying the letter of the law while perpetuating the spirit of the majorat.

The married daughters were excluded from succession to real property in exchange for handsome compensation. The Barracco family was wealthy enough to marry all its girls well, but their rights in the estate, though guaranteed by law, in fact ceased upon their weddings when they received a cash equivalent instead. At Luigi's death, for instance, the family council fixed a *legitime,* that is the share of inheritance to which children were entitled, at 63,170.42 ducats to be provided to each of the twelve heirs out of the assets remaining after deducting the majorat share. The female heirs then could—or rather, had to—transfer their rights in the estate to their brothers and their mother (as guardian of the underage children). Between October of 1851 and January of 1853, all five Barracco sisters performed this "voluntary duty." The actual sale price fixed for each portion was 100,000 ducats (from which the daughter's dowry was deducted)—not exactly a pittance. The integrity of the "property of land, buildings, and livestock" was of indisputable value to the family, important enough to warrant the enormous outlay of 360,000 ducats over a period of just a few years.[32]

5. Division in the Family and Partition of the Estate

Loyalty to the institution of majorat can thus be legitimately considered one of the cornerstones of the Barracco fortune. Its evident erosion during the 1860s was a sure sign that family solidarity itself was weakening. The problems resulted partly from the troubles that broke out during the period of Italian unification and partly from the disproportionate growth of the Barraccos' land possessions, which by then stretched as far as the Terra del Lavoro (today the province of Caserta). The brothers who lived in Calabria, especially Stanislao and Guglielmo, complained that this immense property—which by 1869 amounted to 94,260 *tomolate* (79,178 acres)—was not being managed properly. The Camigliati buildings damaged in the revolts of July 1848, during the wave of peasant struggles, had never been properly repaired; the great olive groves in Petrizia, destroyed by the brigands in 1860–63, had not been replanted. Liabilities and credits, either uncollectable or "extremely difficult to collect," were mounting up apace. The blame for this situation was explicitly

---

32. Teresina and Eleonora were given their dowries together with the inheritance sale price (BA: F [bills of sale and transfer]).

and implicitly attributed to Alfonso, whom Guglielmo reproached for neglecting the administration of the property and paying more attention to luxury and political and social prestige than to business. In effect, Alfonso's thoughts were elsewhere. Italian unity had shifted the interests of the Neapolitan nobility both geographically and politically, making Rome an alternative center. The pursuit of prestige now involved—or, rather, consisted of—obtaining positions of political representation: a strategy that divided the Barraccos who sought to make the family patrimony yield from those who were simply spending it and enjoying the glory. For the first time, tensions among the Barraccos and objections to the policy of the head of the family appeared in written documents: "circulars," evaluations of management, and proposals to divide the estate and sell some holdings to pay debts. On top of all this, in November of 1868 a rather startling gesture came from the mother—a gesture of protest against the privilege of primogeniture, which condemned six of her sons to bachelorhood. Aged and quite sick, Chiara Lucifero demanded and obtained the repayment of her dowry, interest included—6,400 ducats in all—and bequeathed it, as she wrote, to "whichever of her six sons (excluding Alfonso) married first."

In light of these tensions, the Barraccos came to a decision to split up the paternal estate. Alfonso presented his brothers with a report on twenty years of administration: detailed inventories of all the realty, chattels, and livestock, debts and credits, and liquidations of the sisters' inheritance rights.

This change was by no means revolutionary. The original majorat portion was left intact and another smaller portion remained the common property of the brothers under Alfonso's administration; the rest of the patrimony was divided among the seven sons (including Alfonso) in equal shares with joint and equal liability in any future contestation. In reality, the shares were not equal in value, composition, yield, or location, but they did reflect faithfully enough the brothers' personal inclinations and the diversity of their lives, as well as the now highly complex articulations of the family's interests.

While the center of the economic fortune remained in Calabria, Naples and its vicinity was the focus of political and social interest. All the properties situated in the provinces of Upper Calabria (Cosenza) and Lower Calabria II (Catanzaro) were parceled out among the first four brothers: Alfonso, Francesco, Stanislao, and Guglielmo, the oldest and, especially the latter two, most experienced in management. The younger sons Roberto and Maurizio, who had spent little time in Calabria and were to all effects Neapolitans, and Giovanni, who was more interested in politics and art than in agriculture, obtained properties in Naples and in the Terra di Lavoro that were more suitable for amusement than economic profit.

The logic of this partition insured that the unity of the latifondo remained practically intact. The majorat portion left in usufruct to the eldest son included most of the Sila enclosures with the capital in Camigliati, the hillside properties in Rocca di Neto, Rocca Bernarda, Cotronei, Santa Severina, and Altilia, and part of the flatlands in Isola di Capo Rizzuto. The adjacent holdings were all included in the portion assigned to Alfonso in burgage tenure,[33] together with a great many income-producing properties (such as warehouses) in the city of Croton. In this way, the essential part of the Barracco empire was still administered by the head of the family: grain cultivation, most of the cattle and sheep husbandry and dairy production, all the horse-raising operations, the licorice works, and the warehouses and fairgrounds buildings in Santo Janni and Molerà.[34] The shares of the other three "Calabrian" brothers surrounded this core of the "empire" in a semicircle arched between Isola and Croton. Francesco made his home at San Leonardo, Stanislao at Cutro, and Guglielmo at Cotronei.[35] Of the four brothers, however, only Stanislao and Guglielmo actually lived in Calabria. Alfonso, as we have seen, resided permanently in Naples, where the sickly Francesco also lived most of the year. The symbolic old family mansion in Croton gradually deteriorated. The partition left the building and all its furniture in the joint possession of the four brothers (though all the silverware went to Alfonso), but none of them took any care of it. Stanislao lived in Cutro, Guglielmo in Caccuri, and on the few occasions when Alfonso came to Calabria he stayed in his palace in Isola, his house at Spezzano Piccolo, or his lodge at Camigliati.

The properties alloted to Giovanni, Maurizio, and Roberto, the three "Neapolitan" brothers, were located in the Terra di Lavoro and included parks and gardens, reclaimed holdings, and hunting reserves with lodges. Each received a one-third interest in the great warehouses in the port of Naples, a third

---

33. It is interesting to note that the principle of majorat was perpetuated with reference to older legal concepts. In fact, the majorat portion could not be sold; it was inherited together with the title, not necessarily in the direct line of succession.

34. Alfonso's share included most of the livestock: all of the flocks of choice sheep (Merinos, French, and hybrid), the thoroughbred horses, two-thirds of the cattle herds, all of the oxen (except for smaller "caravans" assigned to the three "Calabrian" brothers), all of the donkeys, half of the saddle horses, and half of the draft mules.

35. Most of Francesco's share consisted of the former Tacina fief in the township of Cutro; San Leonardo, where he made his home; other holdings in the same township; and the Camerlongo holding in Rocca Bernardo. He was also assigned a flock of common sheep and a "caravan" of a hundred oxen.

Stanislao, who made his home nearby, received the former Massanova fief in Cutro and the Terrata fief in Rocca Bernarda. His share also included lands in Belcastro, several farms near Croton, some of the Sila properties located in Aprigliano, and Pinicollito Sottano in San Giovanni in Fiore, as well as a flock of common sheep and thirty oxen.

Guglielmo established his headquarters in the fully furnished old castle at Caccuri. His share included the surrounding lands, several holdings in Belvedere and San Giovanni in Fiore, as well as a good deal of livestock: a third of the choice cattle, the other half of the saddle horses and draft mules, and thirty oxen.

of the furnishings and silverware of the palace on Strada Monte di Dio (but not the building itself, which still belonged to Giulia Caracciolo), and a third of its "carriage-horses, carriages, harness and stable equipment."[36]

A few years later, two of the younger sons, Guglielmo and Roberto, married. We can be sure, however, that they were not aiming at the 6,400 ducats they were to receive under their mother's will. Roberto married the wealthy and attractive Artemisia, of the family of Marquis Balbi of Genoa, and Guglielmo's bride brought him a rich dowry worthy of the Barraccos. In fact, she was a Barracco herself and the bridegroom's own niece—Giulia, the daughter of Alfonso and the now-deceased Emilia. After papal dispensation was obtained for the marriage, the wedding was held in 1874 at Alfonso's palace in Isola. The baron consigned the 425,000 lire dowry (the Barracco's usual 100,000 ducats)[37] to his brother/son-in-law and a rich trousseau of clothing, linens, and jewelry to the bride as her exclusive property. We can only speculate on the reasons for this unusual match. Alfonso may have wished to tie this somewhat recalcitrant brother closer to the family interests; Guglielmo was the only competent and energetic manager of them all, and the only one residing permanently in Calabria (Stanislao was ill and died a few years later). Financial considerations may have been involved; the Barraccos needed no new exogamic alliances to sustain their position, and the 100,000 ducats of Giulia's dowry may have come in handy. It may be that the uncle and the niece, who were practically the same age and had grown up together, were in love. Be that as it may, the couple went to live in Calabria, where Guglielmo, besides managing his own property, looked after that of the absent Alfonso, the dead Stanislao, and Francesco in the interest of his nephews: Alfonso's sons Luigi, Errico, and especially Alberto, Giulia's and his favorite. The couple never had children of their own. Thus, everything seemed to have returned to the situation preceding partition of the family property.

As can be readily seen, the partition did not signify the end of the majorat, the breakup of the property, or a radical renunciation of the principle of primogeniture. It simply gave the younger brothers a degree of economic independence, left them free to marry if they wished, and rescaled the productive property to manageable size. In reality, however, it marked the end of rigid, routine, feudal application of the majorat and the privilege of primogeniture,

---

36. The shares assigned to the three "Neapolitan" brothers were about equal in value and composition. The lands were located in the townships of Vitulaccio, Pignataro, Grazianise, and Santa Maria Capua Vetere, and included many parks and gardens, improved holdings with houses, barns, and outbuildings. The warehouses in the port of Naples were located on Largo della Dogana Vecchia.

37. The dowry was paid in cash and notes. The amount was to be deducted from the bride's maternal inheritance (which Alfonso was then administering) and from her future paternal inheritance.

and it subverted the principle of forced concentration of the family to which the Barraccos, like so many other southern (and not only southern)[38] aristocrats, adhered for seven decades after its legal extinction.

6. Continuity and Change

But allowing the cornerstone of the family fortunes to weaken meant that the Barraccos, too, had changed. In the 1870s and 1880s—the last years of Alfonso II and his sons' administration—neither their attitudes nor their economic and social choices changed, but throughout their activities the old spirit of enterprise and innovation was on the wane. On the one hand there was continuity unpunctuated by any strokes of genius, on the other there was some change, a kind of modernization, though not necessarily leading in a positive direction.

Though the principle of primogeniture was definitively abolished in 1865 by the Kingdom of Italy's new Civil Code, the Barracco family continued to adhere to it in practice. The heir presumptive to the baronial title and the estate was Luigi, Alfonso II and Emilia's first child. Their fourth child, Ernesto, had died very young, and, according to tradition, Errico and Alberto had remained bachelors. Only when it was "officially" recognized that Luigi, still a bachelor at the age of almost fifty, would probably remain such did the family's expectations shift to Errico, the second son, already forty himself.

In April of 1884, a magnificent and prestigious marriage was arranged for him with Maria Doria, daughter of Marcantonio, the duke of Eboli. The event was a highlight of the Neapolitan social season.

> The ceremony took place with great pomp in the grand apartment of Palazzo Angri. . . . The godfather of the marriage was Baron Giovanni Barracco, deputy in Parliament; the witnesses were the Prince of Stigliano, the Prince of Ottajano, the Prince of Strongoli and Baron Labonia . . .

reported *La Gazzetta di Napoli*.[39]

It was a brillant and opulent match but also one between two social peers. The marriage contract speaks of "decorum and luster worthy of [Barracco's] name, and equally of the bride's."[40] These were weighty words: in fact, Maria

---

38. A. Mayer, *The Persistence of the Old Regime* (New York, 1981).

39. *La Gazzetta di Napoli*, April 29, 1884.

40. Alfonso Barracco, "as proof of his affection, and to enable his son to sustain the charges inherent in his new status with dignity and prestige worthy of his name and that of his bride," made over to his son the Petrizia holding in Lower Calabria II as well as gristmills and rural buildings in Catanzaro, Simeri, Crichi, and Soveria townships, for a total yearly revenue of 28,280 lire. In addition, the bridegroom received a gift of cash.

Doria was the great-granddaughter of Marcantonio Doria, the powerful prince of Angri, incumbent of Calabria's Barony of Tacina and Massanova, who in the early years of the century had gotten himself so deeply in debt to Alfonso and Luigi Barracco, the bridegroom's great-grandfather and grandfather, that he was forced to make all his property in Calabria over to them (as we shall see in the next chapter).

The principle of primogeniture continued to govern the Barraccos' testamentary practices as well. The main or universal heirs named in the bachelor uncles' and brothers' wills were invariably Alfonso II's sons, particularly Errico and his eldest son, Alfonso III, the individuals who were expected to perpetuate the family name; nieces were usually left cash bequests.[41]

The matrimonial strategies devised for the daughters simply continued along the beaten track: the days of hypergamy and social climbing were over, and the family returned to the practice of social endogamy. Alfonso II's daughters all made excellent marriages in the upper echelons of Neapolitan society, but unlike their aunts' matches none of theirs permitted further social or political ascent.[42] The family continued its traditional practice of liquidating the female childrens' inheritance rights in cash; after Alfonso's death in 1890, the male heirs purchased their sisters' interests in the paternal estate for the goodly sum of 350,000 lire apiece.

The estate continued to grow by purchase and inheritance—the now traditional and conventional means—with no special strokes of genius. Alfonso, Guglielmo, and Francesco bought some state lands, adjacent to their own, which were subdivided and put up for auction after Italy's unification. Other properties came to them by court judgments issued after decades of litigation.[43] Giulia Caracciolo's estate—awaited since Alfonso II's wedding to Emilia Carafa—finally came to the family upon her death in 1875. Having survived her "beloved and ever-lamented sister-in-law," Giulia disposed of her

---

41. Francesco Barracco, who died in Naples in 1878, left half of his estate to his nephews Luigi, Errico, and Alberto, and the other half to his brother Roberto. The nieces Francesca, Amalia, Carolina, and Giulia (Chiara, the eldest, had died very young) inherited sums of money. Only Guglielmo, always the odd man out, made his wife Giulia his universal heir, urging her to look after Alberto, their favorite. Giulia, more respectful of family tradition, made Errico's eldest son her universal heir (BA: F and G [manuscript wills]). I owe the infomation on Roberto's marriage and heirs to the kind attention of Mrs. Giuseppina Emo Pignatelli.

42. Giulia's marriage to her uncle Guglielmo was mentioned above. Carolina, too, married in the family. Named after her aunt Carolina Barracco Pignatelli, princess of Strongoli, she married her cousin Luigi Pignatelli in 1879. Amelia married the duke of San Cesareo, Ettore Marulli; Francesca, the youngest daughter, married baronet Eduardo Pandola.

43. The new purchases were located in the townships of Isola, Rocca di Neto, Rocca Bernarda, San Mauro Marchesato, Celico, Caccuri, and Polligrone. According to an estimate Guglielmo made in 1895, they increased the value of the Calabrian properties (land and livestock) by 475,600 lire.

possessions as she had undertaken to do in the marriage contract, naming Emilia's eldest son Luigi her universal successor and her other male children heirs beneficiary; in addition, she left sums of money to Emilia's daughters. The balance of Giulia's estate amounted to more than 400,000 lire and consisted primarily of lands and buildings in the city and province of Naples (including the mansion at 75 Strada Monte di Dio where the Barracco family had been living since 1849), and properties located in various townships in the Caserta region, in Atena near Salerno, and in Brienza in Basilicata—Giulia bore the titles of princess of Atena and marquise of Brienza—as well as furniture, money, credit notes, and government bonds. Errico Barracco inherited other landed property in 1888 on the death of his cousin Giuseppe, prince of Caramanico and the son of Errico d'Aquino and Emanuela Barracco.[44]

Alfonso II died in 1890. Five years later his still-unwed eldest son Luigi died in Isola, leaving practically the whole estate to his brothers Errico and Alberto. In 1901 Errico and Alberto divided equally between them (each portion yielding 98,373 lire yearly) the succession to the estates of their father, their brother, and their uncle Francesco, leaving the licorice works and the property from the Caracciolo estate undivided and under separate administration for reasons of economic opportunity. In 1903, by a will that could well have been drawn up by the old notary public De Meo in Isola di Capo Rizzuto eighty years before, Alberto (who lived in Paris) made his little nephew Alfonso his universal successor and his brother Errico usufructuary. Giovanni had already delegated the whole administration of his property to his nephew. Alberto died in 1909, Giovanni in 1914, Roberto in 1917, Guglielmo's wife Giulia in 1920, and Errico himself in 1923. Thus, a hundred years after Alfonso Barracco assembled the first core of the empire, the whole estate came back into the hands of a single owner—his great-great-grandson Alfonso.

7. Absentee Landlords

Alfonso II was the last of the Barraccos who, though established permanently in Naples and with little interest in Calabrian affairs, still attended to his image as a Calabrian landowner. He would tour his possessions at the traditional times when landowners put in an appearance—for instance, during the Santo Janni fair in May—and he checked the administrators' accounts once a year. But he was also the one who introduced a political dimension into the family's practices.

Times had changed. With the advent of the Italian state, the prestige that earlier generations had garnered from official honorific titles like "Gentleman

---

44. As his cousin's legatee, Errico Barracco came into lands in Sant'Andrea di Pizzone and San Felice a Cancello as well as a sum of money. In 1900, Maria was paid off in cash and jewels from the Doria estate.

of His Majesty's Chamber" now required election to political office. It is a well-known fact that the latifondisti of Calabria, who had been gravitating toward the liberals for a decade or two, and had eventually supported Garibaldi's expedition to Calabria, won political representation in the very first elections of 1861—Giovanni Barracco was elected deputy in the Catanzaro district, Baron Pietro Compagna in the Cosenza district, Prince Gerardo Carafa di Roccella in the Reggio district—and kept a firm grasp on it for over fifty years.[45] The Barraccos partook from the start, and truly en masse: Alfonso was appointed senator in January of 1861, while Francesco was made knight of the Order of the Crown of Italy and Giovanni was elected deputy. Giovanni maintained his hold for decades; he was elected in one district or another—first Croton, Spezzano Grande, and Catanzaro, later Santa Maria Caputa Vetere—to every one of the legislatures (except the 13th) until 1886 when he was appointed senator. His nephew Luigi joined him in the Chamber of Deputies in 1880 and remained there for five terms until his younger brother Alberto took over in 1895 for another four. Shortly after (1896), Roberto Barracco joined his brother Giovanni in the Senate.[46]

Not that half a century of the Barraccos' service in office left much of a mark in the annals of Parliament, either for the kind of participation they engaged in or for any political innovation. Public office served them on the local level, above all to underline the family's political hegemony and to prevent incursions by the competition; on the national level, it was merely a status symbol. Only Giovanni had a rather brilliant career in Parliament: he was first quaestor of the Chamber for three terms, deputy speaker of the Chamber and quaestor of the Senate, and he promoted and sponsored some legislation, but his main interest was preservation of the antiquities and artistic heritage of the city of Rome not local politics.[47] The other Barraccos, though surprisingly assiduous in their attendance at Parliament—always seated with the Luciferos, the Compagnas, the Berlingieris, the D'Alifes, the Chimirris, and their non-Calabrian relatives and allies (such as the Pignatelli-Strongoli or the Pallavicini)—were heard from but rarely. Certainly they always adhered to the obvious politics of latifondismo—they were rightists until 1882, pro-

---

45. R. De Cesare lists the Calabrian subscribers to Garibaldi's 1860 campaign. The province of Catanzaro contributed more than forty thousand ducats, of which 75 percent came from Croton, city of latifondisti. Barracco's name headed the list, for the sum of ten thousand ducats (R. De Cesare, *Una famiglia di Patriotti: Ricordi di due rivoluzioni in Calabria* [Rome, 1889], cli). On political representation, see, among others, G. Cingari, *Storia della Cababria dall'Unità a oggi* (Bari, 1982), 15 and passim.

46. Luigi Barracco was elected in Spezzano Grande and Cosenza to the 14th, 15th, 16th, and 17th legislatures, Alberto in Spezzano to the 19th, 20th, 21st, and 22d.

47. See, for example, the Senate proceedings for the 16th legislature (*Atti Parlamentari: Senato del Regno,* 10, 26–28, 1264, 1273, 1657ff). See also F. Spezzano, *La lotta politica in Calabria, 1861–1925* (Manduria, 1968).

government with Depretis's *trasformismo,* and partisans of Sonnino in 1904—
and when their own class interests were threatened they were even capable of
promoting or joining political alliances, for instance, during the battles over
land tax equalization, war taxes, and grain tariffs, which we shall discuss in a
later chapter.[48]

With Errico things changed permanently, for he played neither the administrator nor the deputy. For him, Calabria was a distant land, altogether too hard
to reach. The business was by now completely in the hands of the administrators; political defense was entrusted to the more knowledgeable. Errico was
becoming a typical absentee landlord, without a trace of the combative spirit of
enterprise that the earlier generations had shared, while the estate was
deteriorating and the economic crisis of the latter years of the century was
calling for prompt action. His uncle Guglielmo, already ill, wrote to him in a
long letter in 1898 that the burden of debt on the property in Calabria amounted
to almost two million lire, a third of its equity value; that of all the mansions in
Calabria, only the ones in Camigliati and Isola were in a decent state; that the
one in Spezzano Piccolo, uninhabited and in bad repair, contained very few,
and valueless, furnishings; that the Altilia mansion had fallen into disrepair,
and had "only a very little ramshackle furniture"; that the great palace in
Croton, completely uninhabited since 1880, was dilapidated and practically
empty. Errico did nothing, and the same fate struck the castle of Caccuri after
Guglielmo's death. Absent and uninterested, the family also missed the traditional opportunities for profit and now hardly even defended its property. It had
lost a series of lawsuits against the public domain, and was de facto tolerating
encroachments on its lands by more aggressive proprietors or by townsmen.[49]
The Barraccos had been neglected by government officials looking in Calabria
for potential contractors to supply wood for railroad construction. What would
old Alfonso and Luigi have said?

Errico's life was by now that of a high-class rentier. He lived in Naples but
attended all the court events in Rome; his three daughters married men of the
great southern aristocracy, as family tradition dictated.[50] His only son, Alfonso, was still a boy when Errico died at the age of eighty in 1923, still in that

---

48. A. Malatesta, *Ministri, deputati, senatori dal 1848 al 1922* (Milan, 1934), ser. 43; G.
Cingari, *Storia della Calabria,* op. cit., 15, 61–62, 64, 122, 147. Incidentally, both Alfonso and
Roberto were appointed senators for the 21st bracket: the least exalted, since it included "persons
who have paid 3000 lire in direct taxes for the past three years." Only Giovanni was appointed
senator for having served as a deputy in three legislatures (3d category).

49. Decades later, the Barraccos were sentenced to pay rental arrears of *fida, giogatico,* and
alberatura for farming state-owned pasture lands in the Sila. See P. Cinanni, *Lotte per la terra e
comunisti in Calabria, 1943–53* (Milan, 1977); and BA: D and E (court documents).

50. Emilia married Gaetano Caracciolo, prince of Castagneto; Laura married Ettore Carafa,
count of Andria; and Francesca married Paolo Gaetani, eldest son of the count of Aquila
d'Aragona.

same palace on Strada Monte di Dio. Thus, the Barraccos' century-long trajectory came to a stop; like so many other great landed families of the southern periphery, they began as pioneer latifondisti and ended as absentee owners. Yet the choices they made seem rational, typical, and virtually inevitable. The great landed property on the periphery served well as a springboard to attain high economic and social status, but perpetuating it required a presence in the center, both personal—appearances at court and in society, participation in institutional structures, and the attainment of honorific positions—and symbolic—rank endogamy, expenditure on luxuries, and privileges. In the long run, combining the imperative of this presence in the center (and its economic cost) with continuation of an aggressive and innovative entrepreneurial commitment on the periphery turned out to be impossible, and the Barraccos, following a typical path, eventually opted for the former. On the whole, however, the nineteenth century was for them, as for all of Europe's landed aristocracy, a period of flowering and stability. In the absence of agrarian reform, this class was capable not only of surviving political earthquakes and parliamentary reforms but of preserving its influence in local and national politics, maintaining its social prestige, and safeguarding the sources of its economic stability. Its crisis, in fact, came only with the Great Depression of European agriculture at the end of the century.[51]

---

51. The history of southern Italy's landed aristocracy in the nineteenth century was much the same as that of their English counterparts. In England, as Goodwin put it, the nineteenth century was the "Indian summer of the landed governing classes." See A. Goodwin, "The Landed Aristocracy as a Governing Class in XIXth Century Britain," in *Rapports I* of the XIIe Congrès International des Sciences Historiques (Vienna, 1965), 368–74.

CHAPTER 2

The Formation of the Barracco Latifondo

The Barraccos' immense "empire" was assembled over a fairly short period of time between the antifeudal legislation of 1806 and Baron Luigi's death in 1849, at which time the family moved to Naples.[1] It will be recalled that toward the end of the eighteenth century Luigi's uncles had been forced to mortgage the small Arvicello holding in order to scrape up some cash, but their nephew left a landed fortune of 94,260 tomolate, or about 79,180 acres. As was the case for other Calabrian latifondisti, the Barraccos' extremely swift land accumulation drew primarily on uncustomary sources and the opportunities offered by the historical moment.[2] Of course, they did buy some land on the free market in the (so to speak) normal way, but these purchases were fairly rare and hardly significant from the standpoint of acreage; in fact, the aggregate area they purchased recorded in the thirteen bills of sale executed in that period was less than 2,000 tomolate. The major sources of land accumulation, which brought

---

1. Except where otherwise indicated, the sources used for this chapter are documents in the Barracco Archives (BA), particularly Sec. A, vols. 95 and 96 (1, 2, 3, 4), containing cadaster abstracts, bills of sale and exchange, loan agreements, and mortgage deeds; Sec. C, vol. 6 (1, 3, 5, 6, 77), vols. 10, 17, and 20 (3, 4, 11), vol. 28 (2), vol. 29 (1, 2, 3), vol. 30, and vol. 31, containing documents on state-owned properties and their subdivision, the 1811 decrees, copies of the decisions of the Feudal Commission, conveyances of formerly feudal properties, and abstracts from the Provisional Cadaster; and Sec. E, vols. 1–34, containing documentation on lawsuits against individuals, townships, and the government, court verdicts, and public auctions.

2. Ascanio Branca, discussing the origin of the fortunes of the great Calabrian landowners (the Barraccos, the Berlingieris, the Compagnas, and the Quintieris) in the final report on the Agrarian Inquiry, indicated "the suppression of many religious corporations from 1806 to 1815, during the French monarchy, and the sale of their property for modicum prices" (*Atti della Giunta per la Inchiesta Agraria e sulle condizioni della classe agricola* [Rome, 1883], vol. 9, fasc. I, p. xxv). As E. Labrousse remarks, "Le monde de la grande propriété et de la grande exploitation fermière figure en tête des gagnants" in that extraordinary political and economic situation ("Elément d'un bilan économique: La croissance dans la guerre," in Comité International des Sciences Historiques, *Rapports I: Grands Thèmes* [Vienna, 1965], 493).

the Barraccos thousands upon thousands of acres, lay elsewhere: former feudal estates, expropriated Church lands, foreclosed properties, acquisition of credits secured by real property and subsequently foreclosed, encroachment, and the purchase of peasants' allotments. In other words, the Barraccos participated to the hilt in the process of original accumulation in Calabria that had been set in motion and nurtured by the general circumstances of the era: the redistribution of existing wealth by violence, both legal (judicial foreclosures and the acquisition of credits) and illegal (encroachments); the privatization and concentration of land possession (purchases of former fiefs and Church lands); and the failure of attempts at reform (redemption of peasant allotments).[3] The ways and means the Barraccos employed to build and consolidate their latifondo—extraordinarily similar to those used to form great estates in other countries and other eras—are emblematic of the whole great transformation then in progress.[4]

1. Purchases of Former Feudal Estates

The most abundant of the sources on which the Barraccos drew, and the one that eventually formed more than half of the whole latifondo, consisted of properties formerly held in feudal tenure. In those years, the Barraccos came into possession of five Calabrian estates, all freeholds belonging to illustrious members of the kingdom's aristocracy.[5] The stories of these five acquisitions are worth telling, as their common features are of no little interest.

The Caccuri fief, which had been held in the eighteenth century by the Cavalcante ducal family, passed by marriage to the Ceva Grimaldi, a family of Genoa merchants that had been granted a patent of nobility. In 1830, Duchess Rachele, "needing to constitute her dowry," sold the estate (4,571 tomolate, or

---

3. See Marx's classic definition of primitive accumulation in chapter 26 of *Capital*. As Paul Sweezy remarks, Marx's term *ursprüngliche akkumulation* should properly be translated as "primary" or "original" accumulation, to give the idea of a stage in time rather than of a crude and simple process. The period of primary accumulation, though crude and violent, was anything but simple. See S. H. Hymer, "Robinson Crusoe and the Secret of Primitive Accumulation," *Monthly Review* 4 (September 1971): 10–11.

4. See, for instance, for Mexico, F. Chevalier, *La formación de los grandes latifundios en México* (Mexico City, 1952); and D. A. Brading, *Haciendas and Ranchos in the Mexican Bajio, León, 1700–1860* (Cambridge, 1978). A study of a Spanish *latifundo* belonging to the Roca de Togores y Juan family of Alicante in the nineteenth century shows exactly the same swift accumulation, the same sources, the same mechanisms, and the same landowners' mentality in similar historical circumstances. See A.-M. Bernal and J.-F. de la Pena, "Formación de una gran propriedad agraria: Análisis de una contabilidad agrícola del siglo XIX," in *Agricultura, comercio colonial,* op. cit., 131ff.

5. See R. Trifone, *Feudi e demani nell'Italia meridionale: Eversione della feudalità nelle province napoletane* (Milan, 1909).

3,840 acres) to Baron Barracco for 52,816 ducats.[6] According to the land register, it yielded 4,409 ducats a year (this sum, declared for tax purposes, was certainly not overstated), which, capitalized at 5 percent, gave the property a value of about 90,000 ducats. That is, it was worth almost twice the price the Barraccos paid for it.

The Isola fief passed in 1798 from the Marano family to Marquis Ignazio Friozzi, who sold it to Barracco in 1806 for 120,000 ducats in cash plus the baron's assumption of debts incurred by Friozzi for 100,000 ducats at 4 percent interest.

The princely fief of Cerenzia belonged to the Giannuzzi Savelli family. Prince Tommaso was strapped for cash, as he owed 7,000 ducats for the dowry of a daughter engaged to Baron Mollo and annuities to two other children. Already indebted to Barracco for 36,000 ducats, the prince sold him the estate for just 130,000 ducats.[7]

The fief of Cutro and Castella belonged to Don Giovanbattista Filomarino, who was prince of La Rocca, duke of Perdifumo, and baron of Cutro but resident in Apulia. The prince was in debt to the treasury, to the townships, and to private citizens; he owed his son-in-law, Marquis Cita, 10,000 ducats for his daughter's dowry and another 2,400 for the cost of the wedding. Between 1811 and 1817, little by little, the nobleman made the estate's 5,734 tomolate over to Baron Barracco for a total of 77,516 ducats; its assessed value would have been 114,680 ducats.

The barony of Tacina and Massanova had belonged to the Doria family since the sixteenth century.[8] In 1813, the property, consisting of 15,780 tomolata, was encumbered by debts to the treasury and townships and by the 2,010-ducat annuity due to the owner's sister, Marina. The owner, Marcantonio Doria, prince of Angri (whose great-granddaughter Maria would later marry Errico Barracco), began to borrow money from Alfonso Barracco, backing his debts with mortgages on the barony. In 1820, the far-sighted Barracco had Doria delegate him vicarial powers over the barony, whereby he and his son Luigi were authorized to collect rents, attach property, and evict defaulting tenants. Meanwhile, Barracco was buying up Doria's tax and private debts

---

6. Of the total purchase price, 14,756 ducats were paid immediately, and the remaining 38,060 were converted at the duchess's request into a long-term loan yielding 5 percent interest, which would ensure her an annual income of 1,904 ducats (BA: E, F, G [Grimaldi and Cavalcante papers]).

7. This was a kind of homecoming for the Barraccos. One of the Cerenzia hamlets that had disappeared after the disastrous epidemic of 1528 was Bruscano, property of the Barraccos, patricians of Cosenza. See G. Valente, *Dizionario dei luoghi delle Calabrie* (Chiaravalle Centrale, 1973).

8. For the history of the baronies of Tacina and Massanova through the sixteenth century, see G. Galasso, *Economia e società, op. cit.,* 29, 33, 193, 289.

little by little. When the barony was finally sold to Barracco in 1834 for 330,443 ducats, Doria was already in his debt for 275,443.

Thus the Barraccos came into possession of five fiefs in Calabria, enlarging their patrimony by 51,182 tomolate of land in barely two decades. The common features of these acquisitions are highly significant. All five estates were former fiefs, that is, they were part of the approximately three-quarters of the feudal domain transformed by the law of 1806 into freehold property. Their owners were all illustrious members of the kingdom's lately feudal aristocracy: an aristocracy burdened by debts to the treasury, to the townships, and to private citizens and hard pressed to fulfill the basic obligations of its station (contractual dowries, annuities to children and sisters, ceremonial expenses); an aristocracy that did not know how, or was unable, to manage landed property ("They have no notion how to reckon their income or their debts," the old Leopard remarked), could not squeeze out even its assessed income, left rents uncollected, and kept no accounts. Consequently, in all five cases the land was sold for a fraction of its assessed value.

2. Purchases of Expropriated Lands

Between 1806 and 1815, 1,322 monasteries and convents were suppressed in the Kingdom of Naples, 367 of them in Calabria;[9] their possessions, whose aggregate assessed yearly yield was 62,587.20 ducats, were taken over by the goverment and put up for sale. The idea was not new—Ferdinand IV had tried it after the earthquake in 1783, with the Cassa Sacra[10]—but its scale and its effect on the real estate market were unprecedented, for the Church was the largest landowner in the kingdom: according to Antonio Genovesi, in 1760 it owned two-thirds of the farmland.[11] The declared purpose of the sales was to

---

9. P. Villani, *La vendita dei beni dello Stato* (Milan, 1964), app. 1, table 1. Part of the ecclesiastical properties in Calabria had been expropriated and sold in the 1780s during the operations of the Cassa Sacra. See A. Placanica, *Alle origini,* op. cit., passim.

10. On the Cassa Sacra, see, in particular, A. Placanica, *Cassa Sacra e beni della Chiesa nella Calabria del Settecento* (Naples, 1970). Though Placanica judges the attempt to have been substantially unsuccessful (primarily because 90 percent of the lands remained unsold), he sees it as the forerunner of a bourgeois transformation; for Nino Cortese, however, the Cassa Sacra was simply a failure (see "La Calabria alla fine del secolo XVIII," in his *La cultura calabrese* [n.p., 1921]).

11. A. Genovesi, *Ragionamento intorno all'agricoltura con applicazione al Regno di Napoli* (Naples, 1764), reprinted in his *Feudalità, clero e popolo nel Sud attraverso le visite pastorali del '700* (Naples, 1969). But the data found by Franca Assante in comparing the 1743 cadaster of a Calabrian township with the one compiled under Murat are very different from those Genovesi quotes for the kingdom as a whole: in 1742, half of the land belonged to the nobility and only a quarter to the Church. See *Calopezzati: Proprietà fondiaria e classi rurali in un comune della Calabria, 1740–1886* (Naples, 1964).

replenish the treasury's coffers and at the same time encourage the formation of small and midsized ownership, that is, to serve "both politics and morals," in keeping with the old ideals of the physiocrats and the Jacobins, which had survived even in their monarchist heirs.[12] But, despite the low unit price of these lands, other circumstances conspired to keep potential small and mid-sized buyers away and, as Lefebvre notes apropos of the similar phenomenon in France, to reserve state properties "aux anciens privilégiés et à la haute bourgeoisie."[13] The very fact that the auctions were held mainly in Naples tended to exclude middle-class provincials not to mention the peasants. Also, the sales were settled primarily in assignats—government notes and bonds, which obviously were held by the nobility and the wealthy classes, not by the poorer folk. Galloping depreciation sank the real value of assignats, like that of their French counterparts, to around 20 percent of their par value, on the one hand fostering speculation and the appearance of a black market for scrip in the capital, and on the other reducing the price of land to a fraction of its real value. But the regime's urgent need for quantities of money was supreme, so preferential treatment was given to large-scale buyers who could relieve the government of thousands of acres of land at a single stroke. Napoleon Bonaparte, who had been so generous with his brother Joseph, insisted that Murat not only pay the kingdom's debts but also contribute substantially to the cost of the wars.[14] Thus, despite the vision of a happy world of yeoman farmers, the treasury's state of depletion called for the speedy transfer of government property to anyone who could pay for it, namely, the landowners.

Calabria, like the rest of the kingdom, was affected by the *fièvre des biens d'Eglise* with all the characteristics mentioned above.[15] The sales were held during different periods, the first three reserved to payment in assignats, the

---

12. Speaking of "politics and morality," the sycophant Roederer presented the Napoleonic program of agrarian reform as one that made it possible to fight the southerners' laziness—the worst of public vices, fostered by the climate and bad institutions—and at the same time supplied the emperor with a means of getting out of his financial straits. See *Oeuvres du comte P. L. Roederer publiées par A. Roederer,* vol. 4: *Questions faites par l'Empereur à M. Roederer sur le Royaume de Naples* (Paris, 1856), 20. See, in this connection, P. Colletta, *Storia del Reame di Napoli,* ed. N. Cortese (Naples, 1969).

13. G. Lefebvre, "La vente des biens nationaux," in his *Etudes sur la Révolution Française* (Paris, 1954), 232. According to Hildebrand, Joseph Bonaparte and Murat intended to give preference to the great buyers because large estates would have furthered the production of timber and grain for export. See G. H. Hildebrand, *Growth and Structure in the Economy of Modern Italy* (Cambridge, Mass., 1965), 276–77.

14. See A. Valente, *Gioacchino Murat e l'Italia Meridionale* (Turin, 1965).

15. C. Cipolla observes the same mechanisms operating in the secularization of Church property in the fifteenth century. See "Une crise ignorée: Comment s'est perdue la propriété ecclésiastique dans l'Italie du Nord entre le XI et le XVIe siècles," *Annales E.S.C* (1947): 317–22.

other two to cash payment alone. The former, which benefitted assignat holders, far outstripped the latter, and divestment of major properties was practically over by 1810 after three waves of assignat sales; the two cash sales, held in 1809–10 and 1811–15, involved fairly small tracts of land.[16] In the first period of assignat sales, from 1807 to 1810, a very few buyers came into possession of a great quantity of land. In the first wave, from 1807 to 1808, a single large sale was concluded with one nobleman; in the second, from 1808 to 1809, sixty-eight sales were made to only seven buyers, one of whom took fifty-seven of the lots; in the 1809–10 wave, all nine sales were made to only two buyers.[17]

Analyzing the sales from the standpoint of the yield acquired by each contract and by each buyer (table 1),[18] the picture of the extent of land concentration emerges clearly. The "middle class" bought only during the last period of scrip sales, from 1810 to 1815; the 336 sales were made to 194 buyers, and the yield per buyer was relatively low. But even these purchasers belonged mostly to the new government bourgeoisie not to the native petty bourgeoisie.[19]

The Barraccos were among the people who benefitted most from purchasing government properties, though their name appears directly only in the scrip sales of 1810–15 in a single, very large, purchase agreement and three minor

TABLE 1.   Sales of Expropriated Lands in Calabria (yields acquired by contract and by purchases)

Sale Period	Yield/Contract	Yield/Purchaser
1807–1808	5,377.00	5,377.00
1809–1810[a]	340.81	766.82
1809–1810[b]	47.02	924.68
1810–1815	66.18	114.60

[a]Upper Calabria
[b]Lower Calabria

16. The first of these two waves resulted in one sale to one buyer, the second in eighty-two sales to sixty-eight buyers.

17. The greatest buyer in Calabria in the first period, 1807–8, was Baron Emanuele De Nobili of Catanzaro, who purchased 1,365 tomolate (about 1,150 acres) of land at the Sant'Anna Grange near Isola di Capo Rizzuto, formerly the property of the Cistercian monastery of Santo Stefano del Bosco. De Nobili paid 407,800 ducats in scrip for this property, which yielded 5,377 ducats a year. During the subsequent period of scrip sales, in 1808–9, fifty-seven of the sixty-eight contracts were executed by one Salvatore (or Michele) Prisco.

18. P. Villani, *La vendita,* op. cit., app. 9, table 3. See also G. Brasacchio, *Storia economica della Calabria* (Chiaravalle, 1986), 3:103ff.

19. For example, Upper Calabria Intendent Luigi Flach and War Commissioner Luigi Valentoni bought properties yielding 618.60 and 301.06 ducats, respectively.

ones.[20] But the most significant part of this land redistribution took place far from the lights of the capital. Once the former Church lands entered the redistribution circuit, they followed paths outside the public auctions. Some were resold by the original buyers, others that had not been put up for auction were later sold by the Royal Amortization Fund, and still others were sold after the Restoration by ecclesiastical establishments whose property had been partially returned. It was precisely in these purchases far from the public auctions that the Barraccos proved to be eager and aggressive buyers.

Their most sensational acquisition involved the property of Baron De Nobili, who had been the only buyer from Calabria during the 1807–08 auction. By purchasing the huge Sant'Anna Grange, De Nobili, burdened by debt, sought to mend his financial situation. He never managed to do so. Over the ensuing decades, Barracco patiently bought up the credits encumbering De Nobili's property with an eye to cornering the mortgages on the Grange. When the De Nobili family's financial crisis commenced in 1838, Barracco was their major creditor, with rights to a third of the Grange property, and hence he was the one to demand a judicial sale in 1840 and become the major purchaser.

Other properties came to the Barraccos from the successive governments of Naples. Neither the Napoleonic regime nor the restored Bourbon monarchy had a large enough bureaucracy to manage government properties located in the distant provinces, collect rents, and prevent encroachment. Consequently, the French continued to sell off properties in the provinces, and after 1818 the Bourbons transformed them into a source of national income, selling them in exchange for the buyer's undertaking to pay a yearly remittance to the treasury. Thus, between 1812 and 1818, by means of a number of purchase agreements signed with the Napoleonic provincial intendents Martucci and Petroni, then with Pasquale Serra, prince of Gerace and head of the Bourbons' Royal Amortization Fund, the Barraccos came into possession of practically the whole portion of the Altilia estate lying in the townships of Isola and Santa Severina, formerly the property of a suppressed Cistercian monastery. The purchase involved more than 2,500 acres situated adjacent to other Barracco properties and worth about 150,000 ducats (but paid for in assignats or yearly remittances registered in the Great Ledger).[21]

---

20. The 3,106 tomolate (about 2,610 acres) in Sila di Agarò, where the family originated, yielded 1,784.50 ducats a year, but only 89,225 ducats (in scrip) had been paid for them. The three smaller farms in Lower Calabria cost 9,820 ducats and together yielded 196.40 ducats a year. The Barraccos were not new to this kind of operation: in the 1780s they had grown wealthy by buying former Church properties from the Cassa Sacra. See A. Placanica, *Alle origini,* op. cit., 380 and passim.

21. In December 1812, in Monteleone, Intendent Martucci of the Royal Demesne sold Barracco 393 tomolate (330 acres) in Altilia for 9,640.72 ducats (paid in scrip). Between August of 1814 and July of 1815, Barracco bought several holdings in Santa Severina from Intendent Petroni for 10,480 ducats (in scrip). In 1818, he bought the Campolongo enclosure in Isola from the Royal Administration; in August of that year, Prince Pasquale Serra, director of the Royal Amortization

Lastly, the Church itself was selling off properties. From 1815 to 1818, as the Bourbons proceeded to reorganize the government, unsold properties confiscated from suppressed monasteries and convents were returned to their reestablished owners. But, while the revived monasteries and convents— usually the largest ones belonging to the most powerful orders—were situated in or near the capital, the unsold properties lay out in the remote provinces, far not only from the mother abbey but from any other house of the order. Difficult to manage at a distance, left for a decade without any effective owner, and thus subject to occupation and encroachment, these properties were an inconvenience to their new owners who sought to dispose of them as quickly as possible. Accordingly, in 1836, Luigi Barracco was able to buy almost 2,000 hectares (5,000 acres) from the restored abbey of Santa Maria della Pace in Naples, of the order of St. John of God, for only 40,000 ducats, about 60 percent less than the market price.[22]

All told, up to 1837, the Barracco family bought about 5,000 hectares (12,355 acres) of former Church lands for a total assessed value of 334,197 ducats, paying on average half their worth in depreciated assignats or yearly remittances (that is, by installments). Since the owners of these properties— the government or ecclesiatical bodies—wished to get rid of them, their unit price was very low, but their size made it impossible for peasants or local petty notables to make a go of them; only the largest landowners could do so.

The third replay of the same scenario—the sale of Church property confiscated by the Italian state after 1860—was to star the Barraccos once again. These sales were to have a much smaller impact in Calabria, however, because they were too heavily taxed to lead to the accumulation of great wealth and because by then the new latifondi were already firmly ensconced.

3. Foreclosed Properties

In this section we shall describe the aspect of the Barraccos' financial activity involving loans patently aimed at acquiring landed property.[23] Later we shall look into other kinds of lending transactions and the extension of credit to

---

Bank, sold him 2,556 tomolate (about 2,150 acres) in the Sant'Anna Grange of Santo Stefano del Bosco, registered in the Great Book as yielding 5,000 ducats a year; in September, he bought six warehouses and a tower just outside Croton for 1,197.14 ducats. All these properties formerly belonged to the same Cistercian monastery.

22. The lands comprised 4,922 tomolate (4,986 acres) located in the townships of Cutro, Rocca Bernarda, Cotronei, Marcedusa, and Caccuri (bought for 39,000 ducats) and 288 tomolate (about 260 acres) in Verzino (yielding 326.65 ducats a year). The contracts were executed by Don Nicola Gullo, Luigi Barracco's front man in this and other transactions.

23. This section does not include the cases of the debt-ridden feudal lords discussed above.

immobilize and insure a steady supply of manpower,[24] but the loans we shall examine here were all to people who were not employed in any way by the lender. Small-scale lending was not one of the Barracco family's main occupations, and in the whole period from 1806 to 1849 the barons signed only fifty-nine loan agreements for a total principal of 84,696 ducats. The significant fact is that all of these loans, down to the smallest, were backed by mortgages on the debtor's land. In twenty-two cases, or 37 percent of all the agreements, the outcome was the sale, forced or voluntary, of the mortgaged property; in reality the percentage was higher because many of the loans were contracted in different periods by the same people.

These debtors ranged from peasants who owned but a few acres to mid-sized landowners—the local "dons." Debts were frequently contracted by widows and heirs to small estates who needed cash to cover the legal costs of succession and by merchants on the verge of bankruptcy. The mortgaged lands varied in quality and use, and their extension ranged from a couple of acres to hundreds.

The interest rate was never high; often the loan was free for the first two or three years, then rose in the ensuing years, usually to 5 percent, sometimes to 7 percent, and in two cases to 10 percent. The rate appears to have been inversely proportional to the amount of the mortgage: the larger the loan, the lower the interest. There was nothing unusual about this practice, "free loans" being widespread in the Calabrian economy of the time. In this and in other cases, the term certainly implied no charitable activity but concealed liens and obligations to which people in need of cash had to consent. For the Barraccos, the purpose of these transactions was not to earn interest but to acquire the land by which they were secured.

Acquisition of these mortgaged properties enlarged the Barracco estate by about 3,000 hectares (7,413 acres), which, according to the land registers, yielded more than 4,000 ducats a year. The average price paid at auction was around 10 to 15 ducats per tomolata (8.5 to 12.6 ducats per acre), a low price, even for cash payment, especially when, as in many cases, the balance after deducting the debt was a mere trifle.

4. Credit Amassment

Besides making mortgage loans directly, the Barraccos bought up credits granted by others and secured in the same way. As a source of land accumula-

---

24. On earnest money, see A. Placanica, *Moneta prestiti usure nel Mezzogiorno moderno* (Naples, 1982), 30–32; and P. Bevilacqua, "Uomini, terra, economia," in *La Calabria,* ed. P. Bevilacqua and A. Placanica (Turin, 1986), 305. The various functions of credit, the great landowners' monopoly position in the local money markets, and the granting of credit against crops at usurious rates of interest (seed grain at 20 to 25 percent) will be discussed in a later chapter.

tion, this operation was not dissimilar from the type previously described; here, too, the Barraccos, as major creditors, acquired land through foreclosure sales. The difference between the two forms lay in the social standing of the debtors, in the size of the mortgaged properties, and in the fact that in the second case the forfeitors were not inititally indebted to the Barraccos.

Usually they were large landowners indebted to a myriad of small creditors—the not uncommon situation in which the debtor was strong and his creditors weak. Often enough, even a debtor long in arrears could have foreclosure proceedings put off forever if he had political connections, could find more credit, or simply had the means to intimidate his creditors. Any one of the creditors could have initiated foreclosure proceedings had he been able to accumulate enough credits to become the major creditor, but none of them had the means to do so. In short, only a wealthy and powerful creditor could stand up to a powerful debtor; for the ordinary man, having a rich landowner in his debt was both a burden and a risk, and he was happy to get rid of the undesirable credit, even at a loss. The situation of a Baron Barracco was altogether different. Wealthy enough to be able to buy up all the available mortgage credits and patiently bide his time, and powerful enough to fear no intimidation, he could amass them at a highly advantageous discount. These transactions benefitted both small creditors and large-scale buyers, though in different ways: the former received cash for otherwise practically uncollectible credits; the latter got a corner on the "majority share," which would eventually allow him to take over the mortgaged land.

The extraordinary rapacity of these purchases typified this phase of original accumulation: even the smallest credits were bought up provided they were secured by real estate. Let us consider some examples. In 1819, Don Agnello Sculco, a Santa Severina landowner, sold Luigi Barracco a credit against Gennaro Grutther, prince of Santa Severina but a resident of Naples. The prince had contracted the 3,000-ducat debt in 1808, at 8 percent yearly, but had never paid even the interest on it, so that after a decade the total he owed, secured by property in the township of Santa Severina, amounted to 6,476.75 ducats. Don Agnello sold the credit to Barracco for its face value, less than half of that sum.

In 1825, the brothers Luigi and Ferdinando Vercillo, of the baronial family of San Vincenzo La Costa, sold the Barraccos their two-thirds of the Campolongo enclosure; the last third belonged to their brother, Baron Antonio, who resolutely refused to sell. Barracco therefore began to buy up Antonio's debts; reaching the sum of 62,928.49 ducats, he managed to persuade Antonio to sell him not only the rest of Campolongo (142 tomolate) but also the adjacent San Leonardo holding (2,135 tomolate), which netted 1,875 ducats a year. From that time on, Baron Vercillo, now San Leonardo's tenant instead of its proprietor, got ever deeper into debt. In the end, unable to pay the rent, he lost even his harvest and his stock, which were attached by Barracco and subjected to judicial sale.

For many years Don Stanislao Barracco proceeded to amass credits encumbering the properties of Count Carlo Albamonte Siciliano; by 1851 he had 33,500 ducats' worth and thereby came into possession of two "guarded parks" in the Ortella enclosure, which yielded 650 ducats a year.

We have already met Baron Emanuele De Nobili from Catanzaro, the great purchaser of Church property during the French period. Twenty years later, the baron left his heirs mostly debts. In the meantime, Baron Barracco had set about buying up the credits against the De Nobili estate and in four years laid the groundwork for a truly great coup. He acquired credits against the estate held by the Holy Cause of Sesto, near Milan, a substantial but too distant creditor, and held by four other fairly large local creditors who had "neither the strength nor the means to effect the expropriation."[25] And in 1839 he acquired the inheritance rights of the coheirs Tavani, Mesagne, Drammis, and Casolini. Thus, in 1840, Baron Barracco, as assignee of nine large credits against the De Nobili estate, could finally initiate the foreclosure suit. Subsequently, he (and his plenipotentiary Ignazio Larussa) was awarded thirty-eight holdings for the middling price of 289,850.23 ducats.[26]

Some smaller operations were also significant—for instance, a rapid-fire operation carried out in Isola during the summer of 1837. In the two months following the death of the landowner Giuseppe Trapasso, Baron Barracco acquired eleven different credits against the estate from various heirs and creditors, ranging from unpaid dowries and inheritance rights to outstanding loans and interest arrears. On August 31, Baron Barracco, creditor of the estate for 22,937.67 ducats, not only became owner of the contested San Giovanni and Colosimo olive groves but had 13,137.67 still to his credit.

Another operation, conducted by Francesco Barracco, was manifestly paltry, involving a credit of 147.90 ducats held by one Antonio Santo Sacco against Andrea Bruno, a small farmer in the township of Isola di Capo Rizzuto. The insolvent Bruno's tiny property of less than two *tomolate,* yielding 6 ducats a year, was foreclosed. Paltry but significant: the Barraccos were systematically concentrating land in Isola.

---

25. Between 1837 and 1839, the Barraccos acquired the following credits against De Nobili's estate: in March 1837, 57,733.60 ducats from Antonio Elefante de Ruggiero; in April, 20,200 ducats from the Prisco family; in January 1838, a credit of 20,081 ducats, overdue since 1804, from Francesco Ricciulli; and in October, 12,716.12 ducats from Michele De Prezio. The latter was a fairly curious contract, a bet more than a sale: Barracco advanced 958.24 ducats to De Prezio, while the remaining 11,757.88 were deposited with the Gran Cassa d'Ammortizzazione with the proviso that De Prezio would be entitled to the sum if he won his expropriation suit, and Barracco would collect it if he lost.

26. Among these were fifteen holdings totaling 4,656 tomolate (4,716 acres) in the townships of Simeri, Soveria, and Crichi.

The Barraccos' "conquest" of land through the amassment of credits continued into the second half of the century. The gradual ruin of the landed Aspro family of Isola was completed only in 1881; the property of the marquises Ferrari d'Epaminonda was finally foreclosed in September of 1875. But after the "pioneering" stage of accumulation ended, around 1849, the Barraccos pursued this strategy much less intensely.

5. Encroachment and Usurpation

One of the most controversial sources of land accumulation was encroachment. In Calabria this phenomenon was neither novel nor isolated; indeed, encroachments constitute a chapter in Calabria's history that began in feudal times and has still not ended.[27] In the nineteenth century the local term *usurpation* referred mainly to two phenomena: usurpation of common rights and encroachments of land. The first consisted of infringing (or not respecting) public and private easements on particular pieces of land; in practice, the usurper illegally enclosed lands subject to servitudes or freely used municipal or private land for grazing his own stock.[28] The second was the complete appropriation of private, municipal, or ecclesiastical properties, or, most frequently, government domains, made possible by the disorder and fogginess of the statutes; by the omnipresence of multiple ownership rights; by the geographical location of the lands themselves, far from the reach of the law; and by the relative weakness of the victims and the connivance of the powerful.

The locale par excellence of encroachment was—and still is—the Sila mountains, a region of about 100,000 hectares, or 385 square miles, containing forty townships and their respective villages. Part of the southern Apennines,

---

27. See F. Spezzano's "L'origine della grande proprietà terriera in Calabria," "L'occupazione delle terre," and "La riforma fondiaria e l'Ente Sila," in *Quaderni del Mezzogiorno e delle Isole* 38, 39 (1976); P. Cinanni, *Lotte per la terra,* op. cit., 15–19 and passim; and A. Cestaro, *Aspetti della questione demaniale nel Mezzogiorno* (Brescia, 1963). This section draws on the papers contained in the Sila Collection in the Cosenza State Archives, particularly *Stato dei Regi Demani o terre comuni nella Regia Sila,* compiled by Civil Commissioner Pasquale Barletta in 1849, 1850, and 1851; *Descrizione della Regia Sila con gli usurpatori,* 3 vols., by Judge Giuseppe Zurlo (transcribed in 1843); "Sunto ragionato de' titoli esibiti dal possessore ed occupatore della Sila barone D. Luigi Barracco"; and "Stato indicante i terreni non legittimati che si posseggono dal barone Luigi Barracco nella Regia Sila," in the report by the engineer Fergola, dated November 1845.

28. In the Kingdom of Naples, the common rights were grazing, watering, staying overnight, tillage, gathering firewood, quarrying, digging coal, occupying land for homes, gathering acorns and chestnuts, and slaking lime for sale. See L. Lauria, *Demanii e feudi nell'Italia meridionale* (Naples, 1924); G. I. Cassandro, *Storia delle terre comuni e degli usi civici nell'Italia Meridionale* (Bari, 1943); R. Trifone, "Sintesi storica degli usi civici e delle terre comuni nell'Italia meridionale e nelle isole," *Rivista di Economia agraria* 4 (1947); and G. Medici, "Proprietà collettiva, demani, usi civici," *Rivista di Economia Agraria* 3 (1948).

for centuries this wooded upland was thought (rightly or wrongly) to be one of the South's most valuable assets thanks to its summer pastures and its forests of smooth, straight pines, logged for shipbuilding first and railroad construction later. Royal Sila—as it was named in a 1333 edict of King Robert's—was reincorporated into the domain during the French period but was excluded by Joseph Bonaparte from the scope of the antifeudal law. After the failure of a tentative reform of the Sila statute of July 1807, it was immediately privatized: in 1814, Joachim Murat assigned a large portion of these possessions (four enclosures and twenty-eight domains) to the Milanese Domenico Barbaja, builder of the foyer of Naples' famous San Carlo theater.[29] The northerner, having no idea what to do with the mountains of Calabria,[30] promptly sold these possessions to Baron Giuseppe Compagna, and they eventually ended up in the hands of four great landowning families: the Barraccos, the Compagnas, the Grisolias, and the Mollos. Part of Abbatial Sila, too—so-called because it belonged to the powerful monastery of San Giovanni in Fiore—was sold to private citizens after its reincorporation into the public domain during the Napoleonic period.

At the end of the eighteenth century, Royal Commissioner Mercador began a survey of encroachments in the Sila. This monumental work, never completed, was pursued by various commissioners under successive regimes, from the Napoleonic official Giuseppe Zurlo, who produced three impeccable volumes entitled *Descrizione della Regia Sila con gli usurpatori* (all of the copies mysteriously disappeared for forty years, until one was discovered in 1837), to his Bourbon counterpart Pasquale Barletta (1845–48), whose report was published in 1849. All these studies were intended to serve as the basis of proceedings against encroachers, who were repeatedly ordered to leave the occupied lands and provide recompense for their unlawful gains. According to Barletta's investigation, the Barracco family had illegally occupied as many as twenty-two properties in the Sila, which the government ordered them to leave immediately and pay retroactive damages. The Barraccos contested the findings, proposed further investigation, and continued to exploit the lands in the meantime. But their resentment grew against the Bourbons' populist policy in the Sila,[31] especially after the Civil Commissariat, upon petition by the Cos-

---

29. On the Sila law, see U. Caldora, *Calabria napoleonica,* op. cit., 179–84; and *Bollettino delle leggi del Regno di Napoli, 1807–1815* (Naples 1807–15). The Barbaja episode interested even Stendhal during his stays in Naples in 1817 (*Rome, Naples et Florence en 1817*).

30. On the rise of the Compagna family during the Napoleonic period, see R. De Cesare, *La fine di un Regno, op. cit., passim;* U. Caldora, *Calabria napoleonica,* op. cit., 210ff; and R. Merzario, *Signori e contadini in Calabria* (Milan, 1975), 126–40.

31. R. Mascia, *Ferdinando II e la crisi socio-economica della Calabria nel 1848* (Naples, 1973); G. Coniglio, "Note sulla politica economica di Ferdinando II di Borbone," in *Archivio Storico per le Province Napoletane,* vol. 74 (Naples, 1955).

enza townships and villages, voided Barbaja's sale to Barracco and Compagna and ordered them out of twenty-eight holdings. The advent of a new Italian regime seemed heralded by Garibaldi's famous decree of August 31, 1860, which opened all of the public domain in the Sila to the landless. But the Silan landowners appealed to the king of Italy for relief; a survey commissioner was sent in 1862, and the new investigations commenced. Meanwhile, the Sila landowners managed to bottle up the first Sila reform bill, which Finance Minister Marco Minghetti sent to the Senate in 1863,[32] notwithstanding that the highly authoritative voice of Commissioner Pasquale Barletta was raised, in a report addressed to the minister, to denounce the impotence of the peasants "who live in misery" compared with the power of the "rich Calabrian land-owners, led by eight or ten barons" of whom "some are millionaires, and even deputies and senators."[33] When the law was finally enacted, in May of 1876, it was a victory for the encroaching latifondisti, for it legitimized the encroach-ments and abuses at a cheap price, and despoiled the townships of about 50,000 hectares (42,000 acres); that is, it sanctioned the existing situation, due partly to a sort of jaded realism but mostly to the encroachers' political influence on the Left. As soon as his possessions were "legitimized," Baron Barracco sued the government to avoid paying taxes on them because, by virtue of an 1844 statute, "the grants were made free and unencumbered in any way." The suit dragged on (it was still pending in 1887) but became increasingly incon-sequential.

Lawsuits initiated by the townships against the encroachers languished even longer, well into the twentieth century.[34] The Barracco family was in-volved in litigation with as many as fifty-three townships,[35] all related to the same problem. In fact, the Feudal Commission had ruled in 1810[36] on four points: abolition of the former feudal lords' rights to graze stock on private

---

32. The minister of finance submitted the bill to the Senate in 1863; the Sila landowners met in a general assembly in 1864; Guglielmo Tocci published *La questione della Sila di Calabria* in Cosenza in 1866; and the petition was sent to the king, Parliament, and the government in 1869. The Sila Act was finally promulgated in 1877. For an account of the passage of this legislation, see F. Martire, *La questione silana davanti la Camera dei Deputati* (Cosenza, 1872). S. Di Bella's *Terra e potere in Calabria dai Borboni alla Repubblica: La questione silana* (Cosenza, 1979) recapitulates the Sila question.

33. *Relazione circa la Sila di Calabria diretta al Ministro delle Finanze da Pasquale Barletta-ultimo Commissario Civile per gli affari della Sila* (Turin, 1865). See also A. Basile, "La questione silana dal 1838 al 1876," in *Atti del Secondo Congresso Storico Calabrese* (Naples, 1961), 461–80.

34. The lawsuits brought by Rovito, Caccuri, Simeri, and Crichi dragged on into the 1920s and 1930s. The Rocca di Neto suit was decided in 1961.

35. Besides the sources already mentioned, see BA: G (lawsuits and trials).

36. *Leggi e Sentenze della Commissione Feudale,* Bulletin of the laws of the Kingdom of Naples (Naples, 1810); *Collezione degli editti, determinazioni, decreti e leggi di S.M.* (Naples, 1807–15).

property, whether enclosed or not; recognition of local citizens' common rights (wood gathering, watering, gleaning, and so on); confirmation of their *sbarro* servitude (the right to graze stock from April to October on former feudal and ecclesiastical lands); and confirmation of easements of passage. Now—so declared the attorneys for the townships of Cutro, Rocca di Neto, Verzino and Savelli, Isola, Rocca Bernarda, Santa Severina, and forty-seven others—these rights were being infringed upon by the construction of enclosures around the lands subject to these servitudes.[37] The townships also claimed the lands assigned to them by the antifeudal laws, the allotment of which, not completed during the French period, was ignored by the Bourbon government, which either sold them off or handed them back to Church establishments, which sold them in turn.

Church establishments, too, found the lands returned to them occupied by encroachers. The Barracco family was accused of illegal possession of as many as 7,000 tomolate of land belonging to the Diocese Administration, to the Croton Bishop's Table, to the Abbey of Santa Maria del Patire, to the Santa Severina Archbishop's Table, and to the Diocese of Squillace.

Lastly, the great landowners encroached on each others' lands as well. Between 1840 and 1842, the Barraccos and the Compagnas were at odds over their possessions in the Sila. Baron Luigi Compagna of Corigliano, upon becoming sole perpetual tenant of all the property of the Abbey of Santa Maria del Patire, ordered Barracco out of eight lots he had "usurped" in the township of Rocca di Neto. At the same time, Baron Grisolia sued Barracco for usurping the great Laghicello enclosure in the township of Pedace.[38] It may be noted that both Compagna's and Grisolia's names stood out beside Barracco's and Mollo's on all the lists of encroachers in the Sila.

It is impossible to say precisely how much land was "usurped" because it was often unclear whether cases involved actual encroachment or simply ill-defined and contested boundary lines. But even the few cases decided by law leave no doubt about the incidence of usurpation in the process of original accumulation.

---

37. Some of these suits went back to the days of the Cassa Sacra. In 1786, the citizens of Rocca di Neta brought suit in the Supreme Council against Alfonso Barracco, tenant-in-chief of the Charterhouse fief at Santo Stefano del Bosco, complaining that they had been "reduced to a deplorable state," as Barracco prevented them from grazing their stock on the enclosed lands and in general from exercising common rights. See A. Placanico, *Alle origini,* op. cit., 316.

38. The holdings Compagna claimed were Mortelle, Tesauro, Valle della Bruca, Pancari, Pirorosso, Valletorta, Piano di Frasso, and Ponticelli. At the same time, the abbeys of Patire and San Anastasio del Carrà (which together formed the Isola Grange) claimed other properties and tax-farming holdings usurped by Barracco for a total of 8,000 tomolate, or 6,720 acres (BA: E27[4], E28[2]). The papers on the Grisolia suit are in E2(16, p. 24). See also A. Basile, *La questione silana,* op. cit., 464–66.

6. Purchases of Peasant Allotments

The amount of land that came to the Barraccos through purchases of peasant allotments was only a small fraction of their property. This phenomenon is significant, however, because it evidently marks the origin of the so-called proletarianization of the Calabrian peasantry (privatization followed by expropriation) and of capitalist evolution of landed property. As a Neapolitan writer put it,

> A new class of great proprietors has risen up on the wreckage of the barons; after buying up the barons' lands, they have succeeded in evicting the poor peasants from the parcels assigned to them. The peasants thus find themselves deprived of both their allotments and the common rights of pasturage, sowing and wood gathering they used to exercise, practically free of charge, on municipal and feudal domains.[39]

In practice, the mechanism of expropriation took advantage of the myopia and adequacy of the laws. The antifeudal law of 1806 assigned part (usually a fourth) of each old feudal domain to the townships for allotment to the poorest citizens, that is, the landless.[40] The actual effects of this action were quite limited, as in the allotment of the *communaux* in France.[41] The survey commissioners operated in the kingdom only until 1811; the task passed thereafter to the provincial intendents, who gave priority to other concerns (after all, there was a war going on) and in effect ceased to proceed with the allotments. But even the parcels that were actually assigned to the landless did not remain in their possession for long; the peasants wanted to sell, and only a rule imposed from above by Minister Zurlo prevented them from doing so for ten years. The allotments were promptly sold as soon as the restriction lapsed and ended up in the hands of the great landowners who had already garnered their possession by circumventing the law and buying the *jus seminae* and the *jus arandi* in the interim.

To clarify the mechanism, let us examine more closely one of these "expropriations," the division of the Ritani property located in the Castella section of the township of Isola di Capo Rizzuto. On May 1, 1811, the town authorities proceeded to divide up the parcels they had received from suppressed Church and feudal domains. The populace hungered for land, and great

---

39. C. De Cesare, *Delle condizioni economiche e morali delle classi agricole nelle tre province di Puglia* (Naples, 1856).

40. See V. Ricchioni, "Le leggi eversive della feudalità e la storia delle quotizzazioni demaniali nel Mezzogiorno," in Cassa per il Mezzogiorno, Studi e testi, *Problemi dell'agricoltura meridionale* (Naples, 1953).

41. A. Soboul, *Problèmes paysans de la révolution, 1789–1848* (Paris, 1976); G. Lefebvre, *Les paysans du nord pendant la révolution française* (Paris, 1972).

hopes were fixed on the French law. As Vito Doria, attorney for the township in the suit against the encroachers, was to write in his somewhat florid style in 1865,

> The laws against feudalism found the township of Isola in the condition of an oasis in the desert, or better, as its name indicates, an islet in a vast lake. Would it surprise us that an inhabitant of the former, in the Sahara, lacked sand to build his house? Or that an inhabitant of the latter lacked water to slake his thirst? Let wonder cease: the inhabitants of Isola di Capo Rizzuto, though thrown by Providence into the midst of the boundless and fertile lands of the Marquisate, literally have not a stick of wood to cook with, nor a bit of soil to cultivate . . . unless they obtain the grudging consent of the opulent proprietors.[42]

One hundred and fifty Isolans "without a stick of wood" to their name each obtained a share of the 580-tomolate Ritani property that May Day, about four tomolate of good farmland apiece. As Racioppi rightly observed in 1877, the government sincerely believed,

> according to the physiocratic theories still in vogue in the public administration, that if a man had two strong arms and a bit of land to call his own, he could lay his table every day with the Sunday fare of the good king of France. Illusions! Considering how public lands were alloted to the propertyless of every class, possession of a small piece of land— always of the worst quality—does not change the economic condition of the peasants.[43]

Not that the government was totally unaware of the difficulties entailed in implementing this design for promoting peasant ownership, first and foremost the peasants' own desire to sell off their parcels, which they were unable to farm profitably. As we saw, as early as December 1808, Minister Zurlo, aware of the danger that the allotments might end up in the hands of the wealthy, had inserted a clause in the law prohibiting the sale or mortgage of the parcels for ten years after their allotment—a provision that even Racioppi called a "curious clause in the law on the public domain that immobilized these now-stagnant lands."[44]

Exactly ten years went by. On May 11, 1821, nine "communist" beneficiaries of the Ritani allotment appeared at the Barracco mansion in Isola where

---

42. BA: E24(2). Except where otherwise indicated, the sources used for this discussion are in BA: A96(1, 2), E24(1, 2) and E25(1).

43. G. Racioppi, *Contadini e proprietari nel Napoletano,* quoted by R. Villari in *Il Sud nella storia d'Italia* (Bari, 1961), 1:164.

44. Ibid., 165.

notary Francesco Maria Trigani had transferred his office for the occasion. All nine came to sell to the baron—"whole, not measured"—the parcels on which they had not "made any improvements" in those ten years and which "had yielded no profit." The day after, another six assignees sold their parcels according to the same formula, and on the thirteenth, another eleven. In barely six weeks, from May 11 to June 24 of 1821, 47 bills of sale were signed, transferring a total of 136 parcels; another 11 parcels were sold the next February and the last one on June 18, 1822. In all, the baron came into possession of 148 of the original 150 allotments and incorporated in his latifondo 569 of the 580 tomolate that had been divided among the landless ten years earlier. The sellers walked out of the Barracco mansion with cash in hand; the whole operation cost the baron about 6,000 ducats, but, after all, he was one of the few men in the entire kingdom who always had a quantity of cash on hand.

What logic underlay these transactions? What mutual benefits did they bring? For the baron they were, among other things, fine bargains. According to an inventory of the Barraccos' property drawn up around the same time for tax purposes (hence valued on the low side), the average yield of the Ritani allotments was 1.13 ducats per tomolata. This works out to an average value of 22.60 ducats per tomolata, whereas the baron paid an average of 10.40 ducats—less than half of the declared value. So good a bargain was this land that in 1835 Barracco bought the remaining Ritani acreage at an auction in Catanzaro for as much as 27 ducats per tomolata.[45] In effect, the land was good, cheap, and unencumbered. The only obligation weighing on it, besides the national land tax, was a small tax due yearly to the township of Isola, but this was abrogated by the aforementioned decree a year later.[46] Besides being a good buy, the acquisition of Ritani enabled the Barraccos to consolidate their holdings—a crucial factor in the typical wheat-and-livestock operation of the latifondo—and to further labor mobility within its boundaries.

What did the sellers gain? Why did they sell? The answer we read in the bills of sale is always the same: because the land "had yielded no profit." This is evidently a formula dictated by the notary Trigani and included by him in each bill of sale, but was it true? The Ritani property was good land, provided with water by Vallone di Pelacca Creek, suitable for both raising grain and grazing livestock. Why did it yield the peasant owners "no profit"? A closer reading of the sale documents sheds some light.

There were fifty bills of sale altogether, but the sellers numbered 110 (50 women, 60 men), for many of the sales were executed jointly by two spouses

---

45. This formerly ecclesiastical property amounted to 1,776.63 tomolate (about 1,492 acres); Barracco bought it for 48,157 ducats in cash.

46. The 120 ducats due to the township of Isola came to twenty-one grani per tomolata, or little more than eight carlini per allotment.

and their children, or by widows and their children, each of whom owned one or more parcels assigned to them originally and/or inherited from a deceased relative (*never* bought). The bills of sale specified family relationships between sellers, their occupations, and their domiciles. The men all declared themselves "countrymen," that is, peasants except for a tavern keeper, two sailors, a barber, and a Don Giuseppe Pitella. Almost all the women declared themselves spinners; three were peasants and one a "gentlewoman." All but five of the sellers lived in Castella, so the major problem was distance; considering their social condition, they probably had no way of getting to the plots assigned to them four-odd miles away. This obstacle was particularly great for single women; cottage spinning was incompatible with work in faraway fields. Another problem was the small size of the allotments, which made it impossible to raise stock on them; four tomolate (or even eight, considering cases of multiple allotments to a single family) were too few for either grazing or growing feed crops. Lastly, there was the lack of cash to either pay taxes or start farming. Concentrated in the hands of a single owner, the Ritani property yielded 1.13 ducats and more per tomolata, but the same land, carved into parcels, barely yielded the eight *carlini* due for local taxes.[47] The peasants sold simply to get a little cash, but in doing so they sealed the doom of the whole reform project.[48]

Ritani is just one example among many, even in the township of Isola alone. Its significance lies in the fact that the sales were transacted directly between the assignees and the baron. In other cases, the sales formed a sort of chain from the assignee to the baron via midsized landowners. For instance, by 1822, Barracco owned all fourteen of the allotments that had been made out of the little Gabelluccia farm (barely forty-two tomolate), but he had bought none of them directly. Some had been resold to him by Don Ippolito; others were made over to him by Baron Berlingieri, who had bought them from the notary Militi, who had originally bought them from the assignees.[49] Other transactions were much simpler, such as the one in 1821 whereby Barracco acquired *all* the Altilia allotments in the township of Rocca Bernarda (notarized by Giovanni Ricci).

---

47. "The rents due to the townships, the property tax and the lack of means to exploit the land," lamented G. Zurlo in his October 1811 *Inquiry* (quoted in P. Villani, *Mezzogiorno tra riforme e rivoluzione* [Bari, 1973], 207.)

48. E. Blandini, *Per la creazione della piccola proprietà: Risultati di alcune quotizzazioni in Calabria* (Naples, 1913).

49. It was the same story on many other properties as well. The 117-tomolate Cuture holding was partitioned into thirty-nine allotments in May of 1811; in May of 1821, Barracco bought up thirty-six of them through middlemen. All forty-eight tomolate of the small Chiusa holding, which had been partitioned into sixteen allotments in 1811, were in Barracco's hands by 1921; eleven had been repurchased from Castelliti and five came from the Aspro expropriation. All eight shares of the small Sant'Andrello holding (40 tomolate) were bought in 1821 by Notary Trigani, who in this case acted as the front man.

Various dodges were available to the great landowners to get around the law and earmark allotments for future acquisition. The case of General Montigny, who leased peasant allotments en masse and thereby gained an option on their purchase, created some scandal in 1813.[50] Minister Zurlo, seeing the evident loophole in the legislation, sought to extend his ten-year ban to leases, but his proposal was rejected by the Council of State. Baron Barracco was one of the people who took advantage of this loophole. From 1806 until the end of the ban he bought (or leased) the jus seminae and the jus arandi in allotted lands, sometimes paying out large amounts of money by way of "advances." These insured that when the ban ended the assignees would be forced to sell their plots to him and none other unless they could, quite improbably, find the means to pay him back.[51] At times the Barraccos did not even bother to seek a legal dodge around the ban but simply bought peasant allotments outright—as Fortunato put it, "in sales not put in any legal form whatsoever, confiding in the good faith and ignorance of the sellers, in the confusion of boundaries, in the passage of time, and in the acquiescence of local officials."[52]

The amount of land the Barraccos acquired from this source cannot be calculated, though it is reasonable to suppose it was quite little compared to what they acquired otherwise. What the available data make clear is the fact that practically the whole patrimony of the so-called communists ended up in the hands of the Barraccos in the townships where the family's presence was hegemonous. And it should be remembered that this was all modern freehold property, further disencumbered by the law of 1820 of all charges and duties other than the land tax.

7. The Barracco Family Assets in 1849

It is difficult to calculate exactly how much the Barraccos' assets grew from 1806 to 1849 because no complete inventories or registers exist for the period prior to 1822. However, we can compare their assets at three different moments during the period of accumulation: 1822, 1831, and 1849.[53] To complete the comparison, we shall add the asset inventory drawn up in 1868.

---

50. P. Villani, *Mezzogiorno tra riforme,* op. cit., 209.

51. In 1806, Barracco bought the *jus seminae* on 1,196 tomolate (1,005 acres) of the Bugiaforo (or Buciaforo) holding in Isola township, which had been assigned to and partitioned among the landless and some local landholders out of property expropriated from the Croton diocese. Similarly, he purchased the *jus seminae* on 50 tomolate of the Arenace farm and on 1,205 tomolate of the Nastasi holding, which had previously belonged to the local abbey. In this last case, the "advance" paid was all of 2,647 ducats.

52. G. Fortunato, *Il Mezzogiorno e lo Stato italiano* (Florence, 1927), 1:90. D. Camarda di Francia also spoke of "simulated sales" ("I demani comunali usurpati," *La Giovine Calabria,* May 22, 1912).

53. Except where otherwise indicated, the sources used for this section are in BA, particularly Sec. F, vols. 1, 2, and 3.

As we saw earlier, in 1822, Alfonso Barracco took advantage of the 1818 law amending the French provisions on inheritance to constitute a majorat over half of all the Calabrian assets to the benefit of his only son and heir, Luigi, and the latter's firstborn son. The general inventory of the Calabrian assets drawn up for this purpose shows that the Barraccos' yearly revenues from both directly managed and leased farmlands totaled 25,013.24 ducats, of which 12,208.20 came from the properties subject to the majorat.

At Alfonso's death in 1831, when Luigi succeeded to the property and the baronial title, another inventory was drawn up of all the family's rural and urban assets and income of all kinds. At that time, its yearly income from agricultural sources amounted to 59,116.14 ducats.[54]

The third statement of the family's accounts was prepared in 1849 when the estate passed at Luigi's death to Alfonso II and his eleven brothers and sisters. A new inventory was drawn up of personal and real property located in Calabria and of the credits and liabilities due to and from the estate. Its aggregate value amounted to the staggering figure of almost 2 million ducats, with the agricultural property alone yielding 67,291 ducats a year.

Another general inventory was drawn up in 1868 when the Barracco brothers decided to divide up the estate. At that time their income from rural properties in Calabria amounted to 68,500 ducats a year (another 4,525 came from the properties in what is now the province of Caserta).

A comparison of these figures (table 2) shows that the Barracco's income from landed property increased by an average of 1,565.8 ducats yearly over the period of accumulation; in terms of land acquisition, this corresponds to an average of more than 2,000 tomolate a year. The peak period was the decade from 1822 to 1831, when the acquisition of 34.103 ducats of income augmented the estate the elder Alfonso had left by 136 percent. In the ensuing two decades, from 1831 to 1849, the Calabrian properties increased by a further 14 percent. By 1849, the formative period of the Calabrian latifondo had come to an end; over the next twenty years, the Barraccos' properties in the region grew by less than 2 percent.

By 1849, then, the Barracco latifondo had assumed its final shape, transforming the whole pattern of landownership in its territory. Where mixed tenure had once been the rule, and the wide- open spaces of the royal, feudal, and municipal demesnes had predominated, there now extended the modern latifondo, set apart by the physical and legal hedges of private property. Local social patterns, too, were transformed. With the failure of the Jacobin ideal, the peasants were separated from their means of production. In this sense, the

---

54. Capital assets employed in rural industries—"cattle, mares, oxen, and other livestock held in partnership, licorice works, sale of cheese and grain"—yielded an additional 16,960 ducats yearly, making a total of 76,076.14 ducats in yearly revenues.

TABLE 2.   Assessed Yearly Income of Barracco Properties in Calabria

Year	Income (ducats)
1822	25,013.24
1831	59,116.14
1849	67,290.91
1868	68,499.70

historical mission of original accumulation can be considered accomplished.[55] After 1849, the Barraccos' presence in Calabria was characterized no longer by the rapacity of the *conquistadores* but by property consolidation and the rejoining of workers and the means of production in an altogether novel system. In other words, the first steps—concentration and privatization of the land, and liberation and expropriation of the peasantry—had been taken to enable, though not to determine, the development of agrarian capitalism and a modern kind of growth. In any case, it was a metamorphosis that would constitute, in Jerome Blum's words, "the single most important departure from the traditional agriculture."[56]

---

55. Lenin described the Russian process in much the same terms: "the cornering of the land (by purchase or rent), the concentration of production in the hands of a minority, the proletarianization of the majority and its exploitation by the minority who have commercial capital and employ wage labor" (V. I. Lenin, *The Development of Capitalism in Russia* [Moscow, 1974]).

56. J. Blum, *The End of the Old Order in Rural Europe* (Princeton, 1978), 269. Blum attributes great importance to the enclosures and to the concentration of landed property ("the consolidation of scattered strips into unified holdings"), regardless of whether it did or did not really lead to a more productive agriculture (263). A number of scholars have pointed out that land engrossment (*rassemblement, concentrazione*) did not necessarily lead to greater productivity or profitability and sometimes produced the opposite effect (see, for example, J. Thirsk, *Tudor Enclosures* [London, 1959], 12–13; and P. Vilar, *Agricultura, comercio colonial,* op. cit., 234). In the long run, however, as E. Le Roy Ladurie points out, the concentration of property was the more solid foundation for the development of agrarian capitalism (in F. Braudel, ed., *Histoire économique et sociale de la France* [Paris, 1976], 2:796–99.

CHAPTER 3

The Social Territory of
the Latifondo

1. Geographical Territory

The Barracco latifondo lay in the east-central part of Calabria in a sort of dragon shape.[1] The great rounded head filled practically the whole terraced plain in the territory of Isola di Capo Rizzuto and the hills of Cutro before plunging into the Ionian Sea, with one horn touching the port city of Croton. One forefoot crossed the eastern part of the Marquisate to Apriglianello; the other extended westward along the Little Sila slopes to the countryside around Belcastro. The breast reached up along the valley of the Tacina River through San Mauro Marchesto and Scandale into the Silan foothills. A wing bent eastward toward the Ionian Sea, in the territory of Santa Severina, and stretched along the middle and lower reaches of the Neto River to Belvedere di Spinello and Rocca di Neto. The body snaked along the middle and upper Neto valleys through the townships of Cotronei and Caccuri up to the first heights of the Sila. There, at the boundaries of the Marquisate, the dragon's rear leg stretched east to Melissa, crossing the Vitravo River between Verzino and Pallagorio. At San Giovanni in Fiore, the dragon's hindquarters began the climb into the Sila, partly following the Arvo River, partly snaking up the slopes of the Big Sila, to reach the heights between Carlomango and Camigliati, with the tail bending along the western slope of the range. Between Celico and Spezzano Piccolo, it turned south to follow the hills along the upper basin of the Crati River in the area of Serra Pedace, Pedace, and Aprigliano.

The "dragon" stretched more than 60 miles over an area of around 116 square miles. A traveler setting out from the Ionian coast could cross the plains of the Marquisate, the foothills of Little Sila, the rivers and streams of the Sila uplands, and the heights of the range over to its western slopes without ever

---

1. This metaphor of the winged dragon recalls Manual Scorza's description, in *Redoble por Rancas* (Barcelona, 1970), of the enclosure's serpentine progression day after day.

leaving Barracco territory. He would see landscapes ranging from the terraced plains and low hills of the Marquisate, covered with grainfields, orchards, and meadows grazed by prime breeds of sheep, to the vegetable gardens on the way to the port of Croton, and from the game-filled woods in the Little Sila foothills to the uplands with their olive groves, fields of durum wheat, and pastures roamed by large herds of cattle and sheep. Wending his way up the Tacina River, famed for its trout, he would pass through chestnut forests and open pasture, the major product of which was cheese. In the branch stretching eastward through the hills to Melissa were vineyards and olive groves, mineral springs, and several small sulphur and salt mines. In the heart of the Sila reigned forests of beech, fir, and especially spruce, forests spreading between every town and the next (which in many cases lay hours of travel apart), with some signs of a mixed economy: the cultivation of potato and cabbage patches, lumbering, the extraction of pine oil and tar, hunting, and fishing in the lakes. Descending the Tyrrhenian side of the mountains, the spruce gave way to chestnut woods, good for mushrooms and charcoal; rye, potato, and flax fields reappeared, then fig and olive groves, cattle, and sheep.

2. Social Territory

The Barraccos' dragon-shaped estate (see fig. 3) was superimposed on a geographical area with its own "density" in terms of population, history, and culture. The latifondo did not "colonize" an "empty" territory by creating a completely new form of farming enterprise but embraced and incorporated a densely and stably populated region that had long-standing modes of production and distribution, social hierarchies, and models of behavior. The estate never proposed to effect a radical transformation of the existing equilibria—attempts of that kind had failed in other highly populated areas, except when they were supported by government, which was certainly not the case in Calabria—but to harness them for the realization of surplus production.[2] To achieve this goal, it was altogether in the estate's interest to respect the traditions and the specific differences of the areas it had incorporated and turn them to its own advantage. Had they not allowed for the prior history, i.e., the *density* of these areas, the latifondisti could never have succeeded in maintaining social peace in a region famed for its high degree of conflict.

Still, the latifondo was a large-scale enterprise, owning great quantities of land and requiring great quantities of wage labor. It could not but transform its

2. See the discussion of the colonization of "empty" and "dense" territories in P. C. Emmer, D. H. A. Kolff, and R. J. Ross, "The Expansion of Europe and the Transformation of Third World Agriculture," paper read at the Eighth International Congress of Economic History, Budapest, August 1982, 1–3. See also M. Petrusewicz, "Wage-Earners but Not Proletarians," *Review* 10, no. 3 (Winter 1987), 477–88.

Fig. 3. The Barracco latifondo

host territory, redefining and expanding its boundaries. The territory defined by the capitalist-transforming role of the latifondo was wider than the physical bounds of the property and included adjacent rural areas, cities, and towns. This wider range, which we shall call the estate's *social territory,* preserved some features of an ethno-ecological entity but was larger, and perhaps more complex, than the traditional local ecosystems.[3] The "dragon" had fused several different ecosystems (from the mild, malaria-ridden climate of the lowlands to the snows of the Sila) into a single social territory, but above all it aggregated different histories and different mentalities native to Calabria, those of which Rossi Doria speaks: "what we have is not Calabria, but the Calabrias: the Ionian Calabria and the Tyrrhenian, the mountains and the hills, the coast and the interior, the prosperous and the impoverished."[4] The logic of property concentration had spliced the region's historical dichotomy, and the rationality of the dual production of grain and livestock had cemented it. Within the confines of the social territory, the histories of the stable, prosperous, and open communities of Magna Graecia mingled with the closed, austere, and nomadic world of the Bruttii;[5] the decentralized baronial oligarchy with the great statist tradition of Kings Fredrick and Robert; and the feudal world par excellence with the free cities and their cherished autonomy.

The boundaries of the social territory corresponded to the reach of the latifondista Barracco's power; therein he was at once the greatest landowner and the major employer, the point of reference in all the economic and social spheres (opportunities for credit, leases, sharecropping, bureaucratic and legal mediation, favors, and protection), as well as for politics and clientelism; lastly, he came to control (de facto and by appointment) the use of violence and was thus in a way responsible for social peace. All these roles—and this is the key to the modernity of the latifondo—derived from, and bolstered, the first: landownership. But they were also all interlinked, and the relative importance acquired by one or the other depended on the circumstances of the time. In the early stages of the latifondo, the crucial role, as we have seen, was that of the holder of the means of violence (legal or not). During the period of development it was that of the employer, and during periods of crisis it was that of the

---

3. W. Cronon examines transformations and extensions of the boundaries of local ecosystems as agriculture was commercialized (included in the world capitalist system) in seventeenth- and eighteenth-century New England. See his highly interesting essay in ecological history, *Changes in the Land: Indians, Colonists, and the Ecology of New England* (New York, 1983).

4. M. Rossi Doria, *Dieci anni di politica agraria nel Mezzogiorno* (Bari, 1958). See also L. Giustiniani, *Dizionario geografico-ragionato del Regno di Napoli* (Naples, 1802).

5. "[O]n the one hand, the developed world of the coastal cities of Magna Grecia; on the other, the mountainous hinterland populated by the original Bruttii" A. Placanica, "I caratteri originali," in *La Calabria,* ed. P. Bevilacqua and A. Placanica (Turin, 1985), 20.

wielder of political influence and patronage. Taken separately, each of these roles defined the contours of the social territory somewhat differently. Here we shall examine two of them more closely: the social territories delineated by the property per se and by the labor market.

3. Property as Presence

In the beginning, there was the property. Where was it, how big was it, and what proportion of the territories of the various townships did it occupy? Two facts immediately strike the eye in the reconstruction shown in table 3. First, 70 percent of the property of the estate was located in the Marquisate and in the hills lying just inland from the Ionian coast. In the second place, the Barracco property occupied 19.5 percent of these combined areas, whereas in the Sila the percentage was only 9 percent. We can hardly doubt that the owner of a fifth, or even a tenth, of all the local land would in any case be an influential personage in the life of these townships, but just how influential depended on the distribution of property within each. In effect, the distribution was not uniform: while in some townships the Barraccos owned half the land, in others their holdings amounted to but a few acres. The proportion of ownership determined the character of their presence: in townships where they owned more than 20 percent of the land, we may call their presence *dominant;* where they owned from 5 to 20 percent, we shall consider it *leading;* elsewhere it was *minor* (table 4). The varying strength of the baronial presence not only affected the life of the populace accordingly, but it performed different functions within the estate's organization. A *minor* presence often served only to insure geographical continuity—highly desirable for the seasonal livestock drives—or was merely one of the dragon's protuberances.[6] In rural townships like Rocca Bernarda, a *leading* presence set the Barraccos among the few important local landowners; in a city like Croton, it gave them a significant political base.

But their *dominant* presence in seven townships is of greater interest to us because here we can better understand how the latifondo penetrated the existing geographical and social landscape and because here most of the property— eighty-two square miles, or 76 percent of the whole estate—was concentrated. As table 4 shows, five of the townships lay in the Marquisate (Cutro, Isola di Capo Rizzuto, Caccuri, Belvedere di Spinello, and Rocca di Neto) and two in the Sila (Aprigliano and Spezzano Grande). There were some differences, however, in the way the Barraccos were present in the Marquisate and in the Sila.

---

6. The *lesser* presence in Serra Pedace, San Nicola, Pallagorio, San Mauro, and Scandale insured free passage for seasonal livestock drives. Melissa, Belcastro, and Taverna were on the far reaches of the latifondo; Spezzano Piccolo was simply part of the family's inheritance.

TABLE 3. Location and Extension of Barracco Properties by Township

Township	Total area (km²)	Barracco Property (km²)	Percentage of Township Area
Belcastro	52.8	0.13	0.2
Cutro-S. Leonardo	132.0	66.7	50.5
Isola-Le Castella	125.3	62.0	49.5
Cotrone	179.8	10.4	5.8
San Mauro	42.0	—	—
Scandale	53.6	—	—
S. Severina-Altilia	51.9	5.60	10.80
Rocca Bernarda	65.5	9.10	13.90
Casabona	68.9	0.96	1.30
Melissa	50.9	0.96	1.90
Belvedere Spinello	30.2	8.50	28.10
Rocca di Neto	43.6	10.70	24.50
Total Marquisate	896.5	175.00	19.50
Caccuri	57.3	19.60	34.20
Cotrone	78.1	5.20	6.60
Pellagorio	42.0	0.02	0.05
San Nicola	19.3	0.13	0.70
Verzino	45.4	0.96	2.10
Total Sila foothills	242.1	25.90	10.70
Aprigliano	121.3	28.30	23.30
Celico	99.0	9.60	9.70
Pedace	51.5	5.60	10.90
San Giovanni	279.5	15.60	5.60
Serra Pedace	59.2	0.30	0.50
Spezzano Grande	79.6	16.70	21.00
Spezzano Piccolo	48.7	1.00	2.10
Taverna	132.5	1.20	1.00
Total Sila	871.3	78.30	9.00
Total estate	2,009.9	279.20	13.90

In the Marquisate, their presence was not only massive but also capillary. In Cutro township, they owned 50.5 percent of all the land: tracts that had originally belonged to the fief of Tacina and Massanova, extensive properties on the outskirts of town, and a mansion in the center. Most important, their dominion over the outlying villages of San Leonardo (where they owned another mansion), Rosito, and Sant'Anna was complete. In Isola township they owned 49.5 percent of all the land; here, again, the breakdown included a number of urban lots, a palace and other buildings in town, and entire villages in the hinterland (San Pietro, Pedocchiella, Campolongo, Villa Barracco, and

TABLE 4.   The Latifondo Presence by Township (% of territory owned)

Dominant (>20%)	Significant (5–20%)	Minor (<5%)
Cutro (50.5)	Rocca Bernarda (13.9)	Spezzano Piccolo
Isola (49.5)	Pedace (10.9)	Verzino
Caccuri (34.2)	Santa Severina (10.8)	Belcastro
Belvedere (28.1)	Celico (9.7)	Casabona
Rocca di Neto (24.5)	Cotronei (6.6)	Melissa
Aprigliano (23.3)	Cotrone (5.8)	Pallagorio
Spezzano Grande (21)	San Giovanni (5.6)	San Nicola
		Serra Pedace
		Taverna
Total 212.5 km² (76%)	Total 61.1 km² (21.9%)	Total 5.6 km² (2.1%)

Le Castella). In the township of Caccurri, where they owned 34.2 percent of the territory, the Barraccos dominated the town from the castle, as the feudal lord had done before them; in Belvedere di Spinello they held title to all of the village of Polligrone and to a good part of Spinello; and in Rocca di Neto they owned the entire hamlet of Concio in addition to houses, warehouses, and gristmills in the town and its vicinity. Even in Santa Severina, seat of a diocese, where the Barraccos had only a leading presence, they owned the whole village of Altilia.

To sum up, in the Marquisate the Barraccos were ubiquitous. They owned not only extensive lands but whole villages, houses, oil presses, gristmills, licorice works, warehouses, and bakeries. They also owned most of the grounds and buildings where the two major regional fairs were held: the week-long events held in September in the village of Molerà, in Rocca Bernarda, and in May in Santo Janni, located between Santa Severina and Altilia. As we have seen, their property was of the new freehold type, purchased in a market freed of feudal encumbrances, often from the townsmen themselves. In this sense, the Barraccos were simply large landowners, equal to all their fellows in the eye of the law. Yet to the traveler wandering through these districts and asking, like in Giovanni Verga's story "La robba," to whom the villages, the fields, and the flocks belonged, and receiving always the same answer—"to Baron Barracco"—the presence of the latifondo must have given a different impression compared to other properties. The Barraccos seemed to all effects to be the lords of the land. To such an extent did they fit into the age-old social landscape that they might have been mistaken for the old Friozzis themselves, the Doria d'Angris, the Cavalcantes, or the Giannuzzi Savellis.[7]

---

7. The Barraccos were not exactly newcomers to the Marquisate. Centuries earlier, the original Cosenza patrician family had held the fief of Bruscano, a hamlet in the township of

The situation in the Sila was quite different. In the townships of Aprigliano and Spezzano Grande, where the Barraccos' presence was "dominant," their holdings were located far from town, out in practically uninhabited territory: the immense enclosures of Molarotta, Camigliati, and Croce delle Magare in the township of Spezzano Grande, and Capalbo, Fiumarella, Capitano, and Pinicollito in Aprigliano. The same was true in other Sila townships as well: Celico, Spezzano Piccolo, Pedace, Serra Pedace, and San Giovanni. In the towns proper the Barraccos owned townhouses and warehouses, just like the other large local landowners, and were accepted as such—but only as such. In 1814, about a quarter of the population of the Sila and the foothill areas owned at least a small amount of land. In Aprigliano they numbered more than 1,000 (24 percent of the population), of whom 100 or so were "leading citizens"; the same proportion held at Spezzano, with 360 landowners out of a population of 1,576. In the Marquisate, to the contrary, Barracco was the sole landowner in places like Rocca di Neto, Le Castella, and San Leonardo, while there were 10 in Belvedere and 44 in Isola (2.2 percent of the popoulation).[8]

But, if the Barraccos were accepted *inter pares* in the Sila towns, their dominant presence in the outlying districts was resented and opposed. Here lay the great difference between the Marquisate—accustomed for centuries to the presence of great feudal lords—and the Sila, where the appearance of a host of great new landowners (the Barraccos, the Compagnas, the Berlingieris, the Grisolias, and the Ferrari d'Epaminondas) during and after the French decade was unprecedented. Of course, there had always been some private and Church property in the Sila, but most of the land belonged to the Crown, and no sovereign since King Robert's day had ever dared to deliver it into other hands. Significantly, the first to do so was Joachim Murat, a foreign king but most importantly a king both revolutionary and bourgeois, qualities that enabled him to feel free of a sovereign's traditional obligations. We saw in the last chapter that Murat paid the treasury's debts with public lands in the Royal Sila. Hence, between the public lands put up for sale in 1813 and the encroachments facilitated by the general confusion of the times,[9] the free municipalities in the

---

Cerenzia, on the border of the Marquisate; this property was lost after the epidemic of 1528. In the early seventeenth century, Marcello Barracco, collector of revenues for the Calabrian saltworks, resided in Rocca Bernarda; some years later Captain Carlo Barracco, who lived in Isola di Capo Rizzuto, commanded Croton's defense against the Turks. It is doubtful, however, that the memory of the family's presence survived for another two centuries.

8. S. Martuscelli, *La popolazione del Mezzogiorno,* op. cit.

9. In 1814, Murat decreed that the treasury was to settle its debt to Domenico Barbaja, the Milanese patentee of the royal theaters, by assigning him large tracts of the royal domain in the Sila. Barbaja immediately resold the thirty or so properties to several of Calabria's great landowners. In 1868, the Property and Taxes Administration again endeavored to make the Barraccos give up twenty-two properties in the Sila, all presumably usurped (SACS, Sila Collection, *Occupations,* fasc. 3, book 4, 1–4).

Sila found themselves encircled by great landowners who were fencing in lands that had been subject to common rights since time immemorial. Consequently, the municipalities considered the presence of the great landowners illicit on two counts—as proprietors, because King Joachim's divestment of royal lands violated King Robert's edict, and as usurpers—and put up a tenacious resistance to it, employing both legal means (innumerable lawsuits against the usurpers)[10] and their own less-than-legal methods (support for brigands and constant violations of enclosure boundaries). Unlike the intertwined situation in the Marquisate, the Sila enclosures, located as they were in uninhabited areas at a good distance from the towns, were separated from and in opposition to the latter.

Thus, osmosis was the rule in one part of the dragon, hostility in the other. This different relationship could be read in the signs that the owners disseminated, mainly for symbolic purposes, throughout the territory of the latifondo: houses, mansions, fencing, and gates, all decorated with their coats of arms, even if rarely or never used. In the Marquisate, these signs were scattered everywhere, as capillary as the very presence of the latifondo. For a great Marquisate landowner, it was de rigeur to keep a patrician palace in Croton, small, dark, and poor though the city was in that period. Besides the Barraccos's, situated alongside the castle, there were also the palaces of the Gaetanis, the Zurlos, the Luciferos, the Galluccis, and the Morellis. But the Barraccos also kept one in Isola di Capo Rizzuto and one in San Leonardo, as well as mansions in Croton, Isola, Castella, and San Leonardo. A palace with outbuildings, stables, shops, and small houses dominated the village of Altilia, another the hamlet of Spinello in Belvedere township. In Caccuri, the great castle (acquired together with the whole fief that had belonged to the Cavalcante family) reigned over the town with all its feudal entourage, including a church. In the Sila these signs were rarer and of a different character. The patrician homes in San Giovanni, Spezzano Piccolo, and Aprigliano were not particularly imposing; situated among other houses belonging to the major landowners, their role was more practical than symbolic and inculcated no sense of awe. But out in the country the posts erected to indicate the boundaries of the enclosure, and above all to signal the continuous presence of armed guards, sent a harsh and threatening message: private property, no trespassing. More than the others, it was the Camigliati complex—high up in the Great Sila, equidistant (around thirty kilometers) from San Giovanni on the Ionian slope and from Spezzano on the Cosenza slope, built in the middle of the woods in an uninhabited area—that fulfilled a powerful symbolic function.

---

10. From time to time the townships' insistence produced some government action but never to any effect. Some examples: Commissioner Barletta's mission in 1847–48 and the Sila Act of 1876, not to mention the Sila Act passed a century later.

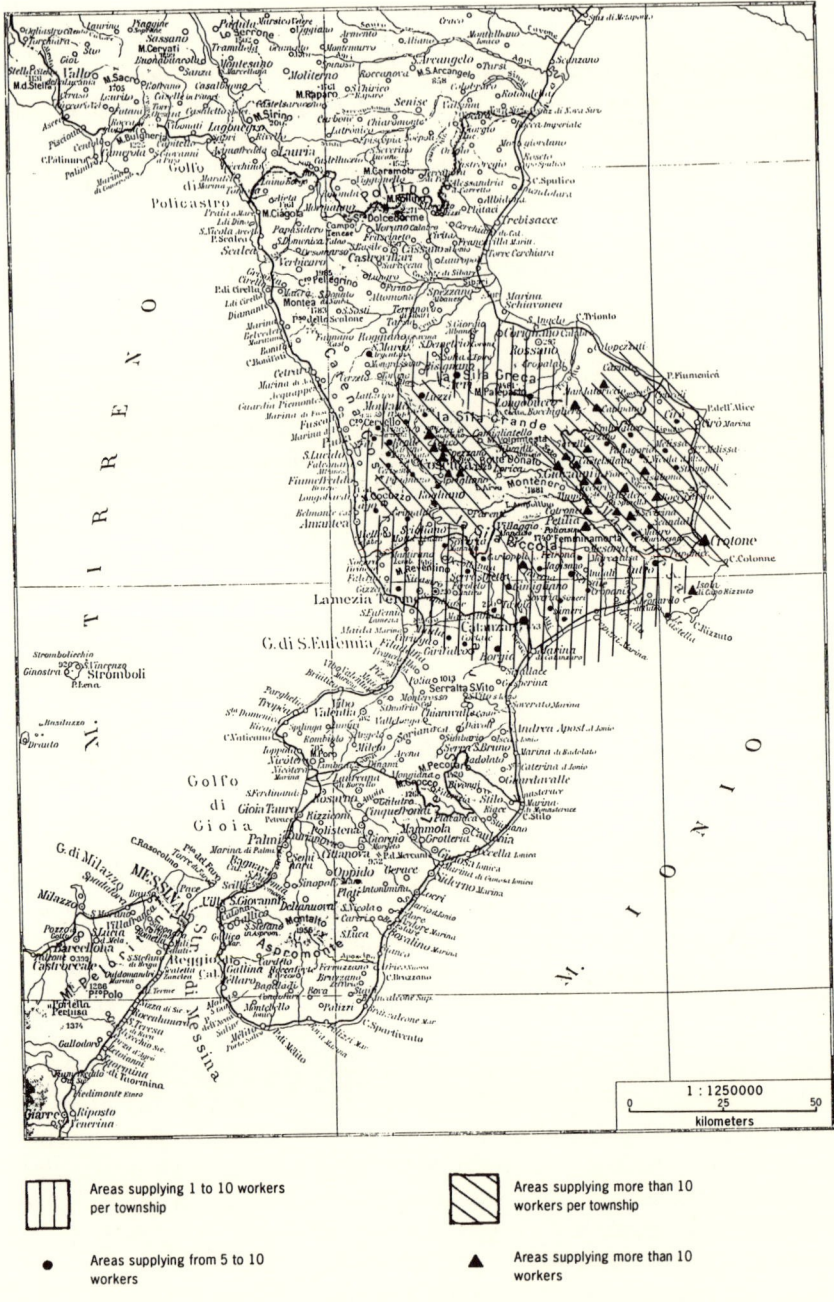

Areas supplying 1 to 10 workers per township

Areas supplying more than 10 workers per township

• Areas supplying from 5 to 10 workers

▲ Areas supplying more than 10 workers

Fig. 4. The social territory: workers' native areas

With its lodge (subsequently enlarged to the size of a large palace), bakeries, stables, blocks of peasant dwellings, bailiff's house, fences, and dozens of armed guards, Camigliati looked more like a stronghold than a country house. From Camigliati—and this was the point—one had the impression of domination in the Sila.

4. The Territory as Manpower Pool

The social territory over which the latifondo exercised the function of employer, and which in turn constituted the reserve of labor for the latifondo, was much larger than that of the property itself. In fact, it included as many as 130 towns, villages, and hamlets. Some, which supplied skilled workmen, were quite distant (the managers of the silk barns came from Reggio, some domestic servants from the Serre, gardeners from Roccella, and pruners from Lauria), but most were situated in the immediate vicinity of the property. The record was held by the upland towns on both slopes of the Sila: three hundred provisionees came from San Giovanni in Fiore and the same number from San Pietro in Guarano, while almost two hundred came from the small towns of Caccuri, Celico, Spezzano Grande, Spezzano Piccolo, and Castelsilano. A slightly wider ring of towns, delimited by Taverna on the south, Scigliano and Aprigliano on the west, Bocchigliero and Mandatoriccio on the north, and Belvedere and Rocca di Neto on the east, with outer points in Isola and Croton, supplied the latifondo with ten to fifty workers each. Lastly, some provisionees—no more than ten per town—came from a still wider ring whose cardinal points were Acri, Cirò, Catanzaro, and Rende. The radius of the outermost of these concentric circles was about sixty kilometers long; at their center was the Great Sila or perhaps the Camigliati lodge.

Outlined on a map, this territory has an ethno-ecological unity of its own: it surrounds the mountain, following the river valleys, and divides the Great Sila from the Greek Sila; it is a large entity composed of different local ecosystems. What marks it off from the latifondo proper is the centrality of the mountain: while the "dragon" of the property was located mainly in the Marquisate, the densest of the "employment" rings was situated in the mountains. To say it with numbers, the latifondo recruited 70 to 75 percent of its permanent workforce and more than 80 percent of its overseers, not from the zones where it had the most property but from the upper and lower Silan districts. This fact, illustrated in detail in table 5, is too constant to be coincidental; it is obviously the result of a conscious hiring strategy. We can only guess at the reasons for this strategy, which surprisingly gave preference to the rebellious and antifeudal mountains at the expense of the docile flatlands; the administrators, for whom it was simply an established practice, never set them out explicitly. It was logical enough to choose mountain men to work with the

TABLE 5. Correlation between Employees' Provenance and Jobs (by decade)

1801–1819	Massari	Herders	Overseers	Administrators	Domestics	Craftsmen	Others	Total
Seacoast	0	9	1	3	0	0	0	13
Line (%)	0.0	69.2	7.7	23.1	0.0	0.0	0.0	
Column (%)	0.0	6.4	5.9	50.0	0.0	0.0	0.0	6.7
Foothills	0	28	0	1	0	0	0	29
Line (%)	0.0	96.6	0.0	3.4	0.0	0.0	0.0	
Column (%)	0.0	19.9	0.0	16.7	0.0	0.0	0.0	15.0
High hills	8	59	11	1	3	1	2	85
Line (%)	9.4	69.4	12.9	1.2	3.5	1.2	2.4	
Column (%)	72.7	41.8	64.7	16.7	25.0	100.0	40.0	44.0
Mountains	3	41	5	1	1	0	3	54
Line (%)	5.6	75.9	9.3	1.9	1.9	0.0	5.6	
Column (%)	27.3	29.1	29.4	16.7	8.3	0.0	60.0	28.0
Provincial capitals	0	0	0	0	0	0	0	0
Line (%)	—	—	—	—	—	—	—	—
Column (%)	0.0	0.0	0.0	0.0	0.0	0.0	0.0	0.0
Other	0	4	0	0	8	0	0	12
Line (%)	0.0	33.3	0.0	66.7	0.0	0.0	5.6	
Column (%)	0.0	2.8	0.0	0.0	100.0	0.0	0.0	6.3
Total	11	141	17	6	12	1	5	193
Line (%)	5.7	73.1	8.8	3.1	6.2	0.5	2.6	100

1820–1829	*Massari*	Herders	Overseers	Administrators	Domestics	Craftsmen	Others	Total
Seacoast	0	6	1	2	1	0	3	13
Line (%)	0.0	67.4	7.7	15.4	1.5	0.0	23.0	
Column (%)	0.0	48.7	2.0	33.3	16.7	0.0	16.6	4.5
Foothills	0	28	4	2	0	0	0	34
Line (%)	0.0	82.4	11.8	5.9	0.0	0.0	0.0	
Column (%)	0.0	15.0	8.2	33.3	0.0	0.0	0.0	11.7
High hills	9	91	27	1	2	0	6	136
Line (%)	6.6	67.4	20.1	0.7	1.5	0.0	4.4	
Column (%)	52.9	48.7	55.1	16.7	16.7	0.0	33.3	46.7
Mountains	6	53	0	1	4	1	2	80
Line (%)	7.5	66.2	0.0	1.3	5.0	1.3	2.5	
Column (%)	35.3	28.3	0.0	16.7	33.3	50.0	11.1	27.5
Provincial capitals	0	0	1	0	0	1	0	2
Line (%)	0.0	0.0	50.0	0.0	0.0	50.0	0.0	
Column (%)	0.0	0.0	2.0	0.0	0.0	50.0	0.0	0.7
Other	2	9	3	0	5	0	7	26
Line (%)	8.0	42.9	12.0	0.0	19.5	0.0	27.0	
Column (%)	11.8	4.8	6.1	0.0	41.7	0.0	38.9	8.9
Total	17	187	49	6	12	2	18	291
Line (%)	5.7	64.5	16.9	2.1	4.1	0.7	6.2	100

(continued)

TABLE 5—*Continued*

1830–1839	*Massari*	Herders	Overseers	Administrators	Domestics	Craftsmen	Others	Total
Seacoast	0	4	7	2	3	1	4	21
Line (%)	0.0	19.0	33.3	9.5	14.3	4.8	19.1	
Column (%)	0.0	1.3	6.2	22.2	10.7	20.0	13.3	38.0
Foothills	0	26	11	1	1	0	5	44
Line (%)	0.0	59.1	25.0	2.3	2.3	0.0	11.4	
Column (%)	0.0	8.7	9.7	11.1	3.6	0.0	16.7	8.7
High hills	11	116	49	4	2	1	8	191
Line (%)	5.8	60.7	25.7	2.1	1.0	0.5	4.1	
Column (%)	57.9	38.8	43.3	44.4	7.1	20.0	26.7	38.0
Mountains	7	82	32	1	7	0	2	131
Line (%)	5.3	62.6	24.4	0.8	5.3	0.0	1.5	
Column (%)	36.8	27.4	28.3	11.1	25.0	0.0	6.7	26.0
Provincial capitals	0	0	1	0	0	1	2	4
Line (%)	0.0	0.0	25.0	0.0	0.0	25.0	50.0	
Column (%)	0.0	0.0	0.9	0.0	0.0	20.0	6.7	0.8
Other	1	71	13	1	15	2	9	112
Line (%)	0.8	63.4	11.6	0.8	13.4	1.8	8.0	
Column (%)	5.3	23.9	11.5	11.1	53.5	40.0	30.0	22.3
Total	19	299	113	9	28	5	30	503
Line (%)	3.8	59.4	22.5	1.8	5.6	1.0	60	100

1840–1849	Massari	Herders	Overseers	Administrators	Domestics	Craftsmen	Others	Total
Seacoast	0	4	6	2	2	1	4	17
Line (%)	0.0	23.0	35.3	11.8	11.8	5.9	11.8	
Column (%)	0.0	1.3	4.3	15.4	5.7	100.0	10.0	3.2
Foothills	0	20	15	3	1	0	5	44
Line (%)	0.0	45.5	34.1	6.8	2.3	0.0		
Column (%)	0.0	6.5	10.6	23.1	2.9	0.0	25	8.2
High hills	9	118	68	5	4	0	7	211
Line (%)	4.3	55.9	32.2	2.4	1.9	0.0	3.3	
Column (%)	45	38.3	48.2	38.5	11.4	0.0	35.0	39.2
Mountains	8	85	27	1	6	0	1	128
Line (%)	6.2	66.4	21.1	0.8	4.7	0.0	0.8	
Column (%)	40.0	27.6	19.1	7.7	17.1	0.0	5.0	23.8
Provincial capitals	0	0	2	1	0	0	0	3
Line (%)	0.0	0.0	66.7	33.3	0.0	0.0	0.0	
Column (%)	0.0	0.0	1.4	7.7	0.0	0.0	0.0	0.6
Other	3	81	23	1	22	0	5	135
Line (%)	2.2	60.0	17.0	0.7	16.3	0.0	0.0	3.7
Column (%)	15.0	26.3	16.3	7.7	62.9	0.0	25.0	25.1
Total	20	308	141	13	35	1	20	538
Line (%)	3.7	57.2	26.2	2.4	6.5	0.2	3.7	100

(continued)

TABLE 5—*Continued*

1850–1859	*Massari*	Herders	Overseers	Administrators	Domestics	Craftsmen	Others	Total
Seacoast	0	6	3	3	3	1	0	16
Line (%)	0.0	37.5	18.8	18.8	18.8	6.2	0.0	
Column (%)	0.0	1.8	1.9	30.0	11.5	25.0	0.0	2.8
Foothills	0	37	20	4	2	1	2	66
Line (%)	0.0	56.1	30.3	6.1	3.0	1.5	3.0	
Column (%)	0.0	11.11	12.3	40.0	7.7	25.0	11.1	11.5
High hills	9	133	89	1	7	2	7	248
Line (%)	3.6	53.6	35.9	0.4	2.8	0.8	2.8	
Column (%)	42.9	40.1	54.9	10.0	26.9	50.0	38.8	43.3
Mountains	10	115	38	1	4	0	5	173
Line (%)	5.8	66.5	22.0	0.6	2.3	0.0	2.9	
Column (%)	47.6	34.6	23.5	10.0	15.4	0.0	27.8	6
Provincial capitals	0	0	0	1	1	0	0	2
Line (%)	0.0	0.0	0.0	10.0	50.0	0.0	0.0	
Column (%)	0.0	0.0	0.0	10.0	3.8	0.0	0.0	0.3
Other	2	41	12	0	9	0	4	68
Line (%)	2.9	60.3	17.7	0.0	13.2	0.0	5.9	
Column (%)	9.5	12.0	7.4	0.0	34.6	0.0	2.5	11.9
Total	21	332	162	10	26	4	18	573
Line (%)	3.8	57.9	28.3	1.7	4.5	0.7	0.3	100

1860–1869	*Massari*	Herders	Overseers	Administrators	Domestics	Craftsmen	Others	Total
Seacoast	0	23	8	3	1	1	1	37
Line (%)	0.0	62.2	21.6	8.1	2.7	2.7	2.7	
Column (%)	0.0	8.9	5.0	30.0	3.1	12.5	8.3	7.4
Foothills	1	21	19	2	3	1	0	47
Line (%)	2.1	44.7	40.4	4.3	6.4	2.1	0.0	
Column (%)	4.5	8.2	11.9	20.0	9.4	12.5	0.0	9.4
High hills	9	121	86	3	11	5	6	241
Line (%)	3.7	50.2	35.7	1.2	4.6	2.1	2.5	
Column (%)	40.9	47.5	54.1	30.0	34.4	62.5	50.0	48.2
Mountains	7	75	36	1	2	1	2	124
Line (%)	5.6	60.5	29.0	0.8	1.6	0.8	1.6	
Column (%)	31.8	29.2	22.6	10.0	6.2	12.5	16.7	24.8
Provincial capitals	0	0	1	0	0	0	0	1
Line (%)	0.0	0.0	100	0.0	0.0	0.0	0.0	
Column (%)	0.0	0.0	0.6	0.0	0.0	0.0	0.0	0.2
Other	5	17	9	1	15	0	3	50
Line (%)	10.0	34.0	18.0	2.0	30.0	0.0	6.0	
Column (%)	22.7	6.6	5.7	10.0	46.9	0.0	25.0	10.0
Total	22	257	159	10	32	8	12	500
Line (%)	4.4	51.4	31.8	2.0	6.4	1.6	24.0	100

(continued)

TABLE 5—*Continued*

1870–1879	*Massari*	Herders	Overseers	Administrators	Domestics	Craftsmen	Others	Total
Seacoast	0	15	14	3	2	2	1	37
Line (%)	0.0	40.5	37.8	8.1	5.4	5.4	2.7	
Column (%)	0.0	7.9	7.4	30.0	4.9	25.0	9.1	8.0
Foothills	2	26	34	2	3	1	0	68
Line (%)	2.9	38.2	50.0	2.9	4.4	1.5	0.0	
Column (%)	12.5	13.8	18.1	20.0	7.3	12.5	0.0	14.7
High hills	7	80	89	4	20	2	9	211
Line (%)	3.3	37.9	42.2	1.9	9.5	0.9	4.3	
Column (%)	43.8	42.3	47.3	40.0	48.8	25.0	81.8	45.6
Mountains	5	55	36	1	3	1	0	101
Line (%)	5.0	54.5	35.6	1.0	3.0	1.0	0.0	
Column (%)	31.2	29.1	18.1	10.0	7.3	12.5	0.0	21.8
Provincial capitals	0	0	1	0	0	1	0	2
Line (%)	0.0	0.0	50.0	0.0	0.0	50.0	0.0	
Column (%)	0.0	0.0	0.5	0.0	0.0	12.5	0.0	0.4
Other	2	13	14	0	13	1	1	44
Line (%)	4.5	29.5	31.8	0.0	29.5	2.3	2.3	
Column (%)	12.5	6.8	7.5	0.0	4.9	12.5	9.1	10.5
Total	16	189	188	10	41	8	11	500
Line (%)	3.5	40.8	40.6	2.2	8.9	1.7	2.4	100

1880–1889	*Massari*	Herders	Overseers	Administrators	Domestics	Craftsmen	Others	Total
Seacoast	1	11	6	1	1	0	0	320
Line (%)	5.0	55.0	30.0	5.0	5.0	0.0	0.0	
Column (%)	5.0	6.0	5.6	14.3	5.9	0.0	0.0	5.9
Foothills	1	35	19	1	1	1	0	58
Line (%)	1.7	60.3	32.8	1.7	1.7	1.7	0.0	
Column (%)	5.0	19.2	17.6	14.3	5.9	100.0	0.0	17.1
High hills	3	73	48	3	9	0	2	138
Line (%)	2.2	52.9	34.8	2.2	6.5	0.0	1.4	
Column (%)	15.0	40.1	44.4	42.9	52.9	0.0	50.0	40.7
Mountains	14	58	25	1	0	0	0	98
Line (%)	14.3	59.2	25.5	1.0	0.0	0.0	0.0	
Column (%)	70.0	31.9	23.1	14.3	0.0	0.0	0.0	28.9
Provincial capitals	0	0	0	0	0	0	0	0
Line (%)	0.0	0.0	0.0	0.0	0.0	0.0	0.0	
Column (%)	0.0	0.0	0.0	0.0	0.0	0.0	0.0	0.0
Other	1	5	10	1	6	0	2	25
Line (%)	4.0	20.0	40.0	4.0	24.0	0.0	8.0	
Column (%)	5.0	2.7	9.3	14.3	35.3	0.0	50.0	7.3
Total	20	182	108	7	17	1	4	339
Line (%)	5.9	53.7	31.9	2.1	5.0	0.3	1.2	100

(continued)

TABLE 5—*Continued*

1890–1900	*Massari*	Herders	Overseers	Administrators	Domestics	Craftsmen	Others	Total
Seacoast	0	6	5	1	1	0	2	15
Line (%)	0.0	40.0	33.3	6.7	6.7	0.0	13.3	
Column (%)	0.0	5.1	5.9	25.0	9.1	—	22.2	6.4
Foothills	1	16	11	0	1	0	0	29
Line (%)	3.4	55.2	37.9	0.0	3.4	0.0	0.0	
Column (%)	11.1	13.7	12.9	0.0	9.1	—	0.0	12.3
High hills	0	45	35	2	5	0	1	88
Line (%)	0.0	51.5	39.8	2.3	5.7	0.0	1.1	
Column (%)	0.0	38.5	41.2	45.5	—	1.1	37.4	
Mountains	8	39	20	0	0	0	2	69
Line (%)	11.6	56.5	29.0	0.0	0.0	0.0	2.9	
Column (%)	88.9	33.3	23.5	0.0	0.0	—	22.2	29.4
Provincial capitals	0	0	0	0	0	0	0	0
Line (%)	0.0	0.0	0.0	0.0	0.0	0.0	0.0	
Column (%)	0.0	0.0	0.0	0.0	0.0	0.0	0.0	0.0
Other	0	11	14	1	4	0	4	34
Line (%)	0.0	32.4	41.2	3.0	11.8	0.0	11.8	
Column (%)	0.0	9.4	16.5	25.0	36.4	—	44.5	13.5
Total	9	117	85	4	11	0	9	235
Line (%)	3.8	49.8	36.2	1.7	4.7	0.0	3.9	100

herds because they were more used to pastoral occupations than others. One other reason could have been that their social characters—individualistic, self-reliant, disinclined to associate with others, accustomed to carrying weapons and to enduring long months of absence from home—made them excellent bosses and overseers.[11] Another likely reason is that during the period of the demographic spread we will be discussing, the workforce in the flatlands was not reproducing at a sufficient rate. It does seem, however, that this strategy also served to moderate the hostile and potentially antagonistic social characters of the Silan territory. The mountain folk—once smallholders, now weakened by expropriations, usurpations, and privatizations, but still jealous of their peasant status ("jealous of the pasturelands") and scornful of the landless farm laborers—accepted the status of wage workers, but (as we shall see) they did so in a sort of alliance with the large landowners.[12] In fact, this strategy was applied only for the so-called *provvisionati,* or permanent employees. For the occasional workers, the braccianti, the geographical distribution was just the opposite; almost all were recruited in the flatlands. But this is a topic we shall discuss later.

5. The Social Territory as the Product of History

In their action of transformation and consolidation, the latifondisti had to take account of other factors that had shaped the social territory. First of all, its history had to be considered. Scattered through the southernmost part of the latifondo, the Marquisate, and the Silan foothills, there were towns that, though of ancient origin and still bearing traces of the Greek structures of self-government, in the nineteenth century were marked mainly by the signs of the more recent feudal presence, which had incorporated them all between the post-Norman period and the seventeenth century and prevailed up to 1806.[13] Although the legislation that abolished feudalism, promulgated from above, had brought in many novelties—some of which soon disappeared, while oth-

11. Numerous descriptions exist of the barons' instrumental use of these local autonomies in times of conflict when they would bring armed herdsmen down from the mountains to put down the peasants' collective actions in the lowlands. See the narratives in F. Jovine, *Le Terre del Sacramento* (Turin, 1982); and V. Padula, *Antonello capobrigante calabrese* (Rome, 1976).

12. F. Piselli and G. Arrighi quote the account given by one of the workers employed on the latifondo: "The herdsmen were quite attached to the owners; they sided with the owners' interests, and their jobs were safe" ("Parentela, clientela e comunità," in *La Calabria,* op. cit., 411). The authors rightly interpret this as proof of division among the various workforces. However, they see in it a strategy that "aimed to achieve exploitation lacking any paternalistic weakness," whereas in my opinion it should be taken as evidence of the effectiveness of the paternalistic relationship.

13. See R. Valentini, *Prospetto istorico-politico delle Calabrie nel Regno di Napoli fino all'età presente* (Naples, 1838); and A. de Rivarol, *Notice historique sur la Calabre* (Paris, 1819). For a fictional account in verse, see L. Stocchi, *Novelle storiche calabresi* n.p., n.d. [ca. 1873]), pt. 3.

ers, less direct, took decades to penetrate local usages—what lasted was the awareness of a certain continuity: when new landowners like the Barraccos acquired properties, in the popular perception they were another link in a long chain of feudal proprietors.[14]

To the contrary, the history of the Silan towns was one of liberty. They were founded for the most part in the ninth and tenth centuries by Cosentines who, fleeing the Saracens and "bad air" (malaria), established new hamlets (*casali*) as outposts of their native city.[15] These Silan towns, though subject to Cosenza's legal jurisdiction, had always remained free of feudal bonds (only San Giovanni was enfeoffed to the Riccis, and that only in the eighteenth century). And they were jealous of this liberty. When an attempt was made to enfeoff them to the grand duke of Tuscany during the period of the feudal offensive in Calabria,[16] all the hamlets rose up in 1647 in the so-called revolt of Celico, a name derived from the name of the town that led the way.[17] Their territories in the mountains and on the high plateau were situated in the midst of royal and communal lands on which they had exercised common rights (de facto and de jure) for centuries.

Accordingly, anyone who aspired to control these lands had to take their

14. In all the villages in the territory, the overlordship had changed hands several times over the centuries, seemingly without breaking the continuity of their history. Isola di Capo Rizzuto, for example, had passed from the Riccas of Taverna to the Catalanos, from the Catalanos to the Caracciolos of Montesardo, and finally to the Friozzis; Castella from the Carafas of Santa Severina to the Carafas of Nocera, then to the Filomarinos; Cutro from the Ruffos to the Filomarinos; Belcastro from the d'Aquinos to the Sanseverinos, the Trivulzios, and the Poerios; San Marco from the counts of Catanzaro to the Carafas, the Ruffos of Scilla, the Sculcos, and the Grutters; and so forth. In the eighteenth century, the Barraccos themselves already owned small fiefs in that district. See BA: Secs. G, E, several volumes; G. Valente, *Storia della Calabria,* op. cit.; and G. Galasso, *Economia e società,* op. cit. Besides, the new landowners surely seemed no worse to the inhabitants of the Marquisate than the old feudal lords, who had had nothing of the "benevolence" of feudalism about them. As H. Swinburne noted in his *Travels in Calabria* (London, 1781), the old barons were "far from considering themselves the protectors, the political fathers of their vassals; to the contrary, they invade their pastures and fields to enlarge their own hunting grounds, and the peasants no longer have enough land or any possibility of producing enough food to live on" (17).

15. Some of these towns grew up or flourished around religious communities, of which the best known were the Abbot Gioacchino's coenobium at San Giovanni in Fiore and the Joachimite communities at Celico and Aprigliano. Many place names in the hills and mountains recall the presence of monasteries and convents: Monaci, Pezzerillo de' Monaci, Abadessa de' Paolotti. The tradition was periodically renewed: in the 1870s, for example, a heretical sect called "the Saints of Bocchigliero" was established in that town (see G. Sole *I. santi di Bocchiigliero: Storia di un movimento ereticale contadino* [Milano, F. Angeli, c. 1990]).

16. F. Braudel, *The Mediterranean and the Mediterranean World in the Age of Philip II* (New York, 1972).

17. Giovanni Barracco, as a Cosenza patrician and man of law, was the person who argued his city's interests at the court in Madrid on that occasion and got the king to void the sale of these hamlets.

history into account. As we shall see, one of the reasons for the success of nineteenth-century latifondismo was its ability to incorporate original local characteristics in its economic strategies.

6. Patterns of Settlement

Another factor that had to be taken into account was the pattern of human settlement, which varied from part to part of the dragon. The differences were noted by the numerous travelers, mainly foreigners, who felt compelled to record their impressions. Ramage, traveling through the flatlands of the Marquisate in 1828, saw a winsome rural world in places where the rolling hills were covered with vineyards and olive groves.[18] A contemporary found the Sila a solitary area where "human beings rarely leave traces" and the forest reigned unopposed.

> The beeches and the pines . . . cling together so as to allow the passage of only a few weak and broken rays of light. . . . Here all is abandoned to nature, and only once in a while do the shepherds cut a few beeches to build their huts.[19]

Although the flatlands, which showed more signs of human intervention, appeared to be more densely populated than the solitary mountain, in reality the opposite was true. But the patterns of settlement in the Marquisate and the Sila were different. Bearing in mind that the population increased sharply throughout Calabria during the nineteenth century,[20] a comparison of the population figures and the territorial extension of the townships crossed by the "dragon" of the Barracco latifondo should give us a better idea of the difference in these patterns (cf. table 6.).

---

18. C. T. Ramage, *The Nooks and By-Ways of Italy,* ed. E. Clay (London, 1965). See also, from the same period, Domenico Cuciniello and Lorenzo Bianchi, *Viaggio pittorico nel Regno delle Due Sicilie* (Naples, 1828); and G. Orloff, *Mémoires historiques, politiques et littéraires sur le Royaume de Naple* (Paris, 1821). From a slightly later period, see Edward Lear's *Journal of a Painter in Calabria* (London, 1847), reprinted in P. Quennell, ed., *Edmund Lear in Southern Italy: Journals of a Landscape Painter in Southern Calabria and the Kingdom of Naples* (London, 1964).

19. L. Petagna, G. Terrone, and M. Tenore, *Viaggio in alcuni luoghi della Basilicata e della Calabria Citeriore* (Naples, 1827), 47–48, quoted in M. Sciacca, *Le terre del Sud* (Rome and Cosenza, 1977), 79. R. Keppel Craven had the same experience: "This mountainous and elevated tract of country may still be considered as one extensive forest . . ." (*A Tour Through the Southern Provinces of the Kingdom of Naples* [London1, 1821], quoted in ibid., 94).

20. Luigi Izzo calculates that the population of Calabria grew from 851,425 in 1820, to 1,130,000 in 1849, and 1,257,883 in 1881, that is, 50 percent in sixty years. See his "Per la storia demografica della Calabria nel secolo XIX," in *Atti del Secondo Congresso Storico Calabrese,* op. cit.

TABLE 6.　Population and Area of Townships Crossed by the Barracco Latifondo: The Marquisate

Township	1814	1849	1861	1881	1901	Area (km²)
Belcastro	962	980	991	1,196	1,409	52.8
Cutro-S. Leonardo	1,872	2,830	2,905	4,556	5,223	132.0
Isola-Le Castella	2,243	1,742	2,964	2,973	2,857	125.3
Cotrone	3,932	5,964	7,168	9,649	9,610	179.8
San Mauro	777	1,016	1,055	1,714	1,770	42.0
Scandale	958	1,254	1,296	1,506	1,467	53.0
S. Severina-Altilia	1,033	1,139	1,305	1,670	1,959	51.9
Rocca Bernarda	600	702	657	1,269	1,299	65.5
Casabona	1,072	1,955	1,936	2,729	2,882	68.9
Melissa	823	1,256	1,541	1,967	2,361	50.9
Belvedere Spinello	745	1,505	1,426	1,430	1,506	30.2
Rocca di Neto	572	712	974	1,323	1,372	43.6
Total	15,589	21,055	24,218	31,982	33,715	896.5
Average density[2]	17.3	23.5	27.0	35.7	37.6	—
Population/Township	1,299	1,755	2,018	2,665	2,810	—

Population and Area of Townships Crossed by the Barracco Latifondo: The Southeastern Sila Foothills

Township	1814	1849	1861	1881	1901	Area (km²)
Caccuri	908	1,009	1,266	1,635	2,002	57.3
Cotronei	1,089	—	—	2,089	2,084	78.1
Pallagorio	560	1,093	1,014	1,139	1,307	42.0
San Nicola	2,052	2,465	2,233	2,685	3,417	19.3
Verzino	846	723	899	1,064	1,261	45.4
Total	5,455	5,290	5,412	8,612	10,071	242.1
Average density	22.5	32.2	33.0	35.6	41.6	—
Population/township	1,091	1,058	1,082	1,722	2,014	—

The first observation concerns population density. While the average over the whole nineteenth century was about the same in the Sila and the Marquisate (twenty-nine people per square kilometer in the former, twenty-eight in the latter), the trends in the two regions were opposite. Over the course of the century, the mountain population, initially 30 percent higher than that of the flatlands, gradually thinned out, while the flatland population increased.[21]

---

21. In 1814, population density in the Sila part of the latifondo was twenty-two people per

TABLE 6—*Continued*
Population and Area of Townships Crossed by the Barracco Latifondo: The High Sila

Township	1814	1849	1861	1881	1901	Area (km²)
Aprigliano	4,328	5,098	4,168	4,071	4,360	121.3
Celico	1,891	2,619	2,448	2,446	2,627	99.0
Pedace	1,550	2,422	1,749	2,046	1,910	51.5
San Giovanni	5,720	9,031	9,239	10,744	12,914	279.5
Serra Pedace	1,263	1,495	1,432	1,331	1,419	59.2
Spezzano Grande	1,576	2,573	2,011	2,160	2,291	79.6
Spezzano Piccolo	1,169	1,572	1,233	1,349	1,360	48.7
Taverna	1,783	2,516	2,255	2,184	2,202	132.5
Total	19,280	27,326	24,535	26,331	29,083	871.3
Average density	22.1	31.4	28.2	30.2	33.4	—
Population/township	2,410	3,416	3,067	3,291	3,635	—

Population and Area of Townships Crossed by the Barracco Latifondo: Summary

Region	1814	1849	1861	1881	1901	Area (km²)
Marquisate	15,589	21,055	24,218	31,982	33,715	896.5
Sila foothills	5,455	5,290	5,412	8,612	10,071	242.1
High Sila	19,280	27,326	24,535	26,331	29,083	871.3
Total	40,324	53,671	54,165	66,925	72,869	2,009.0
Average density	20.0	26.7	26.9	33.3	36.2	—

Population and Area of High Sila Townships

Township	1814	1849	1861	1881	1901	Area (km²)
The "Barracco Sila"[a]	19,280	27,326	24,535	26,331	29,083	871.3
Bocchigliero	3,031	3,729	3,358	3,362	3,109	80.0
Longobucco	5,128	8,209	6,369	3,410	3,760	210.3
Castelsilano	1,033	1,496	1,418	2,047	1,920	39.5
Savelli	2,200	3,758	3,966	4,400	4,194	48.5
Rogliano	3,788	4,845	4,646	4,839	5,252	41.4
Total	34,460	49,363	44,292	44,389	47,318	1,291.0
Average density	26.7	38.2	34.3	34.4	36.6	—
Population/township	2,651	3,797	3,407	3,415	3,640	

[a]Townships crossed by the Barracco latifondo.

The second significant fact was the physical size of the townships. While in both regions the rural town or village remained the dominant form of settlement,[22] the Silan townships were a good deal larger than those in the Marquisate and in the foothills (average areas were 109, 75, and 48 square kilometers, respectively). From the standpoint of the latifondo administration, this meant greater fragmentation in the Marquisate and greater concentration in the Sila: the latifondo's area included seventeen townships in the Marquisate but only eight in the Sila.

The result was a difference in population distribution. In the Sila, population density by township averaged 30 to 50 percent more than on the flatlands: in 1814, the averages were 2,410 and 1,238 people per township, respectively; by the end of the century, they had grown to 3,635 and 2,576.[23]

These summary numerical observations can help us understand why the perceptions of contemporaries were so different and so misleading: the way of life was different in the mountains and in the flatlands. In the Marquisate, with the partial exception of the city of Croton,[24] conurbations were very small. Besides the town proper, the territory of each township included villages and hamlets and still tinier settlements that often lay quite a distance away (the

---

square kilometer but only seventeen in the Marquisate; in 1849, the figures were thirty-one and twenty-three, respectively. See L. Izzo, *La popolazione calabrese nel secolo XIX: Demografia ed economia* (Naples, 1965). In the 1840s, the province's Economic Society lamented a decrease in the population of the Marquisate, attributing it to the noxious air. The tone of the society's reports was highly alarmist: we read of "the lack of trees, the effect of the swamps and the badly-built irrigation works"; in Isola di Capo Rizzuto, "besides [the town's] being ill-situated, damp and without ventilation, many of the springs are unhealthy. . . . Hence the decrease in population should come as no surprise" and "The town of Cutro too suffers the ill effects of swamp air." In Rocca Bernarda, Rocca Ferdinandea and Cotronei, the marshes and the clay soil were said to foster pneumonia and undulant fever. See L. Grimaldi (the society's permanent secretary), "Studi statistici sull'industria agricola e manufatturiera della Calabria Ultra Seconda," *Annali Civili* (1847), fasc. 88, 129–30. But in 1861 population density was twenty-eight people per square kilometer in the Sila and already up to twenty-seven in the Marquisate; the reversal in this ratio was first revealed in the 1881 census. This pattern of growth aroused scholars' interest in the early years of the twentieth century. See *Inchiesta Parlamentare sulle condizioni dei contadini nelle provincie meridionali e nella Sicilia,* vol. 5: the report by Rag. Ernesto Marenghi, the technical delegate, *Basilicata e Calabrie,* pt. 2: "Calabrie" (Rome, 1909).

22. In 1861, 80 percent of the population lived in cities and rural towns and only 11 percent in isolated houses. In 1881, 86 percent lived in cities and towns. Jane Schneider analyzes this pattern of settlement, typical of many areas in the Mediterranean, in her fine paper, "Of Vigilance and Virgins," *Ethnology* 9 (Winter 1971).

23. For practical reasons I have used here only the data on townships traversed by the Barracco latifondo, but my findings would be borne out even taking the whole Great Sila into consideration. (cf. table 6).

24. H. Swinburne had found the city of Croton quite sad looking; he reported that the houses were poor and the streets narrow and dark, with very little animation or commerce (*Travels,* op. cit., 20).

village of Le Castella, for instance, was about ten kilometers from Isola, and the same distance separated San Leonardo from the town of Cutro). Each of these functioned in its own small way on the model of the rural town. The territory was thus sprinkled with communities of which the smallest numbered a few dozen inhabitants and the largest rarely exceeded a few hundred.[25] No distribution of this sort was possible in the Sila because of the severe climate and other dangers, from wolves to brigands. The mountain folk lived in large towns or in villages that were few in number and situated no more than a couple of kilometers away from them.[26] In the distance between one town and another, which might take a whole day's march to cover, there really was nothing besides the mountain, the forest, and pastures: no signs of a human presence except for an occasional sinister and lonely appearance of a stock driver, in midst of the animals.

7. Isolation and Communication

The whole social territory of the latifondo was quite isolated from the great highways. The ancient Via Popilia—the only large road that ran through Calabria before the arrival of the French—lay far to the west. The Consular highway built by the Napoleonic monarchy circled around the latifondo's territory without traversing it,[27] and a short extension of the royal Military highway, built in the mid-nineteenth century, merely linked Mormanno and Lungro. The Sila was still the great problem; any journey through it was bound to be lengthy, solitary, and dangerous. Of the long-planned Sila road, which it was hoped would bring "prosperity to commerce and industry, and therefore to the economy of all these towns," only eighteen miles had been built by 1860.[28] The problem was faced seriously only thirty years later with the formation of the Silan Road Consortium. In short, in 1886, Calabria still had the least

25. ". . . the district of Croton and the vast plain of the Marquisate, where the clay nature of the soil, the lack of trees and the effect of swamps and the badly-built irrigation works make the air noxious. The towns of Croton, Cutro and Isola, with their nearby villages, are the only inhabited parts of the plain; another twenty-six villages can be seen scattered on the surrounding hills and mountains . . ." (L. Grimaldi, "Studi statistici," op. cit., 129).

26. All of the approximately 2,000 inhabitants of the township of Spezzano Grande lived in the town itself; 1,600 of the 1,850 inhabitants of Pedace township lived in the town and 250 a mile and a quarter away in Perito, the town's only hamlet. The population of the township of Celico was divided between the town proper and the hamlet of Manneto.

27. The Consular highway ran south from Naples through Campotenese and Castrovillari to Spezzano Albanese, then followed the Crati Valley upstream to Cosenza, whence it climbed to Rogliano, circled around Sila Piccola, and followed the valley of the Corace downstream to Catanzaro, then wound up to Rossano.

28. The quote is from the governor of Upper Calabria, who hoped for these results from trade among Cosenza, San Giovanni in Fiore, and Croton. See G. Sole, *Viaggio nella Calabria Citeriore dell'800* (Cosenza, 1985), 60–61.

developed road network in all of Italy: hardly more than two thousand kilometers (of national, provincial, and municipal roads), with another four thousand under construction or existing only in politicians' futuristic fantasies. A fortiori, Calabria lacked railroads: although the Southern Railways Corporation was founded in 1861, the Cosenza-Sibari line was built only in 1878, the Catanzaro-Sant'Eufemia line in 1885, and the Ionian line in 1876. The Naples-Reggio line remained under construction until 1895.[29] Getting from Cosenza to Croton or Sibari was thus a perilous, lengthy, and difficult endeavor. From Cosenza to Spezzano Grande you could go "by wheel"—two-wheeled ox carts, two-wheeled wagons drawn by three horses or mules, wealthier travelers in four-horse gigs, the Barraccos in carriages driven by Neapolitan coachmen—but for the rest of the way you would have to ride a mule. Croton's port was silted up and—with engineering works forever postponed—could be used for only a few months each year. Conditions in Paola, Pizzo, and Gioia were even worse, and at any rate they could be reached from our territory only with the greatest difficulty.[30]

The isolation of the rural districts was aggravated by illiteracy. During the 1880s, the region's cities boasted twenty-one junior high schools and five high schools, but 82 percent of the adult population was illiterate. Public elementary schools were attended by barely a fifth of the boys and an eighth of the girls required by law to do so.[31] There was very little publishing, especially at the level of popular distribution; there were no daily newspapers, and periodicals—all in the Italian language—were issued only in a few large towns; in the countryside, not even farmer's almanacs circulated widely.[32] Few letters were sent, even after the townships established post offices. Even traditional channels of communication were scarce: there were few vagabonds and

---

29. Direzione Generale dello Stato, *Il Centenario delle ferrovie italiane, 1834–1839* (Rome, 1940).

30. A constant theme in the prefects' reports to the minister of internal affairs was the government's failure to build planned roads and railways; they rightly saw this as a matter of public order. The local population "hoped to see" construction of the Eboli-Reggio, Cosenza-Nocera, and Lagonegro-Castrovillari railroads and the rehabilitation of the port of Croton partly because these public works would have created jobs. See P. Borzomati, *La Calabria dal 1882 al 1892 nei rapporti dei prefetti* (Reggio Calabria, 1974).

31. G. Vigo, *Istruzione e sviluppo economico in Italia nel secolo XIX*, Archivio Economico dell'Unificazione Italiana (Turin, 1971), ser. 2, vol. 18, and statistical appendix.

32. Besides Cosenza, Catanzaro, and Reggio, where several periodicals of varying political tendencies were published, newspapers occasionally appeared in only a few other towns such as Nicastro, Filadelfia, Croton, Monteleone, and Corigliano. In 1887, only six publications in the region were classified as "miscellanies of popular literature." See G. Masi, "Per una storia della stampa socialista in Calabria," *Historica* 3 (1972): 117–33; C. Minicucci, "La storia di un secolo di giornalismo calabrese," *Corriere di Reggio* (1956–57); Kingdom of Italy, *Annuario statistico, 1887: Stampa;* and *La stampa italiana dal Risorgimento,* and *La stampa italiana nell'età liberale,* ed. V. Castronovo and N. Tranfaglia (1979).

few mendicant friars after the "French decade," while "beggars" resided on a stable basis in the townships.[33]

Nonetheless, communications within the territory were no rarity. The roads were used by seasonal migrants, merchants, muleteers, smugglers, and foreign travelers. Shops in the Silan towns were more or less regularly supplied with products originating in the Marquisate or available in the port of Croton, while the coastal towns received wool, cheese, and cloth from the Sila. Ramage, who in the best Scottish tradition traveled through Calabria on foot, noted that shops in "every part of Calabria" stocked sugar, coffee, English cutlery, and cloth (though in "defiance of fiscal regulations of Government").[34] People complained about the scarcity of weekly and monthly markets, which would have fostered the circulation of small-scale capital, but there were many annual fairs, and the region's three most important ones were held precisely in this territory: Santo Janni in May, Molerà in September, and Decollazione in December. Everything from livestock to labor was bought and sold at these events, contracts were finalized, tenancies were renewed, and laborers were hired or paid off; consequently, just about everybody showed up.[35] Information, too, circulated along the same routes, often blown out of proportion or distorted, as in the case of "rumors about poison-spreading," which the authorities feared more than political propaganda (indeed, such rumormongers were deemed political culprits).[36] Thus, people, goods, and ideas did circulate, though laboriously and irregularly, often blocked by landslides, rain, or snow.

8. Services and Government Intervention

Agrarian credit or support institutions were nonexistent or inadequate. What few there were served the large cities alone. In rural areas, only a few Grain Banks (Monti Frumentari) remained, dwindling in number and in ever-

---

33. S. Martuscelli, *La popolazione del Mezzogiorno*, op. cit., 455–557; *Caratteristiche ambientali italiane: Agrarie, sociali, demografiche, 1815–1942* (Rome, 1943).

34. C. T. Ramage, *Nooks and By-Ways of Italy*, op. cit., 125.

35. A traveler who visited Calabria in 1860 noted "many annual fairs, but very few weekly or monthly markets. Small capital therefore does not circulate; commodities remain unsold for long periods of time, or are lost, and payments are deferred until the next fair" (G. A. Pasquale, *Relazione sullo stato fisico-economico-agrario della Prima Calabria Ultra* [Naples, 1863], 175). See also C. Castellano, "Porto franco, fiere, manifatture e dazi doganali nelle Due Sicilie," in *Studi in onore di R. Filangieri* (Naples, 1959), iii.

36. At every outbreak of cholera in Naples or Sicily, a "deep-felt conviction" spread among the masses that "the local authorities and subordinate agents were administering the poison on secret government orders." During the epidemics of 1846–47, 1854–55, and 1884–85, the diffusion of alarmist news was therefore prosecuted as a political offense (SACZ, Political Trials, Calabria Ultra II, various jurisdictions). For the prefects' reports, see P. Borzomati, *La Calabria dal 1882*, op. cit., 109, 130, 147.

worsening condition; originally a form of aid against usury but subsequently transformed into credit banks, they came to exclude peasants thus defeating their original purpose.[37] The Catholic charities (Opere Pie) and public philanthropies did very little after the legislation of the "French decade" systematically hounded the religious orders out of the countryside. Many towns were left without any monks or nuns.[38] Accordingly, most of the orphan asylums (the Bourbons' public asylums mainly took in abandoned children) and charity hospitals, and all of the Poor Girls Dowry Funds (Monti di Maritaggio), simply disappeared.[39] In 1840, the government created "mendicancy funds" instead and banned begging; all of Calabria's beggars were supposed to hie themselves up north to Salerno. But these measures were a total failure; of the region's twenty thousand beggars, only fourteen went to Salerno. According to prefect Movizzo, what little was left of the Catholic charities after Italy's unification in

---

37. Banco di Napoli opened its first branch only in 1884. In the whole region there existed only 1 savings bank (in Cosenza), as against 106 in Lombardy, only 8 mutual loan companies, and 2 Monts-de-Piété, with deposits totaling 5,500 lire. The Bourbon administrators set great store by the *monti frumentari,* the only credit institutions operating in the rural districts: in 1847, when grain was in short supply, they distributed over a thousand tons of various kinds of grain to the population of southern Calabria. By the 1880s, they existed "only in name. In some cases their funds disappeared due to the negligence of local administrators, in others due to blatant embezzlement"; and they had been "wholly or partially converted into farm credit banks," which were themselves difficult to put into operation due to the lack of "people willing to take on their management." See "Resoconti delle Società Economiche delle province," *Annali Civili* (1836, 1841, 1847); the reports of Prefects Truffi and Reichlin for Upper Calabria in 1884 and 1886, and that of Prefect Movizzo for Lower Calabria II in 1882, in P. Borzomati, *La Calabria dal 1882,* op. cit., 37, 67, 72; and L. Franchetti, *Sulle condizioni dei lavoratori agricoli: Interpellanza parlamentare 1883* (Rome, 1883). See also D. Demarco, *Il Banco delle Due Sicilie, 1808–1863* (Naples, 1958); and *Banco e congiuntura nel Mezzogiorno d'Italia, 1809–1863* (Naples, 1963).

38. By 1814, no monks or nuns were left in Spezzano, Aprigliano, Rocca di Neto, Belvedere, or Isola; even in San Giovanni in Fiore, only a few monks remained, and there was but one small monastery with 7 brothers in Cutro. From this standpoint, the Restoration produced little change because the impoverished religious institutions never returned to the provinces: in 1834, there were but 600 friars and 200 nuns in the whole of Upper Calabria and 460 friars and 300 nuns in Lower Calabria II (F.*** V.*** [pseud.], "Della popolazione dei Reali Domini di qua del Faro all'anno 1834," *Annali Civili* 1837, 10, 108). Nonetheless, traditional forms of communal charity continued: when the family bread was baked, five loaves would be set aside for beggars. The tradition of "St. Joseph's invitation" persisted in some areas, with each family inviting to dinner three poor people who represented the Holy Family (see G. Sole, *Viaggio nella Calabria,* op. cit).

39. Commenting on the 1836 report prepared by Gennnaro Petitti, the provincial intendent for Upper Calabria, Scipione Volpicella, remarked that the Bourbon administration "gave dowries to orphans and poor girls" only on "particularly happy occasions" such as the king's birthday or the birth of the crown prince. *Annali Civili,* 1837/10, 98. After Italy's unification, the provincial administrations appropriated only about 10 percent of their budgets for welfare or charity—sums that would have been totally inadequate even had they been distributed fairly, as in fact they were not.

1860 revealed "serious irregularities, . . . bad management, and partiality in the distribution of charity."[40]

Public intervention was inadequate in other spheres as well. During the 1870s, only one out of three townships had a cemetery, though the French had made them mandatory. Sewers and latrines were lacking, there was no provision for street cleaning or garbage collection, and dwellings lacked chimneys and fire hoods.[41] Despite the relative success of vaccination campaigns,[42] public health remained precarious due to the endemic persistence of malaria and related diseases (undulant fever, pleurisy, bronchitis) and to recurrent epidemics of cholera, which were popularly attributed to unhealthy air produced by the retting of flax with marsh water as well as to bad drinking water. At any rate, the hospitals—few and far between and with very few beds—accepted no malaria or cholera patients. The population increase, fairly strong over the whole century, was neither constant nor uniform. Whereas the population of Calabria as a whole grew 30 percent in the first half of the century, on the coast and in the uplands it actually decreased.[43] The high rate of infant mortality was often attributed to midwives who were ignorant of obstetrics and the principles of hygiene, practiced without a license (there were few authorized midwives), and subjected newborn infants to various treatments "for a

40. P. Borzomati, *La Calabria dal 1882,* op. cit., 67.

41. Of the 419 Calabrian townships, 349 had no sewers or toilets, 107 no garbage collection, and more than half of the houses no firehood or chimney (see Kingdom of Italy, *Statistiche per il 1885*).

42. Mandatory vaccination of the whole population had been introduced by the French; in 1811, Upper Calabria's Intendent Galli praised the progress of the campaign (U. Caldora, *La Statistica murattiana,* op. cit., 26). Lower Calabria's Intendent Grio was less optimistic: "The poor choice of vaccinators—one consequence of the very low pay assigned to them—has pretty much discredited this operation." Among other things, as the vaccinators were "practically ignorant of the condition of the blisters, people say they often caught real smallpox after being vaccinated" (ibid., 46). However, the vaccination campaign seemed "fairly general," even to the Italian officials, and did actually curtail smallpox. See Ministry of Agriculture, Industry and Commerce, Statistics Department, *Annuario Statistico, 1892* (Rome, 1893), 111.

43. The decrease in population during the "French decade" worried the authorities. Michele Galdi ascribed low proliferation to the "weak constitution of the inhabitants of towns located in the marshlands, the excessive number of doctors, indifference to the state of health of people who are about to marry," and "the family economy's established custom of having few people marry" (U. Caldora, *La Statistica murattiana,* op. cit., 27). G. Grio thundered that this custom "frosted over the fervid impulses of love, and totally extinguished the sense of the duty to reproduce" (ibid., 47). In the 1840s, Luigi Grimaldi similarly lamented the population decline between 1815 and 1843 in a host of townships in the province, including Soveria, Simeri, Belcastro, Isola, Castella, Altilia, Belvedere, San Nicola, Verzino, Cerenzia, and Caccuri. Many contemporaries ascribed the lower classes' slow rate of reproduction to poverty. See V. Ricchioni, *La 'Statistica' del Reame di Napoli nel 1811* (Trani, 1942), 126–29. On the later population increase and contemporary accounts, see, besides the sources already mentioned, P. Bevilacqua and A. Placanica, *La Calabria,* op. cit., 65–67.

necessity that existed only in the oddities of their doctrine."[44] The region did have a rather large number of male medical practitioners (physicians, surgeons, barber-surgeons, and leechers), but the peasants, and especially the peasant women, resorted to them only rarely because they resided in the cities ("illness is neglected in the country"), their services were too costly (as there were few publicly assigned practices), and women were traditionally too modest to submit to examinations.[45] Medicines were available, as almost all the townships had their own pharmacies, but so expensive that the people turned to the illegal trade of witches.[46]

Generally speaking, political participation was very limited and was completely dominated in our area by the individual latifondista. During both the Bourbon and Italian periods, until the suffrage extension of 1882 and Crispi's reform legislation of 1889, only the few landowners were entitled to vote in either local or national elections. The peasantry began to be involved in local elections only late in the century and always in a passive and instrumentalized position.[47] There existed no political associations—in the sense of parties— and no cooperative organizations. Mutual aid societies were an urban phenomenon and looked with disgust on the degradation of the rural folk, who in turn

---

44. The treatments in question included manual dilation of the esophagus, detachment of the lingual frenum, application of poultices to the skull, and above all tight swaddling (see U. Caldora, *La Statistica murattiana,* op. cit., 47). In 1834, a third of all children were dying before the age of seven; the percentage was no higher among foundlings maintained at public expense. See F.*** V.*** [pseud.], "Della popolazione dei Reali Domini di qua del Faro," op. cit., 109, 110; and "Relazione del Presidente del Consiglio Provinciale Calabria Ultra seconda, Sig. Ignazio Larussa (Intendente: Sir Gio. Cenni)," in *Annali Civili,* 1847. In 1874, infant mortality was almost 40 percent (see Ministry of Agriculture, Industry and Comerce, Statistics Department, *Movimento dello Stato Civile, Anno 1874* [Rome, 1876], xix, xxxvii). The hill and mountain districts did much better than the regional averages; in San Benedetto, for instance, according to local parish registers infant mortality was only around 20 percent during the same period.

45. In 1811, Upper Calabria had 235 doctors, 86 surgeons, 160 pharmacists, 245 midwives, and 224 bloodletters, "few of them educated, most of them ignorant." By 1885, there were 903 doctors and surgeons in all of Calabria's 419 townships, but in Piedmont there were 1,500 for the same number of townships; the proportion was the same in Lombardy (Ministry of Internal Affairs, Statistics Department, *Annuario Statistico Italiano: Salute pubblica* [Rome, 1886], 40–43).

46. In 1885, only 16 percent of the Calabrian townships lacked a pharmacy, compared with 60 percent of those in Piedmont and 43 percent of all townships in the kingdom.

47. Francesco De Sanctis related, in *Un viaggio elettorale* (ed. N. Cortese [Turin, 1968]), that he had been able to meet all the voters in the towns one by one in the midst of the crowd. In 1875, Michele Campagna denounced electoral corruption in the small districts: voter lists were highly restricted and were controled by one powerful family, which kept its own register with special marks to show that the promised votes had been delivered (*Le elezioni e la legge elettorale* [Cosenza, 1875], 22). See also G. Aliberti, *Ambiente e società nell'Ottocento meridionale* (Rome, 1974).

considered the societies, like the agrarian meetings, notables' associations designed to increase landowners' profits.[48]

9. The Cohesive Fabric of the Territory

In this relatively isolated territory, institutional bonds were thus not very solid, but this fact strengthened rather than weakened economic and social bonds.[49] In the absence of alternatives, social living (keeping economic life in equilibrium, providing for widows and orphans, and reproducing the hierarchies of knowledge, authority, and power) sustained itself almost exclusively through the traditional authority structures, of which the family remained the most important.[50] The handing down of values, the formation of alliances, and the development of strategies for collective protection were facilitated by a high degree of social egalitarianism. In fact, the great majority of the population— the entire population in the smaller settlements—belonged to the same social rank, defined more by its culture and its way of (re)producing subsistence than by its income level.[51]

Thus, families of equal rank exchanged women (brides rarely came from other townships), forming tightly woven networks based on matrimonial swaps. Families (re)produced families and also social cohesion. Practically all the peasants married but not very young: the men at around twenty-six to twenty-nine, the women between eighteen and twenty-two.[52] Widows remar-

48. G. Mastroianni, "Il Movimento Operaio in Calabria negli atti dei congressi regionali," *Movimento Operaio* 5, no. 6 (1953).

49. P. Bevilacqua (in *La Calabria,* op. cit., 296) suggests that these bonds were weak because they were based on the peasant household as a production unit rather than on the standardizing experience of wage labor: "The peasantry consisted in the first instance of farming families, not of a homogeneous social class definable by *prevalent income levels, types of needs, culture and mentality*" (emphasis added). But these units—certainly not institutional—were solid and highly organized productive enterprises that were part of a complex network of social exchanges and were bound by precise codes of behavior. "The nature of their needs, culture and mentality," not weakened by standardization, were strongly unifying characteristics. Their income levels varied (there were rich as well as poor peasants), but their *origin* was homogeneous. See L. M. Satriani and M. Meligrana, *Diritto egemone e diritto popolare: La Calabria negli studi di demologia giuridica* (Vibo Valentia, 1975).

50. Banfield's main mistake was to think that the "familyism" he rightly observed in the Lucanian countryside fifty years later was "immoral" (meaning asocial). In reality, familism continued to perform its traditional functions, though perhaps to a lesser extent than before. See E. Banfield, *The Moral Basis of a Backward Society* (New York, 1967).

51. For example, in 1814, Spezzano Grande's population of 1,576 included 1,030 peasants and 360 landowners, the rest being priests, craftsmen and mendicants; of Isola's population of 1,936, 1,568 were peasants.

52. These ages are younger but not much younger than the averages calculated for all of Western Europe in the preindustrial era: around thirty for men and twenty-six for women. Calabria's not overly early nuptial age disproves the idea that Mediterraneans tended to marry their

ried if still of child-bearing age; widowers often remarried in their deceased spouse's family (a sister, perhaps a widow herself). The average woman's and the average couple's reproductive cycle of twelve years produced an average of five children at intervals of around thirty months—a reproduction rate that hardly seeems to justify the concern of contemporaries. At least one of the children born alive would die before the age of twelve, a mortality not excessively high, which peaked only during epidemics of childhood diseases.[53] Given the high marriage rate, there were few illegitimate births (reported with the usual names of Esposito [exposed], Expurias, Maria Vergine), and those often from the same "fallen" mother; cases of abandoned children (with both parents "unknown") were extremely rare. Children remained under the authority of women (mothers, grandmothers, older sisters, and godmothers) up to the age of eight or nine when the division and sexual segregation of labor began, with the boys starting to go out with the men to the pastures and fields and the girls learning to help their mothers in the household economy.

All members of the family contributed not only to the household's production but to its cash economy as well: the men with steady jobs or day labor, the women with olive harvesting jobs, the girls with "campaigns" in the silk barns and spinneries (all also spinning at home and many raising silkworms on a small scale),[54] and the boys with jobs harvesting olives, fruit, and acorns as well as helping out on the threshing floor. The family's earnings went into a common pool; only the girls were allowed to keep part of their pay for their trousseaux.

Local and family traditions were highly important. Often a town's residents identified themselves with (and reproduced) particular occupations. San Pietro in Guarano, for instance, was a town of shepherds (it supplied 166 to the

daughters off younger than elsewhere because of their obsession with honor, of which women were depositories. See J. G. Peristiany, ed. *Honour and Shame: The Values of Mediterranean Society* (London, 1965).

With "modernization," things changed in this respect too. At the beginning of the twentieth century, both Mortara and De Nobili lamented that men were marrying at a very early age in Calabria, either to procure young female labor for the family farm or, if they were impoverished, because they had nothing to hope for and so gave free rein to their instincts. See V. Mortara, "Le popolazioni di Basilicata e di Calabria all'inizio del secolo ventesimo," in *Inchiesta Parlamentare,* op. cit. (Rome, 1910), 5:3; and L. De Nobili, "Cenni demografici," in D. Taruffi, L. De Nobili, and C. Lori, *La questione agraria e l'emigrazione in Calabria* (Florence, 1908).

53. Often a single couple lost a number of children, a fact that suggests a combination of adverse hereditary factors. Carolina Pizzuto and Domenico Caputo of San Benedetto had eleven children, five of whom died in childhood; Maria Cozza lost five out of ten. During an epidemic, a community of six hundred people would naturally lose three or four children a month (San Benedetto parish registers).

54. P. Moretti, "L'Economia del matrimonio: L'aggregazione domestica in una comunità calabrese del '700," in *Miscellanea di Studi Storici* 3 (1983): 5–29; see also A. Frangipane, "Telai e fucine artigiane di Calabria," *Almanacco Calabrese,* vol. 1 (Rome, 1951).

latifondo) and Caccuri a town of swineherds. These traditions continued, even in the presence of a large farming enterprise, partly because the enterprise recognized the value of the skills they could provide but mainly because their mutually supportive neighborhood and kinship ties set in motion and oriented its manpower recruitment mechanisms. An individual's status in his home town—that is, within his culturally homogeneous residential community—was determined by his family's status and especially by its ability to fulfill its duties toward the whole network of solidarity (both linear and collateral relations). Lastly, the traditional generational and sexual hierarchies were handed down and reproduced in each household. Around the fireplace, in the fields, on the threshing floor, and at the spinning wheel, the eldest members of the family imparted to the younger their own technical knowledge and precepts of life (often "contained," writes Bevilacqua, "in proverbs and apodyptic maxims"). Children were subordinated to the authority of their parents—for instance, the custom of parents acting as "depositories of their children's wages"[55] was widespread—younger siblings to elder siblings, and women to men. The family, foundation of the social order, was a system in an equilibrium that marriage strategies and intracommunity networks, and in a certain sense wage labor as well, were intended to maintain.[56]

The family, like the whole social system that rested on it, was a patriarchal organization. The pater familias occupied a central role, and each member was given tasks to be carried out under his authority. Much of that authority depended on his ability to organize and control the family's subsistence—a subsistence mainly conceived, despite the considerable penetration of the market economy, as the direct fruit of labor (or obtained by barter, exchanges of ceremonial gifts, or remuneration for "custom" jobs). As the great majority of the population were peasants, the patriarch, too, had to be a peasant who possessed the requisite farming know-how—the truest source of authority.

But this whole patriarchal organization began to crumble when, after the great bourgeois reforms, families found themselves with plots of land too small to insure subsistence, which had to be eked out with monetary earnings. Wage labor often took the men out of town and thereby gradually transformed the women into the mainstays of stability and the key elements in the reproduction

---

55. P. Bevilacqua and A. Placanica, *La Calabria*, op. cit. 296. This was also noted by the people who collaborated on the Jacini Inquiry (*Atti della Giunta per la inchiesta agraria e sulle condizioni della classe agricola*, vol. 9 [Rome, 1883].

56. This attachment to traditional structures can be seen at work in the return of the emigrants, in the tendency to seek a wife in one's home town, in compeer networks (*comparaggi*), and in the emigrants' reproduction of home traditions in their new countries. Nicola Misasi sketched a fine, if sometimes excessively somber, portrait of this world; see his *Pagine calabresi*, ed. L. Iannuzzi (Bologna, 1969), esp. "Cola il lupo," "Marco," "In Magna Sila," and "Gelosia." On the daily life of these rural dwellers, see F. A. Angarano, *Vita tradizionale dei contadini e pastori calabresi* (Florence, 1973).

of social relations. Proletarianization thus entailed a threat to the old hierarchi-
cal and patriarchal organization of the transmission of knowledge and of the
sexual division of labor—an organization based on land.[57] Consequently, to
resist proletarianization, heads of families aspired to gain access to land in
whatever way they could, from outright ownership to partial use. They rented
land for payment in kind, often consisting of days of labor,[58] they fought to
preserve the right to use common lands, and they hired themselves out to the
latifondo, attracted by the chance to use a plot of land for a given crop (*cortaglia* and *parasforo*), which was one of the forms of remuneration.

Thus, the great commercial latifondo was implanted in this type of social
territory, gradually, in rational and economic modes that not only allowed, but
fostered, the incorporation of the specific needs, values, and codes inherent in
the preexisting social reality. The latifondo was able to get the patriarchal
organization and the conservative fears of the population to work for it, and it
used them for its own profit in a climate of social peace. In the following
chapters we shall examine these modes and their functionality for the latifondo
system.

---

57. See L. W. Moss, "Mutamenti socio-culturali nel mondo contadino dell'Italia meridionale," *Basilicata* 9–10 (1970): 25–27; and A. Mozzillo, "Il cafone conteso," *Nord e Sud* 7, no. 5
(June 1960): 18–60.

58. G. Arrighi and F. Piselli ("Parentela, clientela e comunità," in *La Calabria,* op. cit., 407)
see this phenomenon in a different, or even contrasting, light, as part of a continuum that, by a
succession of expropriations of small tenants and peasants, "gradually destroyed the foundations
of the household economy." But in the nineteenth century the farm laborers' insistence on obtaining the use of, and access to, land, even for just one crop season, was a concrete way of resisting
both proletarianization and the impoverishment they had known under the ill-conceived French
reform. In fact, they aspired to a generalization of the perpetual leasehold.

PART 2

The Stability of a Production System

CHAPTER 4

The Latifondo Enterprise

1. The Administrative Structure

As Karl Kautsky observed, the modernity of the nineteenth-century latifondo lay in the fact that its various productive activities were concentrated in a single enterprise held together by a centralized administration. Centralization had already augmented the owners' wealth, Kautsky said, and in time would gear into the process of merging individual operations into a single organism regulated by a systematic division of labor and by cooperation.[1] As we have seen, the latifondo's very process of formation was inspired by a modern logic of profit applied to traditional means of production, and now that same logic required a change in land management.[2] The latifondo aggregated a quantity of properties that had yielded little or nothing to their previous owners—erstwhile feudal lords, the Royal Demesne, ecclesiastical entities, and peasant allottees—who had sold them, apart from political considerations, because they were unable to make them pay.[3] Following the same reasoning that Kautsky found in their German counterparts, the Barraccos evidently identified two main causes that made these lands unprofitable: fractioning (the peasants got "no gain" from their tiny allotments); and the two-centuries-old tradition of absentee landlordism, which made rents difficult to collect. In consequence, the latifondisti applied two measures that entailed the largest investment after their initial acquisitions. On the one hand, they merged the unprofitable small

---

1. K. Kautsky, *The Agrarian Question* (London and Winchester, Mass., 1988), 153–59; J. Banaji, "Summary of Selected Parts of Kautsky's 'The Agrarian Question,'" *Economy and Society* 5, no. 1 (1976): 30–33.

2. Other scholars have seen the same logic of profit motivating large nineteenth-century landowners. See, for example, R. Merzario on the Compagnas (*Signori e contadini,* op. cit.), and G. Pescosolido on the Borghese (*Terra e nobiltà: I Borghese, secoli XVIII e XIX* [Rome, 1979]).

3. The Duke of Caccuri complained that while his feudal rents and his income from freehold properties in the territory of Caccuri amounted to 1,934 ducats a year (when he could manage to collect from his tenants), the rents and taxes he and his ducal chamber had to pay amounted to 1,956 ducats (BA: E26[8]). See also sec. 2, below.

and midsized properties into one continuum suitable for a combination of extensive farming and livestock operations, thereby realizing economies of scale; on the other, they appointed agents and administrators dispersed throughout the property and equipped with powers to contract and to collect.[4] These constituted steps—one economic and technical, the other bureaucratic—toward the rationalization of a business enterprise and were aimed at raising productivity not by modifying the nature of the land but by reorganizing it.[5] The result was a unified property administered by a network of salaried managers and overseers—in other words, the birth of the latifondo as an administrative concept, namely, "the Administration of the Calabrias," its title in official documents and ledgers.[6]

The administration was composed of a series of "fiefs,"[7] each run by an administrator, agent, or foreman who reported at fixed dates to the baron or his son in Camigliati, or (after the middle of the century) to the central administrator. It was not long, however, before the network began to stratify into an ensemble of more or less important subadministrations because the agents in charge of smaller holdings, the chief herders and the olive-press managers, being illiterate, reported orally to the nearby "don," who passed their data on in his own reports to the owners.

The administrative network was structured in the following way. At the top was the General Administration of the Calabrias (created in 1849 after the death of Baron Luigi and the family's move to Naples), headquartered initially in Camigliati—a symbolic but somewhat decentralized location—then in Isola di Capo Rizzuto, and finally, after the turn of the century, in Croton. Just below it in importance were the Sila Administration, also with offices in Camigliati, the Marina Administration in Isola, and the Croton Warehouses (or Administration). Since the latifondo included both geographically fixed and "nomadic" (livestock) units, the administration was divided into two kinds of "jurisdiction": by territory and by type of activity. The "territorial" administrations were named for the place where the administrator resided: Altilia, Cac-

---

4. It should be remembered that this was during the period when public domains were being largely privatized and subdivided, and the peasant lands consequently expropriated, as we saw in the last chapter. In this situation, the populace put up only weak resistance to the transformations effected by the Barraccos.

5. This is how Kautsky saw it, that is, in terms of technique and bureaucracy not of "liberation-alienation" of the workforce; similarly, M. Weber, *General Economic History* (1923; rpt. New York, 1961).

6. See E. Turbati, *Rapporti fra proprietà, impresa e mano d'opera nell'agricoltura italiana: Calabria* (Rome, 1931), i.

7. It is interesting that the terminology of the old regime remained in use only as regards subdivisions. The word *fief* sometimes denoted the provenance of a property (for instance, the fief of Tacina and Massanova), but its use also extended to productive and administrative subdivisions (such as the Croton and Concio San Pietro fiefs).

curi, Camigliati, Le Castella, Concio di Neto, Croton, Germano, Isola, Petrizia, Polligrone, Rocca di Neto, San Leonardo, and Spezzano Piccolo. The "nomadic" (livestock) administrations were named for the type of animal concerned (herds of coarse-wooled or fine-wooled sheep, cattle, or goats, or "caravans" of draft oxen) for their chief herder (the Lecce, Scarola, or Bitonti herd), or for principal pasture area (the Marina, Capolongo, or Carlomango herd). Only at the end of the century were they renamed the Cattle Administration or Coarse-wooled Sheep Administration. Other units were named for their specialized activities: the Sties in Altilia, the Warehouses in Croton, the Licorice Works in Neto and San Pietro, Horsebreeding, the Spinneries, the Silk Barns.

The latifondo's administrators, though specialists, were still essentially production bosses and coordinators; they had not yet become the professional managers Kautsky described, charged with administrative tasks alone. The first to climb that rung were the general administrators. Don Luigi Ferrari and Don Saverio Idaro were qualified accountants,[8] responsible mainly for financial matters (they paid local taxes, received cash revenues from unit heads and paid their salaries, and forwarded money—"bronze, silver and paper"—to Naples). The owners, however, continued to pay land taxes and grazing and plowing fees, and they settled the accounts among family members.

The administrative network was integrated in various ways. In the first place, the general accounting system had a physical hub at the annual fair in Santo Janni. This was Calabria's largest livestock fair (particularly for smaller animals like lambs and kids but also for cattle and horses), and the event was taken as the accounting date for yearly rents, large or small, for interest on debts, and for settlements. It was also an occasion on which the landowners traditionally turned out in force: the eldest son of Marquis Lucifero, the eldest sons of the princes of Strongoli, Cerenzia, and Ferraro, Don Vercillo, Don Giudicessa—the crème de la crème of the largest landowners' progeny and deputies. Their parents appeared, too: the barons Barracco, Berlingieri, and Passalacqua, or the Marquis Lucifero, looking to conclude a major deal or sell one another colts of choice breeds, the offspring of famous dams. Buyers and sellers, debtors and creditors, laborers seeking work for the summer season, hiring bosses, itinerants, and the just plain curious—the whole province flocked to the rendezvous in Santo Janni on the third Sunday of May. Logically, the fair was a meeting place for almost all of the latifondo's people. The Barraccos kept an office on the grounds where factors, administrators, and warehousemen arrived during the week to make payments to the owners or

---

8. At the end of the century, the Sila Administration, too, passed from old Don Tommaso Maida to his son, Dr. Luigi, who had a university degree in economics and spent more of his time in Naples than in Camigliati.

their plenipotentiaries. This was where they met to settle accounts, exchange information, and chat.

The administrators communicated with one another in other ways as well, one of which was a sort of "correspondence" consisting of "administration sheets"[9] made out to workers when they entered into regular employment (usually after a trial period lasting two years or so). Each administrator under whom the man served would record all the pertinent data on his sheet along with the amount of commodities, cash, and services he had received against his wages. Thus, for example, Domenico Mancini, the agent in Camigliati, would recognize and complete information forwarded to him by Bruno Carcea in Isola.

Another factor that integrated the administrative network was the frequent exchange of products among units that, though they practiced mixed farming, were not self-sufficient. The Altilia Sties, for instance, would "import" pig corn from Polligrone or from the Rocca di Neto warehouses. Units that did not produce oil, wheat, wine, cheese, wool, broad beans, chickpeas, barley, or oats would "import" these products for their workers' allowances in kind (*minatici*). In addition, each unit could serve as a way station for another's products; oil produced at various presses would be sent to the large facility at Polligrone, whence it departed for Altilia, stopped at Croton, and eventually reached Castellammare or Naples. No monetary transactions were involved until the product reached its final destination, but the intermediate points were linked in a general accounting system in which each adminstrator meticulously recorded the quantities (but not the commercial value) of products received, distributed, and forwarded. The units also traded with each other, as when one sent its products "under commission" to another located in a market area. The agent at Spezzano Piccolo, for example, acted as the Sila jobber for cheese and grain produced at Camigliati but also for white wool sent from Isola. The proceeds on the sale of these products were paid either to the production unit's administrator or directly to the latifondo's central office.

As we have seen, the date on which the administrators ended their accounting periods was usually determined by the natural cycle of the particular activity. Most frequently it occurred in the spring, between May and June, when the accounts were closed for wheat, corn, barley, oats, broad beans, potatoes, flax, linseed, and oil, although for grain the date might vary according

---

9. "Administration sheet issued to chief herdsman Salvatore Bitonti upon his taking up service with the herd on 20 October 1855" was the heading on one typical sheet, which recorded Bitonti's pay—"at eight ducats per month"—and noted his return on October 20, 1856. A sheet from 1894 was identical, except that the pay was "8 ducats per month, or 34 lire" (BA: A65, p. 149, and A68, p. 24).

to the crop schedule and often came at the end of August or in October or November. Seasonal accounts for pastoral products (wool, cheese, and new-born animals) were closed in June and November. Only at the large warehouses in Croton, Messina, Castellammare, and Naples did the accounting year coincide with the calendar year. On the established date the administrators drew a line under the columns in the "commodity account," stating quantities produced, and the "cash account," stating revenues from product sales, rents, and fees (*estagli* and *terraggiere*).

The duties of the administrators varied according to the type of unit they headed, but overall they were absolutely "modern" and extraordinarily similar to those of their contemporary English counterparts. In fact, the difference between the two kinds of enterprise lay not in property consolidation and the modern character of the administrative structure but in the role of the tenant, which at that time was becoming the engine of England's so-called Second Agricultural Revolution, whereas in Calabria it was virtually absent.[10]

But let us go back to the administrators and look, by way of example, at the duties assigned during an ordinary year, 1837, to the head of a major administration, that of Isola di Capo Rizzuto, "burdened" by a series of large holdings: Isola, Castella, San Leonardo, Tacina, Massanova, and others in the territories of Cutro and Rocca Bernarda. In the first place, the administrator organized and managed the unit's operations, which included the wintering of sheep and goats (and pasture management) and the production of wine, oil, and raw silk. He hired workers and overseers, paid wages, and distributed remuneration in kind; he maintained and kept the property in repair and watched the boundaries to prevent encroachments; and he was in charge of the local distribution and marketing of products, as well as arranging for shipments to Naples. In the second place, he managed leases of various kinds: for the production of fruit (figs, pears, olives, acorns, grapes, and "all the fruit" harvested in two vineyards), cropping leases paid in kind (normally two *tomoli* of wheat, equivalent to 3 bushels, per tomolata of land), leases on orchards and small vineyards, and large leases (to Baron Mollo, to Barberio, and to Marquis Berlingieri) that yielded up to 4,000 ducats yearly. In the third place, he managed various partnership contracts on the owner's behalf, from the "one-third share" on olives to the sheep partnership with Morelli. Lastly, he paid sundry rents, local taxes, and surveyors' and notaries' fees, distributed charitable goods, oversaw the "palace pantry," and made purchases in Santo Janni.[11]

---

10. F. M. L. Thompson, "The Second Agricultural Revolution, 1815–1880," *Economic History Review,* 2d ser., 21 (1968): 62–77.

11. Mutatis mutandis, the duties of this administrator were the same as those of the bailiff of a great, directly managed, English estate in the nineteenth century: "They collected rents. They saw to the cultivation of the estate farms, reporting annually to the central estate office . . . and

2. Direct Management, Partnership, and Rental

The three types of operations in which the administrator acted as the owner's agent—direct production, partnership (co-ownership/coproduction), and rental—corresponded by and large to the three forms of management applied on the nineteenth-century latifondo. Of the three, direct production was the one that, after almost three hundred years of disuse, was something of a novelty in the nineteenth century. It was a response to the expanded market for farm commodities resulting from the growth of the population of Naples, the development of soap factories in Marseilles, new perfume industries, a taste for white bread made of soft-wheat flour, and the yen to own real property shared by the enlarged patriciate and the new bourgeoisie.[12] While direct management may have appeared to be the most "modern" form, in reality the latifondista's choice depended on the type of activity, the products' degree of commercialization, and the amount of control he was able to exercise. With few exceptions, choice lands conveniently situated from the commercial standpoint were thus kept under direct management (even if this entailed generalized expropriation, as had been the case in Isola) and were organized into a series of *masserie,* with pastures "assigned to their own industries." Less valuable lands and those located at a distance from the administration headquarters were leased out, and, as we shall see later, the latifondo owner often used the commodities collected from the lessees as rent in kind to supplement the cash wages of workers on directly managed lands with supplies of commodities. Lastly, partnership was the form chosen to manage activities in which control by salaried overseers would have been inefficient; this applied above all to livestock operations.[13]

recommending repairs and improvements. They kept a watch on estate boundaries and prevented encroachments. They settled disagreements between entering and outgoing tenants. . . . They attended the Commissioners and valuers on their rounds of the estate, submitting information about land values and about the capacities of tenants. In general, they were expected to send information of all sorts on request to Alnwick and to carry out all orders emanating therefrom" (D. Spring, *The English Landed Estate in the 19th Century: Its Administration* [Baltimore, 1963], 9).

12. By the end of the century, joint operations had disappeared and long-term leases were on the way out; signs of this process could already be seen in the tensions of the 1840s. See R. De Cesare, *Una famiglia di Patriotti,* op. cit.; A. Guarasci, *Politica e società in Calabria dal Risorgimento alla Repubblica,* vol. 1 (Chiaravalle, 1973); and A. Basile, "Moti contadini in Calabria dal 1848 al 1870," *Archivio Storico per la Calabria e la Lucania* 27, nos. 1–2 (1958).

13. M. Rossi Doria described this correlation between agricultural zones and tenancy arrangements in only slightly different terms. In areas of extensive agriculture, he noted the prevalence of leases paid in grain (terraggeria) and of various forms of sharecropping (such as the Sicilian *metateria*); in areas of intensive agriculture, the predominant forms were cash leases for one or more crops, "improper" forms of sharecropping (mixtures of tenancy and sharecropping), and "proper sharecropping," with the landlord's direct participation in the farm's management ("L'evoluzione delle campagne meridionali e i contratti agrari," *Nord e Sud* 5 [April 1955]: 6–22).

3. The Masserie

Of all the latifondo holdings, the masserie, which involved intensive farming for the market and the use of wage labor, were the most modern and the most productive. The popular image still associated the *masseria* with ownership of a team of oxen and/or of land, that is, with peasant affluence and self-sufficiency. As Vincenzo Padula wrote,

> A *massaro* is a person who has a masseria, and a masseria is a tilled field. The field is his, the goats or sheep that manure it are his, the oxen that plow it are his, and so is the donkey that transports its products.[14]

But, with the reforms of the "French decade," the continuous process of land privatization, the burden of property taxes, the loss of customary rights, the decline of the Grain Banks, and the low prices obtaining during the first half of the century (1817–50), the peasant masseria sank to very little. Of course, some *massari* grew rich, and their sons swelled the ranks of the new service sector ("of craftsmen, lawyers, doctors and priests, to the detriment of the public peace and of public morals," Padula noted ironically[15]), but most lost their land, their oxen, and their money and became *massarotti,* tenants at the service of some large landowner.[16] In fact, the market-oriented latifondo masseria we are concerned with here had more in common with the masseria of the feudal tradition (characterized "by the incidence of expenditures on the budget, and especially the incidence of wages"[17] than with the tendentially self-sufficient peasant masseria.[18]

The Barraccos' six large masserie—of the Sila, of Isola, of Castella, of San Leonardo, of Rocca, and of Croton—were multicrop farms under whose "umbrellas" were collected fifty or so smaller and in many cases more spe-

---

14. V. Padula, "Il massaro," *Bruzio,* June 18, 1864, reprinted in *Persone in Calabria,* ed. C. Muscetta (Florence, 1950), 95–101.

15. *Bruzio,* June 25, 1864, reprinted in *Persone in Calabria,* op. cit., 102–6.

16. G. Giorgetti, however, described the nineteenth-century masseria not as a farm or a form of property but as a form of cash tenancy on bare lands used for planting or grazing and "land on which olive groves exist or are presently being planted" (improvement tenancy) (*Contadini e proprietari nell'Italia moderna* [Turin, 1974], 211–13).

17. Aurelio Lepre has described the feudal masseria in eighteenth-century Apulia (see *Feudi e masserie* [Naples, 1973], 89 and passim). The Pasquale mentioned above, who visited Calabria in 1860, described its masseria as "a farm on which grain is grown in association with cattle-grazing." He considered it of only minor economic importance, however: "In a province where the land is almost all covered with trees, the tilled fields form a secondary part, wherefor they are called masserie." (G. A. Pasquale, *Relazione sullo stato,* op. cit., 78).

18. According to Rossi Doria, it was precisely these commercial masserie, whose number he puts at eight or ten thousand, that were responsible for the 30 percent increase in the number of cattle, horses, and mules (*L'evoluzione,* op. cit., 15–16).

cialized masserie.[19] The masserie were not the only places where farm production was managed directly; various open croplands and *cortaglie*,[20] subject to the traditional collective rotation, were farmed directly in certain years but solely for intensive and market-oriented production.

Let us examine the agricultural (and accounting) year on one of the larger masserie, that of Isola in 1861–62. This very large holding—of approximately 2,500 acres—employed a large number of workers ("cattleherds, massari, swineherds, warehousemen, gardeners, teamsters, overseers") and dozens of gangs of field hands. For the olive harvest alone, eight gangs of boys, or around two hundred people, were employed for as long as six months; the wages of gangs employed in the cultivation of wheat and beans amounted to 13,749 ducats in one year. The farm grew "wheat, barley, oats, flax, broad beans and other beans, chickpeas, vetch, peas, lentils," corn, "citrus fruit and vegetables," olives and grapes, and an attempt to cultivate licorice root was under way. These crops required various kinds of work. For grain and leguminous crops, the fields had to be dressed ("chopping, burning, plowing, harrowing"), then sown, then "hilled and hoed and weeded"; finally, the beans were "hoed and heaped," the hay was cut, the beans were pulled, and the wheat, barley, and oats were reaped, threshed, and transported to the storehouse. Fruit trees and licorice plants were pruned and cleaned, olive trees were "weeded, manured, hoed at the base," and pruned once a year (when the Apulians came), and lupines were planted. Gardens were "manured and irrigated," citrus groves were weeded, vineyards had to be "weeded, pruned, sown with lupines, trellised, hoed, sprayed with sulfur, hilled, tied," and finally harvested in October, after which time the must had to be transported. "Pear, cork and chestnut trees" were planted, grafted, and cleaned; acorns were gathered. Land planted in licorice was dressed with "plow and hoe"; diggers built "cisterns, ponds and ditches." The masseria had a "caravan" of 169 oxen and 97 donkeys, for which

---

19. The Sila masseria included the masserie of Calamauci, Parco di Camigliati, Cuponello, Molarotta, and Vallone. The Isola masseria included those of Vitetta, Braco, Isola, Li Morgoni, Ponticelli, Meolo, San Giovanni, Zumpani, Sant'Andrea, Oliveto, Campolongo, Marina, Corigliatello, Manche, Serra di Bitonti, Ciccio di Varco, Sant'Anna, Rastello, and Colosimo. The San Leonardo masseria included Bugiaforo, Ritani, Palombella, Gabelluccia, Carnevale, Piana Noverella, and Volta del Soverato. The Castella masseria included Ritani, Piano degli Insiti, San Pietro, Gorgione, Liuseti, and Scigliano. The Rocca di Neto masseria included Concio, Belvedere, Brasimati, Setteporte, Juca, and Bruchetto, as well as the masseria of the Morelli partnership. The Croton masseria included no others.

20. Cortaglie were fields manured by local sheep and goats, which were particularly well suited for growing rye. They were located within the Sila enclosures (Carlomango, Calamauci, Molerotta, Pupini, Germano, and Redisole). One frequently used means of remunerating labor was to assign small lots of this type to companies of herdsmen who would share the cost of sowing and harvesting and divide the yield on a prorated basis, the chief herder's share being three times that of the others'. *Cortaglia* was the name given to the arrangement itself, which was similar to the tenant farmer's parasporo.

straw was transported, and hay was "sown, cut, dried, heaped and transported." All these were regular operations for the current year. Then there were maintenance and expansion: the pruners "cleaned the olive trees"; the fence men built and repaired fences and the masons dry walls, storehouses, and dwellings; the ironsmiths repaired the plowshares and shod the oxen; and the diggers "repaired damage caused to citrus trees by flood." That year, 121 plow beams, 1,110 wheel spokes, 18 sowing yokes, wagons, axles, plow and cart components, and a variety of tools were made on the masseria. Moreover, that was the year when two mobile threshing machines arrived with a team of operators, and work had to be started "to accommodate the roads to the machines."

What does this detailed description tell us? The picture that emerges is one of a modern enterprise in which all productive activities were conducted rationally and with due care: the land was dressed for sowing, though not necessarily plowed each time; sown fields were attended to; fallow land was turned over; manuring, weeding, and spraying were undertaken; crops were irrigated and trees grafted and pruned (though some agronomists decried the practice of planting lupines among the olive trees and the grapevines.[21] Infrastructure of all kinds was abundant and kept in good repair. In fact, the masseria had made large investments in modernization: the licorice root plantation, the threshing machines brought from Naples, the road repairs. The whole operation was quite profitable, since it brought in more than 50,000 ducats in 1861–62. Alternating grain and legumes, they could make two crops a year, obtaining 8,000 tomoli (360 tons) of grain, 4,000 (180 tons) of barley and oats, as well as 13,000 *militri* (51 tons) of oil. Yields, though not extraordinary, were high, averaging eight to ten times the seed input, with peaks of fourteen times (the top-quality "majorca" wheat grown on the Camigliati masseria yielded as much as sixteen, eighteen or twenty times the input, oats and broad beans even more).[22]

As we have seen, the incidence of cash outlays, especially for wages, was high on the masserie. In consequence, this form of management was cost effective only on lands that were already suitable for intensive farming: first-rate fields, choice pastures, and orchards. This would not have been so on poorer land such as third-rate fields and range, sterile ground, or woodlands,

---

21. These practices, and the habit of planting grapevines and fruit trees amid the wheat fields, were described by Bolton King in 1903 ("Statistics of Italy," *Journal of the Royal Statistical Society* [1903]: 244).

22. On crop rotation and yields, see G. Porosini, "Produttività e agricoltura: I rendimenti del frumento in Italia dal 1815 al 1922," *Archivio Economico dell'Unificazione Italiana,* ser. 2, vol. 17 (1971); and L. Grimaldi, *Studi statistici,* op. cit. (1847). Yields were comparable to those in the developed agricultural areas of Europe. See S. Van Bath, "Yield Ratios, 1810–1820," *A.A.G., Bijdragen* 10 (1963); and his *The Agrarian History of Western Europe, A.D. 500–1850,* (London, 1963).

which could not have provided yields that high unless their nature was radically altered—an enterprise totally foreign to the logic of the latifondo.

These poorer lands, which made up more than half of the Barracco latifondo, were managed under other systems: partnerships and leases.

4. Partnerships

The fact that an operation was managed in a traditional way, in partnership or under lease, by no means meant that it was marginal. To the contrary, one of the latifondo's core operations, sheep raising, was run precisely through a combination of direct management, with the employment of wage labor, and partnership arrangements. The flocks were owned by joint ventures in which the majority partner was the baron and the minority partner was the "shepherds company," in which the fifteen or so members each owned one share. The company was headed by a chief shepherd (*caporale*) appointed by the baron; his share in the company was the same as the other members' but the baron invested him with a certain power to act in his behalf and some responsibility for management, and he received separate remuneration for these duties. The majority partner contributed the capital (grazing land and flocks) and assumed the overall management; the minority partner contributed all the labor. Operating costs were shared equally by the two partners, although in reality the cash input came entirely from the baron, who advanced his half (fixed in the amount of nine ducats per adult shepherd and from two to six for boys), while the minority partner's share was deducted when the "gain" was divided between the two. This took place at the end of the accounting year, the first of July of every year, in one of two ways. In the first, the "fruits of the flock," consisting solely of secondary products (ricotta cheese, coarse black wool, and part of the yearlings), were divided into two equal parts, while the baron was entitled to all of the proceeds on cheese, lambs, and fine and merino wool. In the second case, the master received a tenth part of the entire proceeds (less products to which the shepherds were entitled as payment in kind), and the shepherds received a tenth of the remainder after deduction of expenses (pails and barrels, salt, transportation, fence building, the wages of occasional helpers, and half of the value of the "gifts" the master "offered" at Carnival and Easter).

These partnership operations were immensely profitable for the baron. In 1837, for example, a flock of 6,500 native sheep and 1,350 merinos yielded Barracco 18,000 ducats as majority partner; that year he had put 394 ducats into the enterprise, plus the grazing land and livestock. The flock had brought in a total of 19,650 ducats, but the minority partner was left with little more than 1,000.[23] That was a good year, but the baron's income was assured even in

---

23. Barracco's proceeds from the flock of 7,850 sheep, valued at 13,700 ducats, were as

bad years when the "gain" in "fruits of the flock" was meager and corresponded to starvation wages for the shepherds.[24] At times, "in consideration of the penurious year," the master would "donate" some expense to his partners, partly to forestall any action by the shepherds themselves, as happened in 1843–44, when those working the Bitonti flock assigned themselves "20 ducats apiece to the master's loss."

Although all the flocks were managed through such arrangements, the ledgers treated them as "direct operations"; in effect, these "partnerships" sui generis were simply ways of managing direct production, not proper partnerships. The majority partner owned all the livestock and grazing land; the regular advance of the shepherds' "share" came to have the appearance of a cash remuneration for labor, that is, a wage. The additional remuneration paid to the chief shepherd and his appointment by the master set him apart from his partners and made him a de facto employee. Lastly, the shepherds' exclusion from a share in the more valuable products permitted the latter to be marketed on a large scale as if they had been masseria products.

The partnerships that the Barraccos formed with other midsized and large landowners, primarily for livestock operations, were on a more balanced footing, so to speak.[25] The largest was the one formed with the Morelli brothers, well-known Sila landowners; in addition, there was one with Marquis Lucifero, another with Giovanni Mancuso ("Gregorella"), another (solely for hogs) with Pasquale Intrieri ("Ciommarella"), and a "joint plant" with Macry. We shall now take a closer look at three of them: the one with the Morellis, who were the Barraccos' social equals, the one with the middle-class Mancuso, and the one with the commoner Intrieri.

The livestock partnership between Luigi Barracco and the brothers Antonio and Michele Morelli was formed on June 1, 1825, originally for a term of three years; in fact, it lasted for thirty. The partners put in a total of 2,200 sheep, 46 horses, and 160 head of cattle (ten years later there were over 3,000 sheep and 400 cattle) with the majority partner (Barracco) contributing two-thirds and the minority partner (the Morelli brothers) one-third. In addition, Barracco leased grazing land to the partnership. The minority partner bore all the operating expenses, including wages and the cost of commodities supplied by Bar-

---

follows: as its owner, he was entitled to 10 percent yearly interest on its value, or 1,370 ducats; for the use of his grazing land and fodder, he was entitled to 15,500 ducats; and the 10 percent share to which he was entitled as a partner amounted to another 1,600 ducats. The flock yielded 19,650 ducats from the sale of the more valuable products: 3,444 lambs, sheep, and kids; skins; 20,000 rounds of cheese; and twenty-nine *cantaja* (about 5,685 pounds) of fine and Merino wool.

24. W. Kula talks about the supply of commercial products during times of famine in *Economic Theory,* op. cit.

25. This situation was similar to contemporary agistments (*soccide*) in Sardinia (see G. Giorgetti, *Contadini e proprietari,* op. cit., 240ff). On agistments in Calabria, see the Branca Report, in *Atti della Giunta per la Inchiesta Agraria,* op. cit., xliii ff.

racco, managed the operation, and sold the final products. Taxes were shared equally. Net revenue (after expenses, rent on grazing land, and interest on capital input) was divided, equally, by products rather than values: the Barraccos were entitled to the choice products, the Morellis to the secondary "fruits." It was a thriving enterprise, yielding gross revenues of up to 17,000 ducats per year, which meant a net profit of 1,000 to 1,500 ducats to be divided equally.[26]

The partnership with Giovanni Mancuso ("Gregorella") was formed primarily for sheep raising, with 2,000 sheep and around 40 cattle, but by 1848 it already had, besides 3,400 sheep, 250 cows and oxen, 15 mares, and 140 hogs—all belonging to the majority partner because Gregorella owned no livestock. Barracco also owned all of the grazing land. The minority partner bore all the operating expenses of the partnership and of an annexed masserie he managed. The division of final products was the same as in the other partnership: the "big" and marketable products went to Barracco, the minor products to Mancuso. Although gross revenue was high—from 13,000 to 19,000 ducats—the partnership often closed its accounts with a loss (especially after 1847–48, the period of peasant unrest) because expenses, too, were high. But Gregorella was the one on the losing end because 60 percent of the expenses consisted of interest on capital (the livestock) and grazing rent payable to Barracco.[27]

The scope of the hog-raising partnership with Pasquale Intrieri ("Ciommarella") of San Pietro was more limited. The "capital" of around 450 head (sows and boars) all belonged to Barracco; Ciommarella managed the whole operation, including the sale of young and adult animals. The minority partner was entitled to only one-third of the shoats born during the year.

In these three examples we can see several features that were common to all the large partnerships regardless of the partner's social class. First of all,

---

26. The shares of deceased partners passed to their relatives. Michele Morelli's went to Filippo Morelli in 1848, then to Gabriele in 1853; Luigi Barracco's went to his sons Francesco and Stanislao in 1849. At the time when the partnership was founded, it owned 2,200 sheep, goats, and hogs, 20 geldings for herders' use, 26 mares, and 160 head of cattle; in 1835, the sheep numbered over 3,000 and the cattle 360; in 1853, shortly before the partnership's dissolution, the sheep were down to 2,115 but the cattle were up to 415.

In dividing up the products, the Barraccos were entitled to the cheese and large animals as well as beans and wheat from lease payments in kind; Morelli was entitled to the secondary products: ricotta cheese, lambs, small animals, diseased cattle, skins and hides, and pork (see BA: E23, but also A71, A72, and A74).

27. Mancuso's responsibilities in the masseria consisted of "the wheat harvest, profit from the Marina, the pulse harvest, barley, wine for the masseria, valuations [*apprezzatura*], olive oil, salt, lard, the smithy, haying, monthly labor [*mesaruli*], rent from the Sculca, grazing rent, fees, repairs, the olive harvest, mule days, flax spinning." Before 1847–48, the net profit to be shared equally could amount to as much as 4,000 ducats, but every year thereafter the partnership showed a loss.

Barracco was always the majority partner, and as such could dictate production guidelines. Second, whatever their operating profit (not always high), these ventures always insured a high "rent" return to the majority partner as owner of the livestock and the grazing land. Third, in the division of the final product, the Barraccos were always entitled to the marketable fruits of the operation. Lastly, but only as regards the large partnerships, the minority partner was responsible for management and operating expenses, while the Barraccos were not required either to invest money or manage labor relations.

Hence, this type of partnership arrangement, too, was hugely advantageous for the latifondo owner. His expenses existed mostly on paper: he owned the grazing land, which could never have yielded 10 percent per annum if otherwise utilized (indeed, there were few alternative uses); and operating costs, in the form of land taxes (in the case of the Morelli operation, these were shared equally by the partners), local taxes, and purchase prices, amounted to hardly a fraction of the rent paid by the partnerships. As we have seen, the arrangement was decidedly less advantageous for the minority partners, whose earnings depended on the amount of profit realized. It was this discrepancy, among other things, that led to the dissolution of all the partnerships in 1853–54, which we shall discuss later.

5. Tenancies

The document entitled "General State of the Family's Rural and Urban Properties and Rents of All Kinds," compiled in 1831, listed not only land "administered directly and used in direct operations" but also land let on lease.[28] These were a very important source of income—the 22,450 ducats a year they brought in amounted to 30 percent of the family's total income from land in Calabria.

Land was leased mainly to large owners, bourgeois, or nobility. In fact, 70 percent of the total rental income came from thirteen large leases, while the other 30 percent came from some *thousands* of small farmers who leased only a few tomolate apiece.[29] At the Santo Janni fair in 1875, for instance, as much as 48,000 lire were collected from only ten tenants, while another 18,000 lire were due from Albani, Zinzi, and Baron Galiani at the Molerà fair.

---

28. These were lands located in the "administration" of Spezzano Piccolo, Sila, the Caccuri fief, part of Altilia, Belvedere, Isola, and Castella. The rented lands were in the barony of Tacina and Massanova (townships of Cutro and Belcastro), on the San Leonardo estate, and on part of the Altilia territory.

29. The rent for land leased "for all uses" or for grazing alone was usually in the form of a flat fee; rent for cropland was determined "by measurement." Stefano Ciacco, a surveyor, was hired for almost 200 days in 1865 "to measure cropland in the Sila and Marina" (Cutro, Petrizia, Altilia, Rocca, Sila, and Spezzano Piccolo). Every year, a surveyor would spend an average of 125 days (at 1.20 ducats per day) making and checking land measurements.

One-use leases were the type given most frequently, and, as we shall see, mainly they were granted to small tenants; large leases were usually "for all uses." In both cases, however, the owner imposed some restrictions on land use and reserved certain rights. Only a very few leases left the tenant completely free; one example was the four-year lease signed with one Giuseppe Trapasso in April of 1823 whereby Luigi Barracco rented Trapasso three properties for a total of 280 ducats yearly, payable in August of every year. That was the whole agreement: an all-use lease, payable in cash, under which Trapasso was entitled to decide what crops to put in and was responsible for managing the land and paying the tax. This quite rare kind of lease can perhaps be explained by the fact that Trapasso was the previous owner of the land he was now leasing.[30] Usually the leases contained a series of restrictive or interdictive clauses. We shall now look at a few typical cases.

In 1822, Barracco leased two holdings, for grazing and tilling, to a wealthy Cutro man for six years at an annual rent of 2,800 ducats. In addition, the lessee undertook to "turn over to Barracco yearly, on a day of said Barracco's choice, all the cheese from the flocks and cattle herds to be installed on said holdings" and further undertook to transport the cheese to Barracco's warehouse in Croton, where it would be paid for at the Santo Janni price.

In 1831, the brothers Don Federico and Don Gaetano Talarico took a lease "for all grazing and tilling uses for three years" on the Campolongo holding for 1,870 ducats plus the Soverito enclosure for 1,400 ducats. Here, again, "all the cheese made from the animals grazed in these districts must be delivered to Mr. Barracco's warehouse in Croton, received by him and paid for at the going price."

In 1827, Luigi Barracco leased two enclosures in the Sila, San Leonardo di Cutro and Germano, to Don Antonio Vercillo, of the barons of San Vincenzo, for tilling and grazing, at an annual rent of 4,800 ducats (800 payable at the Molerà fair, 4,000 at the Santo Janni fair). The lease contained a whole series of restrictions. The lessee was forbidden to keep hogs in Germano and was required to maintain the water supply system and comply with the three-year crop rotation system: "if he intends to plant flax in Germano, he may not do so for two consecutive years." In addition, "the Germano apple orchard crop shall be divided annually" and all (!) the sheep's-milk cheese from San Leonardo "shall be transported to the Barracco warehouses in Croton."

These are three examples of cash leases (payable in gold and silver) given

---

30. Giuseppe Trapasso had sold the three properties—one with tilled fields, one with an orange grove, and one planted with fruit and olive trees—to Barracco in 1817, but he remained their tenant and manager. At his death in February of 1824, his wife and daughters "declared they could not continue as tenants." The landlord thus came into full control of the land and could put it to any use he wished.

"for all uses" to large bourgeois and noble landowners.[31] Yet the Barraccos continued to maintain control over land use and insure proper upkeep;[32] above all, they insured themselves the sole right to acquire all the cheese produced as well as a monopoly on a scarce product (choice apples). Thus, in addition to cash revenue, the leases supplied a quality export commodity at local prices, delivered to Croton, the port of embarkation.[33]

As mentioned above, the most frequent type of lease was for "one use" only. The larger leases were "for grazing" or "for tilling" of any kind; the smaller leases specified the crop. The leases explicitly forbade or restricted other uses and established the owner's affirmative rights—priority in product purchases and delivery to the warehouse, rights of grazing and tilling, and rights of way and of gleaning (the latter two, which required the fields to be kept open and traditional easements to be respected, allowed the owner to retain control of the land). For instance, the lease on one large holding in the territory of Castella, given to Vincenzo Maria Mauro in 1830 "for the sole use of grazing animals of any kind," barred hogs, limited cultivation, and required the cheese output to be sold to Barracco and delivered to his warehouse in Croton.[34] The three-year lease given to Don Giovanni Foresta in 1846 "for tilling" on the Carnevale Soprano and Pozzo Fetido holdings guaranteed Bar-

---

31. Their great quantity of liquid wealth gave the Barraccos a strong hand even vis-à-vis other great landowners. As tenants, they managed to obtain much more liberal terms. In 1843, Luigi Barracco leased "the Vaccarizzi enclosure in Sila for all uses (planting, grazing, even flax growing) for six years" from Don Scipione Giudicessa for an annual rent of 900 ducats, twenty rounds of sheep's-milk cheese, twenty ricotta cheeses, and six pairs of caciocavallo cheese. In addition, Barracco agreed to provide Giudicessa with fifty mule loads of hay a year and allow him to keep on the property two yokes of oxen, five hogs, and a mare with her colts. Having secured these limitations on the owner's rights, Barracco was free to manage the property as he wished. In reality, Giudicessa was in need of cash, and Barracco was able to advance him 800 ducats of the rent at the reasonable rate of 6 percent.

32. Understandably, the landlord would take precautions to insure that crops were properly rotated, that the aqueducts were maintained, that hogs did not destroy the pastures, and that flax (which notoriously wears out the soil) was not overplanted. In 1833, when Don Filippo Bianchi's lease on the Rosito holding ran out, he demolished all the rural houses and carted all the material away. Back in 1822, Barracco had sued this same Filippo Bianchi and his brother Bernardo for 2,800 ducats in rental arrears.

33. In the years from 1835 to 1853, a good part of the tens of thousands of cheeses stored in the Croton warehouse came from similar contracts with twenty-eight tenants, all local notables. Caciocavallo cheese not produced directly was supplied by Don Stanislao Lupinacci and Baron Mollo as payment in kind. After 1854, all the caciocavallo cheese was produced directly.

34. The farm was "leased to Vincenzo Maria Mauro for the sole use of grazing animals of all kinds except hogs [apart from those needed for the hands], it being expressly agreed that none of the land may be planted except for 50 tomolate with the corrals." The rent of eleven carlini per tomolata was payable annually at the fair of Santo Janni. "The tenant must transport the cheese produced by means of these animals to the Barracco warehouses in Croton by way of guarantee and buying option given to Barracco."

racco's grazing rights on unsown land, divided gleaning rights between the two parties, and set the tillage rent at two *tomoli* of wheat per tomolata of land, specifying that the grain must be "clean and free of foreign bodies" ("pebbles in particular") and was "to be delivered every July to the Barracco storehouse in the village of San Leonardo."

The most frequent type of limited-use lease was the small *terratico,* an "imperfect" form of sharecropping found throughout Calabria and in latifondo-dominated parts of Sicily. It gave the tenant (*terraticante*) the use of a particular property for a particular period in order to grow a particular crop, reserving to the owner full rights to the land for the rest of the year and for other uses.[35] For instance, the Nastasi holding was leased for tilling from May to October (compelling the tenants to sow in May and harvest in September) and for grazing from November to May. If the tenant wished to keep an animal on the rented land, he had to pay a grazing fee. These leases were given for one to three years, and the rent was structured in consideration of crop rotation: for one year of wheat cropping, 1.5 tomoli per tomolata; for two years, 2 tomoli; and for three years, 2.5 tomoli.[36]

From the latifondo owner's standpoint, these terratico arrangements were important for several reasons. First, they were a large source of income: until 1861, Rocca and Belvedere tenants were bringing up to 9,000 tomoli of wheat to the Rocca storehouse yearly; Altilia collected around 2,500 tomoli "from Cotronellians, Rocca Bernardians, Caccurians, and Altilians"; and Camigliati collected around 4,000 tomoli of majorca ("from Cupone, Agarà, Colamauci, Carlomango, and Camigliati.")[37] Second, since the lessees were raising "major

---

35. See, in this connection, V. Passalacqua, *La colonia parziaria in Italia sotto l'aspetto sociale, economico e morale* (Palermo, 1890); C. Bertagnolli, *La colonia parziaria in Italia* (Florence, 1877); and G. Arias, *La questione meridionale* (Bologna, 1921), 2:3ff. For a more general discussion, see S. Pace, *I contratti agrari (Saggi di una storia generale)* (Milan, 1952); and G. Giorgetti, *Contadini e proprietari,* op. cit.

36. Not all lands were leased for grain cultivation on a yearly basis. In Castella, for example, fallow land was leased; in Altilia, only summer-crop land; and in Sila, the cortaglie. These short-term leases were usually accorded for planting wheat, rye, or majorca, more rarely for corn and beans. Tenants with leases to plant majorca or rye at Camigliati paid two tomoli per tomolata (three bushels per acre); to plant corn they paid four to five tomoli per tomolata (six to ten bushels per acre, collected at the threshing floor) two out of every three years. The grazing fee for cattle was five ducats per head. In 1869, all the seasonal leases went up 20 percent.

37. Although seasonal leases were used throughout the latifondo, the largest number of these tenants came from Rocca, Belvedere, Cotronei, Caccuri, and Altilia. It is impossible to discover exactly how many they were because the estate ledgers state only the amount of grain each administration collected as rent, and we can only infer the number of leases from these figures. Contrary to what is often said, speculation on wheat in the form of high-interest advances of seed was not a very widespread practice and was not particularly profitable. On the Altilia farm, the "seed wheat given to Altilians, to be returned with a 25 percent increase" amounted to no more than sixty-five tomoli (97.5 bushels); only in Rocca di Neto did wheat given on credit "to the various farmers" come to as much as seven hundred tomoli (1,050 bushels).

crops" (wheat, rye, and majorca), by contract as well as by circumstance, the commodities received in payment of rent increased the Barraccos' stock of exportable goods without any production effort on their part. Third, these leases were no obstacle to the latifondo's seasonal livestock drives, even if their vast number entailed costs for "collection" and "measurement" that would have been unnecessary if the same properties had been leased to large landowners. Lastly, the *terraggiera* played an extremely important social role. Thanks to this access to land, the tenants could provide themselves at least partial subsistence, hence they stayed put and available as a relatively docile workforce. It was mainly for this reason that the guarantee latifondo continued to let land under this type of lease despite the post-1861 growth in direct production, and despite the "crisis" of the years 1887–91.[38] Incidentally, it was for the same reason that the Barraccos maintained (but never multiplied) the perpetual leases—the most secure and coveted form of land tenancy. However, there were only a few of these, and they related only to several holdings of ecclesiastical provenance between Cutro and Isola; although the tenants, secure in their possession, were often in arrears, the leases were maintained because the social price of their termination would have been greater than the economic gain.[39]

The accounts for *terraggiere* often included payments in kind for various "rights" such as multure and oil pressing.[40] As a matter of fact, these rights did not yield much; the dozens of gristmills owned by the Barraccos[41] were kept primarily to grind their own grain ("at the convenience" of the administrations) or were leased to small peasant entrepreneurs who tried to maximize flour

---

38. These years were not only those of the general crisis of the latifondo system (see chap. 8); they were also marked by poor harvests, and the estate was compelled to supply its seasonal tenants with seed carried back from Croton (a reversed flow!).

39. The legislation on the suppression of feudalism, which expressly maintained perpetual leases, was amended on March 26, 1811, by order of the commissioner of land division, to establish the right of landowners (who were entitled to a tenth of the main products of farms held under such leases) to evict tenants who were in arrears. In 1838, Barracco did in fact order tenants residing in the townships of Croton, Isola, and Castella to pay overdue tithes, rents in kind, and other fees. In 1863, however, there were still 287 tenants on the Bosco and Nastasi holdings (2,388 tomolate, or 2,006 acres), and the yearly tithe on these properties rarely amounted to more than 200 tomoli (300 bushels) of wheat, barley, and oats, and a small quantity of flax and linseed. See also D. Demarco, *Le "affittanze collettive" e le trasformazioni fondiarie nel Mezzogiorno d'Italia* (Naples, 1948).

40. Those who had to use the Barraccos' oil presses to press their own olives paid for the service in oil. Besides the modern press at Petrizia, the largest presses were at Isola, Trigani, and Pidochiella (in 1861–62 these "collected" 6,000 cantaja of oil). The rent on small vineyards was sometimes paid in oil, too; flax fields were paid for in kind.

41. The Barretta and Petrizia gristmills were the largest and earned up to 1,900 tomoli (2,850 bushels) a year in milling fees. But the seven mills under the Isola administration (Sant'Anna, Zagonà, Ilice, Ilicicchio, Carazziti, Ponte, and Porcarili) earned an average of only 240 tomoli (360 bushels) a year from 1865 to 1883, after which time the figure declined to 120 to 160 tomoli (180 to 240 bushels).

output with extra work. One such lessee was one Matteo Fardella, a "country-man" from Rocca Bernarda, who in 1837 took a six-year lease on two water mills in that town for a yearly rent of eighty-five tomoli of white wheat with the provision that "in the event no other mills in the town are operating, the rent shall increase by a further fifty-five tomoli."[42]

Overall, leasing was a highly profitable form of management; it partly placated the peasants' hunger for land, brought in large revenues, and supplied the warehouses with export commodities—all with practically no effort by the owner.

It is significant that the latifondo never let land under improvement leases, though they were widely used elsewhere in Calabria.[43] Moreover, leased land by no means escaped the owner's control. Far from becoming an absentee landlord, he enjoyed a number of uses, required upkeep, and procured the major product. Unlike the cases in both nearby Sicily and far-off England, the rents charged within the latifondo enterprise by no means fostered the rise of independent capitalist tenant farmers.[44]

6. Industrial Production of Silk and Licorice

Among the latifondo enterprise's directly managed operations, the production of licorice paste and silk thread deserve separate treatment. These were two industries long and solidly established in Calabria; the know-how was widely disseminated, the raw materials easily accessible, and the market international as well as regional (in fact, demand for licorice and semiprocessed silk soared

42. Fardella could not make a go of it. Six years later, in the hard month of February, Barracco ordered him to pay 120 tomoli in arrears, or the corresponding twenty-two carlini per *tomolo* in cash. In May he attached Fardella's house and a small plot of land in Rocca Bernarda (a quarter of a tomolata, or sixty-four square rods, with some grapevines and fig trees and one olive tree). Michele Fardella—aspiring to become a miller, and more townsman than "countryman," with his home near the main church and his kitchen garden on the outskirts of town—was a typical example of the potential small rural entrepreneur we discussed in relation to the expropriation of peasants' lands. Fardella's main antagonist was the great landowner, who could require payment in February, fix the price per tomolo at the winter rate rather than at the usual eleven carlini, and foreclose on his property.

43. Improvement leases were notorious in Calabria for the very harsh terms they set for the peasants. The first three years of the eight-year leases were rent free, but the tenant was obliged to plant trees on the property; in the ensuing five years he paid rent in cash and/or in kind; at the end of the lease he was theoretically entitled to keep a small fraction of the land but generally had to forfeit it to pay the debt he had contracted in the initial years. See L. Bodio, "Sui contratti agrari," *Annali di Statistica,* 2d ser., vol. 8 (1879): 125; Comizi Agrari, *I contratti agrari in Italia* (Rome, 1891); G. Giorgetti, *Contadini e proprietari,* op. cit.; and G. Candeloro, *Storia dell'Italia moderna,* vol. 2: *1815–1846* (Milan, 1960), 315.

44. On the rise of capitalist tenant farmers in Sicily, see E. Pontieri, *Il tramonto del baronaggio siciliano* (Florence, 1943), 56ff.; on the entrepreneurial activism of the English tenant farmers, see F. M. L. Thompson, *The Second Agricultural Revolution,* op. cit., 72–73.

in the nineteenth century).[45] The Barraccos owned two spinneries and three (later two) licorice works where the organization of production and the truly industrial discipline was such as to make these two businesses entirely different from any other on the latifondo.

A silk spinnery was a true factory, with all the characteristics and horrors that nineteenth-century literature revealed to the wider world. The Barraccos' spinneries were located in the Sila: the modern Fallistro mill between Spezzano Grande and Spezzano Piccolo, and the old Casino works near Castelsilano. The Fallistro spinnery was housed in a large rectangular building with one door and ten large windows. Inside were a French-made twelve-horsepower steam engine, which worked the rollers, a boiler to heat and "vaporize the basins," and a fireplace to "heat the room to the 28–30 degrees [approx. 90° Fahrenheit] necessary to prevent heat condensation." Outside the building was "a cistern suitable to contain the water needed to run the spinnery." It was a murderous environment: hot, humid, unhealthy, and oppressive. Padula was struck by the unhappy silence ("no song, no laughter") that reigned in a Sila spinnery. Shut inside for three months at a time—the duration of a silk "campaign" from the end of June to the end of September—were more than a hundred workers. Almost all were women—fifty-six "mistresses," twenty-eight beaters, twelve unwrappers, and six apprentices. The machine operator, the stoker, and the "director" (an employee who ran a silk barn or an orange grove in the other seasons) were the only men. The factory operated day and night; personnel worked from twelve to sixteen hours a day for the seventy-five working days of the campaign, "excluding holidays and repair days." "As there [were] no dormitories," the women—many of whom came "from a distance"—had to pay rent for a place to sleep in the neighborhood, so that, while spinners' wages were .85 lire a day in Cosenza, "going into the Sila" the women asked for 1.20. These were starvation wages, two times less than those of men in similar jobs (mill weavers or stokers), as they were in all industries of this kind in Italy.[46] And the profits? A "mistress" could work four kilos (8.8

---

45. F. Marincola di S. Floro, *Statuti dell'arte della seta in Catanzaro preceduti da una relazione fatta alla Camera di Commercio ed Arti sulla origine, progresso e decadenza dell'arte della seta in Catanzaro* (Catanzaro, 1880); A. Graziani, "Il commercio estero del Regno delle Due Sicilie dal 1832 al 1858," in *Archivio Economico dell'Unificazione Italiana*, ser. 1, vol. 10 (Rome, 1960) fasc. 1, 27.

46. Bevilacqua, following Arcà, denounces "the exploitation of the social work force . . . pushed to extreme limits" (P. Bevilacqua and A. Placanica, *La Calabria*, op. cit., 262). But the wages and hours stipulated by Barracco were the same as those applied generally. In March of 1884, the mayor of Cosenza made public the wages that were being paid in the spinneries: .85 lire for workers and spinners, half for apprentices and beaters. In 1891, Albert Keller's mill in the province of Cuneo, in Piedmont, was paying spinners 1.10 to 1.20, beaters .67, and knotters .72 for a twelve-hour day. At Forlì, in Romagna, Giuseppe Brasini & Co. was paying spinners .90 to 1.10 and beaters .45 for twelve hours; at San Leucio, in the province of Caserta, near Naples, Offritelli,

pounds) of cocoons a day, producing one kilo (2.2 pounds) of good silk thread in three days, which sold for fifty-seven lire in Milan. Six percent of this went for the cost of labor. Transportation by mule from the Sila to the railhead and thence to Milan (including porterage, canvas, and rope) amounted to fifty centimes per kilo; depreciation, interest on capital, "manufacturing waste," and other expenses cost another 8 lire. Net of these costs, a kilo of silk brought in 44 to 45 lire. There remained the raw material, which the administration reckoned at the current market price of 3.75 lire per kilo of cocoons. It took thirteen kilos—the equivalent of 48.75 lire—to produce one kilo of thread. As a matter of fact, the Barraccos contended in 1880 that the spinnery was working at a loss,[47] and indeed this would have been the case had the cocoons been bought on the open market. However, the fact of the matter was that the mills procured their raw material from the Barraccos' own silk barns in Caccuri, Altilia, and Polligrone.[48]

These silk barns deserve a digression. While a spinnery was a modern industrial plant governed by modern rules and a modern system of exploitation, a silk barn was a place where a rural type of exploitation prevailed. The silkworm growing season lasted three months, from April to the end of June, when the spinneries opened. During that period, the "director" of the barn would stay, with his wife and perhaps an adolescent daughter, at an inn in Caccuri, Polligrone, or Altilia, at his employer's expense; he would fix up the barn, the shelves ("the wooden structures"), and the boiler, hire a stoker, and buy "stock." Mulberry leaves were gathered by gangs of women and children in the latifondo's own groves and transported to the barn by its own mules. The barn work consisted mainly of laying out the leaves for the worms to eat and keeping the shelves clean, and it was done by the wife, the daughter, and three or four other women. The "director's" family earned around five lire a day (the man 2.50 to 3 lire, the wife 1.50, the daughter .65), the hands .80. The Barraccos' silk barns produced not only all the cocoons needed for their spinneries

Pascal & Co. was paying spinners the same rate of .90 to 1 lira and beaters .70 for an eleven-hour day (this mill, which remained open during the winter, at least offered free shelter to workers who lived at a distance). All of the above-mentioned workers were, of course, women, and it is interesting to note that the men who worked in the same mills, though at different jobs, were paid twice as much: stokers 2 lire, overseers 2.50. Even when the jobs were similar, for example, in the weaving process where piece rates were applied, men earned 3.20 to 5.40 lire and women 1.55. See BA: E23(4), F22(1, 2), F23; and *Annuario Statistico Italiano* (Rome, 1893), 474–75.

47. The Barraccos had an interest in showing losses. The spinnery was located in the Fallistro enclosure, which they had bought in 1879 at the judicial sale of the property of the Mollo barons, who were in debt to them (see chap. 2). The Mollos claimed the mill had not been included in the auction lot and had petitioned the Cosenza Civil Court for its return and for payment of damages. See BA: E23(4), F22(1, 2), F23.

48. The market price was real enough. The Barraccos could have sold the cocoons to local traders, as they did the surplus production, for about three lire a kilo.

but also a surplus, which was sold in the local markets. All things considered, the cost of producing a kilo of cocoons was no more than thirty centimes, as against the market price of 3.75 lire. Taking another look at the spinneries' profits with these figures in mind, the picture changes entirely. Considering the real cost of the raw material, every kilo of thread yielded a net profit of 41 lire—a 250 percent return on costs! Every campaign brought in 53,000 lire net.

Note, however, that the immense profitability of this modern factory depended on its being part of the latifondo enterprise. The foregoing calculation of the cost of raw materials is only one demonstration; other aspects are more difficult to translate into immediate monetary terms. Wages, for instance: the Barraccos could pay such low wages for so short a season because they used recruitment circuits internal to the latifondo where families pooled all their income from jobs in the enterprise. In reality, an overseer did not work for a single season but shifted from orchard, to silk barn, to spinnery, and so did his wife and daughters; the workers and the girls were often relatives of other employees.

The production of semiprocessed licorice had many similar characteristics. This too was a modern industrial business, centralized and oriented to markets outside the region: Naples and beyond, especially France, and later Germany.[49] The Barraccos had "always" owned the Neto licorice works, on the Neto River in the village of Altilia, and an antiquated one in Amantea, which was dismantled in 1839. In 1837, they added a large modern plant in the hamlet of San Pietro in Isola. Here the works was housed in a huge hall containing iron presses and copper tables where the paste was rolled out, a hydraulic press, wood-fired boilers, burners to heat the copper cauldrons where the licorice root was kept boiling, and an array of smaller copper basins. The hall was extremely hot and humid, as the licorice "campaign" took place in the spring and summer, from March to October or November. It was also very crowded: shut inside the San Pietro works were around eighty men processing the material, a number of stokers, and fifteen women rolling out the paste, all under the command of one caporale. Outside were watchmen guarding the root, handlers moving the root and the cases of finished product, and suppliers of firewood for the boilers.

The production process was fairly simple and always highly profitable. The initial investment in the San Pietro works was less than 7,000 ducats, and it was already earning 3,000 ducats in its second year of operation. On average the works brought in a profit of 12,000 to 15,000 ducats yearly—a return of around 35 percent. The installation of machinery obviously increased costs, but

---

49. The Barracco trademark was quite well known—enough for others to steal it. In 1873–74, the Barraccos sued one unlicensed user, and at the end of the century they were involved in a commercial suit with Germany and France.

it raised output enormously. A hydraulic press costing approximately 1,000 ducats was installed at the Neto works around 1840,[50] and a powerful steam-driven machine was installed at San Pietro around 1865.

Here too, the secret of high profitability lay in access to raw material and labor within the latifondo circuit. Initially the Barraccos bought licorice root on the Calabrian market or imported it from Basilicata and Sicily. However, prices soared in the late 1830s; a *cantajo* (about 196 pounds) of Sicilian root cost fifteen carlini in 1836 but twelve times as much in 1841 (sea carriage included).[51] Accordingly, the Barraccos' works gradually changed over to "root dug for our own account"—either root that grew wild on latifondo territory[52] or, later, root from the plantations established in Isola in 1872.

The root was dug by gangs of farm hands and carried to the works by the operation's own mule teams, the paste was carried to the Barracco warehouses in Croton by the same means, and the fuel came from the Barraccos' own woods, cut by their *massari* and transported by their own teams and wagons.

Men employed at the licorice works earned forty grani a day (1.70 lire) besides "gifts" of oil and pork; women earned half as much—low pay, like all the other wages in the region.[53] Agents, overseers, and watchmen were regular employees whose tasks varied according to the season, but whose pay, though kept low, was guaranteed all year round.

The licorice works are another example of a directly managed operation capable of exploiting the benefits of a tradition while pursuing the logic of profit. As demand for licorice grew, accompanied by a steep rise in the price of the paste, the Barraccos responded, as we shall see, by quadrupling and modernizing their production.

7. Subsistence Production and Commodity Production

The production of commodities was the main purpose of the latifondo enterprise but not its sole raison d'être. The Calabrian latifondo differed from a

---

50. Luigi Grimaldi reported in 1845 that "the owner [of the licorice factory], Baron Barracco, has bought a very expensive cast iron press, the largest size cast in the Kingdom, and highly profitable for both the product and fuel economy" (L. Grimaldi, *Studi statistici,* op. cit., 113).

51. The cholera epidemics that interrupted trade between Sicily and the mainland also slowed deliveries. See BA: A63, A64, A67, A71, A72, A74, E4(4); and P. Bevilacqua and A. Placanica, *La Calabria,* op. cit. 104, 265.

52. For example, there were plantations at Passanini, Santa Domenica, Ponticelli, Serre Sant'Andrea, Castello di Cotrone, and Petrizia.

53. Wages at the licorice works in Cosenza's hamlets remained at the same low level throughout the eighteenth and nineteenth centuries; the raises that were accorded were absolutely insignificant (P. Bevilacqua and A. Placanica, *La Calabria,* op. cit., 111).

Brazilian coffee plantation, for example. While the latter, a capitalist enterprise implanted multidirectionally in the market, had to buy in order to sell and sell in order to buy, the latifondo, though a player in the market, did not depend on it. The latifondo produced commodities for sale but also bread, meat, wood, and licorice root—that is, goods for its own subsistence, raw materials, and other factors of production. Unlike the Brazilian hacienda, where the working mechanisms could be brought to a full stop by a drop in the price of coffee, the latifondo enterprise self-reproduced. Not even a market depression could cause it to founder or cease to guarantee the masters a high standard of living and the employees a basic subsistence; at worst, its profits might dwindle. As we shall see, this invulnerability of the latifondo economy to the mechanisms of the external market crumbled bit by bit. Though the external market, with the coming of the railroads, entered more and more into the decisions of the masters/managers, it worked to the latifondo's benefit only for a short time.

To understand the force and "freedom" of the latifondo economy in its commercial production, we must therefore examine its extraordinary self-sufficiency.[54] The enterprise produced practically everything needed to live and produce; the only items it purchased, besides labor, were iron, sulfur, salt, coal (for steam-powered machinery), and occasionally machinery. All the rest, including implements (scythes, spades, hoes, plow parts, cauldrons, and so on), was produced on the estate. Consumables were distributed among the masters' tables ("to the palaces," "for the use of the baroness"), the agents' homes, and the workers' cottages through the latifondo network: wages, services, *minatici, linatici, paraspori,* all forms of nonmonetary retribution that will be described later, gifts at Christmas, Carnival, and Easter, and issuances in the fields and at the silk barns, threshing floors, oil presses, and licorice works to gangs of harvesters, sowers, oil pressmen, teamsters, scythers, factory hands, shepherds, and field hands. This was the destination of part of the cheese, wool, lambs, kids, skins, and hides produced by the flocks and the "livestock part-

---

54. Self-sufficiency is a constant feature in the history of successful large-scale farming enterprises. Florescano, for example, quotes a sixteenth-century Mexican *haciendado*'s description of a prosperous hacienda: "A good hacienda must have everything, water, tillage land, pastures, woodland, cactus, quarries, lime-kilns, etc. Thus the products will complement one another. The income from the *pulque* produced by the cactus will help to pay wages and supplies for the laborers. The income from the pastures will help with the harvest. What the Indian charcoal-burners produce in the mountains will help to pay taxes. Some of what the other crops provide will help with extraordinary expenses. Thus the income produced by selling the main harvest can pay for next year's expenses and leave something over for profit. The hacienda that does not have everything is likely to go short. To avoid shortages, one must have everything, and the way to do this is to expand the hacienda" (E. Florescano, *Estructuras y problemas agrarios de México, 1500–1621* [Mexico City, 1971; my translation]). See also *Haciendas, latifundios y plantaciones en América Latina,* ed. E. Florescano (Mexico City, 1975).

nerships."[55] The wheat and majorca harvested on the masserie or by the tenant
farmers and ground in the latifondo's gristmills provided white bread for the
tables of the masters, clergymen, widows, the elderly, and the poor, as well as
some of the employees. The rye was made into daily bread; chickpeas, vetch,
lentils, peas, and beans ended up in the pot or the hog trough; the "pistilli"
beans went to the hogs; the potatoes were for all and sundry, from the palaces
to the kennels; the millet fed the poultry; the barley went to the mules, oxen,
wagon horses, and the animals working at the oil presses and the smithies; the
oats were mostly reserved for the masters' stables in Calabria and Naples; the
acorns from the oak woods went to the hogs; and the pulse went to the cattle.
The oil extracted from the latifondo's olives at its own presses was used in
cooking and dressing food, in lamps, in soap making, at the silk barns and the
spinneries, and in making oil of bergamot. The vineyards supplied grapes to the
wineries (which also made vinegar); they produced about fifty barrels (1,500
liters) of choice wine for the baron's table, and the remainder was distributed or
made into spirits. The orchards produced all the fruit and the gardens all the
vegetables. Every storehouse kept a certain quantity of lard, salami, salt, and
other products needed for latifondo consumption and issuance and to handle
special situations such as the occasional stationing of military and other "public force." Lastly, as we have seen, the latifondo produced its own raw materials: licorice root, mulberry leaves, and silk cocoons; hemp and flax for burlap,
rope, canvas, and the ladies' looms; saddle and harness leather; and wood for
all purposes.

Note, however, that the latifondo economy's self-sufficiency in what may
be called its reproductive function must not be confused with a "natural"
economy. All the products had a market price and were posted at those prices in
the ledgers, and all of them could be sold.[56] In other words, all the products
were commodities, but some, in a manner of speaking, were *more so* than
others—some were destined primarily for the distant market, others partly for
the market and partly for internal use, still others primarily for internal use (and
offered for sale only in bumper years). Of these three groups, the first (comprising wheat and majorca, sheep's milk and caciocavallo cheese, oil, fine wool,
licorice, lambs, and kids) was the one that constituted the latifondo's large-
scale commercial production and justified the assertion that the purpose of the

55. Of the great quantities of various types of cheese produced ("caci, caciocavalli, ricotte,
giuncate, raschi e butirri"), some went "to the mansions" and some to the agents, guards, massari,
and harvesting gangs for Easter and Christmas gifts. Low- and high-grade wool, merino,
lambswool, and ramswool were spun both in the mansions ("for the use of the Baroness") and in
the houses and huts of agents, muleteers, herdsmen, and day laborers. It was the same with lambs,
kids, shoats, pork, leather, and skins.

56. *European Peasants and Their Markets: Essays in Agrarian Economic History*, ed. W.
Parker and E. Jones (Princeton, 1975).

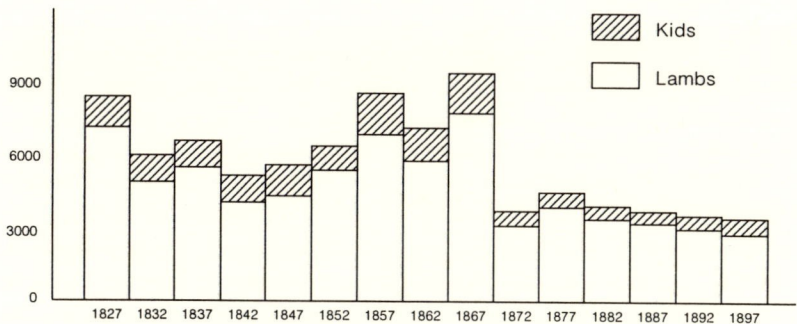

Fig. 5. Barracco livestock production, 1827–97

latifondo economy was to produce commodities. As shown in table 7,[57] yearly outputs were surprisingly high for a single farming enterprise: up to 8,000 hectoliters of oil, over 100,000 rounds of cheese, 4,000 to 7,000 quintals of licorice, and 20,000 quintals of wheat. Of course, this was an old-style kind of production, subject to wide fluctuations resulting from natural cycles and causes,[58] but it was also highly commercialized. It is interesting to note that the commercialization rate (that is, the ratio between quantity sold and quantity produced) remained not only high (75 percent to 100 percent) but also fairly steady, regardless of variations in output or prices. This was equally true in 1843, when output was particularly low, and in 1887, when it soared. The same seven out of ten bags of wheat left for Naples in 1835, when the price was 12.75 lire per quintal, and in 1847, when it was almost twice as much. The same eight- or nine-tenths of the cheese, fine wool, and majorca was sold ("low-grade majorca was given out for *minatici*"), as well as eight out of every ten merino, Swiss, Rambouillet, and hybrid lambs born (the rest being "kept for breeding"), and three-quarters of the kids, young wethers, and fine-wooled lambs. The high and steady commercialization rate means that even in years of poor harvests the large-scale commercial operations produced a marketable

---

57. The first and third parts of table 7 differ as to the time frame used in collecting the data. The third section shows the data for every fourth year, starting in 1827, the first year for which they are available. The first and second sections give the data for every fifth year. Sample years are probably a less reliable basis for finding the trend of production than averages would have been, but they do allow us to appreciate the influence of nature on production (there can be enormous differences from one year to the next) and to see the long-term trend.

58. In J. Meuvret's sense (*Etudes d'histoire économique* [Paris, 1971], passim), so-called subsistence crises are typical of economies subject to very wide seasonal and annual fluctuations, in which everyone has a dirext experience of disastrous harvests and famine.

surplus. Unlike the feudal model, however, where the lord would sell surplus
from the seignorial reserves while famished serfs might have to eat up the seed,
the products the latifondo destined for the market were different from the
laborers' staples (by way of example, they baked rye flour, not wheat; they ate

TABLE 7.   Barraco Livestock Production, 1827–97

Year	Lambs	Kids
1827	7,222	(1,348)
1832	4,655	(1,296)
1837	5,574	1,311
1842	391	(1,299)
1847	4,294	(1,250)
1852	4,752	(1,351)
1857	7,255	(1,305)
1862	5,448	1,804
1867	7,531	1,911
1872	2,889	491
1877	3,634	555
1882	3,270	537
1887	3,007	434
1892	2,633	469
1897	2,548	532

N.B.: estimated figures parenthesized.

Barracco Livestock Inventory, 1827–1902

Year	Sheep	Goats	Cattle
1827	(16,667)	(1,526)	(1,537)
1832	15,438	1,467	1,637
1837	20,785	1,588	1,736
1842	15,325	1,593	1,889
1847	13,188	1,578	1,728
1852	15,257	2,305	1,550
1857	(12,829)	2,488	(1,307)
1862	10,318	2,618	1,112
1867	10,391	2,886	1,047
1872	6,827	303	772
1877	7,549	346	1,071
1882	7,297	287	1,143
1887	6,783	336	1,182
1892	4,894	348	1,092
1897	4,566	359	1,038
1902	3,221		

N.B.: estimated figures parenthesized.

TABLE 7—*Continued*
Barracco Export Production, 1827–1903

Year	Oil (hl)	Cheese (rounds)	Grain (*tomoli*)	Licorice (quintals)	Wool (quintals)	Caciocavalla Cheese (pairs)
1827	—	—	—	—	—	3,592
1831	—	—	—	—	—	4,364
1835	2,163	95,031	25,202	1,273	27	4,300
1839	3,041	111,500	17,185	4,412	103	9,078
1843	1,934	86,614	29,367	5,036	78	9,650
1847	4,259	56,741	27,977	7,516	181	4,908
1851	6,449	52,979	32,264	2,278	219	(4,125)
1855	3,537	33,904	46,446	1,915	316	5,735
1859	2,781	35,333	24,449	1,658	200	8,036
1863	3,042	26,873	36,029	3,093	125	10,166
1867	3,101	34,746	32,567	4,313	162	11,259
1871	4,999	12,047	30,220	3,333	110	8,133
1875	4,265	14,071	29,268	2,645	110	6,093
1879	4,805	14,487	21,732	1,991	124	4,890
1883	4,776	10,181	25,874	4,167	99	5,163
1887	8,249	9,604	15,285	4,204	68	3,378
1891	3,992	11,762	13,911	4,287	(7)	6,195
1895	2,101	9,128	18,169	2,877	52	6,204
1899	1,313	7,565	8,799	1,559	55	4,506
1903	1,081	6,010	10,037	1,506	(27)	2,430

N.B.: estimated figures parenthesized.

pork, not lamb, and cottage cheese rather than hard cheese; and they spun coarse wool, not fine).[59]

The second group consisted of what may be called large-scale mixed production destined partly for internal consumption and partly for the market: rye and coarse wool (important staples that were traditionally part of workers' remuneration in kind), potatoes, silk cocoons, hides, and skins. The enterprise produced considerable quantities of these commodities (from 6,000 to 10,000

---

59. Besides its great cash crops, the estate produced oranges and hogs for sale on a medium scale and oil of bergamot on a small scale. The specialized ("garden type") production of oranges ran to as much as 660 tons, "all sold out" for up to four thousand ducats a year. Commercial production of oranges made its first appearance in the ledgers in 1867, and it grew swiftly and steadily. From 1867 to 1875, annual production more than quadrupled, going from 250,000 pieces of fruit (about 44 tons, the sweet Calabrian oranges being quite small) to 1,135,000; in 1874, the record year, over 3,656,000 oranges—more than 660 tons—were sold. Receipts increased from 625 to 3,845 ducats. In 1872, lemons were added to the estate's list of crops; in 1873, two new groves (presumably planted at the beginning of the boom) came into production and in 1875 a third. Unfortunately there are no data on production in the ensuing years. The hog operation produced around 650 suckling pigs, 600 of which were sold, yielding from ten to twelve thousand ducats. On the other hand, barely 169 pounds of oil of bergamot were produced in 1871.

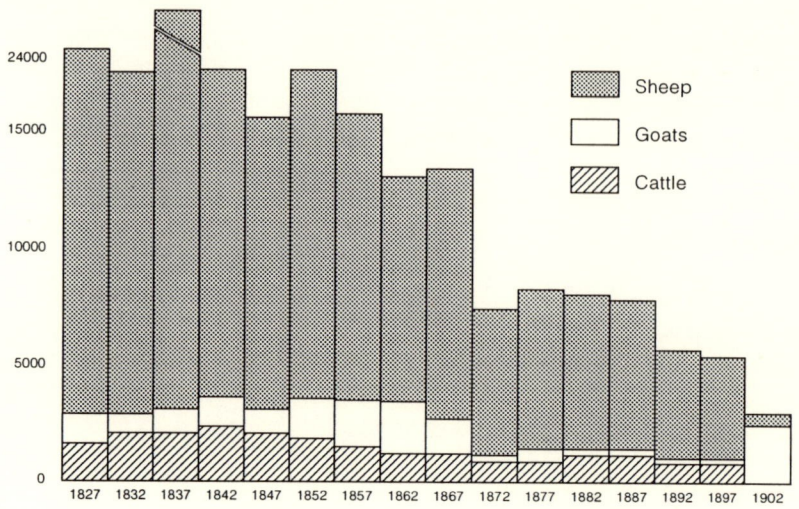

Fig. 6. Barracco livestock inventory, 1827–1902

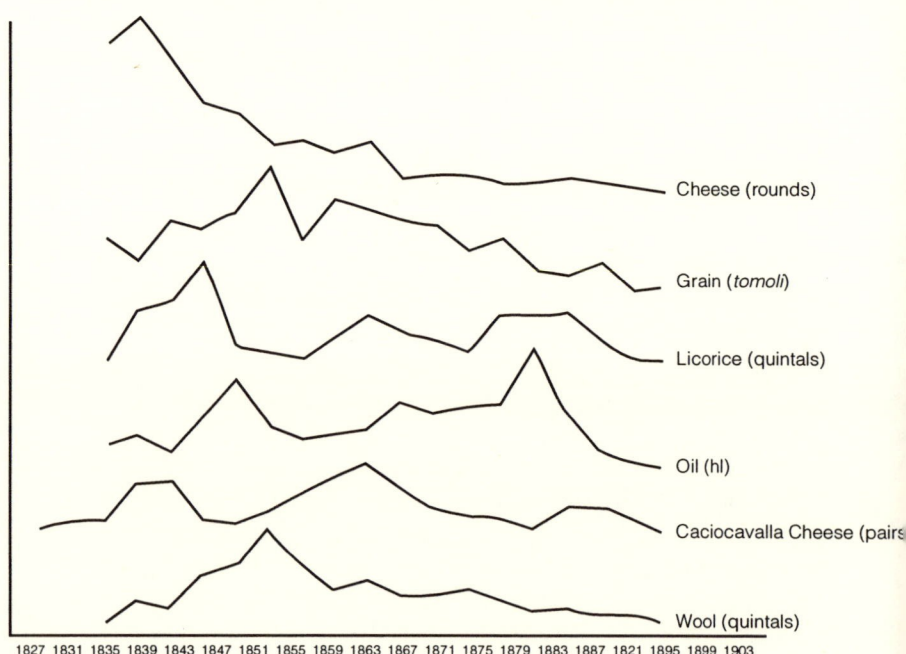

Fig. 7. Barracco export production, 1827–1903

tomoli of rye, from 100 to 200 quintals of coarse wool, and around 2,000 tomoli of potatoes), and the part sent to market brought in a substantial amount of money. Commercialization rates for these products averaged from 10 percent for cocoons to 50 percent for rye, but, unlike the case for large-scale commercial production, they varied according to the amount produced. The primary purpose of this production was to meet the requirements of the enterprise, hence fixed quantities were destined for distribution (as workers' remuneration, charity, and gifts) or for use as processing materials, while the amount of surplus sent to market varied.

The third group comprised large-scale production for internal use only: flax and hemp for burlap and ropes; barley, oats, pulse, corn, chickpeas, vetch, and pistilli beans for livestock feed; and broad beans and wine for the workmen's dinners. Here, too, we are talking about large quantities—around 3,000 tomoli of broad beans, 4,000 to 5,000 of barley and oats, 750 hectoliters (almost 20,000 gallons) of wine—of which occasional surpluses from bumper harvests (like Isola's 10,000 tomoli of oats in 1848) were sold at a profit.

Up to now we have been talking about the production of food, raw materials, and semiprocessed goods. In fact, the latifondo produced neither finished products nor luxury goods, even if many of its products were of high quality. The only exception was the horse-breeding operation, the products of which brought extremely high prices in Bourbon Naples and, according to De Cesare, triumphed at the racetrack.[60] The operation, which was located in Calabria, stocked fifty or sixty mares, several hundred colts, one or more Arab mares, English studs to strengthen the breed, half-bred, and other horses.

8. The Markets

The line dividing large-scale commercial production from mixed production corresponds almost exactly to the line dividing two markets: one extraregional, the other local.[61] In fact, the large-scale commercial production was destined

---

60. Intendent Michele Galdi, listing the "Barracco of Cosenza" breed of horses in the Murat statistical compendium, described it as "overly thin, ungainly, good only for carting and for breeding mules," and "lacking studs" (U. Caldora, *La Statistica murattiana,* op. cit., 104). But the Barraccos invested heavily to improve the breed. In the 1840s, their inventories show that the breeding farm was run diligently (with listings of each mare's name, age, description, paternity, and offspring, studs' names, and pedigrees) and that the stock had been improved through the import of English studs. De Cesare writes that the horses most highly esteemed at the races in Naples were "those of the Barracco breed, and most of all Rischio, of whom Filippo Palizzi painted a splendid portrait, and the beautiful [*bellissima*] Egeria, who always refused to stand to stud" (R. De Cesare, *La fine di un regno,* op. cit., 357).

61. The term *export* is used here in the sense of taking something outside a given market—in this case the regional market is the one we are considering to be local. As the development of a national market in the Bourbon kingdom was far from complete (for instance, duties had to be paid

mainly for the metropolitan market (Naples and thence often abroad), the mixed production (and a fortiori the surplus of noncommercial crops) for the local market.

These two markets were governed by differing mechanisms that imposed differentiated behavior on the commodities themselves. For the large Calabrian producers, the metropolitan market corresponded to the world market. It represented an unlimited demand (or so it seemed for eighty years), but they had to submit to the prices, units of measure, and quality standards it dictated and to the rule of delivery to customers' premises. Like the Polish lords studied by Witold Kula, and unlike many southern landowners described by John Davis,[62] the Barraccos used no brokers in their relations with the metropolitan market but sold their products directly to large traders and trading houses. This implies the existence of storage facilities and transportation systems, hence the necessity of a logistical and organizational network. In Calabria, this was provided by the existing latifondo network. Export products (licorice, fine wool, oil, cheese, durum wheat, and majorca) were brought out of production areas via the latifondo's "internal" means of transport—ox, mule, and wagon trains—stopping temporarily if necessary at one of the intermediate storage facilities (Altilia, Caccuri, or Isola), and proceeding to the Barraccos' large warehouses in the port city of Croton (or, rarely, to Castella where there was a small port).[63] At Croton, under the supervision of the head warehouseman, they were prepared for final shipment. The licorice was packed in cases, the wool was baled, and the oil was transferred from jars to casks and barrels; everything was counted, weighed, and recorded in Neapolitan units of measure. The goods were loaded (by the Baron's men) onto the various types of vessels laying over in the port, or, later, onto the "mail steamboat" or the railroad, destined for Messina, Milazzo, Castellammare, and, mainly, Naples.[64] Upon arrival in

---

on goods transported from one town to another), the character of the Naples market was different from that of the Calabrian market, though they lay within the same monetary and fiscal boundaries.

62. W. Kula, *Economic Theory,* op. cit.; J. A. Davis, *Merchants, Monopolists, and Contractors* (New York, 1981).

63. Wheat was brought to Croton "in July from the Marina threshing floor, by three watermen's boats, and from the Piana threshing floor by cart. In August, majorca from the Isola storehouse by mule and ox train."

64. Though sea carriage was an outside service, the vessels that belonged to the shipowners (*padroni*) De Campo, Arpante, Accetta, De Luca, Cafiero, and De Angelis in fact remained at the almost exclusive service of the Barraccos, especially from March to November when they sailed these routes two or three times a month. Bills of lading were drawn up a couple of months beforehand and specified the loading date and location, destination, insurance, and freight. In 1820, the "price of the voyage" by *padron* Michele del Vasto's brig *Il Cattolico* from Croton to Castellamare was 79.76 ducats. This was no great sum, considering that the vessel was carrying 4,000 tomoli (6,000 bushels, or 180 tons) of wheat. See BA: E14(1), E17(8, 9).

these ports, the goods remained in the Barraccos' hands. In Naples the family owned a large building in the port district, rented huge warehouses on Customs Street, and employed a salaried sales agent; in the other ports they rented storage facilities. The goods were put in the care of, and sold by, a family member, an agent like Gregorio Macry in Castellammare, or a large operator like Don Francesco Fiorentino, a Messina licorice trader who was both customer and agent.

By contrast, the Barraccos had no influence at all on prices, nor did they appear to care particularly about them; they sold at whatever prices obtained at the moment in the Naples market as a result of the play among a vast spectrum of markets and the manipulations of the capital's trading "giants."[65] At most they tried to avoid paying duties (this is why their cheese was often shipped to Castellammare rather than to Naples). They exported in any case, even if Naples prices were not always or necessarily higher than local prices. As is shown in table 8, prices in so imperfect a "national" market could fluctuate sharply from place to place, even if keeping to the same trend. We must not think that the Barraccos were altogether insensitive to these variations, but since they were not seeking speculative profit their behavior was neither greatly nor swiftly influenced thereby. For instance, if wheat exports decreased during the early 1860s, the reason was fear of brigandage not the better prices obtaining locally (although later on, when the spread became systematic, the latifondisti's business behavior changed accordingly, as we shall see). On the whole, the Naples market was beautifully simple for the Barraccos. For each product they dealt with one or two major buyers, the same ones year in and year out; prices were whatever they were, and payments were fairly prompt.

From this standpoint, the local market was much more complex. More than one market, it was a whole variety of local markets because sales were concluded out in the fields and orchards, among the herds or in the warehouses, as well as at the fairs and the great open markets in Cosenza and Catanzaro. Large traders often reserved products—rye, oranges, wool, lambs, kids, and shoats—by paying an advance months prior to their materialization, taking delivery at the agreed time at the warehouses or the fairs of Santo Janni and Molerà. In this case the goods were transported to the delivery point at the producer's expense, by the usual ox or mule trains, carts, and muleteers, but often the traders, especially the smaller operators, came to pick them up in the

---

65. In this connection see J. A. Davis, *Merchants,* op. cit., 75ff. There were seven "giants" in the Naples wheat business: Forquet, Volpicelli, Buono, de Martino, Perfetti, Falanga, and Montuori. Though dependent on the government's foreign trade policy, according to Davis these houses were able to control the wheat supply and thereby manipulate prices. For example, all of the commercial agents operating in Barletta in 1842 were in the employ of the de Martino brothers.

TABLE 8. Prices on Local, Naples, and All-Italy Markets, 1812–1900

Year	Oil (lire/quintal)			Sheep's-milk cheese (lire per *cantaio*)		Grain (lire/quintal)			Licorice (lire/*cantaio*)	Wool (lire/quintal)		Caciocavallo cheese (lire/*cantaio*)
	Local	Na	It	Local	Na	Local	Na	It	Na-Me	Local	Na	Na
1812						25.50		30.28				
1813						13.60		23.87		123.25		
1814				119.00		26.50		25.56		142.80		
1815				119.00		29.75		38.24		104.55		
1816	104.72			89.25		36.55		49.16		104.55		
1817				96.69		38.25		41.97		114.33		
1818	104.72			104.13		21.25		22.48		114.33		
1819				98.18		16.15		17.81		114.33		
1820				95.20		19.97		20.43		114.33		
1821				71.40		26.35		21.96		114.33		
1822	47.60			71.40		16.02		17.53		105.40		
1823	107.10			80.33		12.75		16.40				
1824	107.10			71.40		11.47		10.01		142.80		
1825	107.10			89.25		13.17		18.33		104.55		
1826	95.20			59.50		12.75		21.63		135.45		
1827	95.20			59.50		14.45		22.20		123.68		
1828				73.10		17.85		22.20				
1829	119.00			75.86			18.70		22.60		123.68	
1830	71.40			77.35			13.60		20.69			
1831	95.20			78.84			12.75		20.69		114.33	
1832				74.38			18.70		20.84		114.33	
1833	119.00			74.38			16.15		19.63		114.33	
1834	95.20			78.84			14.16		17.81		123.68	
1835				83.30			12.75		15.85		114.33	
1836				80.33	108.38	12.75		19.25	102.00	133.45		
1837				77.35	116.88	13.17	21.88	99.88	127.50		142.38	
1838				84.79		18.70	21.55	102.00	138.13		127.50	

1839	114.24		87.68		19.00	21.93	99.88			123.25	
1840	114.24		89.25		17.85	21.85	99.88	114.33		140.25	
1841	114.24		104.13		18.70		19.57	102.00	123.88		
1842			92.23		14.45		20.59	102.00	135.45		
1843			92.23		23.80		20.35	89.25	135.45		
1844	171.36		83.91		15.94		18.45		123.88		
1845	95.20		87.76		12.75		19.79				
1846	119.00		92.23		13.60		23.00				
1847	80.92		90.74		23.80		31.05				
1848			92.95		14.45		26.11		148.75	153.85	
1849	92.82		93.71		15.30		23.28		142.80	165.85	
1850	57.12		95.20		14.45		19.19		123.88	204.85	
1851	57.12		99.03		15.30	18.53		133.45			153.00
1852	66.64		96.69		17.85	14.45	21.67	140.25	133.45	208.25	148.75
1853	89.96		86.28		25.50	18.19	29.05		133.45		
1854	80.32		93.71	119.00	26.50	23.40	34.55				
1855	101.15	119.00	83.30	120.06	24.65	18.70	31.53		133.45	265.63	
1856			111.56	129.62	21.25	18.70	31.77		99.88	212.50	170.00
1857			86.28	145.35	22.10	21.25	20.88		114.75	174.50	
1858			86.28		28.90		28.81		174.50		
1859			89.25		20.40		22.93			212.50	
1860			105.61	158.10	26.50	22.95	25.23	191.25		212.50	172.13
1861		124.71	86.28	140.25	22.95	25.50	28.68	180.63			212.50
1862		100.91			20.40	23.00	29.52	182.75	157.25		144.50
1863	79.04			148.75	19.55	22.95	26.36	199.75	142.80		206.13
1864	54.74				20.40	19.55	25.57	212.50	144.50		
1865	67.98		145.78	165.75	19.80	18.70	24.01	180.65	144.50	233.75	
1866	68.00		148.75		23.80	25.50	27.30		148.75		
1867	61.88		123.46	127.50	25.50	25.50	31.24	144.50			
1868			148.75		27.62	25.50	31.69		146.63		
1869		92.34	166.60	161.50	20.40		25.69			233.75	
1870		92.34	165.11		22.10		27.67		159.80		229.50
1871	89.53		148.75	170.00	24.65		31.36				
1872	68.00		119.00		26.35		32.77		171.28		

(continued)

TABLE 8—*Continued*

Year	Oil (lire/quintal)			Sheep's-milk cheese (lire per *cantaio*)		Grain (lire/quintal)			Licorice (lire/*cantaio*)	Wool (lire/quintal)		Caciocavallo cheese (lire/*cantaio*)
	Local	Na	It	Local	Na	Local	Na	It	Na-Me	Local	Na	Na
1873	88.00	99.96		119.00		34.00		36.96		142.80		
1874	59.50			148.75	153.00	32.30		37.35		142.80	233.75	
1875	79.33			148.75		26.35		28.27		153.00		229.50
1876		92.34		148.75	165.75	22.50	21.25	29.49		142.80		
1877	93.30			148.75		30.60		34.40		153.00		
1878		106.70		148.75		29.75	24.65	32.13		142.80	174.25	195.50
1879	80.90	101.15	160.00	148.75	146.73	28.55		27.67	235.88			
1880			150.00	148.75		26.56	24.65	32.99	238.00	266.43		199.75
1881			140.00	148.75		22.10		27.19				
1882		89.49	120.00	148.75	155.12	18.30		26.24	235.75			
1883			125.00	148.75	155.12	21.25		23.81	238.00	209.53	161.50	196.35
1884	78.06		135.00	148.75		19.13		22.29	235.88			
1885	78.40		130.00	148.75		18.70		22.01	238.00			
1886	78.40		120.00	148.75		19.55		22.85	242.25	152.15	121.55	
1887			125.00	148.75	165.73	18.70		22.80	238.00	233.45		204.55
1888		71.40	120.00	148.75		20.40		22.85				
1889			120.00	148.75		21.25		24.36		133.45		
1890			120.00	148.75		18.90		23.96		123.68		
1891			110.00	148.75		21.25		25.98		135.45		
1892			105.00	148.75		25.50		25.30				
1893			110.00	148.75		20.40		21.98				
1894	80.92		105.00	148.75		17.85		19.66				
1895	93.77		105.00			15.30		20.00				
1896			95.00			17.42		19.50				
1897	85.68		108.00			19.55		25.60				
1898			108.00			24.65		31.00				
1899	99.86		120.00			19.55						
1900			124.00			22.10						

Na = Naples prices; It = all-Italy prices; Na-Me = Naples and Messina prices.

production areas, buying ricotta and sheep's-milk cheese directly at the Sila warehouse in Camigliati, wine and vinegar at the Altilia cellars, rye at the warehouses in Spezzano Piccolo, wheat at the Rocca di Neto warehouses, cocoons in Altilia and Caccuri, and linseed in Isola. Hundreds of animals, bales of wool, hides, and skins were carted to the fairs in Santo Janni and Molerà, hundreds of kids and young wethers to the Decollazione fair.

The variety of goods traded locally (in some cases only locally) was quite large, as it included all the products of the Baracco latifondo except for caciocavallo cheese, licorice, cotton, and high-grade sheep's-milk cheese. Rated according to the amount of revenue each type brought in, first came the livestock (lambs, kids, sheep, cattle, mules, and hogs), then grain and citrus fruit, oil, wool, silk cocoons, and lastly wine, potatoes, oats, corn, ordinary cheese, ricotta, flax, leather, and skins. When expedient, the farm and orchard managers, warehousemen, and foremen themselves acted as sales agents, and they were rewarded from time to time "for good work in selling." They negotiated prices, collected advance payments, kept "memory notebooks" to record "promises" made and "earnests" received, then turned the cash over to the baron or his clerk at the fair.

The price situation at any one time was a patchwork. The price of wheat sold at the Rocca di Neto warehouse could vary from one day to the next; there was a going price (*pubblica voce*), but also others above or below it. In August of 1829, the mayor of Isola certified that white wheat was selling for 1.60 ducats per tomolo, but that same month the local Barracco warehouse was selling at 2.20; conversely, while Croton's municipal clerk announced in 1848 that the going price for majorca was 2.10, Barracco was selling at 1.90. In 1819, in the depths of the postwar depression, Luigi Barracco's agent sold wheat to a large trader at eighteen carlini per tomolo; a year later, though prices had risen, the same agent sold the same product to the same trader at sixteen carlini. The largest buyers sought to agree on the price before shaking hands on the contract and paying a deposit, but sometimes the price was referred to as the going rate (*la voce*) at delivery time. In short, prices varied according to the season, the month, the place, the buyer, and the quantity of goods available in the warehouse. Large producers were obviously able to influence local prices to some degree. For instance, in 1863—a relatively good year for oil production but also a "brigand war" year—the Barraccos shipped less oil than usual to Naples (1,213 hectoliters, slightly more than a third of their production) and dumped the rest on the local market where the price immediately fell from seventy-nine to fifty-five lire per quintal. However, they seem never to have used this power for speculative purposes; even in the local market, the Barraccos were interested primarily in finding advantageous outlets, and in the amount of their total revenues, rather than in the prices of individual products.

9. The Traders

Just as the nature of the metropolitan and the local markets differed, so did the traders who operated in them. In the Neapolitan market the Barraccos did business with the largest houses in the kingdom. They sold their oil to the brothers Andrea and Pietro Rocca, "traders, bankers and shipowners,"[66] and to Zolese, De Chiara, and Bruni, also large oil dealers. Later on, in the 1850s, they sold to Albert Rauth (or Routh), an operator who had dominated the licorice export trade in the previous decades, and still later they sold to Casimiro Fiesco and Giovanni D'Amore, who had a monopoly in Castellammare (D'Amore also dealt in cheese), and to a Mr. Kolme. Besides D'Amore, their caciocavallo and sheep's-milk cheese was sold to Don Camillo Visconte (or Viceconti) and a Mr. Coppola. Raffaele Sava, who had supplied uniforms to the Bourbon army before Italy's unification, continued to deal in cotton and wool. The Klentz house bought wool and licorice from Barracco. Besides Rauth and Klentz, their customers for licorice were Forquet, one of the seven "giants" of the grain trade, and, under the successor political regime, Langrafà and Wolf and Stolt. Before the Klentz era, the Barraccos sold wool to Lorenzo Zino (known primarily as a timber trader but also as a promoter of various stock corporations) and later to the Gervasi brothers. For thirty years, starting in 1855, grain was sold to the Falangas and the Montuoris, two other "giants" of the grain trade who, like the Roccas, had been shipowners during the Bourbon period. All of these operators belonged to the tiny elite of great Neapolitan traders rated credit-worthy—some of them even in the top classification—in the lists kept by the Chamber of Commerce.[67] Many of them, like the Klentzes, Rauth, Wolf and Stolt, were foreigners (the Forquets, like the Roccas, were originally from Genoa but long-time residents of Naples).[68] Business relations between these "giants" and the Barraccos were apparently based firmly on their mutual advantage: the producer guaranteed a constant supply of goods, the trader guaran-

---

66. R. De Cesare, *La fine di un Regno,* op. cit., 318.

67. On the lists of credit-worthy operators, see J. A. Davis, "The Case of the Vanishing Bourgeoisie," *Mélanges de l'École Française de Rome* 88, no. 2 (1976): 862; and his *Merchants,* op. cit., 14. Among the twenty names listed by the Advisory Chamber of Commerce in 1838 as "worthy of credit at the Royal Customs in Naples" were the following Barracco customers: Forquet, Leoffler & Klentz, Rocca Brothers, K. J. Routh, and Volpicelli. In 1859, Forquet, Falanga, Montuori, Rocca Brothers, and Volpicelli were included on the list.

68. Based on the censuses and the "credit-worthy" lists, Davis calculates that there were about 250 merchants in the city of Naples. Half of the houses listed in the "exceptional" bracket were foreign owned, though they usually had a strong base in Naples. See J. A. Davis, "The Case," op. cit., 861; and his *Merchants,* op. cit., 13–16. See also G. Galasso, "Professioni, arti e mestieri della popolazione di Napoli nel secolo decimonono," in Istituto Storico Italiano per l'Età Moderna e Contemporanea, *Annuario* 13–14 (1961–62): 107–79.

teed a market for the entire production. Most likely the Barraccos were in a way protected from the monopolists' hegemony and domineering described by Davis,[69] because they had their own warehouses in Naples, controled transportation as far as the capital city, and did not deal through brokers. The absence of brokers is significant, mainly because of its rarity. In fact, in the years immediately following the Restoration, when the latifondo was still being organized, the Barraccos did use brokers, especially one Giuseppe Capua, a "venture merchant" from Castellammare who also had interests in the pasta industry and bought grain and cheese from the largest producers in the Marquisate—Barracco, Lucifero, Berlingieri, and Galluzzi—on forward contracts usually signed at the beginning of April. The producer had only to deliver the goods "to the shore" in Croton, and Capua took care of all the rest: chartering vessels, transportation, insurance, storage at the port of destination, and sale. But by 1829, when Capua's business collapsed,[70] the latifondo network was already complex and extensive enough for the Barraccos to be able to do without brokers. From then on, although they sometimes chose to sell mainly oil to a broker in Croton,[71] they preferred to use their own salaried or commission agents, and thus keep tight control over the terms of sale of their products, without ever actually becoming traders themselves. Some of their agents—Don Nicola Gullo in Naples, Don Fiorentino in Messina, and Gregorio Macry and later his son in Naples and Castellammare—were traders or medium- to large-scale entrepreneurs in their own right.[72]

---

69. Davis presents this period as one in which the Neapolitan growers were fighting a losing battle to keep from falling under the total control of the merchants. Price was one of the elements, but the merchants' "monopoly" was based on their monopoly of storage facilities in Naples and along the coast and their control of sea carriage, especially for export (J. A. Davis, *Merchants,* op. cit., 69–70).

70. Giuseppe Capua's bankruptcy was quite dramatic. Unable to pay his debts, he was sentenced by the court to three years of imprisonment. After his release, Capua was forced to sign all of his credits and his dockside warehouses in Castellamare over to Luigi Barracco (and to his agent Nicola Gullo, who was also Marquis Francesco Lucifero's agent). See BA: E14(1, 7), and, for the failure, E17(9).

71. J. Millenet mentioned this during the 1830s: "The olive-oil trade is controled by the great merchants who buy directly from the landowners" (*Coup d'oeil sur l'industrie agricole et manufacturière du Royaume de Naples* [Naples, 1832], 426). For example, in the 1860s, Gaetano Bruni, descendent of a Neapolitan oil merchant who had been the Barraccos' customer, bought large quantities of oil in Croton and shipped them to Naples by steamboat. Vincenzo Adavia, a great Taranto merchant, also bought oil in Croton for resale in Apulia in partnership with Michele Basile, a shipowner.

72. Gregorio (Grégoire) Macry and his French partner François Henry were founding members of the Sebeto Company, the first civil engineering firm of its kind in the kingdom. See J. A. Davis, *Merchants,* op. cit., 110–40; and BA: file entitled "La Compagnia Sebezia."

The world of the local traders was by contrast a potpourri. For each product there was usually one large buyer, a handful of medium- and small-scale buyers, and an indeterminate number of tiny operators whose names were not recorded. In their diversification of commercial interests and their geographic mobility, the large regional traders imitated the Neapolitan houses in miniature. In 1859, when Santo Ranieri began dealing with the Barraccos, he was an oil dealer based in Reggio and Villa San Giovanni. In 1864, he shifted all his operations to wheat, flax, cocoons, and oats, and in 1867 he made his first purchase of produce—250,000 oranges—from the Rocca groves. In the following decade, when, as we have seen, citrus production grew tenfold and European demand for Mediterranean fruit was on the rise, Santo Ranieri gradually abandoned the grain, flax, and cocoon trade and became the Barraccos' sole buyer of citrus fruit. His contracts, which were now signed before harvest time (in October), provided for the sale of "all fruit from the Isola and Rocca groves" (that is, all of the latifondo's citrus acreage) and not only fixed the price but entitled Santo Ranieri to oversee the harvest or even to "harvest the fruit himself" with gangs paid by the latifondo.

Another example of a large local trader was Raffaele Mammone of Cardinale, who dealt in small livestock—mainly lambs but also goats, old sheep, wool, and hogs. His contracts, too, guaranteed him in advance (usually in March, with delivery in May at Santo Janni), at an established price, "all the lambs from the five lambings," or "all from San Leonardo and Ritani." He had first choice of female lambs "after we have chosen 450" breeding ewes and rams "after the shearing." There were others, too: Romualdo Punzo of Croton, a wholesale livestock dealer who bought cows, "proprietory breed oxen, Morelli breed, foreign breed, sick or lame animals," hogs, and a little wool, too; Domenico Poerio of Polistena, who bought "old and second-rate rams, fine and coarse-wooled, after shearing . . . and old fine-wooled sheep from both flocks after shearing" and occasionally also served as the baron's sales agent; Don Alessandro Scigliano of San Giovanni, a kid trader who would reserve all the kids, "both early and late," in October; and Giuseppe Pane, who bought billy goats, young mules, and mares (each listed by name).

After the large traders came a whole group of smaller traders and dealers. Don Nicola de Luca, Pietro di Paola, Don Francesco Cribari, Francesco Calvello, and Filippo Carvelli were all, at different times, Aprigliano wool dealers who supplied the numerous craftsmen of their area. Giuseppe Ajello owned a large store in Catanzaro and bought oil from the Petrizia press (sometimes the entire output). Isola merchant Vincenzo Funaro bought wine from the latifondo; the tanners of Acri and the curriers of Taverna bought hides and skins; and the butchers of Isola, Croton, Cosenza, and San Giovanni bought hogs, lambs, and kids. The Barraccos also sold to other large breeders: Don

Gaetano Ferrari Epaminonda, Baron Berlingieri, Baron Felice Zezza, and Baron Palizzi.[73] In Calabria, as we have seen, the Barraccos also sold directly to consumers; in Naples, this would have been unthinkable.

Transactions, too, were more complex than in the Naples market. Products might be sold by measure or en bloc, "by word" before "sprouting" or after the harvest, at the market or in the warehouse, at prices fixed in advance or according to the going price at delivery time. Santo Ranieri, for instance, bought grain according to availability, cocoons en bloc, oranges by quantity, and flax by weight. Payment might be by note, as in Naples, in gold, silver, and copper, or by an exchange of credits noted in the books.

Relations between producer and traders were highly personalized both in Naples and in Calabria, though in different ways. In the seemingly anonymous metropolitan market, the Barraccos actually sold to only a few well-known houses; the Roccas, the Forquets, the Falangas, and the Montuori's frequented the same companies, banks, and industrial concerns as the Barraccos, if not the same drawing rooms.[74] The Calabrian traders, even the small operators, were the ones the Barraccos ran into repeatedly at the fairs or on the streets of Croton, Isola, or Spezzano. Though a Capua might go bankrupt, or a Baron Zezza have trouble paying his notes, in general the Barraccos' network of business relations was low-risk.

Thus, the latifondo enterprise—modern, multifaceted, diversified, rational, and clearly market-oriented—distinguished itself from other large nineteenth-century agrarian enterprises on the periphery, like the plantations: not only was it was not enthralled to the market, but it operated therein with considerable autonomy. Although its raison d'être was to produce commodities, the enterprise also produced its own subsistence and maintained a web of trading relations and a clientele that ensured its survival and legitimacy.

---

73. In 1860, Gaetano Ferrari Epaminonda of Cosenza bought "645 ewes, rams, etc., of the Barracco breed"; Berlingieri regularly bought Swiss cows for his own farm; Felice Zezza bought heifers; and Palizzi bought heifers and calves.

74. For example, the Sebeto General Insurance Company, with which the Barraccos had considerable dealings in Calabria, was connected with Fourquet's bank. But in Naples the Barraccos belonged to the aristocracy's liberal-progressive circle, initially friendly to the reform-oriented prime minister Luigi De Medici, then to the king's brother Leopold. Members included also some high-ranking Bourbon officials such as the younger prince of Ottajano (De Medici's nephew) and Marquis Nunziante, promoters of a number of industrial ventures (the Sebezia bank for small and medium-scale investors, a railroad contruction company, and so forth). Stanislao Barracco was one of ten members of the watchdog commission on railroad construction (R. De Cesare, *La fine di un Regno,* op. cit., 254, 274, and passim; J. A. Davis, *Merchants,* op. cit., 151–59). In 1884, the prince of Ottajano was a witness at Errico Barracco's wedding (*La Gazzetta di Napoli,* April 29, 1884).

CHAPTER 5

The Workforce and the Relations
of Production

1. The Workforce

All workers on the Barracco latifondo were wage earners. By itself, this affirmation tells us little about the character of the production relations in the enterprise. Wide use of wage labor in agriculture did not begin in the nineteenth century, but during that century it spread in the peripheral areas of Europe such as Russia, Hungary, and the Balkans and was often applied because it cost less than unfree labor.[1] Thus, to note the universality of wage work on the latifondo is only a first step toward understanding the character of its production relations, it still does not allow us to speak of the effective proletarianization of the workforce or, by consequence, of the capitalist character of the latifondo system.[2]

---

1. The Spanish Crown, for example, sought from the sixteenth century onward to institute the wage system in the Peruvian viceroyalty as the general and regulated form of remuneration for Indians who rendered untypical, special, or voluntary services. On the other hand, the nineteenth-century latifundia of the Andes studied by Martinez Alier used wage labor because it was cheaper than servile labor. See R. Mellafé, "Evolución del salario en el virreinato peruano," in Banco de la Republica, *Boletin Cultural y Bibliográfico* (Bogotá) 9, no. 5 (1966): 853–68; J. Martinez Alier, *Relations of Production in Andean Haciendas* (London, 1972); CIDA, *Agricultural Labor in a Latifundio Agriculture* (Washington, D.C., 1968); Su Ching, *Landlord and Labor in Late Imperial China: Case Studies From Shandong* (Cambridge, Mass., 1978); and F. Katz, "Labor Conditions on Haciendas in Porfirian Mexico: Some Trends and Tendencies," *Hispanic American Historical Review* 54 (1974): 1–47. In Europe, a transition toward the great farming enterprise based on wage labor occurred in all of the regions touched by the Napoleonic conquest. See J. Blum, *Noble Landowners,* op. cit., 41–62; and J. Kochanowicz, "Changements dans le méchanisme du foncionnement des exploitations paysannes en Pologne à l'époque napoléonienne," *Annuario dell'Istituto Storico Italiano per l'età moderna e contemporanea,* 33–34 (1983): 74–89.

2. This is G. Arrighi and F. Piselli's assumption in "Capitalist Development in Hostile Environments," *Review* 10, no. 4 (Spring 1987): 649–751. The same may be said for many other studies of the phenomenon in Latin America. See, for example, R. Baztra, in *Estructura agraria y*

In a close reading of the ledgers, the general presence of wages appears to be a rather superficial aspect of the condition of workers on the latifondo. In the reality, it was often submerged and contradicted by the priorities and hierarchies of a complex network of exchanges, needs and expectations hidden behind the terms in which wages were expressed. While in the long term, the extension of wage work certainly played an important role in the transformation of social relations both within the enterprise and in its social territory, in the short and medium terms the reality of these relations was perceived more through the nonuniformizing aspects of the wage condition. In other words, social differentiation among workers was not determined by their wage levels; indeed, except for the thick borderline between "managerial" and manual labor, they were surprisingly egalitarian. As we shall try to demonstrate in the following pages, the far more important distinctions were those between employees working at fixed salaries—the "provisionees" (provvisionati)—and those hired at occasional wages, namely, the farmhands (braccianti).

The provisionees (so called because they were *provided for* and received *provisions*) occupied a very conspicuous place in the enterprise. The ledgers speak only of them, and we know not only their names and birthplaces but also their relatives employed on the latifondo; not only their wage rates but their monthly receipts, their debts, sicknesses, accidents, and dismissals. These were people with steady, though frequently seasonal, employment (in the latter case they were rehired year after year for a particular season) at all levels, from swineherd to administrator, who not only enjoyed all the privileges of the guarantee system but could extend and transmit them to the other members of their families. Within this category we find an extremely strong trend toward professional longevity, hereditary occupations and jobs, and professional endogamy. On the job, the provisionees assumed control of whole production cycles, recruited and trained new workers, and often kept the accounts of their particular operation. All these tasks were highly valued, obviously by the master but also by the provisionees themselves who could thus perpetuate their peasant autonomy. In a way, the provisionees constituted a sort of intermediate and mediating stratum between the owners, on the one hand, and the farmhands and the social territory on the other. As we shall see, this position sometimes exposed them to criticism and suspicion, in part because as foremen they had to play the role of buffer whenever social tension mounted.

By contrast, the farmhands constituted a category of altogether precarious workers. Their names were conspicuously absent from the ledgers; they appeared only as numbers in gangs of men, women, or children under the name of

---

clases sociales en México (Mexico City, 1975), who writes that the capitalistic agrarian enterprise arises "en un proceso de descampesinización y de sustitución del sistema de pago en trabajo (u otras formas precapitalistas) por el sistema de salarios" (16).

the provisionee responsible for forming them for specific tasks. As we shall see, the reverse side of this anonymity was the absence of a personalized relationship with the master, hence a greater propensity for resistance and struggle.

In spite of the fact that the use of provisionees was, all told, quite cheap as well as highly advantageous in terms of loyalty, responsibility, and good service, there were far fewer of them on the latifondo than there were farmhands. While every year, thousands of people were hired by the day, week, or month (Franchetti, too, noted the extraordinary number of day laborers), the provisionees never amounted to more than 600—about 20 percent of the total workforce (see table 9).[3] These numbers are somewhat misleading because, unlike the hands hired for short periods, the provisionees were employed on a yearly basis, for lengthy seasons, or, often, for two consecutive seasons. In effect, the latifondo preferred to employ provisionees whenever possible, but not all of its sectors lent themselves equally well to their engagement. It must be remembered that the wage-earning provisionee in some way represented a transition between, and combined elements of both, the traditional peasant, who was independent even if subject to feudal obligations, and the modern wage worker. Due to the reorganization of production processes that took place during the formation of the latifondo enterprise, in some sectors there was no longer room for any autonomy on the part of the workers, while in others the traditional organization was maintained. Of the two principal sectors in the latifondo economy, grain farming, which saw the development of a sharp division of labor and vertical control of production processes, belonged to the former category; stock raising, which continued the traditional modes of production on a very large scale, belonged to the latter. In fact, as table 10 shows, farming was based mainly on the labor of the braccianti, and barely 5 to 7 percent of the latifondo's provisionees were employed in it, while 50 to 73 percent of them worked in stock raising. This dichotomy corresponds to the one between the mountains and the lowlands that we have already described. During the 1860s and 1870s, when the latifondo economy accentuated its orientation toward grain production at the expense of stock raising, the number of provisionees decreased, as we shall see, and the number of farmhands increased. Administration, supervision, and domestic service were other sectors suitable for the use of provisionees because they entailed a delegation of authority or implied highly personalized, even intimate, relationships.

---

3. We cannot calculate exactly how many hands were employed year by year on the estate because the sources show only the names of the foremen, the total amount of recruitment pay, and wage balances. Knowing the average amount of daily wages, we can suggest that the estate employed about two thousand people a year.

TABLE 9. Provisionees Working on the Barracco Latifondo (by decade)

Decade	Number
1810–19	193
1820–29	291
1830–39	503
1840–49	538
1850–59	573
1860–69	500
1870–79	463
1880–89	339
1890–99	235

TABLE 10. Provisionees by Job

	1801–19	1820–29	1830–39	1840–49	1850–59	1860–69	1870–79	1880–89	1890– →
Farming	11	17	19	20	21	22	16	20	9
Column (%)	5.7	5.8	3.8	3.7	3.7	4.4	3.5	5.9	3.8
Stockraising	141	187	299	308	332	257	189	182	117
Column (%)	73.1	64.3	59.4	57.2	57.9	51.4	40.8	53.7	49.8
Oversight	17	49	113	141	162	159	188	108	85
Column (%)	8.8	16.8	22.5	26.2	28.3	31.8	40.6	31.9	36.2
Management	6	6	9	13	10	10	10	7	4
Column (%)	3.1	2.1	1.8	2.4	1.7	2.0	2.2	2.1	1.7
Domestic service	12	12	28	35	26	32	41	17	11
Column (%)	6.2	4.1	5.6	6.5	4.5	6.4	8.9	5.0	4.7
Crafts	1	2	5	1	4	8	8	1	0
Column (%)	0.5	0.7	1.0	0.2	0.7	1.6	1.7	0.3	0.0
Other	5	18	30	20	18	12	11	4	9
Column (%)	2.6	6.1	6.0	3.7	3.0	2.4	2.4	1.2	3.9
Total	193	291	503	538	573	500	463	339	235

Besides this correlation between types of work and forms of contract, there was another (discussed by Arrighi and Pisellli) between the place an employee came from, with its particular kind of social organization, and the type of contract he was likely to be given.[4] In fact, from 70 to 75 percent of the

4. See G. Arrighi and F. Piselli, *Parentela, clientela e comunità,* op. cit., 367–487. On the other hand, it was logical for the inhabitants of the lowlands to work in the fields and for the local petty notables—better educated and more familiar with the cash economy—to become administrators and warehousemen.

TABLE 11.   Provisionees by Provenance

	1801–19	1820–29	1830–39	1840–49	1850–59	1860–69	1870–79	1880–89	1890– →
Coast	13	13	21	17	16	37	37	20	15
Column (%)	6.7	4.5	4.2	3.2	2.8	7.4	8.0	5.9	6.4
Low hills	29	34	44	44	66	47	68	58	29
Column (%)	15.0	11.7	8.7	8.2	11.5	9.4	14.7	17.1	12.3
High hills	85	136	191	211	248	241	211	138	88
Column (%)	44.0	46.7	38.0	39.2	43.3	48.2	45.6	40.7	37.4
Mountains	54	80	131	128	173	124	101	98	69
Column (%)	28.0	27.5	26.0	23.8	30.2	24.8	21.8	28.9	29.4
Provincial capitals	0	2	4	3	2	1	2	0	0
Column (%)	0.0	0.7	0.8	0.6	0.3	0.2	0.4	0.0	0.0
Others	12	26	122	135	68	50	44	25	34
Column (%)	6.3	8.9	22.3	25.1	11.8	10.0	9.5	7.3	24.2
Total	193	291	503	538	573	500	463	339	235

fixed workforce was recruited in the mountain and high hill towns compared to 4 to 8 percent on the coast and 17 percent in the low hills (see table 11). By contrast, almost all the farmhands came from the lowlands.[5]

To give some order to our description of the world of the latifondo's workforce, we shall rank its members on a scale ranging from the least to the most "dependent," from the most to the least "wage-earning," from the farmhands to the shepherds operating in partnerships. This scale in no way represents a "historical march" toward proletarianization.[6] In fact, we cannot assume that the most "wage-earning" work can be equated with the most dependent because the most "wage-earning" workers were at the same time the ones at the farthest remove from the master, while the most autonomous were also the ones most deeply enmeshed in paternalistic ties.

---

5. As will be remembered from table 5, an average of 60 percent of the mountain dwellers worked in stock raising, supplying three-quarters of the relevant workforce; 30 to 36 percent of the hill and mountain dwellers worked as overseers in various operations and another 6 percent as heads of purely farming activities. The coast and the lower hill areas supplied about 15 percent of the overseers but *no* head of a purely farming operation. At the management level, however, 50 to 70 percent of the agents and administrators came from the lowland towns and the hills, while only 7 to 10 percent came from the mountains. Other kinds of jobs had their own geographical regularities: the cooks, for example, all came from Naples or Sicily and the craftsmen from the larger towns.

6. See E. Le Bris, *Capitalisme négrier: la marche des paysans vers le prolétariat* (Paris, 1976); and, from a different point of view, J. Lopreato, *Peasants No More* (San Francisco, 1967).

2. Braccianti: Wages and Subsistence

As we have seen, the use of braccianti was mostly limited to farm work.
Moveover, braccianti remained such perpetually, whereas in stock-raising, for
example, young hands hired by the month were later promoted to provisionees.
Almost all of the farm work, directed and overseen by provisionees, was
performed by the hands. Their most intensive season was between May and
October—the cycle of the Pleiades, according to Hesiod, between harvesting
and plowing—but there was work to be done all year round. In the late autumn,
the grainfields and vineyards were dressed; in winter, oranges and olives were
harvested, the oil pressed, and fences built; in the spring, olive and mulberry
trees were planted, cleaned, and grafted, and potatoes and licorice root were
planted; summer was reaping time. The grape and potato harvest followed, and
the cycle came around to the starting point once again.[7]

Sexual and generational division of labor followed rural tradition. Men
did the work that required the most muscle power (such as spading, hoeing, and
reaping) or know-how (such as pruning); women harvested grapes, olives,
mulberry leaves, and acorns; and children picked olives, oranges, bergamot,
licorice root, and mulberry leaves and helped on the threshing floor. The hands
worked in gangs formed for specific jobs, and since the division of labor was so
thorough there were hundreds of such gangs, from the smallest, for spade
work, fence building, and tree cleaning; to the midsized gangs of pickers, made
up of 20 or 25 women and children; to the huge gangs of mowers (from 30 to
60 men) and reapers (in 1868, Angelo Valente headed one that numbered 138
men). Each gang lasted just as long as it took to finish its job, rarely more than
fifteen or twenty days (only the boys, the fencebuilders, and the tree pruners
sometimes worked for a couple of months at a time). Occasionally, laborers
were brought in from the outside. For a few more highly specialized jobs, like
pruning, or later oil pressing, workmen were "imported" from Apulia; when
the local labor supply was insufficient, it was supplemented by short-term
immigration from adjacent territories.[8] But generally speaking the gangs were
composed of local people. Those, in turn, brought their relatives and neighbors
into the latifondo's circle. Thus, for example, the hundred men from Polligrone
who "cut and cleaned" in the Barraccos' fields in their township would return
home at night to eat and sleep. The whole population would turn out at the
latifondo's oil press and threshing floor for the usual songs, gossip, and court-

---

7. Each of these jobs entailed a series of tasks, which, at a very advanced stage of the
division of labor, were carried out by separate gangs of day laborers. Wheat fields, for example,
had to be plowed, harrowed, and sowed; grapevines had to be hoed and pruned; and harvesting
involved scything, binding, carting, and threshing.

8. See Arrighi and Piselli, *Capitalist Development,* op. cit., 687.

ing. The men and boys worked until late, the women and girls brought the evening meal, and the master sent over the wine.

Wages were low: .60 ducats and a little coarse wool per month for a boy, 10 grani a day for an olive picker, and 25 or 30 grani a day for men (except for specialized workmen, who earned 40 or 50 grani per day of work and 25 per day of travel). According to a law enacted by the French, "workmen's wages during reaping and grape harvesting were to be fixed by local officials," but, although the latter did publish wage schedules, they never bothered to check whether these were being applied. At any rate, the wages paid by the Barraccos were no lower than the rates paid elsewhere.[9]

On the whole, then, the labor performed by the farmhands was poorly paid, anonymous, and precarious. These characteristics, combined with the fractioning of tasks, the gang-based organization and the time wage, apparently point to an effective proletarianization of their working conditions, thus giving the agricultural sector—which, as we know, was highly market-oriented—a modern capitalist character. But the picture changes if we take as the indicator of proletarianization the degree to which subsistence depended on the wages and the hands' own perception of their condition. Their wages, in fact, were neither the exclusive nor the primary source of their families' subsistence. Given the short seasons and the wage levels, their pay could not have sufficed in any case. A family of farm laborers who pooled their earnings (the husband working in one or two gangs, the wife picking grapes and olives, the daughters tending silkworms and working in the spinnery, the sons picking fruit and olives) could have made about forty ducats a year, whereas the minimum necessary for a single adult's decent subsistence (without counting clothing, rent, taxes, salt, or tobacco) amounted to around thirty-six.[10] But, if the farm-

---

9. These wages for grape cultivation and harvesting, for pruning, and for various kinds of field work were identical to those paid for similar jobs on the masserie in the Vesuvian area a century earlier and in nineteenth-century Apulia. See R. Romano, *Prezzi, salari e servizi a Napoli nel secolo XVIII, 1734–1806* (Milan, 1965); G. Carano-Donvito, "Prezzi e compensi nel Mezzogiorno e in Puglia ai primi del secolo XIX," *Rivista di politica economica* (1933), fasc. 11; and *Dizionario delle Leggi del Regno di Napoli,* 3:54.

10. This calculation is based on the following estimate of an adult's minimum monthly consumption.

	Ducats
Half a tomolo of rye (about .75 bu.)	1.25
One-eighth of a tomolo of broad beans (about 11 lb.)	0.20
One *rotolo* of pork (about 2 lb.)	0.22
Lard and olive oil	0.60
One round of cheese (about 3 lb.)	0.35
Figs, tomatoes, chestnuts, etc.	0.40
Total	3.02

hands, though poor, were not reduced to indigence (the fate of their descendants, of which Salvemini spoke with such passion),[11] it was because they did not depend on their wages alone. Like their better-studied Latin American brothers, the *peones sedentarios,* they were members or heads of small household economies that consumed self-produced food and were largely independent of the monetary economy.[12] Let us take the observations Vincenzo Padula set down in 1864 as an example.

> I visited one after the other those smokey hovels where the families of the populace live jam-packed together. . . . To the right of the door, a donkey chewing his hay . . . then a pig rummaging in the trough, and roosters, hens and chicks scratching here and there . . . a peasant so poor he has to wait until hog-slaughtering season to eat a bit of fresh meat.[13]

While pitying the "poor peasant," Padula also described the elements of his tiny household economy. Besides the home-fattened pig (or *frisinghella,* a dialect word that Padula thought worthy of the Crusca Academy's great dictionary) slaughtered in the winter, the donkey, and the chickens, Padula found

---

This budget, as I said, would have provided a decent subsistence. In reality, the peasants' diet was often much poorer: they would sell their rye and eat chestnut-flour bread, and meat appeared on the table only on very rare occasions. In addition, this estimate assumes that all the food would have been bought at market prices, hence it takes no account of what the household would produce on its own or acquire by barter. But, nothwithstanding its rudimentary character and the wide (though balanced) two-way margin of error, it does help us understand the problem of the relationship between wages and subsistence, that is, the degree of proletarianization of the laborers. Furthermore, this estimate more or less agrees with the one F. Galiani calculated in 1780: "Today, if you were to value in cash what a man and his wife, without children, need and receive, they cannot live on less than eight ducats a month . . ." (*Della moneta,* ed. F. Nicolini [Bari, 1915], 321). Considering that Galiani was talking about the costlier situation in Naples, and that the prices of foodstuffs remained substantially the same (cf. R. Romano, *Prezzi, salari e servizi,* op. cit.), the four ducats per capita in Naples correspond to three in the country.

11. G. Salvemini, "Guerra al Latifondo" and "La questione meridionale," reprinted in *Movimento socialista e questione meridionale,* ed. G. Arfè, op. cit., 71–89 and 237–39. For the distinction between poverty and wretchedness, see O. Hufton, "Life and Death Among the Very Poor," in *The Eighteenth Century: Europe in the Age of Enlightenment,* ed. A. Cobben (London, 1969), 293–310.

12. See the discussion of *inquilinaje* (corresponding to the Calabrian *provvisionati*) and peones on the nineteenth-century Chilean latifundo in A. J. Bauer, "Chilean Rural Labor in the 19th Century," *American Historical Review* 76, no. 4 (1971): 1059–84. But Franchetti, too, noted that in Calabria "few peasants live solely or almost solely on food they produce on rented land, just as only a few . . . live solely on daily wages" L. Franchetti, *Condizioni economiche ed amministrative delle province napoletane* (Florence, 1875), 78–79.

13. Padula's beautiful "L'ostracismo dei porci," originally published in *Bruzio* on May 4, 1864, was reprinted by C. Muscetta in V. Padula, *Persone in Calabria* (Rome, 1967), 45–50.

occasional goats, a ewe with lambs in the high hills, a vegetable garden with a few olive trees, and sometimes a small field, three or four tomolate held under a term or perpetual lease.[14] The women spun and wove cotton, coarse wool, flax, and broom for the family's use and rounded out its income by spinning silk and raising silkworms at home.[15] Barter was a widespread practice, both as exchange between neighbors and at the small local fairs. Access to common rights that had somehow survived the attack of privatization provided firewood and acorns and made it possible to keep some livestock. These farm laborers, then, represented a mixed figure long recognized by agricultural historians.[16] More than agro-proletarians, they were small, poor peasants who managed to provide for their own subsistence,[17] at the cost of overworking and underconsuming, but were compelled to earn wages, too, in order to meet cash expenses: rent (through this was often paid in kind), land tax, salt, and tobacco. Their wages were low, but the alternative was to earn nothing at all from the seasonal surplus resource that was their labor power.[18]

3. Hierarchies: The Caporali

Immediately after the farmhands on the "wage-earning" scale came the foremen engaged to oversee people, things, and activities. These men— provisionces whose wages were not only expressed in monetary terms but actually paid in cash—were hired by agents and administrators, and their task was to form and direct gangs of laborers. Usually the man was a resident of the town where he was to form a gang, chosen because he had direct knowledge of both the land involved and the men to be hired (often they were his relatives).[19]

---

14. Perpetual leases, the kind tenants valued the most, were by then infrequent in southern Italy, but they did survive here and there and were to gain importance after the enactment of new legislation in 1919.

15. See P. Moretti, "L'economia del matrimonio," op. cit., 12–13.

16. Gunnar Myrdal found it appearing frequently in the agrarian history of Southeast Asia (*Asian Drama,* vol. 2 [New York, 1968], 1055).

17. Perhaps they were no worse off than their ancestors under feudalism, if we are to believe Galanti's description of them in 1792: "The peasant is the lowest of the nation: he is a beast of burden who is allowed just enough to keep going: cornpone, cabbage soup seasoned with salt, bad wine" (G. M. Galanti, *Breve descrizione della città di Napoli e del suo contorno* [Naples, 1792]).

18. These are exactly the same considerations that led the Flemish peasants studied by Mendels to weave linen at home: their pay, though very low, was a necessary supplement for survival and "a vent for a surplus resource which, in Flanders, was a seasonal labor surplus" (F. Mendels, "Agriculture and Peasant Industry in 18th-Century Flanders," in *European Peasants,* ed. W. N. Parker and E. Jones, op. cit., 179–204).

19. Thus, Fortunato Stampo, head of the Sila diggers, was a native of San Giovanni in Fiore; Ignazio Staino, from Spezzano Piccolo, organized labor gangs in the Sila; Annibale Mazza, from Rocca di Neto, organized gangs of olive pickers; and Francesco Settino, overseer of workers from Isola di Capo Rizzuto, was from Isola himself. Sometimes, however, foremen recruited in the

The qualifications that the administrators were mainly looking for in a foreman were organizational capacity, honesty in handling money, and practical knowledge of the tasks to be supervised and directed. In fact, most of these men were known to the administrators for their previous work on the latifondo, often as herdsmen. For some, the job of foreman was a step up in an internal "career" ultimately crowned by the position of agent.[20] During his first year of service, a foreman had to prove he truly had the aforesaid qualifications, and in fact 26.7 percent of them failed the test (one Vincenzo Macrì, for instance, was fired because he could not put twenty-five men together for the reaping). But, as table 12 shows, those who passed became, to all intents and purposes, lifetime employees, for 20 percent of them actually continued as foremen until their deaths. This professional longevity seems quite extraordinary not only because there existed no contract binding an administrator to hire the same foreman year after year (in fact, there existed no contract binding him to do anything at all) but also because the work was seasonal. The six-to-eight-month "seasons" worked by the foremen were, in any case, longer than the jobs of individual gangs.[21] And, though the foreman was paid for a season's work, he had access to the latifondo's network of material and intangible privileges all year round; in fact, and "by right," a foreman belonged to the latifondo structure. The seasonal character of his job took nothing away from the authority of a foreman, who enjoyed a notable margin of autonomy and discretion in organizing and managing production and even in the final sale of the output. After being charged with performing a job, the foreman took care of every aspect. First he would assess the extent of the job and its costs. Then, equipped with cash provided by the administrator, he would go from town to town and to the large fairs (Santo Janni in May, Molerà in September, Decollazione in December) to recruit people for the next season, advancing them a small sum

---

mountain villages were sent to organize gangs far from home; this was the case for Francesco Ciambrone, from Magisano, who headed a gang of fence builders in Isola, and for Raffaele Antonio Cinnante, from Spezzano Piccolo, who organized hoeing on the Ionian coast. We have already discussed the correlation between employees' geographical origins and their jobs on the estate.

20. After eighteen years' service as foreman, in 1849, Raffaele Antonio Cinnante was promoted to agent at the San Pietro licorice works. Pasquale Liotta, an overseer, became the agent in Rocca di Neto in 1840. In 1874, after working thirteen years for the Barraccos, Tommaso Giacco "improved his condition by going with others to act as agent." In 1891, Antonio Milizia, thirty-two years a guard and overseer, obtained a well-paid "sinecure" as caretaker in the Croton mansion for the remaining fourteen years of his life.

21. Foremen of "winter gangs," such as those recruited for spading and hoeing, worked from October or November to April or May; "summer gang" foremen worked from April to September or October.

TABLE 12. Length of Overseers' Employment on the Barracco Latifondo

Years of Employment	Number	Percentage
1 year or less	20	26.7
2–5 years	22	29.7
6–15 years	17	22.6
16–25 years	4	5.3
over 25 years	12	16.0
Total	75	100

of money.[22] At the proper time, he would call up his people and take them to the job site where he not only directed the work but took part in it, too. He would arrange for transportation, material, repairs, and more rarely for food and wine (this was usually the administrator's task). Once the job was finished, he would pay the people and either break up the gang or take it to another job site.

Unlike their subordinates, the foremen were paid by the month. Their wages varied according to the type of gang. Those who oversaw men were paid almost twice as much as those who oversaw women and children; foremen of specialized workers earned more than foremen of plain laborers.[23] The average pay was about seven ducats a month "flat" (that is, with no other form of remuneration); extra work was paid for separately.[24] Only a very few foremen received a *minatico* of one tomolo of grain per month, and only one man, Raffaele Cinnante, a future agent, enjoyed *jussi* (a variety of rights and usages) as a foreman. These wages, like everything else on the latifondo, were subject to little change. In 1814, a head fence builder named Filippo Monaco was paid

22. Piero Bevilacqua complains that the practice of advance recruitment hindered the mobility of the workforce (*La Calabria,* op. cit.). This seems not quite convincing, for the laborers had few alternatives, and those they had involved the same kind of jobs (working for Berlingieri rather than Barracco) for the same pay. Then, too, recruitment pay was so low—from twenty grana for a child to two ducats for a man—that it could simply be returned, without penalty, if anything better (also with a salary advance) turned up. It is true that the system allowed landlords to freeze the labor market, but at the same time it permitted the peasant household to plan its cash income.

23. Overseers of women and children earned from four to six ducats a month and overseers of men from seven to nine. Mauro Scatamacchia, who brought a gang of twenty-five pruners from Apulia every year for a quarter of a century, earned fifteen ducats a month besides his traveling expenses: the same as an administrator. The foremen of gangs of licorice-root diggers and carriers earned the same pay; Gaspare Sapia, a foreman in Roccella, received an extra eight ducats a month for "keeping a horse."

24. Many men who moved from other jobs to help with the harvest were paid a lump sum of six to twelve ducats. Giovanni Romano, for one, was rewarded with a "special gift" for "the care and precision put into the sale of fruit from the Rocca groves."

25 grani a day; eighty years later, one Pietro Costabile was making one lira in
the same job; only the currency unit had changed. A man's wages changed only
if his tasks changed, that is for example, if a planting foreman became head of
the whole process of cultivating licorice root, as happened to Gaspare Sapia in
Roccella.

The system of gangs—formed in the same way, with the same number of
people, the same tasks, and the same knowledge from time immemorial—was
often criticized for its conservative immobility.[25] It had its merits, however. It
enabled the seamless, low-cost operation of a traditional type of agriculture and
the perpetuation of rural lore within a gigantic modern structure. And, in a
certain sense, the custodians of that lore were the foremen: men of the people,
peasants and faithful retainers, despite their condition as wage earners. The
same, if need be, also served as a buffer between labor and ownership that
could be useful in damping potential conflict.

4. Management Staff: Administrators, Agents, Warehousemen, and Directors

The latifondo's top management staff was not very numerous. Besides the
general manager, who resided in Croton (and later in Isola), each holding was
headed by an agent or administrator, each large commercial warehouse by a
chief warehouseman, and the industrial enterprises (licorice works, spinneries,
and silk barns) by directors who reported to the general manager. Despite their
mercenary character, the positions of the administrators were invested with
considerable powers, mainly because they represented the owner's authority
and handled thousands of ducats, a fact from which they derived also a certain
prestige. It was the administrators who made all the decisions on current
production and who paid, collected, and renegotiated leases, debts, and credits;
they were the immediate employers who hired and fired lower-ranking provisionees; they often negotiated the prices and concluded the sale of products
grown on the holdings they managed. Within the social territory they were the
ones who acted as liaisons between the owners and local government institutions, on the one hand, and between the latter and the population on the other,
providing services, granting privileges and credits, procuring permits, collecting taxes, and so forth. The warehousemen, those stationed in the port cities of
Croton and Naples, but also those in Rocca Ferdinandea and Spezzano Piccolo,
centers of local commerce for products of the Ionian coast and the Sila, handled

---

25. The system was said to perpetuate backward and "unintelligent" techniques of agronomy and to discourage innovation. Just about everyone complained about this—in the Murat
statistical compendium (see U. Caldora, *La Statistica murattiana,* op. cit.), at landowners' meetings (see J. Jacini, *Atti della Giunta,* op. cit.), and in the Economics Societies (see V. M. Greco,
Rendiconto della R. Società Economica della Provincia di Calabria Citra [Cosenza, 1864]).

the storage and sale of the latifondo's most marketable commodities, destined for export. Consequently they had access to very large amounts of money.

Who were these managers? Obviously there was a class hierarchy within the category. The top administrators who headed the most commercialized holdings were members of the local gentry, small landowners for whom a salaried job was essential (and the job of agent coveted) to both their subsistence and their class reproduction. But often enough the agents who ran holdings with only local cash circulation were men who rose to their posts on a career ladder internal to the latifondo. Biagio Biafora, for instance, had been a warehouse manager for ten years before becoming administrator of Isola di Capo Rizzuto. Raffaele Caruso had served for ten years as guard and foreman in Altilia before becoming an agent; his was a fairly typical career.[26] The warehouse managers had the same social roots as the smaller agents: men of the people but with a tradition of employment with the Barraccos (the warehouseman Gaetano Ajello, for example, was the son of the Altilia agent).

The Barraccos were fortunate in their choice of managers. The central administration was headed for almost a century by only two men, Don Giacomo Riccelli, who served from 1814 until his death in 1853, and Don Luigi Ferraro, who served from that year until 1907. Both retained full control over their business affairs until the end, and only a faltering of the writing hand betrays their age.[27] The important post of agent in Camigliati, which included the general administration of affairs in the Sila, was filled first by two generations of the Mancinis of San Giovanni in Fiore, Giuseppe and his sons Luigi and Domenico (while their uncle Felice Antonio was the agent of another holding), then by Don Tommaso Maida for more than thirty years; in 1898, when Don Tommaso, "due to his advanced age, could no longer continue to act as agent," the job was inherited by his son, Dr. Luigi (the first employee in the history of the latifondo to have a university degree in agricultural economics). Actually, lengthy service in top positions and their inheritability were the rule. Michele Cancelliere served as agent in Altilia for forty years, assisted by his son Vincenzo, heir apparent to the job; in 1861, Raffaele Antonio Cinnante left his job as manager of the San Pietro licorice works (he died after thirty-seven years of employment with the latifondo, of which twenty-two were spent as

---

26. A typical promotion was from overseer to agent. This was the case for Luigi Ranieri in Petrizia, Leonardo Rizzuto and Antonio Perrone in Rocca di Neto, and Gaetano Pizzuto in Spezzano Piccolo. Before becoming agent at the San Pietro licorice works in 1839, Raffaele Antonio Cinnante had served there for years overseeing the work of hoeing the plants and digging the roots.

27. Nevertheless, for a good part of this period the members of the family—first Barons Alfonso and Luigi, then Stanislao and Guglielmo as their elder brother Alfonso's agents after the partition of the property—continued to exercise direct control over the estate's management (see chap. 1).

agent) to his son Francesco; and Gaetano Pizzuto, the agent at Spezzano Piccolo, was succeeded by his son Giuseppe. The important post of warehouse manager in Croton was occupied by five consecutive generations of Cantafaros: Francesco, Raffaele, a second Francesco, Alfonso, and Luigi in 1900 (their given names denote their attachment to the Barracco family). Overall, 60 percent of all the managers remained in service for more than fifteen years, and in only three cases did their employment last for less than three years.

Generally speaking, the managers were paid fairly well, with salaries varying according to the importance of their jobs. Those assigned to less important posts earned from 60 to 120 ducats a year, those heading large administrations such as Isola or the Sila earned 200 to 240 ducats, and general managers up to 380.[28] One cannot say that they became wealthy. The conspicuous presence of the master (or his sons or brothers) kept them confined to a subordinate role and reduced the possibility of extra earnings; the sociopsychological phenomenon of substitution found in the large Sicilian *gabelle* was absent from Calabrian latifondism. They did, however, lead comfortable and secure lives, those on the smaller holdings living much like well-to-do peasants, those in the larger administrations like the rest of the middle class. They lived in well-built stone houses owned and maintained by the baron for this specific purpose in every seat of administration. Some had many rooms, were surrounded by orchards and vegetable gardens, and even today, in Isola or Camigliati, stand out due to their bourgeois and well-to-do aspect. Through the latifondo's usual channels, the managers bought grain, hogs, fine white wool, flax, citrus fruit, wine, as well as spirits, shotguns, and timepieces ordered from Naples and paid rent for garden plots, orchards, and pasturage (fida, giogatico, and erbaggio). Giacomo Riccelli and Tommaso Maida sent their sons to Naples University, Don Pasquale Perri sent his to the seminary, and Don Luigi Ferraro's daughter married well in the capital. Whatever their salaries, they all enjoyed access to the latifondo's guarantee structures and could expect, with age, to be granted a lifetime pension by the master or, in the event of his death, a bequest.

It was precisely the type of work they performed that determined the more monetized character of the managers' remuneration (only a few received a monthly minatico of one tomolo of grain, a liter of oil, and two heads of cheese and, despite their prominence in the world of the provisionees, ranked them on the scale of pay dependency just above the farmhands and the foremen.

---

28. Don Luigi Ferraro, in Croton, was paid 380 ducats starting in 1880. Dr. Maida, in Camigliati, was paid 1,200 lire, or 280 ducats, plus a per-diem of half a ducat. The Croton warehousemen (or, de facto, the Cantafaro family) received 180 ducats a year.

5. Farm Labor: Massari and *Acquaroli*

The only group in the farming sector that enjoyed traditional participatory treatment was the one made up of massari and waterworks men. We have already described the role of the masserie in the latifondo. Some, like the large, market-oriented masserie in the lowlands, were venues of capitalist production, characterized by high productivity and specialized in commodities destined for distant markets; here, however, there were no massari, because the organization of the enterprise was vertical, based on braccianti and run by administrators or agents. Others, however, like the Sila masserie, though situated within enclosures and provided with irrigation systems, consisted mainly of second- and third-rate cropland and were therefore rather marginal, producing commodities for local use: flax, rye, and potatoes. These Sila masserie were the ones run by massari, who had complete charge of the cropland, the adjacent grazing land, and logging in the surrounding forests (Sila pine was highly prized for ship masts and later for railway ties), and they also took part in other farm work outside their "own" masserie. Always to be found alongside the massari were the acquaroli, the men responsible for keeping up, and above all guarding, the waterworks built in the Sila's larger enclosures (Camigliati, Germano, Frassineto, Soverato, Ritani, and Tacina, significantly improved in the 1830s).[29]

The massari and the waterworks men were fixed provisionees (the former hired by the year, the latter by the month), but in reality they were a cross between sharecropping peasants and wage workers.[30] Their nominal pay was

---

29. The notorious water problem had long obsessed those who practiced agriculture in Calabria and those who observed it. Not a single work on agronomy or government investigation failed to discuss it, from the Murat statistics to the studies by the Department of Bridges, Roads, Waters, Forests, and Hunting, headed by former lieutenant Carlo Afan de Rivera. In their reports to King Murat, both Matteo Galdi, for the province of Upper Calabria, and Pietro Colletta (or the statistician Giuseppe Grio for him) ascribed enormous importance to the water system and its improvement as a way to remedy the unhealthiness of the air and end the endemic malaria as well as to benefit agriculture. In the Bourbon period, an 1839 law on land reclamation (actually implemented only in 1855) reaffirmed the government's duty to intervene in this area—a duty earlier recognized in the French laws of 1806–7, which also offered incentives to landowners in the form of loans at extremely low rates of interest. See U. Caldora, *La Statistica murattiana,* op. cit.; and C. Afan de Rivera, *Considerazioni sui mezzi da restituire il valore proprio ai doni che la natura ha largamente conceduto al Regno delle Due Sicilie* (Naples, 1833). See also R. Ciasca, *Storia delle bonifiche del Regno di Napoli* (Bari, 1928); G. Travaglini, "Il controllo delle acque e la difesa del suolo," in *La Calabria,* ed. Bevilacqua and Plancanica, op. cit., 695–718; and, for our own century, P. Bevilacqua and M. Rossi Doria, *Le bonifiche in Italia dal 1900 ad oggi* (Bari, 1984).

30. This spurious character—the peasant-wage-earner—was quite common in commercial farming in the eighteenth and nineteenth centuries, though the combinations of mandatory and contractual labor, wages, and quantity of assigned land varied according to local conditions. "In

thirty ducats a year (or around three ducats a month)—a very small amount, which, in terms of daily pay, was no more than a farmhand's wages. But what allowed a massaro to consider himself, and be considered, socially superior to a farmhand was the fact his job entitled him, as Franklin Mendels put it, to "a non-monetary dividend in the form of security and prestige," and, most important, to access land in the form of a *parasforo*.[31] This term meant the right to grow a crop (rye or flax) on a given amount of masseria land—eight tomolate for a head massaro, three (or one for flax) for an ordinary massaro or a waterworks man.[32] In addition to the land, the owner supplied the necessary draft animals and tools, while the cropper supplied all the seed and labor. The sharecropped plots were harvested at the same time as the masseria's enclosed fields, and the cropper contributed a "reapage fee" (seventy-five grani per tomolata) to the laborers' wages.

Not that they earned much in economic terms: three tomolate yielded from ten to twelve tomoli of rye,[33] of which three were deducted for seed and the rest would barely suffice for the family's daily bread (calculating the usual 500 grams a head) if the massaro did not sell it at the low postharvest price and eat chestnut-flour bread instead. Often they sold the seed as well, then had to "borrow" more from the baron at the seasonal price, which was 60 percent higher than the summer price.[34] They paid a "grass fee" for each cow or ox and an "acorn fee" for each hog they grazed on the master's land, and they bought leather, coarse wool, meat, and cheese from him.

All the above transactions were simply ledger entries, with no real circulation of money. The massari saw hardly any cash at all, just two ducats by way of recruitment pay in April or October and a balance of four or five ducats at the

---

different parts of the world, landowners have sometimes found fit to compensate labor, wholly or partially, by letting laborers have the usufruct of a small plot of land," writes M. Mörner, who studied the phenomenon in Denmark, Sweden, Norway, the Germanies, Egypt, South Africa, Ecuador, Peru, and Chile (M. Mörner, "A Comparative Study of Tenant Labor in Parts of Europe, Africa, and Latin America, 1700–1900," *Latin American Research Review* 2 [1970]: 3–15.

31. F. F. Mendels, "Agriculture and Peasant Industry," op. cit., 197.

32. We shall see later how the parasporo gradually disappeared as a mixed form of share-cropping. With the extension of grain farming during the grain boom of the 1860s, the barons little by little incorporated the paraspori in the true form of masseria, transforming the massari into simple wage earners. See E. Sereni, *Il capitalismo nelle campagne, 1860–1900* (Turin, 1975), passim.

33. These calculations, based on the ledgers of fixed laborers, agree with those of G. Porisini, in *Produttività e agricoltura,* op. cit.

34. The massari sold their crop and seed at the postharvest price of 1.10 to 1.20 ducats per tomolo but "borrowed" seed from the baron at the spring price of 1.75 to 2 ducats per tomolo. Seventy percent of all Barracco's massari had to resort to such "borrowing" sales at least once over the years, and many of them could never break out of the vicious circle.

end of the accounting year.[35] Yet some of them did manage to develop a small-scale entrepreneurship that reminds us of the old kind of massaro. Vito de Fazio, a head massaro before he became an agent, formed a small hog-fattening partnership with the master, rented a small farm in Celico from a parish priest named Jacino, and put aside the considerable sum of forty-five ducats to buy a pair of gold earrings for his wife. The great majority, however, lived like those whom Padula called the massarotti—poor people, half peasants and half wage workers.

Besides access to land, which in any case gave them social status, the greatest benefits of a massaro's job were stability and inheritability. 80 percent of the massari and waterworks men kept their posts for more than five years and almost half for more than fifteen. Many of them, in their old age, were given jobs that required less physical effort. Francesco Intrieri became a domestic servant, and in 1885 Michele Granieri was "made a shepherd on the coast due to his age," more for the gentler climate than for the ease of the task. The position was hereditary. The Cassano family of San Benedetto, for instance, passed the job of waterworks man on the Ritani and Soverato enclosures down from father to son for almost a hundred years; the first Filippo began in 1818, while the last great-grandson, Francesco, died in 1899.

The last members of this group of farm workers were the vegetable gardeners and orchard men. The former had about the same treatment as the massari, with slightly higher wages and a slightly smaller parasforo. By contrast, the orchard men belonged to the most "advanced" sector; as heads of the highly commercialized production of "Portuguese" and bergamot oranges, they were treated more as managers than as massari, with good wages but no parasforo, though at the time of sale they were entitled to keep a share of the lemons and "Portuguese" oranges at a lower price.[36]

---

35. The estate ledgers, to which the administrators posted all wages due to a worker, all advances of seed, and all sums of cash and commodities he received for "harvesting" or "for need," give an accurate picture of the composition of wages. The massari and the water linemen bought hides from the landlord, from four to ten pise of low-grade wool (thirty-five to eighty-eight pounds), cheese, ricotta cheese, pork, and sometimes a suckling pig for Carnival. For the right to graze stock in the landlord's pastures and woods, they paid a yearly fee (*fida* or *erbaggio*) of 4 to 5 ducats per head of cattle and 2.5 ducats per hog (*ghiandaggio*). In the second half of the century, when the number of water linemen had increased substantially, their parasporo was replaced by a monthly minatico consisting of a tomolo of rye, a quarter tomolo of beans, and a *litra* of oil (about 2.6 quarts), plus a *prestazione* of two pise of low-grade wool yearly.

36. Vegetable gardeners earned from forty-two to forty-eight ducats a year and had the use of one tomolata of parasforo. Orchard workers earned from six to nine ducats a month. The amounts of wine, vinegar, spirits, and "wheat" entered to their accounts in the ledgers are indicative of their higher standard of living.

6. Laborers in Livestock Partnerships: Shepherds and Goatherds

The sector on the opposite end of the wage-earning scale from the farmhands was livestock production, dominated as it was by the use of provisionees in a variety of participatory relations with the baron. The shepherds were well-known figures in the wild landscape that so fascinated nineteenth-century travelers: romantic and solitary protagonists, together with the animals, of the ceaseless and repetitive migration of huge flocks from the mountains to the lowlands and from the lowlands back to the mountains. To the reformist writers of that day, the seasonal stock drive, though part of the Calabrian landscape from time immemorial, seemed to be the epitome of sadness, fatalism, and resignation—qualities that in reality they saw in the men who accompanied the animals ("Fatalism is our shepherd's religion," wrote Padula).[37]

In fact, huge flocks predominated in stock raising. Although they all belonged to the great landowners, their management was a web of ancient covenants and the modern wage contract, the typical example being the live-stock partnership described earlier. Let us go back to that particular version of these partnerships, in which the shepherds themselves played the role of minority partners, to examine it from the workers' standpoint. As will be remembered, this type of partnership worked like all the others: the baron put in the capital (flocks and grazing land) and the minority partner the labor, with current expenses split fifty-fifty. A company of shepherds was made up of about fifteen men, each with one share in the company, headed by a *caporale,* a term whose military overtones effectively reflected the power of command these captains held over a unit of animals and men. At the beginning of the season, the first of July, the master advanced his half of the flock's expenses in an amount fixed at nine ducats per adult shepherd (somewhat less for youngsters and boys). The division of profits between the two partners took place during the two periods of product sale, at Saint Peter's Day and the end of the season in June. It could be done in two ways: either the "secondary" yield from the flock (ricotta cheese, coarse wool, and some of the yearlings) was divided into two equal shares, or the shepherds received one-tenth of the total net proceeds. In both cases, the "profit" each shepherd received was anywhere from seventeen to twenty-five ducats, depending on the year (the head shep-

---

37. He quoted a rustic proverb as an example: "Black sheep, white sheep; if you're destined to die, you die; if you're destined to live, you live" (V. Padula, "Bilfolchi, giumentieri, pastori, caprai e vaccari," in *Persone in Calabria,* op. cit., 137). On pre-Enlightenment descriptions of the nomadic Calabrian landscape, see F. Braudel, *The Mediterranean,* op. cit. For an example of the Enlightenment point of view, see G. M. Galanti, *Nuova descrizione storica e geografica delle Sicilie* (Naples, 1788). For the nineteenth century, see A. Mozzillo, *Viaggiatori stranieri nel Sud* (Milan, 1964); and M. Sciacca, *Le terre del Sud,* op. cit. The term *herdsmen* includes shepherds, goatherds, cowherds, muleteers, swineherds, and horsemen.

herd received the same share as the others).[38] As in other cases described, this money had already been spent in advance. The shepherds had to pay for the construction of fences, for the wages of their hired hands, for half of the value of the master's Christmas and Easter "gifts" to them (beans, oil, and pork), and for the lambs and kids they bought from the latifondo administration. The head shepherd also paid a grazing fee for a mule, mare, or cow kept on the baron's pasture land. For the shepherds, the major attraction of the arrangement was therefore not the tiny profit they could earn but their entitlement to a cortaglia (similar to the parasporo granted to massari), that is, tillage of a plot of manured land on one of the Sila enclosures (Carlomango, Molerotta, or Pupini). This consisted of two tomolate per man and six for the head shepherd "to be sown and harvested at the collective expense of all the shepherds, and the net yield to be divided pro-rata, [the head shepherd's share being] triple that of the others."[39]

A shepherd led a rather segregated and spartan life. However, unlike the image that the novelist Corrado Alvaro has given us of the shepherd alone on the barren uplands of the Sila, he was a member of a very close-knit group, an all-male one in an all-male cultural universe. The sons started very young, at age eight or nine, to accompany their fathers or older brothers on the seasonal stock drives and to learn the tasks of a *curatulu* and a *furisu*. In the summer, when the shepherds were up in the Sila, they could return home for a visit once every two weeks, by rotation, but in the winter, when they were down on the coast, the distance from their villages and the difficulty of travel on the muddy roads made such visits impossible, and they spent up to six months without seeing their womenfolk. Living in the company of men and animals gave rise to a whole corpus of popular raillery on the sexual pastimes of shepherds and the "caprices" of their wives—whose needs, both material and sexual, they were unable to satisfy—and on their oafishness and ignorance of social customs, but the derision was mixed with a certain envy of their independence and freedom.[40]

---

38. Though the formulation may suggest a great difference, the resulting values were comparable; the difference depended only on how the "yield from the flock" was defined. In the first case, it consisted only of the secondary products: ricotta cheese, low-grade black wool, and part of the yearlings; all the proceeds from cheese, lambs, and fine merino wool were excluded from the partnership with the shepherds. In the second case, the shepherds' tenth part was calculated on the basis of the net proceeds, namely, the earnings on all the products of the flock (except those to which the shepherds were entitled by contract), less expenses (for pails, barrels, salt, transport of the cheese and wool, and—the item most significant from all standpoints—the landowner's tenth).

39. BA: A66, sheet 1 (the hiring of head shepherd Marino Castiglione). Sometimes the administration charged the usufructors 1.36 ducats for harvesting, but more often the shepherds' companies managed their plots by themselves.

40. They were ridiculed in popular rhymes: "When the shepherd goes to Mass, he squats

Like the shepherds, the men who worked in the latifondo's goat-raising operation (much smaller than the sheep-raising sector) were at the same time the baron's minority partners and his wage-earning employees. In these partnerships, he supplied the grazing land and paid two-thirds of the expenses and all the wages; the minority partners—five or six men plus the caporale—bore the remaining third of the expenses and supplied all the labor. The proceeds from the sale of kids and females, net of a portion to which the goatherds were entitled, went to the baron, while the proceeds from skins and ricotta cheese was divided in the same proportions as the expenses: two-thirds to the baron and one-third to the minority partners. Unlike the shepherds, however, the goatherds had no access to land, and, although nominally they earned more (twenty-five ducats a year for the men, thirty to forty for the head goatherd), they were poorer than the shepherds. Their wages, like the shepherds', were often gone before they received them—spent on such items as grain, beans, cheese, and skins or deducted for the meat of dead animals (*carnaggio*).

7. Labor in Directly-Managed Livestock Operations

Only part of the Barraccos' famed cattle-raising operation was managed in partnership with other great landowners;[41] the remainder of the cattle, as well as all the oxen, horses, and mules, were managed directly by the Barracos and had been since the earliest days. The livestock organization was based on herds and stock farms that employed a large number of cowhands, oxhands, stablemen, wranglers, and muleteers. Their "contracts" differed from those of the shepherds, since the very nature of this operation (a cow being worth much more than a sheep) ruled out many types of profit-sharing arrangements, but the men's autonomy in managing the stock and their job security made these wage workers resemble the shepherds and their companies more than the farmhands.

The roaming cattle herds were tended by groups of cowhands (six or seven men and four or five boys) headed by a caporale who, as with the sheep flocks, directed the care of the stock and the production of cheese during the drives. He was the person who selected the cowhands and monthly helpers in

---

down on the floor with his nose touching his feet"; as so infrequent a worshipper, he would mistake the Communion wafer for "a piece of cheese"; and his wife, whose material and sexual needs he could not satisfy, was bound to be unfaithful ("she sends you bull's horns"). Yet his life was intriguing in a way: "The shepherd was seen at Easter, eating fresh ricotta cheese," said the town dwellers with envy, to which the shepherd would reply, "But he wasn't seen in the month of March, when he was cursing all Christ's saints."

41. The Barraccos had been lauded in the Murat statistics (see U. Caldora, *La Statistica murattiana,* op. cit., 106–7), and their cattle breeds earned prizes under the Bourbons.

September at the Molerà fair, paying two ducats to each man to secure his services for the winter season on the coast.

Oxen and cattle raising were separate operations. The oxen were grouped in "caravans" tended and managed by oxhands (or head oxhands), assisted by suboxhands. The "caravans" had to provide services and transportation for the whole latifondo. Initially there were two "caravans," one based in the Sila and the other in Polligrone, but after the property was reorganized in 1868 all the draft animals and all the hands were concentrated in a single operation, which sent out teams upon request.

The horse- and mule-raising operation was geared to two sets of needs, luxury and production. The first—requiring horses for hunting, drawing the family carriages in Naples, riding, exhibitions, and very special gifts—was met by a famed breed of fine horses, held in great account by the baron, sired by English and so-called king's breed stallions. The second—ordinary breeding, draft, transportation, mounts for agents and armed guards —was met by sturdier breed of mares and mules, prized for their strength and resistance to the harsh climate.[42] The two kinds of stock were entrusted to two distinct groups of provisionees. Stallions and brood mares were stabled during the winter and tended by trained grooms, selected with care and well remunerated, who were assisted by stableboys and, during covering and foaling, by specialists called in from the Abruzzi. Ordinary mares and colts were kept on the range and tended by wranglers who also broke them and arranged sales. The mules, grouped in "caravans" tended by muleteers, were used for transportation, travel, and the May field work. One small string was kept permanently at the Croton house for carrying goods from the warehouses to the port and the railroad; the others were on the range summer and winter. While the stablemen were chosen one by one by the head horseman, with frequent intervention by the master, the wranglers formed a partnership with the baron. The caporale was responsible for hiring "winter" and "summer" wranglers at the Molerà fair, and besides his wages he was entitled to "a part" of a mule colt (he might take one animal every other year or redeem its value in cash). Lastly, the muleteers formed fixed yearly or seasonal groups; their wages were paid partly in cash, partly in kind, and sometimes they had the use of one or two tomolate of arable land.

Finally, the Barracco latifondo had a large and important hog-raising operation, often overlooked because it was not part of the export sector and also (since "fattening a hog" had always been a standard part of the household economy) because these animals were associated with the self-sufficient economy. But hogs were frequently the object of local cash and noncash transac-

---

42. "Though raised in the marshlands, the mares hardly ever get sick," intendent Galli noted in 1812 with some surprise (U. Caldora, *La Statistica murattiana,* op. cit., 53).

tions. In the first place, large quantities of shoats were sold in February and March because, while only a few families could afford to keep a sow for breeding, many bought a shoat for fattening. In the second place, since "a suckling pig at Carnival" was the master's most frequent gift, he distributed hundreds of them. Lastly, the latifondo itself consumed a huge quantity of pork products. Part of the "hog stock" remained with the individual administrations, and another part was kept in partnership with other landowners, but the largest part was managed directly at the great sties in Altilia and Polligrone, tended by swineherds headed by a chief swineherd. The swineherds, too, are often overlooked, perhaps because their social standing was lower than that of the other provisionees.[43] Yet the "hog administration" employed from seventeen to twenty regular provisionees, whom the chief swineherd hired as usual at the Molerà fair (for the butchering and farrowing periods he hired extra monthly help). Here, too, there was a profit-sharing arrangement; besides their wages in cash and in kind, plus a "free shoat" every year, the swineherds were entitled to raise their own animals with the master's stock, paying a per-head fee (which was doubled in the case of a sow).

The last figure inseparably associated with the flocks and herds (but also with the townhouses and farmhouses, barns and pens, storage facilities and industrial buildings) was that of the armed guard. In wooded and mountainous Calabria, livestock was constantly exposed to danger; losses due to wolves, foxes, and brigands ran into the dozens in normal years and could soar when a particularly harsh winter or political unrest increased the daring of man and beast. The weapon used against these predators, but also against other people's livestock if it strayed onto the property, was the shotgun. It was an ambiguous weapon that the master assigned exclusively to his guards, keeping its ownership for himself and retaining tight control over its employment by adding his own rules to the legal restrictions. There were always plenty of guards on the payroll; they were stationed at every warehouse and mansion, with every flock and herd, on every farm and hunting preserve, at the licorice works, and in the fields. They numbered from thirty to thirty-six in "normal" times, twice as many in "hot" periods (from 1847 to 1850 the latifondo employed seventy guards, and in 1870 there were eighty). The lives of the guards followed the cycle of the activity to which they were assigned. Besides insuring security and control they participated in the work itself, especially in jobs carried out in the most intensive seasons, like haying, reaping, and oil pressing. Nonetheless, being armed with the master's guns and riding his horses, the guards were seen by the other workers as his men and accordingly distrusted.

---

43. Oddly enough, the people of Calabria, who loved pork and hogs and believed that St. Anthony Abbot had tended them, looked down on swineherds.

What was the standard of living of these people? Except for the shepherds, whose incomes varied according to the "profit" produced by their partnerships, all the other livestock workers earned fixed wages paid in cash and in kind, in varying proportions. Almost all were provisionees hired and paid on a yearly basis; the only exceptions were the oxhands and the horse and colt wranglers, also provisionees but hired for a seven-month season (from the end of April to the end of October in the Sila and from the beginning of October to the beginning of April on the coast). However, their wages, too, were fixed on a yearly basis. Of all these men, the only ones to be paid almost wholly in cash, and quite well, too, were the horsemen, who earned anywhere from 72 ducats plus a minatico of grain to 150 ducats "flat." All other wages were paid largely in kind. As we have seen, participatory benefits were quite limited. Some of the cowhands and all the oxhands and guards were given a parasporo of two or three tomolate in the Sila, planted in rye or flax; mare wranglers were entitled to "a part" of a mule colt (redeemable in cash) and "a free mare" every once in a while; and swineherds got "a free shoat" per litter (the caporale was entitled to two sows and eighteen shoats). Much more important, however, was the part of the wage paid in kind, as either a monthly minatico consisting of rye, beans, oil or lard, cheese, and sometimes wine, or a yearly "supply" of rye and coarse wool. These provisions were supplied in quantities that insured, or almost insured, subsistence. In some cases, during the winter, when provisionees had no yield from their paraspori, the master would distribute "food expense" or the corresponding amount of cash. In addition, herders had the ambiguous benefit of "carnage," namely, the meat skins and hides of animals killed in accidents, which they had to pay for but obtained at a discount. Other benefits attaching to their employment are more difficult to translate into monetary terms. Workers kept their own cattle, mules, horses, and hogs on the master's land for a small grazing fee, and swineherds could raise their own hogs along with the master's, again for a fee. Stablemen were given the family's old shoes and clothing. Only a small and fairly uniform part of their wages was expressed in cash: from twenty-four to thirty, or in some cases thirty-six, ducats a year, and somewhat more for the caporale. Like other provisionees, the men working in livestock operations actually received very little cash because their wages were often spent before they saw them on items purchased from the master: grain and millet, hides and skins "good for tanning" (that is, to make clothing), coarse and fine wool, cheese and ricotta, shoats and pork.[44]

---

44. The chief cowhand earned thirty-six ducats a year, a minatico of fifteen tomoli of rye (about 22.5 bushels), and two shoats (one for fattening, one for breeding). Ordinary cowhands earned twenty-four ducats plus two pise of wool and a monthly minatico of a liter of oil. They kept a few cows and a mule or mare on the landlord's pastures for a grazing fee and a few hogs for an "acorn fee"; often they were allowed access to fields in the enclosure, paying a "flax" or "harvesting" fee. They had to divide up the price and the meat of dead animals: the chief herdsman would

8. Longevity and Familism in Livestock Operations

We have already mentioned, apropos of the latifondo's management personnel, the professional longevity and familistic patterns that characterized some sectors of the latifondo organization. In no sector were these two features so widespread, indeed universal, as they were in grazing. In effect, the shepherds' and goatherds' companies and the groups of cowhands were so long lived that the flocks and herds to which they were assigned became known by the names of their respective chief herders, who in turn became identified with the flock or herd with which they spent their entire working lives. In fact, the ledgers speak of Lecce's, Scarola's, Bitonti's, or Bonanno's flock or herd rather than the merino flock, the coarse-wooled flock, or the cattle herd. Sixty percent of the head shepherds remained with the same flock for more than twenty years after serving as subordinates. The brothers Gaetano and Salvatore Bitonti held their posts as head shepherds for thirty-nine and forty-three years, respectively, and Francesco Bonanno held his for forty years. From 1836 to 1870 (when it was merged with the coarse-wooled flock), the goat herd was run by only two *caporali,* Giovanni Battista Alessio and Nicola Panza, who had a number of

---

take the veal, leaving the adult animals to the hands.

When they worked in the Sila mountains, oxhands were paid 2 ducats a month and were given two pise of wool a year and a parasforo of land (three tomolate for a chief herdsman and two for an ordinary hand) in one of the enclosures. During the wintering in Polligrone, wages were 30 ducats per year for the chief herdsman and 2.5 per month for hands (for seven months), with a monthly minatico of one tomolo of wheat, one of broad beans, a round of cheese, and a liter of oil. They rounded out their wages by transporting oil and licorice.

Horse herdsmen earned 72 ducats a year plus a minatico of wheat, or just 150 ducats in cash. Grooms earned 5 to 7 ducats a month, a minatico of wheat, beans, oil, cheese, and lard, plus a *cannata* of wine a day (about 2.7 pints). The experts from the Abruzzi were paid an additional fifteen grani a day (the "treatment"). Stablemen earned 3 ducats a month, boys 2 ducats.

Mare and colt herdsmen earned 2 ducats a month (for seven to nine months) plus a monthly minatico of a tomolo of beans and a cheese, as well as ten tomoli of rye and two pise of wool a year. The chief herdsman also received "a part" of the offspring (or the corresponding 25 to 27 ducats); this could, though rarely, result in his owning a mare of his own.

Muleteers were paid an average of six ducats a month, plus a minatico of wheat, beans, lard, and oil during the winter in the Marina and food expenses during the summer in the Sila, and the same ten tomoli of rye and two pise of wool a year.

Swineherds received 24 ducats a year, a monthly minatico of oil, and one shoat per year. Head swineherds received 48 ducats and two sows per year, plus eight shoats from the October litter and ten from the April litter. In addition, they received the income from the sale of their own newborn hogs to the landowner: 3.75 ducats for those born in October, 2 for those born in April.

Guards earned three ducats a month and a minatico of a tomolo of wheat, beans, and a cheese, or alternatively three ducats plus food expenses for those who moved up to the Sila in the summer and a parasporo of three tomolate of cropland. Their service during seasonal farm work was paid separately by a "gift" of six ducats for the olive harvest and as much as fourteen for the sale of oranges.

relatives working under them. Of all the head cowhands, not one had worked for less than twenty years; Antonio Librandi served for forty-eight years (twenty as caporale), Francesco Renzo ("Boscarello") for forty-one (thirty-four as caporale), and Tommaso Lamanna for thirty-six as caporale.

The fact that employment in livestock operations was dominated by families further strengthened the trend toward family specialization and job inheritability. Familial networks extended both vertically, or diachronically, creating dynasties of workers similar to the ones we have already noted among the agents and warehousemen (the reader will recall the Cantafaro dynasty of warehousemen in Croton), and horizontally, or synchronically, fostered by the operation's extensiveness. The networks were based on patronage as well as kinship, since the chief herdsmen could choose workers at their own discretion. The caporale himself, appointed by the administration, was usually chosen within the existing group, with clear priority given to the son of the dead man to be replaced. The caporale in turn hired his own sons, nephews, and brothers. Boys began at a very early age to accompany their older relatives to the pastures, initially receiving only a minatico in kind; later they were promoted to monthly workers and ultimately to full membership in the company. At least 30 percent of the men in each of the shepherds' companies, in fact, were members of the same family—at one time Salvatore Bitonti's flock had six other Bitontis working with it—and 85 percent were from the same town. For example the management of the hog administration was monopolized for a hundred years by one family, the Ciampàs of Caccuri.[45]

In the second half of the century, many of these characteristics underwent fairly radical changes, which gradually reduced the forms of partnership, limited the shepherds' decision-making authority, and accentuated the trend toward specialized production. The Barraccos began to transform their livestock operations as early as the late 1840s for reasons to be discussed later. The partnerships with the shepherds were terminated between 1846 and 1851, and those with other landowners (the Morelli, the Macrys, and De Lucro) in 1853. In 1849, a single "hog administration" was created; in the 1860s, the cattle

---

45. Ignazio Scarola served as chief shepherd of the Marina flock from 1815 to 1833 (in the same years, his nephew Tommaso Corigliano had the same job with the Carlomango flock). After that date, the job passed through three generations of the Bitonti family: Salvatore (1833–58), his sons Antonio (1858–64) and Rosario (1864–76), and Rosario's son Salvatore (1876–1902). Gennaro Lecce ran the Campolongo flock for twenty years. Then in 1835 it, too, came into the hands of the Bitonti family, with the job of chief shepherd passing from Salvatore's brother Gaetano (1835–56) to Gaetano's son Giovanni (1856–73), then to his grandson Antonio (1873–87). In 1887, it went to another Gennaro Lecce, great-grandson of the first.

Aniceto Ciampà of Caccuri joined the latifondo as a swineherd in 1813, bringing his son Giuseppe with him. Giuseppe became chief swineherd in 1839 and head of the sole hog-raising administration in 1849. He served in this position until his death in 1870, after which it went to his son Vincenzo and in 1892 to Vincenzo's son Giuseppe.

herds were joined in a single unit; in 1870, the goat herd was merged with the flock of coarse-wooled sheep; and in the 1880s, all the sheep were brought together in two huge flocks.

Termination of the partnerships resulted in the disappearance of participatory arrangements and the herdsmen's transition to wage work. The shepherds became fixed provisionees; commodity supplies and cortaglia became less important now that only a few men were entitled to them, and they vanished altogether in the last five years of the century. The parasfori granted to guards and oxhands were also eliminated. With the concentration of livestock operations, however, larger numbers of herdsmen were needed for each unit (the flocks were now tended by eighteen to twenty shepherds and seven or eight monthly hands, the cattle herds by thirty regular cowhands and seven to nine monthly hands), thereby altering and broadening the functions of the caporali. The men who headed the new flocks now had to pay the shepherds' wages, keep the accounts of their operations, handle expenditures, and distribute the portion of the products to which the shepherds were traditionally entitled (a so-called basket that included ricotta and sheep's-milk cheese, rye, leather, and pork). The man who headed the cattle herd was now responsible for managing several thousand bulls, cows, steers, heifers, and calves, for overseeing the production of cheese, meat, and leather, for local sales of sick and dead animals, and for shipping livestock and products destined for distant markets overland to Croton (and later by rail or sea directly to Naples or Rome). These new tasks and the stronger market orientation of the livestock operations required the caporali to possess additional qualifications; in fact, the younger generation knew how to read and write, keep accounts, and use the telegraph.

A further consequence of the monetization of relations of production and the disappearance of participatory arrangements, and of the broader responsibilities assigned to the caporali was a general growth in monetary wages. By the end of the century, sheep and cattle drivers were earning from 120 to 144 ducats a year with no other benefits, simple shepherds from 48 to 60 ducats plus the traditional "basket" of products, oxhands 72 ducats, and muleteers and guards 9 or 10 ducats a month "flat." In other words, the minatico, too, had been eliminated.

These transformations—the disappearance of participatory arrangements and assignments of land and the gradual disappearance of payments in kind—were all furthering the monetarization of relations of production. By the end of the century, the process had been completed with the attainment of a purely monetary wage. These transformations went hand in hand with the concentration of operations, the increase in the workforce assigned to each flock or herd, and the faster pace of labor turnover and dismissals for disciplinary reasons. In short, these are the characteristics of a process of capitalist transformation, to which we shall return later.

9. Domestic Workers

A large part of the enterprise's accounting records was devoted to the highly variegated world of domestic workers (where women appear once again). This is hardly surprising. For one thing, the line dividing the latifondo's requirements as a productive enterprise from the owners' private needs was both fuzzy and flexible, for another, the concept of the domestic was by no means well defined. Everything that had to do with houses, stables and kitchens, journeys and rounds, hunting and amusement was posted in the latifondo accounts. In consequence, most of the staff—stewards, personal servants, laundresses and ironers, cooks and scullions, doorkeepers and gatekeepers, household guards, coachmen and outriders, gardeners and caretakers, gamekeepers and houndkeepers—were provisionees of the latifondo. Only the ones who were physically closest to the masters—the valets and the personal maids, the ladies' gentlewomen and the girls' handmaidens—were provided for out of personal funds.

A special place among all this staff was occupied by armed men, who included not only the household guards, *armigeri,* but also the coachmen and the gamekeepers, the caretakers and the gatekeepers. Obviously these were not the only men who bore arms on latifondo territory with the master's blessing— there were also agents, administrators, warehousemen, surveyors and their assistants, and curates on their rounds—but they were the ones whose weapons were used directly for the master's protection. They could be distinguished at a glance from the range guards and watchmen because of the fine-quality rifles and double-barreled shotguns they carried on their shoulders—weapons they owned but had bought in Naples through the latifondo administration, which paid for repairs and procured firearm permits.[46] Living in the master's houses and accompanying the family on its travels, these men, particularly the household guards, were to its members what the range guards and watchmen were to its property: a small army that insured security and protection. No journey was undertaken in Calabria without such an escort.[47] The Barraccos, like other great landowners, always employed a fair number: at least four "mobile men" (attached to the masters wherever they went), who became six or seven in uneasy times, plus the same number of "set men" stationed permanently in the palaces of Croton, Isola, and Naples. The occupation of private policeman was

---

46. The shotgun was an expensive "tool of the trade." In 1871 Michele Pizzuto and the brothers Antonio and Giovanni Biafora paid seventy ducats apiece for theirs. A double-barreled shotgun never cost less than twenty-two ducats.

47. Tales of the dangers of traveling in Calabria abound to the point of monotony. In 1900, the mayor of Cortale recalled that during his childhood any trip, even just to Catanzaro, had to be kept secret: "Armed guards, a necessary escort of the faithful, would be called out at midnight. . . ." (see S. Romano, *Histoire de l'Italie du Risorgimento à nos jours* [Paris, 1977], 41–42).

one of great trust and, besides loyalty, required certain physical characteristics. Consequently, it was not a family trade in the sense we have described for other provisionees. A "family of household guards" like the Biaforas, with the father Matteo in the Sila and the sons Antonio and Giovanni in Naples and Croton, respectively, was something of an exception. As a rule, the men were chosen from among employees who had given some proof of loyalty: range guards or foremen with several years of service. Chosen preferably from families already linked to the Barraccos by a tradition of working ties, in the last analysis, these men, too—sons of range guards or brothers of shepherds—belonged to the horizontal and vertical family networks that constituted the linchpin of "fidelity."[48] They, too, remained in service for decades on end, and when age lessened their efficiency they became doorkeepers in the master's palaces and houses.

Other armed domestics included the coachmen—all Neapolitans who traveled to Calabria with the masters for the summer season (part of their salaries was paid monthly to their wives or mothers in Naples); the outriders who accompanied the master's horse or carriage; the gamekeepers who looked after the hunting preserves in Soverato, Ritani, Altilia, and Infantino and organized frequent shoots for the masters and their guests; and the houndkeepers.[49] Lastly, there were caretakers and doorkeepers guarding the master's palaces during his absence; these men were less close to the baron's family than were the household guards because, although they lived in the palace during those spells, sometimes for eight months on end (from September or October to May or June), they moved out upon the master's arrival.

Armed domestics were paid rather well: from the caretakers' seven or eight ducats monthly to the gamekeepers' ten or twelve. The guards were also entitled to a parasforo of three or four tomolate of land planted in flax and a minatico of chickpeas, vetch, and millet.[50] When away from home (often for six months or a year at a time), they received an extra seven ducats "for living expenses" besides their travel expenses; those who did not live in the palace were given another twelve or eighteen ducats "for rental of the summer dwelling." Their standard of living was thus rather high for the social class to which

---

48. The father of household guard Michele Pizzuto had worked as a Barracco guard for forty years, and his brother had the same kind of job; Pasquale Ceraso was the son of a shepherd who had served 25 years; and Domenico Intrieri had four brothers who were permanent laborers on the estate.

49. "The lack of other pastimes in almost all the towns of the province, and the implacable idleness of the lives of the wealthy in those parts, make them resort eagerly to the hunt," wrote Intendent Michele Galdi in 1812 (U. Caldora, *La Statistica murattiana,* op. cit., 49). Beaters for the boar hunt were hired by the gamekeepers, who personally paid out the wages for this and similar kinds of day labor.

50. After 1844 and the disappearance of parasporo, armed guards earned 96 to 108 ducats a year, with an additional 7 ducats a month for traveling and living expenses.

they belonged. For a good part of the year they lived in the palaces (enjoying access to the master's pantry), their salaries were paid almost entirely in cash, and they made only occasional purchases of a little wool, wine, and weapons. Proximity to the master's person procured them various gifts: clothing, shoes, and other signs of appreciation. The gamekeepers and houndkeepers, for instance, received tips of as much as sixteen ducats apiece on the occasion of a special hunt (during the king's visit or the prefects' tours). The baron's nearness created an interdependence between master and servant that could become intimacy. *Armigero* Giovambattista Laratta looked after the old baron Alfonso, confined indoors "due to his great age," for five years; Pasquale Ceraso—prototype of the character described by Tomasi di Lampedusa—was a "friend" to the baron whose hounds he trained for twenty-five years; and Filippo Caputo always accompanied the younger members of the family on hunts.

The domestic staff proper was extremely numerous; the houses and palaces literally swarmed with servants whose comings and goings made these places resemble a town square. They were all salaried provisionees but organized in a rigid hierarchy at the top of which stood the majordomos and the personal attendants, whose work required a certain savoir faire beyond the grasp of country folk. In fact, the people recruited for these jobs were sons and daughters of the small local nobility; they were trained in the master's houses and often stayed for their whole lives. Next came the palace servants, frequently in direct contact with the masters, followed by the "rural" servants stationed in country houses rarely visited by the family, and lastly a multitude of menials and chore boys brought up and trained in the houses, often themselves children of servants. Here we find women en masse: maids taking care of the palace linen, laundresses, ironers, the young ladies' servants (not their personal maids), other women serving the stewards, the valets, and the personal maids, and maids-of-all-work. And all around them was an array of widows forced by indigence to "work off" the aid they received from the Barraccos.[51]

The kitchens in the Croton, Caccuri, Isola, and Altilia palaces were a world unto themselves. The chefs were all from Naples (except for one from Catania) and usually moved to Calabria only for the "master's season," leaving

---

51. Some were gentlewomen, like Donna Gabriella Lancellotti. As a widow with a small child, she received "three measures of flour every month, and one and a half tomoli of legumes and three *litre* of oil at Christmas" for supervising the ironing and doing other small tasks for the baroness before her son, Don Giovannino, was hired as a secretary-companion for the young Barraccos. Caterina Scino, widow of Luigi Guarascio, a guard, "worked off" the debt her husband had left her. Caterina Castagnino-Minelli helped out with the household tasks in exchange for "a monthly allowance of six ducats . . . so you can pay for a place in the school where your son Vincenzo studies."

their families behind. The bread and pastry makers, skilled workers under the direct supervision of the stewards, were almost always from Cosenza or—by an odd coincidence—Brescia. The undercooks and scullions were local boys who never remained in these jobs for more than a few years.

Almost all the domestics were fixed provisionees who generally remained "with the family" for decades, many until their deaths. Their salaries, though highly differentiated in amount, were all made up in the same way: part in cash and part in a "treatment": room and board in the master's house or the equivalent in cash when the family was away. The stewards, personal servants, and chefs earned nine or ten ducats a month plus the "treatment" ("staying in the house . . . in the family's absence . . . [one received] a further six ducats per month for living expenses"); as of 1864, their salaries rose to fifteen or eighteen ducats monthly "flat." All these people were paid in cash, with deductions for clothing, boots, cigars, and coffee ordered from Naples through the administration, in the case of the cooks a portion (30 to 60 percent) was paid directly to their families. Palace domestics earned seven or eight (later ten) ducats, and undercooks and lower-ranking servants four or five ducats clear, with the administrator supplying them with clothing and shoes. Rural domestics had the same treatment but also the advantage of being able to keep their own mules and hogs in the master's barns, rounding out their salaries by rendering services with a mule team, selling shoats, or helping in the farm work.

Many of these were actually lifetime salaries because it was the custom among patrician families to grant elderly servants pensions in the amount of their previous salaries provided they remained in the house. As a rule, old retainers were mentioned in the family wills and sometimes the bequests were quite substantial.

On average, women were paid half as much as men. In Naples as well as Croton, Altilia, and Caccuri, they earned, with few exceptions, 2 ducats per month, with never a raise, plus another 2 ducats per month during the family's absence, as an equivalent to the "treatment." These extremely low salaries were paid mainly in cash, with rare deductions for purchases of cloth, wool, or a shoat. On the occasion of a maid's wedding or her child's baptism, it was customary for the young ladies of the house to make her a gift of ten pise of wool. Scullions were given 3 ducats per month plus the "treatment," which in the 1880s became 5.5 ducats "flat." All kitchen staff were dressed and shod at the administrator's direction (but at their own expense).

10. "Intellectual" Labor

This picture of the world of the latifondo's workers would not be complete without the clergymen, secretaries, surveyors, appraisers, lawyers, notaries, and physicians. Some of these were regular employees (registered in the lists of provisionees); others provided services that were in constant demand.

The job of a secretary, which made one a "don," was not overly toilsome, was well paid (around twenty ducats per month), conferred a certain prestige, and entitled one to the use of a vehicle, an old-age pension, and the certainty that after his death "care and friendship" would be shown to his widow, children, and grandchildren. In fact, this position was highly coveted by the members of the local bourgeoisie and was characterized by both professional longevity and familism. For instance, Don Carlo Maida, brother of the Camigliati administrator, served as secretary for thirty years, until 1884, notwithstanding that he had been receiving a pension equivalent to his salary since 1879; Don Giovanni Gianfreda "died in service" after twenty years of seniority, "bequeathing" his post to his nephew, Francesco Pellicori.

That clergymen should appear on the latifondo's payroll may seem surprising, for they had their ordinary prebends to live on. The Barraccos paid them in the following way: an annual stipend of 80 to 90 ducats for officiating at daily and Sunday mass in the family's private chapels (on the Belladonna holding, in San Marco, on the former Caccuri fief, and in San Pietro), 50 ducats a year for *misse legate* or masses by bequest, and a further stipend of 150 ducats if they were engaged in educating the family's male offspring. Like other middle-class employees, the clergy were paid in cash (Don Antonio Monaco was the only one to have a parasporo of three tomolate in the Sila) and took advantage of the administration to invest their savings and make purchases: from wine to a subscription to the magazine *Civiltà Cattolica,* and from hogs to silverware.[52] As part of the family entourage, the clergymen benefitted from the exchange network of gifts, from chocolate to horses, and often received bequests from family members. Baron Luigi erected a statue costing 130 ducats on the tomb of Don Tommaso De Martino, the family priest for twenty-eight years, and left 2,000 ducats to Don Costantino Lopez provided that he would "continue the education of his grandson Luigi."

Professionals who were not in the Barraccos' sole employ but whose services were frequently requested were entered in the lists of provisionees. Veterinarians had a small regular monthly stipend of ten ducats, plus fees and transportation for services as needed. Surveyors and land appraisers, who worked from 120 to 150 days a year producing reports submitted in the encroachment trials and measuring leased plots, were paid from one to two ducats a day (depending on who provided transportation) plus a small monthly sti-

---

52. Don Costantino Lopez, for example, had the administration invest 5,000 ducats for him in government bonds, buy silverware in Naples, and take out magazine subscriptions. Don Francesco Saverio Tambieri, a numismatist, had collector's items sent to him from Naples through the administration.

pend. Lawyers and notaries, whose services were needed practically without
pause for reports, statements, briefs, bills of sale, and other contracts, were
remunerated with varying fees and stipends. The usual fee was five ducats a
day plus transportation, stationery articles, and a sort of "corruption fund"—
cash on hand to grease the palms of court officers and judges—though Angelo
Forlani, a family lawyer from 1812 to 1844, earned a straight thirty ducats a
year plus a "fee for his labors," while another lawyer, Don Vincenzo Biondi,
earned five hundred. The regular availability of physicians and pharmacists
was assured with yearly gifts of fattened hogs and privileged access to the
latifondo's internal market, while their services were paid for as needed.[53]
Lastly, the Croton telegraph operator, Don Bruno Ferrante, was paid only for
his telegraph services, as one would expect, but his assistent Gianmaria, based
in Isola, was on the roll for a yearly gift of hogs and wool worth twenty ducats.

11. Craftsmen

Finally, within and around the latifondo worked a whole bevy of master craftsmen. Though listed in the ledgers of provisionees, they were not employees of
the Barraccos but worked on their own account in the adjacent towns or "on the
road," or they arrived "on call" from the cities, sometimes a considerable
distance away. An enterprise the size of the Barracco latifondo needed their
services continuously. Master blacksmiths and their "fellows" supplied dozens
of tons of iron and steel to the palaces, farms, and stables, making and repairing
plows, presses, hoes, and other farm tools, house and field gates, harness shafts,
pipe fittings, barrel hoops, and plowshares, not to mention shoeing the horses
and mules. Tinsmiths supplied copper and tin plate, built and repaired boilers,
and supplied various implements to the palaces, farms, licorice works, and silk
barns. Woodwrights supplied and worked wood, fabricating dozens of plow
shafts every year, constructing carts, heavy wagons, and harness shafts, and
building and repairing woodwork in the houses, including the palace in Naples.
For structural work, the master carpenters often brought along gangs of masons
who traveled as needed from Isola to Croton, from San Leonardo to Camigliati,
and so forth. Housepainters, always from Cosenza and considered socially
superior to other craftsmen (their names were preceded by a "Don"), came with
their apprentices to paint or repaint the house walls, doors, and windows (in
anticipation of the king's visit in 1833 all the palaces in Caccuri, Isola, Altilia,
Croton, and Camigliati were repainted) and to wallpaper the interiors. Master
plasterers resurfaced the palace walls and repaired the indoor decor. Master

---

53. For instance, in 1870, the Croton pharmacist Don Giuseppe De Majo bought thirty-two
below-standard mares for only 2,000 ducats; on the market, they would have cost him 3,200
ducats.

stonemasons, whose services for nineteenth-century Calabrian buildings were in more frequent demand than those of bricklayers, laid foundations for houses, presses, sewers, and wells, and even for steam-driven machinery; they supplied and installed mill wheels, including the steam-driven mill wheels at the licorice works. Charcoal makers prepared and delivered charcoal. The latifondo's livestock operations required the services of tanners to cure goatskins, pigskins, and cowhides, and of saddlers and harness makers to make saddles, bridles, and halters, reins and traces, collars and girths, cruppers and breechings. Then there was an array of more adventitious craftspeople—tailors, seamstresses, shoemakers, clock makers, tinkers, linen embroiderers (this work was normally done by the girls in the orphan asylum "patronized" by the Barraccos)—and suppliers of a host of other services, from snow dealers (much on the scene between October and May) to itinerant master craftsmen.

Seen from the standpoint of its long-standing and organic relationship with the latifondo structure, the world of the craftsmen may appear overly homogeneous, but in actuality it was highly variegated. Some worked by themselves, others in small groups of no more than four, some with fellow craftsmen, others with apprentices, many in family groups.[54] Almost all the master craftsmen came from cities or fairly large towns with artisan traditions. Some of these, like Croton, Spezzano Grande, San Giovanni in Fiore, and Aprigliano, were situated in the latifondo's social territory, or nearby, but others lay at some distance. Giannantonio Barilaro, for instance, an iron worker and master blacksmith who served the Isola, Petrizia, and Polligrone farms for twenty-five years, lived in Serra San Bruno, seventy kilometers south of Catanzaro. The tinsmiths were traditionally all from Lauria, a city in the northern tip of the province of Cosenza; all the painters and one cabinetmaker were from Cosenza; and many of the tanners and master saddlers came from Acri, a town known for this craft tradition, located in the Greek Sila but on the far side of the mountains.

In the work relations between these independent craftsmen and the latifondo, we find the same characteristics of longevity and familism already noted in connection with the fixed provisionees. And, since in both cases these features can be ascribed to the artisan tradition (in which trades and clients are hereditary) not to baronial paternalism, the ledgers were not mistaken in treating these craftsmen in the same way as they did the provisionees because those

---

54. Master carpenter Pietro Lupia of Spezzano Grande had three other master carpenters working for him; carpenter Filippo Calvello worked with his partner Francesco Marrazzo and son Franco; mason Rosario Scalise's gang included three other partners; the painter Don Romeo Bevacqua had an apprentice; master saddler Tommaso Fragasso worked with an apprentice, a partner, and two sons; stonecutters always worked as families (such as the Calabrese brothers of Taverna and the Costanza brothers of Rogliano); and snow suppliers worked in partnerships of two or three.

features generated the same kind of behavior in both groups. We find the same master blacksmiths, tinsmiths, carpenters, harness makers, and saddlers at work for decades on end (one master craftsman, Faragasso, "saw to saddles and other objects" in Camigliati for fifty-two years), and after their death we find their sons.[55] The craftsmen, like the provisionees, were often paid in kind. Some got wheat, barley, flour, or bread, others got flax, wool, or hides, and still others got cheese, salt, oil, beans, potatoes, or pork. Some grazed cows in the Barraccos' pastures. All these items were posted against "job notes." In short, the craftsmen received little cash and owed large debts to the latifondo.

Their pay varied in both form and amount. Most (blacksmiths, tinsmiths, and woodwrights) were paid against "notes" stating the price of materials plus the agreed price of the job; others (masons, painters, and saddlers) were paid by the day, plus travel expenses if appropriate. Tanners, stonemasons, and farriers were paid by the piece (hide, millstone, well, or horseshoe) and masons often by the month.[56] How much they actually earned is not easy to establish. The yearly income of a master blacksmith or woodwright, for example, averaged from 200 to 250 ducats, and sometimes reached 600, including the price of materials, but how much of this went for expenses? Master craftsmen paid by the day earned forty grani, with travel and inn expenses paid; "fellows" earned only ten, except for saddlers and painters, who were paid better.[57]

Lastly, the provisionees' ledgers list a few owners of small boats, which the latifondo thereby insured would be available, as needed, in addition to its own vessels and to supplement the brigantines it hired for shipments to Naples. Besides the usual hire per voyage, these boat owners received a small monthly stipend of three or four ducats, which kept them and their crews available eight months out of the year.

Such was the world of the latifondo workforce, made up entirely of wage earners except for the traditional craftsmen and professionals. But what was the meaning of this generalized conversion to wages?

In his analysis of latifondism at the end of the last century, Karl Kautsky assumed that the general use of wage labor was one of the *preconditions* that

---

55. Master blacksmith Rosario Laratta was succeeded by his son Rosario, Jr., tinsmith Gioambattista Rossi by his nephew Nicola Capelluccio, and carpenter Filippo Calvello by his son Franco and eventually his grandson Filippo.

56. Iron cost ten grani per *libbra* (fourteen grani/lb.) or four ducats per cantajo and hardware about sixteen grani per rotolo (eight grani/lb.). Paint and wallpaper were bought from druggists. Leather for saddles and harnesses was produced on the estate; the administrators had the hides tanned before engaging saddlers and harnessmakers.

57. It cost sixty grani to fit a horse with a new shoe and ten to fix an old shoe. Timber cost an average of ten grani per cantajo, while planks and beams were bought by the *palmo*. A tanned saddler's hide cost from sixty to seventy-five grani. A simple millstone cost three ducats, a steam millstone up to twenty-six. A steam-engine sump cost seventy ducats. A rotolo of snow (about two pounds) cost four grani (two hundred ducats' worth was bought a year!).

made the modern latifondo a capitalist enterprise.[58] But it seems more accurate to speak, as Eric Hobsbawm does in reference to the industrial labor in the nineteenth century, of two stages in the conversion to wages. The first, lasting until around 1880, was dedicated to partially learning the ground rules. The workers did learn to think of labor as a commodity, but they still established its price, quantity, and quality according to noneconomic criteria whenever they could.[59] The latifondo system was a structure typical of this phase. The generalized use of wage labor undoubtedly constituted a fundamental difference between the latifondo and preexisting agricultural structures,[60] but the wage per se seemed not so much the homogeneous and anonymous equivalent of working time or ability as it was a new way of expressing ancient relations that had been neither homogeneous nor anonymous. In short, however modern the nineteenth-century latifondo may have been, it was not a factory.[61] The generalized wage condition was not the outcome of a supposed proletarianization of the countryside; to the contrary, in the short term it actually seemed a way to prevent or slow that process. The only people who were paid by time and in cash, had an anonymous relationship with the master, and were excluded from the paternalistic network were the farmhands—the very same people who, not coincidentally, did not depend on their wages for either subsistence or social status. By contrast, the provisionees, whose survival did depend on their earnings and whose social status was determined by their employment on the latifondo, were in a rather "imperfect" wage condition. Part of their "wage" actually consisted, in fact, of the shared profits of their "companies" while another part was made up of goods and services. Their relations with the master were characterized by a high degree of intimacy, longevity, and loyalty; and their remuneration took account of personal differences and needs. By an apparent paradox, the farmhands—in their own and their beholders' eyes the most "proletarianized" workers of all—were by no means proletarians,

---

58. The second precondition, according to Kautsky, was the commercialization of the estate's products. To these, in the modern era, were added the centralization of production and management, the division of labor, and cooperation among the various units of the latifundium. See K. Kautsky, *The Agrarian Question,* op. cit., 95–132; J. Banaji, "Summary of Selected Parts," op. cit., 30–33; and M. Petrusewicz, "Wage-Earners but Not Proletarians," op. cit., 471–72.

59. E. Hobsbawm, "Customs, Wages and Work-Load," in *Laboring Men* (New York, 1967), 405–35. M. Rossi Doria uses the same time frame for the agrarian transformation in *L'evoluzione delle campagne,* op. cit., 16.

60. Some of the conditions on the Calabrian latifondo were different from those Kautsky described, especially the degree of mechanization and the intervention of credit institutions. See K. Kautsky, *The Agrarian Question,* op. cit.

61. It is becoming evident, from numerous recent studies on various forms of industrial paternalism, that even the employees of the nineteenth-century factories were not quite as anonymous and interchangeable as they were assumed to be in discussions of the "industrial army." See P. Joyce, "The Factory Politics of Lancashire in the Later Nineteenth Century," *Historical Journal* 18, no. 3 (1975): 525–53; and E. Hobsbawm, *Laboring Men,* op. cit., 407–9.

whereas the provisionees—protected, profit sharers, and peasants (albeit wage earners)—were objectively in the conditions of proletarians.

In reality, on the nineteenth-century latifondo wages were neither the measure of things nor the determining factor in social status. Subjectively and socially, the "imperfections" of the wage condition counted more than the wage itself, for they were what guaranteed the survival of the whole family and enabled the "wage earner" to retain control over his physical and cultural reproduction. It was precisely the imperfect configuration of its relations of production that enabled the latifondo enterprise, with its social organization, to form a *latifondo system.*

CHAPTER 6

The Guarantee System and the System's Guarantees

1. Reciprocity: Cornerstone of the System

The workability of the latifondo system depended primarily on the masters' and workers' recognition of reciprocity in their relations. From the owners' standpoint, reciprocity was a matter of duties; it was the provisionees's duty to work well, respect the owners, and be disciplined, obedient, and loyal; it was the master's duty to treat them well and protect them. From the provisionees' standpoint, it was perhaps more a reciprocity of rights: the master was entitled to loyalty, gratitude, and good service, but the provisionees were entitled to help, gifts, job security, and consideration of their family needs. A master who offered good terms and kindness could legitimately expect to be repaid with loyal and honest service. Although the entire latifondo economy was based on the wage relation, the underlying system of social guarantees was thus one of expectations and duties wherein needs and acquired rights were recognized. This system had little in common with the mercantile concept of exchange between equal values but much in common with the peasant's view of exchange. It had benefits for both sides: the latifondista could take advantage of the opportunities afforded by the nineteenth-century development of capitalism without having to pay the full price in terms of surveillance, punishment and wages; the provisionees could still be peasants, at least in part, with all that meant in terms of control over their own lives. These converging interests in preserving the peasants' status and mentality resulted in a reconciliation, embodied in the system of social guarantees, between the apparently contradictory aspirations of the latifondo, as a commercial enterprise, and of its social territory, which tended toward self-sufficiency, conferring on the latifondo system its peculiarly nonbourgeois character.

It should be clear that we are talking here about a "tacit dimension"; the guarantee system was the outcome not of any plan conceived by the latifondista or the workers but of a whole history of tinkering with tradition, of establishing certain practices as "rights," of a never explicitly articulated balancing of mutual benefits.[1] To achieve what we might call a balancing total in the calculation of mutual benefits, there had to be agreement on the legitimacy of the needs and expectations of both sides; in other words, each side had to recognize the fears and priorities the other felt to be essential. What wage-earning peasants feared most was proletarianization: severance from the land and from the ensemble of their traditional knowledge. In a sense, they feared it even more than plague or famine,[2] for these disasters had a collective and inexorable character, while proletarianization was equivalent to individual loss of control over one's life. For a variety of reasons, however, the latifondo had no interest in proletarianizing its workforce. In the first place, it would have deprived the latifondo of the basic element in its economic rationale, that is, the "unlimited" supply of cheap labor.[3] In fact, a worker whose subsistence depended entirely or mainly on his wages would no longer be willing to accept less than subsistence pay. In addition, a peasant freed from his tie to the land would have been likely both to seek better-paying work elsewhere and to demand higher wages. Third, he would have become a potential subversive, inclined to demand and rebel,[4] forcing the ownership to set up costly policelike controls, to deal with potentially bloody conflicts, or at least to bargain with the workers. Lastly, a peasant who became an agrarian proletarian would rightly have had no interest and taken no satisfaction in working the master's property diligently. The danger here was not necessarily sabotage (though that was a

---

1. The difference between the "guarantee" system and the paternalistic system is discussed in the introduction. See also E. Genovese's now-classic definition of paternalism in his *Roll, Jordan, Roll* (New York, 1974); and the onging debate in the journal *Slavery and Abolition* (starting in 1980).

2. Precapitalist society had very few means of coping with collective disasters such as epidemics and famine. At the same time, the very sense of inevitability of these catastrophes and their collective, nondiscriminatory nature made them in a way more human and more bearable. Proletarization led to the individualization of risk and solitude vis-à-vis market forces, that is, hunger became an *individual* risk and experience. K. Polanyi stresses the difference in the social perception of threats to survival: "It is the absence of the threat of individual starvation which makes primitive society in a way more human than the market economy, and at the same time less economic" (*The Great Transformation,* op. cit., 164).

3. A. Lewis's concept of an "unlimited supply of labor" ("Economic Development with Unlimited Supplies of Labour," *Manchester School* [May 1954]: 139–91) may be used here if we bear in mind the significant absence of personal types of bonds, of serfdom, in the southern agrarian system and the equally significant presence of cities and towns offering alternative work opportunities. See M. Aymard, "Amministrazione feudale e trasformazioni strutturali tra '500 e '700," *Archivio Storico per la Sicilia Orientale* 71, no. 1 (1975), 17–42; and J. Kochanowicz, "Historia wsi włoskiego południa," *Przegląd Historyczny* 75, no. 1 (1984): 119–25.

4. "The peasant who becomes a city dweller" (that is, one who loses his peasant characteristics) "immediately becomes a proletarian who is not yet, but can be, organized," wrote A. Gramsci (*La questione meridionale* [Rome, 1966]).

possibility) but rather a daily resistance to wage work, consisting at least of the failure to apply one's knowledge—what the masters rightly called negligence. Had this become systematic recalcitrance, it would have forced the master to create an extensive and costly system of expert overseers charged with defining individual tasks and continuously checking their execution.

An evolution of this kind was anything but impossible or impractical; indeed, it had occurred on the great German estates and South American plantations,[5] and later it occurred in Calabria itself. Hic et nunc, however, such an upending of the latifondo's very rationale would have appeared costly and pointless since the system worked quite well as it was.

Hence, there was a converging interest of master and workers in preserving the latter from a proletarian fate. At stake was not wage work per se but wage work without proletarianization. For a wage worker to remain a peasant, three conditions had to be satisifed: he had to retain some access to land; he had to keep some control over the production process, in the sense of being able to apply his traditional knowledge; and this knowledge, not money, had to remain the source of his authority within his family and his social environment. These three conditions had much more weight than ownership of the means or tools of production in creating a sense of psychological and economic security, which in a peasant family counted more than overfatigue and a purely cash income. The nineteenth-century latifondo succeeded in providing that sense of security through a web of protective mechanisms, noncash rewards, illusions of continuity, and the personalization of objectified relations—in short, through the guarantee system.

2. Expropriation sans Expropriation: Access to Land

The Barraccos favored the provisionees' access to land. On first sight this would appear in stark contrast with that ferocious process of land privatization and expropriation of the rural population, described in chapter 2, of which the Barraccos had been among the chief protagonists. Large-scale expropriation had indeed occurred, but peasant access to land had been reorganized during the process, creating the illusion of an expropriation without expropriation. Let us explain.

The French laws, like the timid reforms of the government of united Italy, were intended to foster peasant smallholding: a design stemming from the lawmakers' vaguely physiocratic views, and which they thought reflected the age-old aspirations of the peasant masses. In reality, the peasants aspired not so much to legal *ownership* of land as to its free and hereditary *use*. It was not because they rejected the concept of ownership—to the contrary, they had

---

5. K. Kautsky, *The Agrarian Question,* op. cit.; J. R. Mandle, "Plantation Economy: An Essay in Definition," *Science and Society* 35, no. 1 (Spring 1972): 49–62.

enthusiastically welcomed the apportionments of the French decade, Garibaldi's promises, and the allotments assigned to "communists"—but because of their bitter experiences with these schemes. The allotments—too small, lacking irrigation, and too far from the villages—could not be made profitable, while property taxes stripped the new owners of their savings, putting them at the mercy of loan sharks. As we have seen, the result was that the peasants sold their allotments, often to latifondisti, as soon as the restriction on alienation expired, though without giving up the hope of using the land itself.

The latifondisti, for their part, had an interest in granting land use to the inhabitants of their social territory. Once the real property had been consolidated for stock and grain farming, the latifondo still had vast expanses of marginal land available: poor and ill-situated, underused in the latifondo economy, and, therefore, of little value in an imperfect market situation. But these very same lands, if assigned to families of provisionees, accomplished a series of economic and extraeconomic objectives. First of all, they constituted an important, if not the major, source of subsistence for such users,[6] whose wages, automatically transformed into an extra source, could therefore be kept low. Second, the land assignments allowed the workers to perpetuate their peasant identity and thereby helped keep the peace on the latifondo. Third, assignments ad personam as part of the overall remuneration of labor on the latifondo motivated loyalty to the master. Moreover, grants to provisionees often involved uses and easements that rural folk had practiced for centuries, *cuiusdam consuetudinis universalis,* by the law of universal custom, and their reinstatement, albeit individualized, created an illusion of continuity in custom and usage. Last but not least, the assignments brought the Barraccos tillage fees, leaving intact their grazing rights and all the affirmative easements of way and gleaning.

Access to land took various forms. Those preferred by both the users and contemporary reformers were perpetual sharecropping and perpetual leases.[7] Sharecroppers paid the landlord one-tenth of the major annual crop (excluding beans), while the landlord retained the right to graze his stock from October to April (the cropper paid a fee to graze his); the right to glean was usually rotated on a three-year basis, two years for the cropper, the third for the master (who would further assign it to landless people). The terms of perpetual leases were similar, but in addition the lessee was entitled to subletting the holding, provided that the land and appurtenances were kept in good condition.

---

6. For discussions of the rationality of a peasant family's economic calculations, see A. V. Chayanov, *The Theory of the Peasant Economy* (Madison, 1986); W. Kula, *An Economic Theory,* op. cit.; and J. Scott, *The Moral Economy of the Peasant* (New Haven, 1976).

7. G. Salvemini, however, was critical of these ("Guerra al latifondo," op. cit., 238).

It is obvious why the peasants were partial to this type of lease: the rent was low and proportional to the harvest—terms preferred by all peasants[8]—and land use was de facto hereditary, the sole conditions for lease renewal being loyalty to the master and prompt payment of rent. But perpetual leases and sharecropping were infrequent[9] because the latifondisti considered these forms of land assignment overly constrictive. Indeed, they was to be found mainly in the outlying areas of the Croton Marquisate, where the 1806 laws abolishing feudalism preserved preexisting tenancies of this kind.[10] But in areas where they had not been firmly established under the old regime, where the density of the peasant population was low enough for them to be revoked without creating "unrest," or where the municipalities failed to safeguard the distribution of allotments—in short, wherever possible—the latifondisti chose other forms of land assignment.

A much more widespread way of giving latifondo workers (and other people) access to land was the terratico, a small tenure—usually located in hilly or coastal country—on which cropping rights were granted for three-year periods.[11] For the peasants, this type of lease was much less advantageous than the perpetual lease in that the term was short, the rent (terraggiera) was a fixed amount whatever the harvest, the landlord kept all grazing rights on the cropland, and land use was restricted. For the same reasons, such a lease was advantageous for the latifondista: its short term allowed him to use it to "reward" loyal workers and "punish" the "negligent," and the return was actually far from insignificant, especially considering the lack of any real alternative

---

8. James Scott analyzes the reasons for this preference for proportional rather than fixed rent. In the first case, tenant and landlord share any losses; in the second case, the tenant family can be ruined by a succession of poor harvests (*The Moral Economy,* op. cit., 44–45).

9. This was the case at least as regards the permanent laborers. But large and medium-sized landowners frequently granted each other perpetual leases. For example, the Barraccos were emphyteutic tenants of the Berlingieris and the Luciferos of the Barraccos, and the Barraccos were subtenants of the Di Paolas and the Vercillos of the Barraccos.

10. The huge Bosco estate in Isola township was almost entirely rented out. In 1863, there were 287 tenants on its 2,388 tomolate (2,006 acres), of which one-fifth were considered untillable; the directly-managed Isola masseria occupied only 137 tomolate (115 acres) but of choice land. In Rocca di Neto, seventeen tracts amounting to 321 tomolate (of which a third were "woods, marshes, and sterile land") were under perpetual lease to the same number of tenants.

11. This widespread form of small tenancy was described in chapter 4; here I shall simply recall its salient features. The terraggiera, or rent in kind with reference to the acreage tilled for the main crop, varied according to the quality of the land and the type of crop. For a rye crop, and more rarely for wheat, the average rent was one or two tomoli per tomolata (about three bushels per acre); for corn it might run to as much as four or five tomoli per tomolata (charged at the threshing floor). The Barraccos retained grazing rights on arable land; the tenant had to pay a fee to pasture his own animals on it, and he was often forbidden to keep hogs on it. The terraggiera of "dry grain free of foreign bodies" was supposed to be delivered in July to the nearest Barracco storehouse, though usually the landlord's agents collected his part right on the threshing floor.

use for these lands, which—given the low prices of rye and corn—it would have been unprofitable to manage directly.

But the most widely practiced forms of land transfer on the Barracco latifondo were the parasforo and cortaglia, which we discussed in the last chapter. Unlike the other leases, these assignments of cropland were linked directly and solely to work on the latifondo. A massaro would be given three tomolate of parasforo, a shepherd (being a massaro as well) two tomolate of cortaglia, and a waterworks man several *linate*. In other words, use of the plot was part of the regular remuneration for a particular type of work, and anyone who left the latifondo or changed his job lost it. As will be remembered, the owner's only direct gain was a small percentage of the harvest, but there was the usual indirect gain as well: he saved on wages, tied the workers to the latifondo, and obtained a return on second- and third-rate land located in the most remote parts of the Sila mountains without giving up any grazing rights.

Perhaps the most curious form of "expropriation sans expropriation" was the granting of so-called jussi. These were ancient customary rights of wood-cutting, grazing, gleaning, watering, quarrying, and lime slaking. The latifondisti had appropriated those rights in the manner described earlier and began to grant them by way of special privileges and rewards for services, not to the community but to their own chosen employees, administrators, and agents. As beneficiaries, these people automatically had an interest in obstructing community claims to the ancient rights.

Not that the latifondisti denied their employees access to ownership of real property (they had neither the means nor any interest in doing so), but it is plain that they did not encourage it. The cases in which the baron granted workers credit for land purchases were extremely rare,[12] which was in the absence of credit institutions an effective impediment. What the Barraccos favored were ways of assigning land use that left them broad control and could easily be reversed, a prerogative of which they made extensive use during the wheat boom of the 1860s.

3. Job Security

That a peasant family will value security over fatigue, and that one of the major components of security is the guarantee of jobs, has been amply demonstrated by Chayanov. This type of cost-benefit calculation, like all the peasants' calculations, applies not to individual people at given times but to whole

---

12. They were also special cases. Luigi Biafora, an old servant, obtained six hundred ducats from his employer to buy a kitchen garden at Monastero della Pace; Pasqualle Pirelli, a specialized gardener, bought one at Setteporti in annual installments paid by the administration. Don Antonio Monaco, chaplain and tutor, obtained a loan to buy a holding for his brother Francesco.

families over the year.[13] To maintain its stability, a guarantee system thus had to guarantee job security not only to heads of families but also to other members: women and youngsters, the elderly and the sick, and even to "extra" relatives (nephews, uncles on lengthy visits, and so forth). This security, extended to the whole elastic labor surplus, induced the peasants to work for wages considerably lower than the theoretical market price and to comply with the owner's concept of "good work."

Within the latifondo administration, this guarantee applied explicitly to the category of fixed provisionees but indirectly to the farmhands as well. In fact, the latter—who, as we have seen, were recruited year after year in the same villages, by the same bosses, and for the same jobs—were presumably the bosses' relatives, friends, and neighbors. The silk barn managers hired their wives and daughters year after year, the spinning women returned season after season, and likewise the tree pruners, the fence builders, and even the workers hired by the month for livestock operations.

In the case of the provisionees, the ledgers offer a wealth of detail that enables us to understand how the system of guaranteed employment worked.

First of all, one was rarely fired. Job security was best represented by the fact that, as a rule, the latifondo dismissed no one (this practice changed in the 1860s for reasons we shall discuss later). As table 13 shows, until 1860 the number of dismissals per decade amounted to no more than 3 percent of the whole labor force (and less than 1 percent in the first four decades). Nonetheless, the very low dismissal rate did not mean that the labor force was static; turnover was indeed rather high (as table 14 shows, it sometimes reached the level of 50 percent), because many provisionees quit their jobs, either voluntarily, to seek their fortunes elsewhere, or compelled by the draft, jail terms, or sickness. But those who resigned did so knowing not only that they could come back but that they could do so more than once. One example of this is the case of Vincenzo Benevento of Campana, a cowhand who quit in 1854 after thirty years of service, returned the following year but remained for only one year, left again and returned ten months later, remained "in service" for slighty more than a year, left once again, and returned in September of 1861 to work for four consecutive years. Finally, after quitting again in 1865, he returned no more. We have no idea what Benevento was doing during his absence, but the fact is that he found his old job waiting for him no less than four times and at the same wages.[14]

Practically everyone was guaranteed a chance to be rehired: sick people,

---

13. A. V. Chayanov, "The Socio-Economic Nature of the Peasant Farm Economy," op. cit., 144–45.

14. Pietro Gigliotti, a Caccuri swineherd, quit three times in twelve years, and he, too, was promptly rehired.

TABLE 13.   Job Security on the Barracco Latifondo

Decade	Workers	Dismissed	Rehired	Never Rehired	% Workers Never Rehired
1801–19	193	1	0	1	0.5
1820–29	291	0	0	0	0.0
1830–39	503	1	0	1	0.2
1840–49	538	11	0	11	2.0
1850–59	573	19	3	16	2.8
1860–69	500	69	4	65	13.0
1870–79	463	98	7	91	19.6
1880–89	339	48	0	48	14.2
1890–99	235	40	0	40	17.0

TABLE 14.   Workforce Turnover on the Barracco Latifondo

Decade	Workers	Resigned	% Turnover
1801–19	193	3	1.5
1820–29	291	8	2.7
1830–39	503	70	13.9
1840–49	538	120	22.3
1850–59	573	206	35.9
1860–69	500	251	50.2
1870–79	463	224	48.4
1880–89	339	131	38.6
1890–99	235	89	37.9

draftees, convicts, even those who had been dismissed. In 1853, when the Pinicollito enclosure in the Sila was broken up and the livestock partnership with the Morellis was dissolved, all of their respective guards and shepherds were given other jobs on the latifondo. Even men who had been fired for disiplinary reasons were allowed to resume their jobs. Guard Pasquale Scarpelli, for instance, was fired by the Isola administration in 1882 after having been caught stealing crates of olives, but despite this offense, he was rehired the same year at Petrizia.[15] Jail was considered a normal fact of life. After serving their terms (usually one year or less), ex-convicts went back to work on

---

15. Water lineman Francesco Saverio Miranda, fired in June of 1870 for abandoning his post, was back at work in September and kept his job for the next twenty years. Francesco Filippelli, a cowhand from Bocchiglieri, was fired in 1856 for carrying a switchblade knife but was rehired in 1860 (though he lasted only a year, for in July of 1861 he took up brigandage instead).

the latifondo, often at the same fiduciary jobs; one Petrizia guard named Pasquale Imbrogno actually continued to receive his salary while serving three months' time in 1853.[16] For young men called up in the dreaded military draft, the certainty that they would find their jobs waiting for them upon their return was a fundamental consolation; depending on the government and the political climate, military service might last from a few months in the militia to more than two years in the army, and it might funnel off all the young (and not so young) men who hadn't the means to pay for a "replacement."[17] Not only were ex-servicemen able to return to the latifondo but they were sometimes promoted to better jobs (the army having made men of them!).[18] By the same token, people who took sick and could not work for months on end were able to return to their jobs when well enough (though often far from completely cured).[19] Luigi Lavia of San Pietro, for instance, spent seven years on sick leave out of his ten on the latifondo.[20] This guarantee was especially important during the epidemics that periodically hit whole areas. In 1867, twenty workers were sick for five to seven months; in 1874, another epidemic laid low many of the Caccuri people; and in 1884 dozens of workers were out for four to five months. And the guarantee system offered more than just job security. Besides having access to the services of physicians and pharmacists (whom we shall discuss later), many sick workers collected all or part of their regular wages,

---

16. They came back to their jobs even after serving long prison terms. Gaspare Sapia, an overseer, and Luigi Giannotta, a guard, were rehired after four years in prison and remained in the Barraccos' service for another seventeen and forty years, respectively. Many of the men rehired after prison terms were long-time employees; Vincenzo Marasco, a Casino guard from 1880 to 1898, spent a month in jail in 1887; cowhand Luigi Toscano, employed from 1822 to 1842, did a year's time in 1834; and Rocco Guarascio, a guard from 1830 to 1869, did nine months in 1841–42. It is interesting that having a record did not seem to influence these men's employment at all; they were not only rehired, but they were put back in their same fiduciary jobs (as guards or herdsmen).

17. Giuseppe Chiodo, a guard, was drafted for only a few months, from May to August of 1863; Salvatore Jaconis, another guard, "was called to arms" for a month and a half in 1883; and Francesco Saverio Teti served in the militia from August to December 1870. But Gennaro Lucente, a domestic servant, had to serve from February of 1872 to November of 1874.

18. For example, Francesco Intrieri was working as a guard when he left for the militia in February of 1864, but he became a domestic servant when he came back in 1866. Gaetano Bernardo was an apprentice swineherd before he was drafted in 1849, but he was granted an adult's salary when he came back two years later.

19. The nature of the disease was only rarely specified; most often the books note simply tertian or "autumn fever," almost certainly malaria, but two cases of pleurisy and one of apoplectic seizure are mentioned.

20. Lavia became ill in 1872, a few months after being hired as a guard. He went back to work in 1874 but fell sick again almost immediately and was absent for another four years. Back on the job in 1878, he fell sick once again in January of 1881, returned to work after seven months, and finally died "in service" in November of 1882.

or—more frequently—at least their minatico.[21] In other cases, the sick person "served through an intermediary," usually a family member, but remained the "job holder" for administrative purposes.[22]

When sickness or accident left a worker with a permanent disability that made it impossible for him to perform his old job, he would often be transferred to a less wearing or less mobile job situated in a healthier locale. Thus, guard Natale Jusi, lamed by a gunshot in 1873, obtained a doorman's job two years later "in consideration of his misfortune," and Vincenzo Arnone, suffering from malaria, was sent to be a gamekeeper in the Sila "for a change of air."[23] Similar provision was sometimes made for people who had grown old in service,[24] but as a rule age and consequent diminished efficiency were taken as acceptable costs of the guarantee system's proper operation, and elderly provisionees simply remained at their posts until their deaths. Indeed, death was the reported cause of severance for one out of every seven latifondo employees.

As a whole, what we have here is an extraordinary lifetime job guarantee; what is more, it was a guarantee extended through the "kinship network" to the faithful worker's relatives. After the first year of a man's employment, the younger members of his family—sons, stepsons, nephews, and brothers—could all benefit from this privilege. The absolutely general practice (if not the principle) was to avoid alienating, in any sense, the active and potential workforce.

---

21. Angela Maria Spina, a servant of Donna Giulietta's, received full wages during the eleven months she "spent sick in her own home" in 1883–84. Luigi Giannotta (the guard who spent four years in prison) also was paid full wages during the seven months he was not working in 1888. But *canettiere* Nicola Granieri, who went home "to cure his apoplexy" from May to September, 1887, received only his minatico (he died of this disease in 1896). Gaetano Marano, a guard, received his minatico for four months in 1884; Giuseppe Monaco for three months in 1827; Pietro Staino, a servant, for six months in 1853; Giovanni Spina, a water lineman, from October 1864 to April 1865; Dionisio Lumare, a threshing-machine stoker, for almost all of 1867; canettiere Vincenzo Perri for five months in 1878; guard Matteo Pulia for seven months in 1867–68; and Giovanni Spadafora for five months in 1867. Only a very few of the fiduciary workers rehired after illness had received no pay at all during the interval: guards Giovanni Girimonti and Domenico Luria, both sick in 1874; and gamekeeper Michele Turano, absent for three months in 1882.

22. For example, shepherd Francesco Bonanno, nicknamed Nervo, had his brother Lorenzo stand in for him from October 1848 to June 1849; canettiere Luigi Valentino was replaced by his brother Giovanni in 1874; and so on.

23. Muleteer Giuseppe Cannata, unable to drive the mule trains after a fall in 1864, became overseer of the hog-fattening operation in Isola two years later. Gaetano Librandi, an elderly servant, was sent to Naples with Don Stanislao for two years "to follow a cure"; in 1869, after a long illness, Nicola Panza, a chief goatherd, was made overseer at the Altilia piggery, a job that did not require him to go out droving.

24. As the climate in the Sila became too harsh for water lineman Michele Granieri, he was transferred to the coast in 1885. After forty years' service as an overseer, in 1898, Antonio Milizia obtained the sinecure of doorkeeper at the little-frequented Croton mansion.

Still, dismissals did occur every once in a while, and the system had its "sticks" as well as its "carrots." Prior to 1860, dismissals were so rare (see table 13) that bookkeepers felt it necessary to record their cause. What kind of fault or misdeed could lead to dismissal during the period of stability?[25] One was perpetration of a crime against latifondo property: one gardener was fired "because he is a thief," another man "because he is a thief and undisciplined," still another for having "stolen crates of olives," and a whole group "for damaging the holm-oaks at Santa Anna." Another reason was disorderly conduct: one guard was dismissed "for drunkenness," another for "bad conduct," still another for "very bad conduct," an overseer for his "incredible refusal to obey the baron's order," and two "because [they] carried a switch-blade knife." Plainly, what was being punished by dismissal was not unfitness for a given task but rebellious behavior and damage to latifondo property. An offense of the first kind (lack of discipline, bad conduct, "incredible opposition," and bearing unauthorized weapons) could easily lead to one of the second (theft of the owner's "belongings" or criminal association for purposes of damage or misappropriation). As we shall see later, however, the same behavior and acts were tolerated, and the guilty protected, when they were not directed against the latifondo. The "stick" of dismissal was not meant, then, to punish or eliminate rebellious attitudes and violent acts per se but only to direct them elsewhere, to protect the latifondo's property and its hierarchy of power against them.

4. Authority Structures

Among other things, the guarantee system succeeded in creating an interdependence between the community and the latifondo such that in the eyes of the wage workers, the land, authority within the family, rites of passage, and economic control remained integrated.

Access to land (the peasantry's traditional means of autonomous reproduction), limited though it was, perpetuated the illusion that the wage worker had control over his own reproduction, that he remained a peasant. This, in turn, allowed the latifondo's provisionees to retain a position of authority within the peasant community. As is commonly known, although an individual's standing in a preindustrial society like Calabria's was not completely independent of his economic power, it depended largely on his degree of autonomy in productive activities or his peasant status. This, in turn, following

---

25. I have excluded the period after 1860 from this analysis because the reorganization of the latifondo after partition of the family's property and the changes made in types of production during the agrarian crisis led to layoffs of a new kind. These changes are discussed in chapters 1 and 8, respectively.

the paradigm of rural "familism" described by Arensberg ("land, blood and local standing"), enabled reproduction of the patriarchal hierarchy within the family's life.[26] Peasant fathers retained the authority of masters and teachers over their children, something they could not have done under conditions of full wage alienation.

What is significant is that in part this pretense held within work relations on the latifondo itself: exactly where the peasant was operating as the purest form of wage worker. Yet the logic of the guarantee system made it possible to preserve the remnants of the traditional authority structure, the most important of which were ancestral working practices and the supremacy of the father.

All production activities on the latifondo (with the sole exception of the licorice works) were conducted with traditional methods well known to the peasants "not because they knew the theory, but because they were guided by a sort of inveterate practice,"[27] who had been applying them since time immemorial on their own lands and those of the masters. The masters, who were anything but ignorant of the science of agronomy and its innovations, retained the old ways because they realized that these were more than just the dying vestiges of ancient usages.[28] Although nineteenth-century modernizers railed against the uneconomical practices of fallowing, extensive grain farming, nomadic stock raising, and plows that "looked like a legacy from the Greeks," the workers were all perfectly familiar with them; expropriating their traditional knowledge would have created a potentially subversive frustration that the latifondisti intended to avoid. *Rebus sic stantibus:* any countryman hired by the latifondo was perfectly able not only to control the production process entrusted to him but also to pass his knowledge on to the younger generation. This is where the working principles of the latifondo system incorporated the reproduction of patriarchal authority, allowing a wage-earning father to preserve the same authority over his children that he would have had on his own farm. Indeed, organizing work in a way that perpetuated traditional patriarchal authority was so fundamental to maintaining the masters' power that rural "familism" had been taken as a cornerstone of the latifondo structure. The point at which the two systems met was in the recruitment and training of

---

26. C. M. Arensberg, *The Irish Countryman,* op. cit., 76ff.

27. G. Grio of Monteleone, quoted in U. Caldora, *La Statistica murattiana,* op. cit., 94.

28. The Barraccos' bent for modernization will be discussed later. Here we need only note that back in 1811 even Grio was forced to admit that "they do spend a little time reading about the principles of agriculture"; that Luigi Barracco was a member of the Agrarian Society and had many works on agronomy in his library; and that Roberto Barracco was to be one of the founding members of the Association of Landowners and Agriculturists of the Neapolitan Provinces. Still, the only significant innovation the Barraccos made on their estate before the end of the century was the installation of a threshing machine to replace the heavy stone dragged by oxen around the old threshing floor.

young workers, which occurred mostly through family channels. At the center was the adult male provisionee who brought a boy of nine or ten—a son, younger brother, nephew, or brother-in-law—with him to work and started his apprenticeship. At first the novice earned no wage; his presence was barely noted on his sponsor's "administration sheet" and was acknowledged only with a small gift of pork or rye. A year or two later, when the boy had begun to get the hang of the work, he would start earning a minatico, always handed over to the sponsor. After another year, the father (or other sponsor) would begin to collect a small wage for the minor's work; over the next seven or eight years, this wage would grow by one or two ducats yearly until the young man, now about seventeen, reached the salary level of an adult worker, at which point he was "issued a sheet" and freed, for accounting purposes, from paternal tutelage.

This kind of system had advantages for both sides. The latifondo secured a constant flow of qualified labor whose training cost it practically nothing (the tiny wage paid to these youngsters was more than repaid by their work), while all responsibility for their lack of experience or exuberance fell on the shoulders of the adult workers, who, besides teaching the boys their jobs, trained them in discipline and loyalty. And the system enabled the men to keep control over their sons (as their masters) and power within their families, as it recreated occasions for the boys' traditional passage from maternal to paternal tutelage (from household chores and female company to training in farm work and exclusively male company).[29]

Besides this support for his patriarchal power in the family, the "faithful" worker also acquired a certain power of patronage in recommending his relatives for latifondo jobs. Over the long run, this very widespread practice produced kinship networks—horizontal-synchronic (brothers, brothers-in-law, and *compari*) as well as vertical-diachronic (grandfathers, fathers, and sons)—that involved upward of a quarter of the latifondo's entire workforce (see table 15). In some families, working for the Barraccos was a tradition with an incidence much higher than the averages indicated in the table. The most emblematic case is that of the Intrieri family of San Pietro in Guarano, of which as many as sixty-three members worked as shepherds on the latifondo between 1815, when the brothers Pasquale, Gaetano, and Domenico, and Domenico's young son, Francesco, were first hired, and 1898, when Alberto, the last of them, died.[30] It is hardly surprising, then, to find certain occupations taking

---

29. C. M. Arensberg speaks of "old fellows [who] will walk to the pay-off to collect for themselves the wages their sons have earned" (*The Irish Countryman,* op. cit., 58). "In the persons of . . . old men, . . . the integration of the community is accomplished" (137).

30. Twenty-three Ajellos from Casino worked for them, all cowhands and all related to each other; eighteen members of the Bitonti family from San Giovanni, as guards, foremen, and overseers; thirteen Panzas from San Pietro, almost all guards; and so forth.

TABLE 15. Incidence of Kinship Relations on the Barracco Latifondo (1801–89)

Sector	No. of Employees	Employees with Relatives Present	Percentage
Farming	102	25	24.5
Stock raising	1,357	339	25.0
Management staff	35	8	22.9
Domestics	145	42	29.0
Overseers	646	171	26.5
Craftsmen	22	1	4.5
Boatmen	11	6	54.5
Other	85	13	15.3
Total	2,402	605	25.2

TABLE 16. Horizontal and Vertical Kinship Networks (1801–89) (provisionees with at least one relative also employed on the latifondo)

Kinship Network	1801– 19	1820– 29	1830– 39	1840– 49	1850– 59	1860– 69	1870– 79	1880– 89	1890– 99	Total
Horizontal	29	20	24	11	12	7	10	1	0	114
Line (%)	25.4	17.5	21.1	9.6	10.5	6.1	8.8	0.9	0.0	
Column (%)	44.6	35.1	27.6	19.6	14.3	13.5	30.3	14.3	0.0	25.7
Vertical	36	34	61	45	72	45	23	6	3	325
Line (%)	11.1	10.5	18.8	13.8	22.2	13.8	7.15	1.8	0.9	
Column (%)	55.4	59.6	70.1	80.4	85.7	86.5	69.75	85.7	100	73.2
Nonspecified	0	3	2	0	0	0	0	0	0	5
Line (%)	0.0	60.0	40.0	0.0	0.0	0.0	0.0	0.0	0.0	
Column (%)	0.0	5.3	2.3	0.0	0.0	0.0	0.0	0.0	0.0	1.1
Total	65	57	87	56	84	52	33	7	3	444
Line (%)	14.6	12.8	19.6	12.6	18.9	11.7	7.4	1.6	0.7	100

the form of *chasses guardées* of one or another family. Just like the Intrieri shepherds, the trade of swineherding, for instance, was dominated by the Laudaros and the Gigliottis of Caccuri in the first half of the century, and by the Samàs of San Nicola and the Feras of Rocca di Neto in the second half. The tendency to form "dynasties"—to transmit trades, jobs, loyalty, and authority vertically from father to son—became stronger over the course of the century. This can be seen from table 16, in which we consider only provisionees who had at least one relative working on the latifondo, distinguishing the horizontal kinship network (siblings) from the vertical (fathers, sons, and grandchildren). In fact, while in the early decades (1801–30) approximately 40 percent of these provisionees with relatives on the job belonged to the horizontal networks and

57 percent to the vertical networks, from the fifth decade on, more than 80 percent of them were part of a vertical network (the decrease in the aggregate numbers of people involved in kinship networks starting in the seventh decade will be discussed below).

In other words, the latifondo organization established itself by reinforcing the kinship-based system of recruitment, training, and heredity. In fact, the kinship networks became extremely important for the system's stability. In the first place, they encouraged specialization by "clans" and occupational endogamy and handed down a tradition of loyalty, good service, and (inter)dependence. Moreover, they reproduced the stratifications existing within the workers' world. Sons and younger brothers of foremen often became foremen themselves, either in the same administration, through inheritance, or in a parallel operation: several generations of Ciampàs served as head swineherds, and generations of Bitontis and Lecces were chief cattle herders. The same mechanism operated at the management level; the administrator Luigi Mancini was the son of the agent Giuseppe, nephew of the chief warehouseman Felice Antonio, and brother of Pasquale, an administrator in Naples. As table 17 shows, these kinship networks were strongest in the sectors characterized by the greatest autonomy: 56 percent of all family relationships were concentrated in the livestock sector, the most independent of all; 28 percent in surveillance; and just 4 percent in farming, which was dominated by casual labor. Lastly, the distribution of family relationships by provisionees' area of provenance (table 18) confirms the previously mentioned correlation between type of work and area of origin; the incidence was very high for workers who came from the mountains and the high hills (74 percent in all) and very low for those who came from the coast (3.4 percent).

Overall, *padroni* and *padri,* the masters' and the fathers' workers had a mutual interest in maintaining the traditional patriarchal authority and patronage system. That interest was job security, on the one side, and reliable labor supply on the other.[31]

5. Access to Special Services

It was easy enough for the guarantee system to stand in for absent or inadequate civic structures in its social territory, and to make itself the indispensable mediator between workers and social services. As will be recalled, health providers, lawyers, and notaries were not necessarily on the latifondo's payroll, and theoretically they practiced their professions over the whole social territory, but the absence of specific infrastructure made access to their services

---

31. For the relationship among paternalism, patriarchy, and mastership in the slave system, see E. Genovese, *Roll, Jordan, Roll,* op. cit., 5–6, 134–36, 662. For the Irish peasant patriarch, see C. Arensberg, *The Irish Countryman,* op. cit., 54–55, 69–70 and passim.

TABLE 17. Kinship Networks by Job

Kinship Network	Farming	Stockraising	Oversight	Management	Domestics	Craftsmen	Others	Total
Horizontal	2	106	36	3	13	0	6	166
Line (%)	1.2	63.9	21.7	1.8	7.8	0.0	3.6	
Column (%)	8.0	31.3	21.1	37.5	31.0	0.0	31.65	27.4
Vertical	23	230	134	5	29	1	10	432
Line (%)	5.35	53.2	31.0	1.1	6.7	0.2	2.3	
Column (%)	92.0	67.8	78.4	62.5	69.0	100	52.6	71.4
Nonspecified	0	3	1	0	0	0	3	7
Line (%)	0.0	42.9	14.3	0.0	0.0	0.0	42.9	
Column (%)	0.0	0.9	0.5	0.0	0.0	0.0	9.1	1.1
Total	25	339	171	8	42	1	19	605
Line (%)	4.1	56.0	28.3	1.3	6.9	0.2	3.1	100.0

TABLE 18. Kinship Networks by Area of Provenance

Kinship Network	Seacoast	Foothills	High hills	Mountains	Provincial capitals	Other	Total
Horizontal	2	5	54	30	1	22	114
Line (%)	1.8	4.4	47.4	26.3	0.9	17.3	
Column (%)	13.3	16.1	24.4	27.8	33.3	33.3	25.7
Vertical	13	25	166	77	1	43	325
Line (%)	4.0	7.7	51.1	23.7	0.3	13	
Column (%)	86.7	80.6	75.1	71.3	33.3	65.2	73.2
Nonspecified	0	1	1	1	1	1	5
Line (%)	0.0	20.0	20.0	20.0	20.0	20.0	
Column (%)	0.0	3.2	0.5	0.9	33.3	1.5	1.1
Total	15	31	221	108	3	66	444
Line (%)	3.4	7.0	49.8	24.3	0.7	14.9	100

very difficult for the less informed and for rural folk. Let us take medical care as an example. The province was, as we have seen, relatively well supplied with physicians and surgeons (around one per thousand people), but the problem was not so much the number of doctors as the scarcity and small size of hospitals, the rarity of publicly funded area practices, and the cost of medications.[32] In this situation, the latifondo's mediation was critical. A sick worker could turn, directly or through the administration, to any doctor, who would treat him all the more willingly because the employer was certain to pay the bill. The employer did not foot the bill—the amount would be entered against the worker's name in the ledger and gradually reimbursed through a deduction from his wages—but the worker would not have to pay cash on the spot in a time of trouble. A man like Filippo Caputo would certainly not have been able to pay sixty ducats in cash to physicians, surgeons, druggists, and the hospital in 1866 when he was earning only thirty a year and his wife took sick, too; nor would Filippo Abate, whose sickness in 1852 caused him to lose his yearly income from running the silk campaign, have been able to pay out thirty ducats; nor would chief goatherder Giovanni Battista Alessio have had the cash to pay "a woman to nurse him during his illness"; nor would guard Natale Jusi have been able to pay hospital expenses greater than his yearly earnings; nor

32. According to Intendent Galli, there were 235 physicians and 86 surgeons in Upper Calabria—an altogether respectable ratio for a population of 350,000 (almost 1 per 1,000). Intendent Grio found the same situation in Lower Calabria: 455 physicians and surgeons for 460,000 inhabitants. But, notwithstanding the French administration's insistence that "each township provide in its budget for the expense of universal doctors and surgeons" (see Grio's report, quoted in U. Caldora, *La Statistica murattiana,* op. cit., 43–44), only a very few did employ a general practitioner (see chap. 3).

would the hundred other workers who turned to the administration for help of this kind at least once in their lives. Often the person in need of medical care was not the worker himself but a relative: not only his wife or child but his mother-in-law, a sibling who lived elsewhere, or a *compare;* the fact that these "debts" were recorded as a matter of course shows that they were customary. In some cases, the latifondo would forgive a man's debt for sickness or pay a hospital bill itself.[33]

But druggists, who were licensed to write prescriptions and to sell quinine and similar medicines often administered in this land of seasonal diseases, were needed even more frequently than doctors. Every large town had its own druggist.[34] Besides dispensing human medicines, they supplied veterinary specialities, vaccinated children, and kept a stock of cooking spices and "opiates," imported tobacco, purgatives, and even paint and dye. It was in its relations with druggists that the guarantee system attained the most developed form of its contribution to social costs. With some, the latifondo had a sort of standing agreement (the ones with Don Giuseppe De Majo in Isola and Don Vincenzo Camera in Croton continued for decades), under which the druggist supplied whatever the enterprise and individual workers might need. Once or twice a year, upon presentation of their prescriptions, the administration would settle the entire bill, footing one-third of the workers' and their relatives' pharmaceutical expenses.

The latifondo's mediation was also a boon for anyone who needed a lawyer. It was often the case in this generally litigious society[35] in which, at the same time, a countryman would be unable to handle the cost of a trial or suit in the courts of Cosenza or Catanzaro without assistance. The latifondo administration allowed its people to consult its own lawyers—Poerio in Catanzaro and Bosco in Cosenza—and paid the bills, which were beyond the limited resources of such clients,[36] especially men awaiting trial in jail and thus deprived of income. This access to qualified legal aid with deferred payment was of immense value.

The latifondo played the same role in workers' relations with notaries. This was another hovering presence in the lives of Calabria's people, who, whether or not they owned any property, had to turn to notaries to draw up wills

---

33. Pasquale Turano, a servant from Caccuri, was forgiven a debt of seven ducats incurred for an urgent call made by a doctor from San Giovanni; Natale Jusi was forgiven one for twenty-five ducats for hospital expenses after he was accidentally shot; and servant Angela Maria Spina's mistress paid for her hospitalization in Croton.

34. According to the Murat statistical compendium, there were 160 in Upper Calabria and about 200 in Lower Calabria.

35. See, for example, *Annuario Statistico Italiano,* year 1 (1878), 284–85.

36. The sum of twenty-four ducats paid in 1859 to defend cowhand Nicola Bracone's son equaled the father's yearly wages; the fifty ducats due from shepherd Pietro Staino for his brother's defense were far and above his wages.

and marriage contracts, divide estates, attest marital status, certify loan agreements and bills of sale, and update or revise mortgages. Again, it was a boon for the latifondo's people to have access to the services of Notary Biondi or Notary De Meo and to defer payment of fees and expenses.

Less frequent, but certainly very convenient, was the latifondo's mediation with churchmen. Domestic servant Filippo Perri, for instance, applied to the administration in 1843 for help in obtaining dispensation to marry a cousin from the archbishop of Santa Severina. Others sought help to carry out a vow when ready cash was lacking or it was difficult to get to a market where religious articles were sold.

In addition, the latifondo acted as a lending institution, an important role and one much in demand in this region where there were but a few *monti di pietà* and *monti frumentari* and practically no branches of city banks, and confraternities played no financial role whatsoever.[37] People in need of credit turned to individuals with money—local loan sharks or the wealthy Barraccos themselves. The financial transactions the administration performed, willingly or not, consisted of extending small or medium-sized loans, accepting savings deposits, granting "invisible" credit on the books, and tolerating debts.

Small loans were extended interest free to trusted employees for a specific purchase (a cottage, a mare),[38] to help out a relative, or to pay a note or debt.[39] Such loans often took the form of advances "on the year's yield" or sales.[40] Larger loans usually carried 5 percent interest, the current rate in the kingdom. There was no usury involved; in effect, these larger loans were favors granted to faithful administrators and clergymen to enable them to buy private or government bonds.[41]

---

37. On the monti frumentari, see, for example, D. Winspeare, *Ragionamento sui monti frumentari nelle provincie meridionali* (Naples, 1875); G. Fortunato, "I Monti Frumentari nelle provincie napoletane," *Rassegna Settimanale* 5 (1880); and G. Fortunato, "La trasformazione dei Monti Frumentari," in *Il Mezzogiorno e lo Stato Italiano*, op. cit.

38. Chief herdsman Gennaro Lecce borrowed sixty ducats in 1819 to buy himself a house; Luigi Biafora, a servant, borrowed 200 ducats in 1823 for the same purpose. Agent Gaetano Pizzuto borrowed thirty ducats in 1824 to buy a donkey; Bruno Greco, a massaro, did the same. Filippo Caputo borrowed thirty ducats to buy a mare, Giacinto Zinnante ninety-six ducats for a mule, guard Giovanni Angiolillo 100 ducats for a colt, and later another forty-three for a mule.

39. Francesco Ciambrone borrowed seventy ducats his wife needed, Michele Pizzuto 100 ducats for his brother, and Fortunato Comito thirty-four ducats for his son. Sixteen ducats were paid for a debt owed by Tommaso Lamanna's brother and thirty-six for Marino Castiglione's son. Over two years' time the administration paid thirty-seven ducats' worth of notes given by Antonio Angotti and even a note for eighty-five ducats given by Rosario Cerminaro.

40. Massaro Vincenzo Muto borrowed seventy-two ducats in 1871 as an advance on his year's wages "for a necessity that has arisen"; every year the administration advanced to Donna Vittoria Cortese the sale price of her mules without interest; Caterina Scino "worked off" the loans she had obtained.

41. The 2,000-lire interest-free loan granted in 1878 and 1879 to chief guard Pasquale

The credit transactions carried on the enterprise's books mirrored the kinship networks discussed earlier. Part of a man's wages might be sent to relatives residing elsewhere, credits and debits might be transferred from one man's account to another's, or a deceased man's estate could be reckoned and divided among his heirs. Some employees used this facility to pay for their children's education, those whose jobs kept them far from their families would have their monthly pay sent home and some settled debts to acquaintances in the same way.[42] Entries marked "payable by" or "payable to," which appear in the ledgers with exasperating monotony, testify to this "banking" function performed by the latifondo.

More rarely, but very significantly, the administration acted as a savings depository. Rarely, because few workers were able to put anything by and if they did, the amount of their savings was pathetic; significantly, because it shows that the latifondo administration was considered a safe custodian and could be trusted to deliver a deceased man's savings to his heirs. Some people had the administration set aside a fixed sum from their wages year by year, others made deposits from time to time, usually after concluding a small sale. Overall, the amounts involved were paltry, indeed; the largest deposit was two hundred ducats.[43]

Pirillo, nicknamed Guerra, was an exception. Others bore 5 percent interest: a ten-year loan of eight hundred lire to agent Luigi Mancini; 500 ducats lent to cook Giovanni Crescenzio; the large sum of 3,566 ducats lent in 1855 to Don Costantino Lopez, a priest and the children's tutor, to buy a living; and other loans for purchases of government bonds.

42. Such loans enabled herdsman Fortunato Amelio to pay for his brother's seminary education and Don Pasquale Perri to pay for his son's. Secretary Don Riccelli received one to send his son to law school in Naples; chief herdsman Salvatore Bitonti to help out his brother Gaetano on a monthly basis; and the priest Don Lopez to support his nephew Marcello in Naples. All the provvisionati who were far from their families regularly had money sent to their mothers, wives, daughters, sons, brothers, sons-in-law, or brothers-in-law, either month by month or as a lump sum. Cook Giovanni Cicchini earned eight (and later ten) ducats a month, "of which six ducats a month to be paid by Don Alessio Tricarico to his mother in Naples"; after his mother's death, the money went to a brother and a sister. Other payments might be ordered, too. Cowherd Francesco Fole had 1.7 ducats a year paid to a friend, and mare herdsman Fortunato Amelio had a debt to his brother-in-law paid by installments.

43. Guard Pietro Lancino deposited 80 ducats with the administration in 1836, surveyor Stefano Ciacco 59 ducats in 1877, guard Filippo Caputo 199 ducats in 1863, and servant Pietro Antonio Tavernise 164 ducats in 1875. Chief herdsman Antonio Bitonti was able to save 10 ducats a year this way. At the death of water lineman Giovanni Miranda, the administration turned over to his widow the 17.4 ducats he had saved over twenty-eight years. After thirty-five years of labor, agent Mancini left the sum of 662 lire deposited with the administration, which divided it among his heirs. The savings of the priest Don Martino, who died intestate, were paid to his sister Cecilia upon the baron's decision.

6. Indebtedness

To consider debt as a form of guarantee may seem odd. Debts are usually seen as an encumbrance and an effective constraint on workforce mobility leading indeed, to a "debt peonage" on the great South American haciendas.[44] But in the latifondo economy the encumbering aspect of debt was subordinate, in the workers' eyes, to its positive aspect. The fact that the master would tolerate a worker's debt interest free and accept continuous renewals was seen as positive recognition of the man's status.[45] Indeed, what with one thing and another—book transfers of moeny, credits, transfers of debts from one account to another, and advances for "needs incurred"—indebtedness was a fairly common condition among the provisionees; 32 percent of them contracted a debt with the latifondo at least once in their lives (42 percent of those hired before 1870), and half remained in debt for the rest of their working lives. Many started work on the latifondo already burdened by a debt; sometimes these were obligations they themselves had contracted ("the old debt"), but most often they were inherited from a relative—father, stepfather, or elder brother—in accordance with the practice (also noted by Arensberg in Ireland) known as generational progression of debt. If a man died in debt, his liabilities were passed on to his principal heir. Francesco Intrieri's case was typical. Son of the shepherd Domenico Intrieri, he began work in 1819 with a twenty-three-ducat debt inherited from his father and, when killed in an accident in 1829, left his own son a debt of fifteen ducats. If there were more than one heir working on the latifondo, the deceased's debt was shared among them in the same proportions as his estate. At Pasquale Turano's death in 1841, for instance, his forty-four-ducat debt was divided equally between his sons Giuseppe, a guard, and Domenico, a domestic.[46] The system of recruitment through family connections and the concept of collective liability thus produced and reproduced indebtedness.

---

44. A. J. Bauer, "Chilean Rural Labour," op. cit., 1059–84; R. Baztra, *Estructura agraria y clases sociales in México* (Mexico City, 1975).

45. Arensberg remarked that "The debt, like the dowry, can and does become a measure of status, too. . . . The debt descends with the land or the shop from father to son. It moves onward with the progression of the generations. Many a small farmer pays off bit by bit the family debt of a parent or relative" (*The Irish Countryman,* op. cit., 175).

46. Shepherd Luigi Intrieri began work in 1846 with a small debt of 2.57 ducats inherited from his brother Michele. Michele Parise began in 1839 with a debt of 6.7 ducats inherited from his father. In 1863, Gaetano Ajello found himself saddled with 26.4 ducats his father Giacomo had incurred. Swineherd Aniceto Ciampa inherited his stepfather's debt of 17 ducats in 1813, Giovanni Spina his father Francesco's debt of 16 ducats in 1824, Giovanni Romano a debt of 4 ducats from Antonio Romano in 1850, Luigi Giannotta 10 ducats from his father in 1846, and so on.

The administration tolerated even permanent debt; it charged no interest and did not punish arrearage. On no occasion was an indebted worker refused any of the usual services or required to pay his debt through a wage deduction. However, workers' debts were almost always relatively small, not above a man's yearly wages. The only recurring case of large debt involved military draftees. For a family who wished their son to avoid the service, a substitute might cost as much as 250 ducats, a huge sum, which the administration would pay in a lump sum. The draftee would reimburse the debt (usually together with a relative) in annual installments over six or seven years, until his debt was down to 20 or 25 ducats.[47]

Half of the debtors managed to pay off their debts during their working lives, some through wage deductions, others in a single settlement, perhaps by presenting the master with a mule or colt from their own stock. Of the ones who remained permanently in debt, two examples are Giuseppe Tropea, who started on the latifondo with a paternal debt and took thirty-five years to get free of it, and Filippo Siculo, who in fifteen years of work never managed to pay off his.

What happened to a man's debt if he left the latifondo, took another job, or was fired? Only in 3.6 percent of these cases was the debt eventually paid; that is, only eleven workers paid their debts in cash or kind sometime after severance. Occasionally, the administration attempted to get its money back by accepting a pledge or impounding livestock. Very rarely, in pitiful or long-standing cases, it might cancel the debt,[48] but all told, with cancellations and more or less voluntary repayments, only 5 percent of these debts were paid; in 95 percent of the instances, they remained outstanding. Sometimes a debt would "wait" for years, but as soon as the former employee resumed his job or was replaced by a relative there it was, the old debt back on the "sheet." But in most cases a debt would be "passed on" to an heir (or a succession of heirs) or to another latifondo worker, with or without explanation. It is understandable that after the hog driver Luigi Intieri had "passed on his credits" to his four sons for a score of years, they should have shouldered their father's debt (of only five ducats) at his death, but why should Pasquale Turano have had to pay Luigi Tarasi's debt? Why did Pino Saino inherit Giovanni Cinnante's? The ledgers

---

47. This was more or less the tolerance threshold, although the average debt was around eight to twelve ducats.

48. Gaetano Forte had had to give a necklace as collateral for a debt of fifteen ducats. Giovanni Periti undertook to pay seven ducats a month. When Tommaso Riccelli, who had borrowed thirty ducats to buy a mare, was fired a year later, he had to forfeit the animal in payment of his debt of forty-six ducats. In rare cases, debts were forgiven: warehouseman Gaetano Ajello began work encumbered with a twenty-six-ducat debt of his father's; when Gaetano retired in 1874, his debt (now fifty-eight ducats) was "forgiven in consideration of his and his father's long service." Guard Michele Covello was forgiven his thirty-one-ducat debt upon his retirement in 1854, and Gaetano Panza his thirty-seven-ducat debt when he was arrested in 1871.

give no explanation; evidently the habit of thinking in terms of family groups instead of individuals was so ingrained that the bookkeepers felt no need to justify the peregrinations of debts.

The low value of these debts and the ease with which they were "passed on" would seem to rule out the existence of any form of debt peonage in the latifondo system. Debt did, however, forge still another tie between master and worker. On the one hand, debt was a hold the latifondista acquired over the worker and his family; on the other, it created in the debtor a sense of gratitude toward his tolerant creditor. And it was precisely as proof positive of this tie that debt constituted an integral part of the guarantee system.

7. Protection against the State

In a splendid scene in *Le Terre del Sacramento,* a mother, seeing a conscription officer approach, cries to her son, "Make a break for it! The Fatherland's coming!"[49] Peasant populations generally saw state-imposed obligations as abuses of power; the government was an estranged presence that materialized in taxation, the draft, and the administration of justice. The government was there to demand, impose, and punish, never to give or help. The government always showed a menacing face, and it was—is—commonly thought that no ordinary soul could hope to stave off the Leviathan without the aid of a powerful patron. It so happened that the most powerful person in the district was the latifondo owner, who, though one's master and creditor, was a known element, part of a network of social relations governed by comprehensible codes of behavior, and it was his aid that a latifondo man would seek when the government was barking up his tree. Often it was simply financial aid; one asked the baron's help in paying tax arrears in time to avoid confiscation of one's cow or vegetable garden (a debt owed to the master himself was, as we have seen, much less cause for concern).[50] Persons who owned a little property might try to meet their obligation by resorting to a local loan shark. At any rate, the baron's protection was vital in the most important affairs, especially in relations with the provincial law and the army.

A man who had the benefit of the latifondo's guarantee network was in a distinctly privileged position with respect to the law-enforcement system. He was defended by an attorney, his case was attended to while he was in jail, in many instances he would receive financial aid, and the administration worked

---

49. F. Jovine, *Le Terre del Sacramento,* op. cit.

50. For instance, in 1831, the baron paid fifty ducats owed by Rocca di Neto agent Antonio Perrone's father to the Cosenza tax bureau. Luigi Ferrara had to resort several times to his employer's help to pay his taxes.

for his release by defraying court costs and by more or less open bribery, which ranged from "gifts to the judge" to smaller "gifts to prison guards."[51]

When a young man was called up for military service, there were but few choices. Sometimes a "gift" could get him released (the baron got chief cattle herder Tommaso Lamanna's grandson released with one of 40 ducats), but usually the man whose name was drawn in the draft lottery either left to do his service or provided the already mentioned "exchange for the army," that is, he paid for a substitute recruited from among the poor peasants' sons whose names had not been drawn.[52] A substitute cost from 100 to 250 ducats—an immense sum compared to a man's wages. Still, thanks to the baron's administrators, who arranged the deals and advanced the price, such "exchanges" were frequent.[53]

To enjoy these forms of protection, a provisionee did not need to hold an important position in the enterprise; employment with the latifondo over a long period of time or following a family tradition was sufficient. Gaspare Sapia, whom we have met before, worked thirty years for the Barraccos, broken only by a four-year stint in jail; Pasquale De Carlo, after being saved from conscription in 1859, served the baron until his death in 1896; and so forth.[54] The traditional bond linking these men to the Barraccos gave them a legitimate expectation of help and protection, which in turn strengthened the existing bond. Besides a material debt, these poor folk often ran up a debt of gratitude to local potentates who sided with them against what they perceived as arbitrary government.

---

51. The large sum of 279 ducats was spent for the cost of overseer Gaspare Sapia's trial in 1846 (not counting the lawyer's fee); part went for "the gift to the judge." In 1881, when a group of shepherds was prosecuted in Croton for seizing a great quantity of wine from a ship that had gone aground nearby, the baron paid their trial costs and their fines. Other "gifts" were less costly: 20 ducats "to have [the Cosenza court] acquit" the son of cowherd Nicola Bracone, and 25 ducats to free Pasquale "Folino" Turano's son Giuseppe.

52. Engaging a stand-in for one's military service was a common practice in other countries as well. E. Guillaumin describes it in France under the Second Empire and the Third Republic (*La vie d'un simple* [Paris, 1904]).

53. In 1838, an "exchange" of 221.6 ducats was paid for Pasquale Fusaro, a shepherd from San Pietro, son of a shepherd and future father of another two. Pasquale died ten years later without having managed to pay off his debt. In 1847, 240 ducats apiece were paid for Rosario, son of chief herdsman Salvatore Bitonti, and for Domenico, younger brother of Salvatore Greco. In 1849, 200 ducats were paid in Cosenza for Pasquale Zaccano's son; in 1851, 100 were paid for Pasquale Scalise's. By 1859, the price had risen to the 240 ducats paid in exchange for the young muleteer Pasquale De Carlo.

54. Tommaso Lamanna worked thirty-five years as a cowhand and chief cow herder and "gave the latifondo" four sons. Salvatore Bitonti was one member of the San Giovanni family, which supplied it with eighteen faithful servants over the century; so, too, the Grecos, the De Carlos, the Intrieri, the Zaccanos, the Turanos, and so forth.

8. Pensions, Bequests, Widows, and Emergencies

Due to his advanced age, he cannot continue to work as an agent, so Don Alberto, in consideration of the long time he served with love, faithfulness and honesty, and by a letter written March 25, 1898, to Don Luigi Ferraro in Isola, granted him as a lifetime annuity the same stipend he had received as agent in Camigliati.

The subject of this entry was Tommaso Maida, agent in the Sila for thirty-five years, who in 1898 "passed on his powers" to his son, Dr. Luigi. Although old age pensions were not among the most widespread forms of security, Don Tommaso's case was by no means an isolated one. To take another instance, his brother Carlo, who had worked as a secretary, received a pension of 180 ducats from 1879 on, and upon his death the lump sum of 233 ducats was paid over to Tommaso. Superannuated provisionees were not automatically entitled to a pension; it always depended on the baron's decision. No criterion was ever set forth for the assignment of pensions but we can infer one by analyzing the beneficiaries. They were all long-time employees of higher than average rank whose jobs kept them in close contact with the baron, and usually they came from families with a tradition of working for the Barraccos. In practice, pensions were granted to agents, administrators, tutors, and domestics, often under the condition that they remain in the household.[55] The masters' wills always provided for elderly and faithful employees (clerks, domestics, coachmen, and riders, though rarely shepherds and massari) with bequests ranging from small sums to ones as large as the 300 ducats Baron Luigi left to the domestic Domenico Mancini.

Regular protection of widows and orphans was rare, and in any case limited to those of white-collar employees, but help in specific cases of need was frequent.[56] The possibility of obtaining help in need from a deceased relative's employer strengthened the image of a right acquired through faithful service, and, indeed, the ledgers continue to note, for years after an employee's

---

55. Baron Luigi's will made his legacy to Don Costantino Lopez, the children's tutor, conditional on his "continuing the education of his grandson Luigi" and the sixty-ducat annuities assigned to many servants conditional on their not leaving the house.

56. The estate took care of Donna Peppina Laratta, widow of secretary Don Giovanni Gianfreda, and her nephew Franco Pellicori. The administration generously advanced money to Donna Vittoria Cortese of San Giovanni and helped her manage her business. Donna Gabriella Lancellotti was granted a monthly ration of flour, plus oil and beans at Christmastime. Caterina Castagnino Minelli, daughter of an elderly swineherd and widow of another employee, received six ducats a month to help pay for her son Vincenzo's education. In the same way, Giovannino Lancellotti was enabled to finish his law studies in Naples. Guard Luigi Guarascio's widow received a fixed monthly sum of "charity," which she had to "work off."

death, gifts of bread, flour, oil, pork, or cash made "in memory of ——" to his relatives.

The same obligation-expectation mechanism worked in a variety of emergency situations, of which ready credit and debt tolerance are just two examples. In general, the ledgers speak of "aid" requested by employees for a variety of reasons—sickness in the family, theft, accident, or death—and granted in all cases of "legitimate need."[57] Such "aid" always figures as a personal act of "charity" by Don Luigi, Don Checco, Don Stano, or Donna Giulietta. The item that appears most frequently is "seed grain aid," as a gift after a poor harvest or a loan to be repaid after the next harvest (different from the interest-bearing advances of seed discussed earlier). Seed grain aid was given in small amounts (from one-half to two tomoli of rye, with the specification that it was "for sowing") and was easy to obtain—in a bad year, such as 1818, a score of workers might be granted this benefit—but priority was given to workers whose wages consisted partly of land use. By lending them a hand in poor years, the latifondo assured both immutability of the wage structure and continuity in the cultivation of paraspori belonging to the large, directly managed masserie and enclosures. With an occasional gift worth no more than a couple of ducats, the master thus accomplished three purposes: he calmed the workers' worries, perpetuated the structure of labor relations, and insured the continuity of production activities.

9. Intangible Needs

The needs of any society, even the materially poorest, go beyond mere survival. Foremost among a society's legitimate *intangible* needs[58] are the *social needs* of community life, which, though distinct from needs relating to individual subsistence, survival, and protection, are nonetheless real needs of individuals or single households. Such is, for example, the need to meet traditional obligations and community expectations, whether ritualistic-religious or secu-

---

57. "After a fire in which he lost five tomoli of wheat," Rocco Guarascio received the identical amount as a gift. One worker was given five ducats "because that amount was stolen from him"; another was given three ducats that "Pugliese had stolen from him." Giovanni Battista Lopez, nicknamed Macchione, was given four ducats "for his release from prison." Gaetano Panza received a gift to console him for his arrest, Giuseppe Mancuso "for his dying wife," Maria Mutarelli "for household expenses," Pietro Milizia "to buy potatoes he needs," Matteo Puglia "for his illness," Giuseppe Sciullo for a forty-eight-day leave of absence, Saverio Malizia to travel to Cosenza to visit a son in prison, and Gaetano Tarasi "for a carriage to take him home sick" a few days before his death.

58. I borrow this very appropriate term from G. Levi, *L'eredità immateriale: Carriera di un esorcista nel Piemonte del Seicento* (Turin, 1985).

lar.[59] Some of these—weddings, deaths, prescribed holidays, dowry settlements, and commitments of a ritualistic-religious nature—appear frequently in the latifondo ledgers. Such needs, though normally predictable, had to be attended to in little time. For instance, settling a girl's dowry and assembling her trousseau were urgent problems in a society in which social spaces for unmarried women were practically nil and a girl who reached the age of twenty-five without marrying was fated to remain so for the rest of her days.[60] Carnival and Christmas had to be celebrated every year, and a deceased person obviously had to be honored with a funeral, however modest. A family that lacked the wherewithal to fulfil these obligations had to procure it somehow, even at the cost of incurring a debt. Here the latifondo appeared once more in its providential role but not only that of the understanding creditor. The administration, well aware of the subjective and social importance ascribed to the satisfaction of these needs, would come through with a suitable gift or a supply of appropriate commodities charged to the worker's account. The financial value of these actions depended on the social standing of the family involved and its closeness to the masters. In 1880, when the Barraccos' old coachman and rider Gervasio Magliocco gave his daughter in marriage, the baron advanced him the large sum of 500 lire for her dowry and another 275 to furnish a home for her in Naples. In 1867, the baron made Don Luigi Ferrari a present of sixty-five ducats for his daugher's trousseau and contributed another ten toward the wedding feast, whereas Carolina Laudari, a servant, received only 10 pise of wool for her daughter's dowry, and a chief herder got five ducats for "his son's wedding favors." Christmas and Carnival gifts—usually food stuffs—were distributed according to the same principle: majorca, hogs, and good olive oil to white-collar employees, pork and rye to simple provisionees. But the principle applied to all faithful workers, without exception. Even people who were not currently employed on the latifondo but remained within its sphere of influence were entitled to aid and holiday gifts.

The latifondo recognized the legitimacy of ritualistic-religious commit-

---

59. There is now a vast literature on the structure of needs in peasant societies. See F. Piselli, *Parentela ed emigrazione* (Turin, 1981); A. Chayanov, *Theory of Peasant Economy,* op. cit.; J. Scott, *Moral Economy,* op. cit.; E. P. Thompson, "The Moral Economy of the English Crowd," *Past and Present* 50 (February 1971); the subsequent debate in *Past and Present* 54 (February 1972), and 58 (February 1973); and M. Aymard, "Autoconsommation et marché: Chayanov, Labrousse ou Le Roy Ladurie?" *Annales E.S.C.* 33:6.

60. The custom of fairly early marriage seems to have been followed throughout the Mediterranean. See J. G. Peristiany, *Honour and Shame,* op. cit.; J. A. Davis, *People of the Mediterranean* (London and Boston, 1977); and P. Moretti, "L'economia del matrimonio," op. cit. It was otherwise in the peasant societies of northwestern Europe (see L. Stone, *Family, Sex, and Marriage* [New York, 1977]).

ments and would step in if an employee had trouble meeting them; for one man it would pay "the cost of candles" to be lit in church, for another his "alms to the Greek Madonna," for still another his contribution to "the funeral of the parish priest," and so on, even advancing a fence builder the eighty ducats he had "pledged for the Chapel of Saint Blaise." Upon the death of an employee or a member of his family, the administration would offer the bereaved either a contribution toward funeral expenses or a gift of money. Sometimes the latifondo itself took charge of a funeral, as for "the burial and other expenses" of Michele Cervino, who was killed by brigands in 1864, and of Benedetto Pizzuto, a guard for thirty-seven years, who was given a fine thirty-three-ducat funeral. It was also customary for the latifondo to pay for the celebration of a mass in a local church for the soul of a "deceased old servant."[61]

10. Gifts and Rewards

The terms for gift and reward—*regalo* and *regalia*—appear very frequently in the latifondo documents. Rewards included remuneration in cash or kind for work over and above a worker's regular tasks ("reward for harvesting work"), performance bonuses ("reward for care and precision in selling products"), seniority bonuses ("reward in recognition of his father's and his long service"), rewards for a particular character trait ("granted a hunting license because he is well mannered"), and advances on pay raises. Gifts proper were expected and handed out in holiday seasons (Christmas, Carnival, and Easter) and on special occasions.

A present made without a specific explanation in the ledger might simply attest to affection—a concept that, in the context of master-employee relations, was not univocal. When young Luigi and Errico Barracco gave cleric Don Costantino's nephew a fine horse (valued at two hundred ducats), their gift was a token of their affection for and gratitude toward their old tutor, but in most cases the master's presents went to subordinates not personally known to him. What kinds of gifts were made? Cash was given only rarely, and then by family members who had no role in the enterprise (Lady Barracco, Miss Giulietta, the count of Aquila); the master himself gave trifling "things"—wool, oil, cheese, or shoats—rarely worth more than six ducats. And, while such gifts went to provisionees of all categories, they arrived infrequently (perhaps two over one's entire working life but never more than four) and never before one had been on the job for at least five years.

---

61. The usual contribution of 5 to 20 ducats for funeral expenses was paid to the widow or orphans. Ten to 15 ducats would go to a worker who had lost a close relative, with the specification that the gift was "for his dead father [or child, brother, or wife]." Occasionally special outlays were made as tokens of esteem, such as the 130 ducats spent in 1846 to erect a statue on the tomb of Don Tommaso Martino who had been the family priest and the children's tutor for twenty-six years.

Still, these gifts, though rarely made and of little material value, played a precise and important role in the guarantee system, for they were instruments of differentiation within the world of the provisionees. As we have seen, other kinds of rewards were considered de facto entitlements, but a benevolent and apparently nonreciprocal gift attested to the master's personal affection. In a way, the gift as "pure" token of affection was the crown piece of the guarantee system. On the one hand, it reinforced behavior and character traits desired by the master, and on the other it put a sheen of sentiment on his power to give. The behavior and traits that the gift "affectionately" encouraged were the same ones that gave access to the system's facilities: lengthy service, family tradition, and loyalty to the master. We have already discussed the first two, and their functionality hardly needs further illustration, but the concept of loyalty calls for special attention. The latifondista judged a worker loyal, hence worthy of enjoying all the privileges of the guarantee system, if he was *willing, constant,* and *well mannered.* A willing worker was one who was docile and could be put to different uses; he was *willing* to take on jobs other than his regular work over the course of the year (to help out in harvesting or at the oil press, for instance) and *willing* to travel (typically required for the seasonal stock drives), accepting long separation from his family. "Constancy" referred to his attitude toward his employment with the latifondo; a *constant* worker was one who sought no other job opportunity and maintained an unbroken relationship with the latifondo. In this sense, absence due to an inevitable necessity such as military service or a jail term did not compromise the image of constancy; this is why draftees and convicts could continue, as we have seen, to have full access to the guarantee system's facilities. Lastly, "well manneredness" described behavior toward the latifondo. A *well-mannered* worker was obedient, sober, honest, and nonviolent; that is, he contributed to the social peace on which the system's stability rested. It is worth repeating that this trait referred to a man's behavior toward the latifondo; however else he may have behaved outside its sphere did not affect his rating in this respect. A "thievish" man, for instance, was so described only with reference to the master's property; theft, manslaughter, and brawling that did not affect the latifondo itself were seen as accidents, and the guilty party was still deserving of the master's protection.

It will be noted that the character traits that made up "loyalty"—willingness, constancy, and good manners—were not directly related to the importance of one's job (although the loyalty index was generally higher among white-collar employees), hence the *loyalty reward* that consisted of full access to guarantee facilities did not depend on one's rank. While an agent's credit might be higher, his hospital bed softer, and the gifts he received costlier than a muleteer's, he came by these benefits neither more easily nor more frequently than a muleteer did. Moreover, only in very rare instances did loyalty bring material advantages, which depended on one's type of work; in general, rewards for loyalty consisted solely of unrestricted admission to the guarantee system.

The fact that the guarantee system fostered and rewarded loyalty, conservatism, and aspiration to family security obviously contributed to their persistence among the cultural values of this society. But to believe, as Edward Banfield does, that this *collective* mentality was the symptom of a fatalistic attitude of passive acceptance, of an "immoral familism," is to have missed its deep social motivations.[62]

---

62. E. Banfield, *The Moral Basis,* op. cit. Banfield's thesis has been too widely criticized for it to be discussed again here. As to this particular topic, I would merely point out that it is a mistake to equate poverty with wretchedness and backwardness and to mechanically apply indicators of American-style participation and protest—and only a very few at that, regarding volunteer associations and political organizations—to a context in which these phenomena are totally absent. See also A. Pizzorno, "Familismo amorale e marginalità storica," *Quaderni di Sociologia* 2 (1960).

PART 3

The Decline of the Latifondo System

CHAPTER 7

The Rationality of the Latifondo System and Its Long-term Dynamics

1. A System in Equilibrium

The latifondo system was neither an inefficient and obsolete white elephant, as the literature of the early twentieth century would have it, nor a necessity imposed by nature, as its nineteenth-century supporters averred. For most of the nineteenth century it remained a model of rationality. By practicing the most traditional form of agriculture—a combination of grain and livestock farming —the latifondo achieved a whole set of goals: scale economies permitted maximum output with full (though not intensive) use of available land; and the traditional alternation of land uses took advantage of the mild winter climate and at least partly avoided the problems of summer aridity, maintaining ecological equilibrium and assuring safe and constant profits.[1]

The latifondo economy was a simple one, and its organization was elementary, but these characteristics should not be mistaken for backwardness or apathy. On the contrary, the Barracco enterprise was perfectly capable of innovating both its technology and its organization, and it was sensitive to market signals. Its simplicity was geared to optimal and rational resource use, and it served two purposes, one social, the other economic. By basing its operations and organization on the guarantee system (that is, by incorporating traditional practices, long-standing customs, deep-seated hierarchies, and ac-

---

1. Ascanio Branca pointed out the rationality of these crops, "which, though less profitable in terms of their aggregate cash value, are exposed less to seasonal changes; in those days, when arable land and pastures were worth very little, they yielded sure and constant profits" (*Atti della Giunta per la Inchiesta Agraria,* Branca Report, op. cit., xxvii). Even Rossi Doria admitted that this agriculture constituted "an admirable cycle linking the mountains and the plains, summer and winter, in harmony with the climate and nature's own cycle of fertility. . . ." M. Rossi Doria, *Riforma agraria e azione meridionalista* (Bologna, 1956), 10–11; E. Azimonti, *Il Mezzogiorno agrario quale è,* ed. G. Fortunato (Bari, 1919); and F. Barbagallo, *Stato, Parlamento e lotte politico-sociali* (Naples, 1976), 2–3.

cumulated social wisdom) the latifondo system succeeded in preventing class polarization and insuring virtually unbroken social peace in its own territory.[2] And, by avoiding investments in fixed assets, the enterprise was able to convert capital rapidly from one form to another, adapting easily to the ups and downs of the market while preserving a notable degree of autonomy.[3]

2. Peace on the Latifondo: Armed Defense

The records register only a handful of violent actions, individual or collective, directed against the Barraccos' property. Still, the region was characterized by a fairly high level of conflict. In addition to civil suits involving unauthorized grazing, distraint, unpaid debts, and foreclosures, the local courts judged a great many charges of affray, battery, theft, manslaughter, murder, rape, resistance, and smuggling.[4] This was a common enough situation in the South: latent conflict with government institutions, endemic war among the poor, and peace between rich and poor. Most of the credit for the social peace reigning in the latifondo's territory—an achievement extraordinary especially at times of uprisings and brigandage—should go to the guarantee system. It performed its major function of insuring peace and preventing contestation of its hierarchy of power, by rewarding loyalty and punishing rebellious behavior and offensive actions. But it would be ingenuous to credit the guarantee system alone; the Barraccos' persons and property were also defended and protected by shotguns—"organized" shotguns entrusted to a small private army of field and household guards and watchmen. These guns were different from the ones a peasant might own in that they were better and they were legal. The single- and double-barreled shotguns the guards carried, purchased in Naples through the latifondo administration and kept in good repair at its expense, were better than the sawed-off shotguns and harquebuses the peasants used,[5] and they were protected by regularly issued permits procured through the master.

The law not only permitted but encouraged the formation of such private armies as a means of governing and controling the possession of firearms, a perpetual concern of nineteenth-century governments in a region where peasants habitually kept guns to defend livestock and humans against "wolves,

---

2. Martinez Alier finds the same factors underlying the stability of the *latifundo* system in southern Spain (*La estabilidad del latifundismo* [Ruedo Iberico, 1968]).

3. On this question, see G. Valenti, "L'Italia agricola dal 1861 al 1911," in *Cinquanta anni di storia italiana* (Milan, 1911), 2:104–5.

4. The Barracco estate was involved in some way in only three or four of the numerous criminal cases (see SACZ, Grand Criminal Court of Calabria II).

5. Michele Pizzuto and the brothers Antonio and Giovanni Biafora bought their shotguns in 1871 for seventy ducats apiece; a double-barreled shotgun never cost less than twenty-two ducats.

foxes and brigands" (and often for other purposes as well). The first to regulate gun possession were the French, who, in the midst of a war of conquest, and mindful of the experience of 1799, introduced the police legislation that required anyone who carried a weapon for either hunting or defense to obtain an annual permit from the local authorities (and pay a fee of 2.42 ducats). These laws were retained by both the Bourbons and the Kingdom of Italy, and, while they doubtless reduced the presence of firearms (axes, knives, and clubs are mentioned more frequently in the criminal trial records),[6] they also created the conditions whereby large landowners, who had the cash to pay the fees (2.42 ducats was more than half the average worker's monthly pay), could establish nearly oligopolistic control over them. A Barracco, for instance, would procure, pay for, and renew at least fifty gun permits a year.[7] The members of the "armies" thus formed were protected by both the law and the latifondo.

Here, by way of example, is the story of Sabato Fumo, of San Benedetto, a latifondo guard charged with attempted murder. In September of 1822, "acting in his capacity of guard in the employ of Baron Barracco," Fumo seized some cattle he had found grazing on the baron's land. They belonged to one Don Vincenzo Spina and were tended "by his herdsman Giuseppe Vonà." Vonà accused Fumo of "penning . . . only my cattle" and letting other people's range at will. With the words "I'll show you whether I'm going to free them," he pulled "his ax out of his belt," whereupon Fumo fired at him point blank with "the firearm commonly called *pallottini,* a shotgun," reloaded the weapon, and then, "as many people had run up," fled to avoid arrest. Vonà was permanently disfigured.[8]

At the end of the trial, which was held eight years later, the court found Fumo guilty of inflicting a "serious wound" but recognized that he had acted "in his capacity as [Barracco's] guard" and sentenced him to a mere seven months in jail.

Sabato Fumo had worked as a Barracco guard since 1818, and he was kept on as an *armed* employee for years after that fateful September. His brother Antonio was also a guard, and in later years his grandson Vincenzo worked in

---

6. Charges of theft and illegal possession of weapons might be tried before the grand criminal courts in the provincial capitals. Some people argued, perhaps out of personal interest, that the restrictions "increased the population of wolves, foxes and boars . . . [and were] damaging to flocks, people and fields" (see U. Caldora, *La Statistica murattiana,* op. cit., 48, 75).

7. The prefects were always reporting that they had increased oversight of gun permits and the number of seizures, but the amount of rustling did justify their issuing more permits, which they explained as being "due mainly to the summer season, when people feel more strongly the need to guard the fields, and to carry arms in order to protect life and property" (Prefect Movizzo of Lower Calabria II, "report" dated June 1885; P. Borzomati, *La Calabria dal 1882,* op. cit., 149). Each province issued from three to four thousand gun permits.

8. SACZ, Great Criminal Court, 1824, 85–87.

the palace kitchens. In other words, as far as the latifondo was concerned, Fumo's action had been a quirk. Moreover, the court had acknowledged that a person acting as the baron's guard was allowed to use weapons, just as a policeman was, and, by giving him a light sentence, ipso facto recognized the latifondo's institutional character.

We have seen already that the Barraccos' "army" was made up of a rather large number of men, all loyal to the master because their very nearness made their service and loyalty highly personal.[9] But, if armed defense and the guarantee system could be really effective in times of peasant uprisings and brigandage, it was partly due to another factor: such forms of popular rebellion were directed not so much against the latifondisti as against the government, at once interventionist and absentee.

3. Peace on the Latifondo: Brigandage and Peasant Uprisings

Ever since the publication of Eric Hobsbawm's *Primitive Rebels* in 1965, there has been a tendency to interpret all popular uprisings of the nineteenth and twentieth centuries in terms of a primitive class struggle.[10] Hobsbawm's thesis

---

9. Loyalty to their master could lead them into conflict with the local populace, especially during years of turbulence. "In the memorable year of 1848, when the terrifying idea of communism had overcome men's reason," a nineteen-year-old shoemaker from Isola, imbued with "hatred for Barracco's property," tried to burn down one of the baron's woods. The property was saved thanks to the prompt action of guards Benedetto Pizzuto, Michele Covelli, and Filippo Caputo (whose deed earned him promotion to the rank of household guard), but the young man was sentenced anyway to eight years in irons for arson (SACZ, Grand Criminal Court, 1849). Many accounts speak of these conflicts of loyalty. G. Arrighi and F. Piselli mention several that took place in the Marquisate ("Parentela, clientela," op. cit., 410–11).

10. E. Hobsbawm, *Primitive Rebels* (New York, 1965), especially the chapter on "The Social Bandit." See A. Blok's criticism, "The Peasant and the Brigand: Social Banditry Reconsidered," *Comparative Studies in Society and History* 14, no. 4 (1972), 494–503; and Hobsbawm's reply in the same issue. The same interpretation is given in *Il brigantaggio meridionale: Cronaca inedita dell'Unità d'Italia,* ed. A. De Jaco (Rome, 1969); and A. Scirocco, "Fenomeni di persistenza del ribellismo contadino: Il briganntaggio in Calabria prima dell'Unità," *Archivio Storico per le Province Napoletane* (1981): 245–79. For interpretations of southern Italian brigandage in political terms, see A. Lucarelli, *Il brigantaggio politico nel Mezzogiorno d'Italia* (Milan, 1982); L. M. Greco, *Annali di Citeriore Calabria* (Cosenza, 1872); A. de Custine, *Mémoires et voyages* (Paris, 1830), 398–99; P. Calà-Ulloa, *Della sollevazione delle Calabrie contro a' Francesi* (Rome, 1871); and R. Church, *Brigantaggio e società segrete nelle Puglie* (Florence, 1899). The romantic image of the brigands appears in J. Rambaud, "Fra Diavolo et le commandant Hugo," *Revue napoléonenne* 13 (1913); C. Bianco di Saint Jorioz (who sees Calabria as a historical model of guerrilla warfare), *Della guerra nazionale d'insurrezione per bande applicata all'Italia: Trattato dedicato ai buoni Italiani da un amico del paese,* 2 vols. (Malta, 1830); and B. Croce, "Angiolillo (Angelo Duca) capo di banditi" (1892), reprinted in *La rivoluzione napoletana del 1799* (Bari, 1953). Croce was later inclined to the "degenerative" interpretation ("La fine di Mammone," *Archivio Storico per le Province Napoletane* 30 (1905): 468–80). See also E. Wolf, *Peasant Wars*

provides a social interpretation of rebellion at the expense of a political or ethical one. It combines a consistently progressive view of history with true compassion for the people, and it has the merit of rediscovering in the "people without history" the protagonist of its own actions. This is why it has enjoyed great success with historians of southern Italy (and not Marxists alone).[11] Nonetheless, his thesis actually recasts the people as an *unwitting* actor. Sanfedist or Vandean, driven by a sacrosanct thirst for social justice, the people choose the wrong means—self-defeating means—out of ignorance or incapacity, allowing themselves to be manipulated by the reactionary forces of throne and altar locked in battle against the forces of progress.[12]

Applied to nineteenth-century Calabria, this thesis does not explain why, during sixty years of "social" brigandage, landed property suffered so little damage. There can be no doubt that, although Robin-Hoodism was a diffused model of behavior, landowners were not the main target of Calabria's brigands, who did not operate at all as class vanguard. To the contrary, though brigandage, as Fernand Braudel wrote, had existed in Calabria since time immemorial, its nineteenth-century course echoed political rather than social crises. Unfortunately, contemporary assessments of the number of brigands operating in the region over the century are unreliable, for different phenomena were labeled "brigandage" in different periods. But, if we take these estimates simply as an indication of orders of magnitude and compare them with the numerical data on trials before the Great Criminal Court of Catanzaro (table

---

of the Twentieth Century (New York, 1969); E. Wolf, *Europe and the People Without History* (Berkeley, 1982); and B. Moore, *Social Origins of Dictatorship and Democracy* (Boston, 1967), 75 and passim.

11. Study of the *Parlamentary Reports*—all written from a positivistic and progressive point of view—has supplanted research into what the protagonists themselves had to say. Historians (even F. Molfese in his exhaustive *Storia del brigantaggio dopo l'Unità* [Milan, 1974] have tended to accept the idea that at a certain point "brigandage turned into roguery," neglecting, or even ridiculing, the declarations of bandit chieftains like Crocco, the contents of bills posted by brigands in the towns, eyewitness accounts, and the romantic historiography of the period. This interpretation is not shared by the new school of southern historians of the 1970s, whose most significant contribution remains E. M. Capecelatro and A. Carlo's essay *Contro la "Questione Meridionale"* (Rome, 1972). Their thesis is an invitation to rethink the whole history of southern Italy in the nineteenth century, but in fact their study focuses almost exclusively on the structural aspect. Works such as C. Ajanello's *La conquista del Sud* (Milan, 1972), on the other hand, are conceived as testimonies rather than research.

12. Hobsbawm treats misguided rebels with much sympathy and understanding: the peasant masses, unwitting and unassisted, were not responsible for their own mistakes. The fault lay rather with the progressive forces, which were unable to pass a real agrarian law, endorsed the Jacobin ideal of the small freehold farm (and perhaps a large one for themselves), and never could understand the people's deep attachment to their "superstitions." The act of rebellion, though tragically misguided, redeems the people from the brutishness generated by poverty and ignorance. It would be interesting to review in these terms the argument between Salvemini and Gramsci on the autonomous role of the southern masses and the "social bloc."

TABLE 19.   Political and Brigandage Trials in Catanzaro Province, 1821–1900

Year	Political	Brigandage
1821–1830	8	34
1831–1840	6	26
1841–1850	63	172
1851–1860	61	53
1861–1870	178	480
1871–1880	35	216
1881–1890	20	10
1891–1900	9	5
Total	380	996

19),[13] we can see at least that brigandage intensified during times of political crisis, reform efforts, and war. In 1810, Intendent Galli counted 30,000 brigands in Upper Calabria along, whereas the 1821 records mention barely 190 in the whole region, and the 1862–63 records cite some 100,000 men and a few women.[14] The discrepancies can be explained not so much by reason of ideological conflict as by the fact that these periods coincided with a larger presence of the government and its representatives: native or foreign soldiers, policemen, tax collectors, land surveyors, teachers, and judges. Their presence simply multiplied the number of opportunities for conflict with local populations (harassment of women, offense to religious images, impoundment, requisitions of "bed, board, and fire" from tax delinquents, conscription), incidents usually followed by the flight of the local person involved, who, rather than take his chances with an alien "and unjust" judicial system, preferred to turn brigand.

In consequence, these agents of the government (but not the king, its symbol)[15] were held reponsible for the conditions that turned people into

13. The Great Criminal Court of Catanzaro held 1,376 trials on political charges and brigandage under the Bourbon and Italian monarchies (SACZ, Lower Calabria II: Political Trials and Brigandage).

14. U. Caldora, *Fra patriotti e briganti* (Bari, 1974); U. Caldora, *Calabria Napoleonica,* op. cit.; F. Solimena, *Francesi, giacobini e briganti in Calabria: Un processo verbale del 1807;* G. Cingari, *Brigantaggio, proprietari e contadini nel Sud, 1799–1900* (Chiaravalle, 1976); J. Rambaud, *Naples sous Joseph Bonaparte* (Paris, 1911); F. Gaudioso, "Orientamenti per una storia del brigantaggio postunitario nella provincia di Cosenza," *Calabria Contemporanea,* 14, no. 3 (1974): 98–165; J. Gelli, *Banditi, briganti e brigantesse nell'Ottocento* (Florence, 1931); M. Milani, *La repressione dell'ultimo brigantaggio nelle Calabrie, 1868–69,* (Pavia, 1952); M. Petrusewicz, "Society Against the State: Peasant Brigandage in Southern Italy," *Criminal Justice History* 8 (1987).

15. This does not mean that government intervention was not desired on these or other occasions. In 1848, the peasants of Calabria were clearly trying to send a signal to the king, in the

brigands, and their persons and property were the most frequent, and most applauded, targets of the brigands' *vendetta,* revenge. As soon as a band set foot in a town, it proceeded, with the population's at least passive support, to burn down the soldiers' barracks, the property registry, and the headquarters of the police, the National Guard, or the Royal Carabineers—"the headquarters of our eternal enemies," as Crocco put it.[16] In this perspective, opposition to the local landowners simply took a back seat. This is why, despite some incidents of plundering or robbery, and notwithstanding their fears, landowners as such suffered little damage at the hands of the brigands, so little that they were suspected of connivance.[17] The Barraccos were afraid—they traveled with six-man escorts and stationed guards in their homes—but their property was seldom raided by brigands.

It is true that Barracco property was plundered on two occasions, but even if these episodes were labeled "brigandage" they were actually more in the way of looting by people who simply seized opportunities offered by the historical moment. The first such occasion occurred in the summer of 1806. Calabria was already "at war,"[18] the French garrison had left Cosenza, and the province was overrun by French, English, and Neapolitan troops, some marshaled and some dispersed, and by brigands. Like other landowners, the Barracco family had departed for Naples, leaving their homes under thin guard. On July 5, pillaging broke out in the Sila and simultaneously in Spezzano Piccolo, Rocca di Neto, Altilia, and Isola; in Camigliati the "brigands" seized stores, flocks, farm equipment, household furnishings, money, and silverware. They were joined by people from nearby towns who "carted away" the booty.[19] Losses were

firm belief that the common usages were rights protected by the monarch as well as by custom. But the "good king" was always surrounded by evil and corrupt officials—a recurrent idea in popular revolts, as G. Rudé demonstrates in *The Crowd in History* (New York, 1964).

16. The stories, ballads, and anecdotes about the brigands still told and sung today narrate ambushes laid for soldiers, policemen, false witnesses, corrupt judges, government officials, and tax collectors. Basso Tomeo, the "King of the Countryside," was said to have a real penchant for burning down French barracks with the troops inside. Crocco recalls seventy-five murders in his autobiography, about fifty of them of government agents. Musolino, "the last brigand," killed seven carabinieri, a judge, a mayor, false witnesses, and his own "crooked" lawyer. Vincenzo Padula has his Antonello proclaim, "To heal the sores of our unhappy Calabria . . . the headman's ax should first dispatch the Intendent, the King's Attorney and the Mayor, and lastly the menials and the clerks in City Hall" (*Antonello capobrigante calabrese,* op. cit., 13).

17. Progressive intellectuals as well as government officials entertained this suspicion. See M. Petrusewicz, "Signori e briganti: Repressione del brigantaggio nel periodo francese in Calabria," in *Storia e cultura del Mezzogiorno* (Rome, 1977).

18. A. Mozzillo, *Cronache della Calabria,* op. cit.

19. On July 5, in the Sila, "twenty-two brigands from Longobucco seized five shotguns and two pistols," says the Camigliati agent's report to the baron; at noon "thirty-six brigands from Marinelli plundered the pantry and the storehouse," tied up the unfortunate agent and two other men, and made them hand over two hundred ducats in cash. The events on July 10 were more

considerable (though Alfonso Barracco, given special powers by the French, later managed to recover a good part of the loot,[20] but there is no evidence to suggest that landowners in general, or the Barraccos in particular, had been specifically targeted by peasants or "brigands"; the looters seem simply to have seized the chance to raid poorly guarded property in uncertain times.[21]

The second episode occurred forty years later when Baron Alfonso was long dead and Baron Luigi was sixty. During the 1840s, peasants from townships on the flanks of the Sila were protesting against encroachments of common lands by the great landowners: the Barraccos, the Berlingieris, the Compagnas, the Cosentinis, the Giudicessas, and the Mollos. In April of 1841, the inhabitants of Pietrafitta, Spezzano Grande, Spezzano Piccolo, Macchia, and Casale attempted to break and sow land in the Barracco enclosures. In 1848, this unrest swelled into a great movement to reclaim (occupy) the land. In July, peasants from the Cosenza side of the Sila uplands seized the rich latifondisti's

---

serious: the "brigands" came en masse, removed all the furniture from the Camigliati house, "found the hiding place with 30,000 ducats in cash and 10,000 ducats in silverware," then "began to wreak havoc in the buildings and took the belongings," including all the hardware on the farm; one "Pio Sciaverta even took twenty-two cow chains." At this point the "whole population of Celico" arrived "with carts" and "took away" rye, beans, and cheese, while three "brigands" (two men and a youth) "took two flocks of young sheep from Scarola's stock." At Spezzano Piccolo they took "belongings from the mansion, beds, and linen."

20. Testifying before a commission that was investigating the patriots' losses, Barracco claimed that in addition to the property already listed, he had lost "6,000 sheep and goats, 400 pair of cattle, thirty pair of mares, 150 plow oxen, 4,000 tomoli of rye, 2,000 of barley, 1,000 pair of caciocavallo cheeses." He put the total damage at 198,000 ducats, which he asked the provincial intendent to compensate. In reality, Alfonso Barracco's losses amounted to much less, because "going through the province" with the truly extraordinary powers the French had granted him in September of 1806 (and subsequently further enlarged), he managed to get back a good part of his property. For instance, one Pietro Scanello from Santa Severina "promised [in writing!] to return 200 ewes with their lambs, cheese, and milk, which had come to him indirectly during the brigandage"; so, too, his fellow citizen Vincenzo Mazzei and many others, who signed notes and accounts specifying what had come to them and what they were willing to return. A number of horses bearing the Barracco brand were recovered in conflicts with the bandits and returned to their owner.

21. Nor are there any indications that the Barraccos were attacked by the brigands because of their friendliness to the French. This idea was maintained by General Verdier, who in the meantime had become friendly with Alfonso. Verdier managed to persuade Saliceti, the minister of police, of it, and a few years later it enabled him to obtain compensation for his friend, "to help him out of his economic difficulties." Alfonso Barracco, wrote Verdier, "suffered the hostility of the Bourbon court and his property was plundered by the brigands" *because* he had been loyal to the French since 1799. See BA: G1(2), the "Statement issued by the Commission charged by the Provincial Intendent with Verifying the Patriots' Losses," dated Cosenza, October 13, 1807; G1(5), a letter from Verdier to Barracco, dated Cosenza, September 10, 1806; a letter from the intendent to Barracco, dated December 22, 1806, mentioning the opinion of Saliceti; letters from General Amato, commander of the province after Verdier's departure and a distant relative of the Barraccos; and various lists and notes.

flocks, notably those belonging to Baron Barracco, and began to hoe the enclosures with the intention of drawing the king's attention to the usurpation of state lands, reclaiming customary common rights ("to cut hay in their common lands"), and forcing the usurpers to pay grazing fees.[22] The Silan latifondisti were targeted qua usurpers not qua latifondisti.[23] Incidentally, over the following year, the baron and his partners recovered all the thousands of animals that had been seized, with the help of "troops," the National Guard, and the Gendarmerie, and municipal authorities, or by paying ransom to "the malfeasants."[24] But that summer of 1848 the baron's family left in terror for Sorrento, and in the absence of the masters the inhabitants of the nearby towns seized the harvest, stores, flocks, household furnishings, and buildings in Altilia, Isola, Aja di Ponticelli, Polligrone, and Rocca Ferdinandea, damaging houses, outbuildings, and vineyards.[25] "Criminal" occupation, division,

---

22. In this connection, Basile quotes a significant report submitted by Ferdinando Barca, commander of the National Guard in Pedace and an eyewitness to the events: "As soon as they reached the Sila area, [the peasants] built a huge wooden crucifix, on which they all laid their right hands and swore to claim all the rights they believe to be theirs"; he unhappily concludes that "lives are at stake, because [the peasants] do not know the law" (A. Basile, *Moti contadini,* op. cit., 87 and passim). But the action was in some degree effective, because another landowner whose flock had been seized, Cosentini of Aprigliano, at once declared himself willing to pay the grazing fee. On the uprising of 1848, see, in addition to the works mentioned above, G. G. Rossi, *Storia dei rivolgimenti politici nelle Due Sicilie, 1847–1850* (Naples, 1851–52); A. Basile, "La questione silana dal 1838 al 1876," in *Atti del Secondo Congresso Storico Calabrese* [Proceedings of the Second Conference on Calabrian History] (Naples, 1961), 461–80; M. Borretti, "Storia delle occupazioni di terre in Calabria Citra," in *Chiarezza,* vol. 3 (Cosenza, 1964); G. Valente, "Le condizioni ed i moti dei contadini in Sila nel 1848," *Rassegna Storica del Risorgimento* 3–4 (1951): 679–90; and T. Pedio, *Contadini e galantuomini nelle province del Mezzogiorno d'Italia durante i moti del 1848* (Matera, 1963).

23. The only instance in which Barracco was targeted as a specific object of hatred, and his property chosen for an attack, was the above-mentioned attempt to burn down the woods in Isola, and in that case his property was defended by his own employees.

24. About "fifteen thousand sheep, mostly merinos, a thousand cattle, six hundred horses, six hundred plow oxen, besides goats and hogs" were seized from Luigi Barracco. In a claim submitted to the minister of internal affairs, the baron said his loss amounted to "over two hundred thousand ducats," with "the destruction of the finest breeds of horses, cattle, and merinos introduced into Calabria." But in reality he got back almost all his livestock, while the investigation of the encroachments on Sila lands and the claim that they belonged to the public domain was postponed until after the conclusion of Commissioner Barletta's investigation.

25. The inhabitants ("reprobates") "of the countryside of Celico and Pedace, and other people from Pietrafitta and Aprigliano" set themselves to plundering. In Altilia, 130 cheeses and about two hundredweight of grain were "plundered" and the vineyards badly damaged (they produced no harvest in the next three autumns). In Isola and on the Ponticelli farm, 86 cheeses were taken (about 258 pounds); in Polligrone, 4,172 *militri* of oil (about 16.3 tons); in Rocca Ferdinandea, 245 tomoli of millet (about 367 bushels). The partnerships with Morelli lost sheep, cattle, and two oxen. The damages produced by vandalism were perhaps more serious. An affidavit dated January 1850 claimed that "In the riots of July 1848, not only was all the personal property

and cultivation of common lands occurred the next summer, too, but this time they did not involve Barracco property; however, the great gristmill in Rocca Ferdinandea was looted, and around twenty-five hundred tomoli of grain were lost.

Significantly, latifondo property was practically unscathed by the wave of "brigandage" in the 1860s, though it was most intense in the latifondo's own district. The whole province was in turmoil; court records speak of dozens of armed "bands" operating against the government and against the state. Whether charged with attempted murder or political agitation, with robbery or with praising the Bourbons, they were all prosecuted for brigandage.[26] In July of 1861, peasants armed with hoes set out to occupy Camigliati land but were stopped on the way by a company of infantry and a unit of the Mobile Guard of Cosenza. One peasant was killed and twelve were arrested, but the property was kept safe.[27] In the midst of all this tumult, the brigands destroyed a few olive groves, extorted a little money, killed one guard and enrolled two of the Barraccos' long-faithful herders—all in all, mere nothings. The oil output seemed unaffected, the brigands' relatives continued to work for the Barraccos, and the dead guard's son was hired in his father's place.[28]

---

existing in the Camigliati farm buildings sacked and destroyed, but the buildings themselves were vandalized and rendered uninhabitable. . . . The baron's house in the town of Spezzano Piccolo was also plundered." See the document notarized by A. Militi in Croton, January 11, 1850. Reports and notes on plundering and damages and on negotiations with the "rogues" are in BA: F1(5), A71, A72, A74.

26. In the decade from 1861 to 1870, the Grand Court of Catanzaro tried 480 cases of brigandage (see table 19), triple the number in the decade from 1841 to 1850. Often whole groups of men and women were charged with joining in "armed bands" against the government and the state, "conspiring against the government," destroying registers of vital statistics, posting bills, making speeches "against the present government" and against the new king, going through the towns "singing the praises of the Bourbons, waving flags, and invoking the return of the sovereign Francis II," perpetrating "attempts on life, arson, robbery, and kidnapping," and trying to overthrow the government by force. Some of these "brigandage" trials involved dozens of defendants: a band of 54 men from Cotronei and Scandale; one of 59 from Taverna, Soveria, Zagarise, Albi, and Simeri; one of 17 from San Giovanni and Santa Severina; one of 36 from San Giovanni, Casabona, and Zinga; one of 141 men, women, friars, and notables accused of an "attempt to change the form of government, participation in an armed band, and sacking a warehouse in Rocca di Neto"; and so on.

27. According to *Il Calabrese,* the journal of the Cosenza romantics, the peasants, "carrying hoes and other tools . . . went to occupy land in the Camigliati zone." This was in July of 1861. In fact, land occupations almost always took place in July, just after the harvest. But summer was also the season when the adventure of brigandage called. Padula spoke of youths who "hurried the advent of summer so as to go into the mountains." On the peasant revolts of 1860–61, see G. Racioppi, *Storia dei moti di Basilicata e delle provincie contermini nel 1860* (Bari, 1910); and A. Basile, "Un episodio del movimento contadino nella Sila del 1860 e le vicende del feudo demaniale Frisone," in *Calabria Nobilissima,* vol. 13 (Cosenza, 1959).

28. According to Guglielmo Barracco, the brigands destroyed the olive groves of Petrizia,

If the Barraccos ever had much to fear from the brigands, it would have been during the French period when Alfonso was given the task of suppressing brigandage in the province. In that moment, in fact, Barraccos represented the government. As will be recalled, the baron was most reluctant to accept that assignment and distinguished himself only once, in 1809, by capturing two members of the Scarola band.[29] The appointment of General Manhès as commander in chief of the army in Calabria and head of the High Police, in September of 1810, brought the situation to a head because the future "hangman of Calabria," hostile as he was to the great landowners, whom he suspected of connivance with the brigands, forced them to act "for the destruction of brigandage."[30] But over the next two years Barracco managed to transform his role from one of brigand hunter in the government's behalf to informal head of the district—a role the brigands respected. In the summer, the Barracco palace in Camigliati was headquarters to "all landowners of the coastal district who own property in the Sila," who gathered "to fight the bands of scoundrels . . . safeguard the harvest . . . [and] protect work, lives, and property."[31]

In all the events we have mentioned, the Barraccos worked to keep peace on the latifondo. In July of 1806, though they knew perfectly well who the looters were, they named no names despite General Verdier's explicit requests;

---

and some of the warehousemen and agents had to offer "gifts to prevent the warehouse from being broken into during the brigandage wave of 1861." Two cowhands, Francesco Filippelli and Vincenzo Gigliotti, "went off to be brigands." In February of 1864, Michele Cervino, twenty years a guard, lost his life in a conflict with the brigands.

29. Once, in September of 1809, four brigand chieftains and their bands seemed to be preparing to burn down Camigliati, but nothing actually happened. By capturing two members of the Scarola band, Barracco earned a name for himself with the French without making too many enemies in the war-torn territory. The complicity of "uncle" General Amato, turned out to be highly useful: Bruno Lupinacci, one of the men arrested, was presented as "the famous brigand," and the king was informed of the loyalty and courage shown by Baron Alfonso in the conflict.

30. Manhès, whom Murat rewarded with the title of count of Rocca di Neto, enjoined Barracco to act "for the destruction of brigandage" using both weapons and other "means to make the brigands surrender." See BA: G1(6), Manhès's letter to Barracco from Cosenza, dated December 8, 1810. The tone of the correspondence subsequently softened. Manhès issued the baron a pass. In January of 1812, he wrote to confirm that he had "received two mules," thanked the baron, and asked their price. Three days later he sent Alfonso gun permits for himself and his son Luigi and congratulated him on receiving justice "in your business" (the application for damages).

31. Armed with his special pass, which forbade any military authority to arrest or interfere with him except on direct orders from Manhès, and with gun permits for himself and Luigi, Alfonso acquired considerable personal power both in the district and with the administration. In correspondence dated February and March 1812, after the war had ended, Deputy Intendent De Riso asked Luigi Barracco to certify the loyalty of certain candidates for the post of elementary-school teacher in Isola, gave and requested information on a confidential report to the minister of police, asked Luigi about a priest's character, and discussed proposals for the upcoming elections, even forwarding to Luigi copies of several mayors' reports and asking him to investigate. See BA: G1(5).

later, in testimony given to the damage claims commission, they spoke generically of "brigands."[32] The Barraccos gradually recovered their stolen property without bringing charges, allowing those in possession simply to declare that they had "received them indirectly." Lastly, they took no revenge on the families involved; close relatives of men known to be guilty of looting continued to work on the latifondo.[33] Thus, even if they were occasionally direct victims of criminal deeds, the Barraccos understood that the acts of Calabrian brigands or insurgents were not aimed at the landowning class but at the state, the government, the National Guard, the Royal Carabineers, and tax collectors.[34] They also understood that the antistate character of brigandage was a safeguard for their own interests, and they did all they could—to the extent of arousing suspicions that they were aiding and abetting—to prevent the "brigands" from shifting their sights.

But the reign of peace in the latifondo's territory by no means implied that the latifondisti and the populace shared any general interests. On the contrary, in their politics the Barraccos always stood with the side diametrically opposed to the people's, and their liberal views were never democratic or populist. This separation between the wealthy bourgeoisie and the progressive nobility, on the one hand, and the peasant masses, on the other, had been brewing throughout the eighteenth century; it was finalized, as Aurelio Lepre rightly indicates, with the revolution of 1799 and Sanfedism.[35] During "the decade" the latifondisti sided with the French; in 1848, with the so-called democratic party, which opposed peasant claims as well as the Bourbons;[36] in 1860–61, with the

---

32. Before the month was out, the baron's agent reported that "Pietro Barretta, Antonio Intrieri, and his son took two flocks of young sheep"; the "brigands from Celico" were led by "Don Domenico Rizzuto, Michele Patrone, Pietro Passarello, Nicola Granieri's son Giacomo, and the son of Miranda from Manneto"; "Motiscella's son Giacinto took all the hardware . . . and Pio Sciaverta . . ."; and so forth.

33. Three members of the Granieri family, four Mirandas, and Tommaso and Giuseppe Petrone were employed on the estate; all were related to "brigands" the agent had recognized. The Intrieri family remained the most loyal: sixty-seven of its members, including "Antonio the Pistol," were employed by the Barraccos over the course of the century, although one of them, Pasquale, left in September of 1848 "to become a brigand."

34. In only one instance did the rebels' actions take on an explicit connotation of class struggle: the band of fifty-nine brigands from Taverna, Soveria, etc., was charged with "conspiracy and attempts against a class of people," namely, the landlords.

35. A. Lepre, *Storia del Mezzogiorno nel Risorgimento* (Rome, 1969), 60–66.

36. In 1848, they had opposed both the king and the people; the popular uprisings of 1848–49 shared many of the characteristics of traditionalist movements that appealed to monarchs against usurpers and "evil agents." Ferdinand, with the usual Bourbon paternalism, had granted pardons to hundreds of peasants guilty of occupying lands, and, through the work of Pasquale Barletta, civil commissioner for Sila affairs, tried to get the usurped lands back into the public domain. The Calabrian landowners, already flirting with the liberal cause (the Barraccos seem to

Savoias more than with Garibaldi and after unity with the progovernment rightists.[37] Nonetheless, only after the final defeat of brigandage and the stabilization of the Kingdom of Italy did the peace that had always reigned on the latifondo, through all the troubles, begin to break down.[38] The first sporadic

---

have offered the Bandiera brothers support in Croton), never forgave the king for this. See F. S. Nitti, "Il grande dissidio della vita italiana: L'Italia del Nord e l'Italia del Sud," in *Scritti Politici* (Milan, 1980), esp. 144–45. The Barraccos' politics coincided with that of the so-called democratic party, which in Calabria engaged in agitation parallel to the popular uprising. No Barracco seems to have taken part in the provisional government in Cosenza, although the family supported it and gave aid to the prisoners. (But Antonino Basile says that "in the rising of 1848, among the rebels who were members of the provisional government in Cosenza were some of the richest usurpers of the Sila: the Lupinaccis, the Barraccos, the Collices, and so forth" ["Moti contadini," op. cit., 100].) However that may be, other members of Calabria's nobility were directly involved: the Morellis, the Vercillos, and the De Risos. In 1849, Marquise Maria De Riso was charged in Catanzaro with "incitement against the government and public actions to spread discontent." The marquise seems to have ordered one Giuseppina Prestirà to let loose "a pig that was made to wander about the town of Baraccone with a red ribbon around its neck" (SACZ, Lower Calabria II: Political Trials and Brigandage). The Bourbon police were not known for their sense of humor.

Ironically enough, while Tommaso Antonio Lamanna, one of the Barracco's administrators, was arrested in Catanzaro a few years later for being "found in possession of a facetious sonnet against the king," his young master Giovanni was heard in the salons of Naples reciting a poem in praise of Agesilao Milano, guilty of an assassination attempt against the king. See R. De Cesare, *La fine di un Regno,* op. cit., 254. Milano, a young Albanian from San Bendetto Ullano, made his attempt on December 8, 1856, as the king was reviewing his troops on the parade ground.

37. In Naples, the two Barracco brothers belonged to the liberal and pro-Piedmont milieu that gathered around the king's brother, Don Leopoldo (husband of a Savoia) and included Camillo Caracciolo, Cesare and Alfonso Casanova, Carlo and Luigi Giordano, Arenolfi, D'Afflitto, Gallotti, Antonacci, the Pandola brothers, and Antonio Capecelatro. In Calabria, the Barracco family, along with other millionaire landowners (from the Morelli, Compagna, Guzzolini, Quintieri, and Labonia families), contributed to Garibaldi's expedition, and they supported and subsidized (though they did not join) the fiercely anti-Bourbon liberal committees, which for some time had been heading their documents with the Savoia arms. The Barracco family gave the Cosenza Committee "ten thousand ducats, besides fodder and oxen for the rebels, and they gave ten thousand ducats to the Catanzaro Committee as well." The members of the Cosenza Committee included Donato and Carlo Morelli, Baron Francesco Guzzolini and his son Angelo, Baron Pietro Compagna, Giuseppe Boscarelli, and Mazzei, all Sila usurpers, and the Cosenza citizens Carlo Compagna, Raffaele Persiani, and the Frugiuele brothers. In August of 1860, Garibaldi was the Morellis' guest at Rogliano (in the same mansion that had given Ferdinand II hospitality in 1844) where he appointed Donato Morelli governor of the province and issued the famous "Rogliano decrees" on the flour tax, the price of salt, and common rights. See R. De Cesare, *La fine di un Regno,* op. cit., 128; R. De Cesare, *Una famiglia di patriotti,* op. cit., cxxxi; A. Guarasci, *Politica e società,* op. cit., 59ff.; and G. Procacci, *Le elezioni del 1874 e l'opposizione meridionale* (Milan, 1956).

38. There was a sharp increase in litigation all over the South in the period following Italy's unification. The number of criminal cases appealed to the Supreme Court from the Neapolitan provinces rose from 2,298 in 1863 to 32,975 in 1875. See *Annuario Statistico Italiano,* Administration of Penal Justice, Court of Cassation, 276–77.

signs of a popular antagonism directed specifically against the Barraccos appeared in the latter part of the 1860s. In 1867, the outcome of the electoral race in Croton between Giovanni Barracco and young Gaetano Cosentini was contested, with popular support tilted sharply toward the latter.

[T]he people put Barracco to flight, beseiged the baronial palace, broke its windows with a volley of rocks, and shouted "Down with Barracco!" and demanded "division of the land . . ."[39]

reported Vincenzo Padula in *Bruzio,* ascribing the people's rage to the ever-vital issue of the Sila, recently exacerbated by Parliament's legitimation of the encroachments and the definitive depletion of common land by privatization.[40] The novelty of the Croton populace's demonstration lay, however, not so much in the vitality of the Sila question as in its targeting of the wealthy latifondista Barracco. On another occasion, during the so-called flour-tax riots in the winter of 1868[41] (the tax was a particularly large problem in districts where workers were paid in grain) peasants who refused to pay the tax at three gristmills owned by the Barraccos maintained that they did not intend to further enrich the baron.

These incidents were signs of antagonism rather than class conflict and still less open conflict. The 1860s were boom years, and the increased production of grain offered many job opportunities. There were no farm workers' organizations and no strikes;[42] the republican uprising of 1870 did not touch the latifondo's district. Nonetheless, its peace seemed threatened.

---

39. V. Padula, *Persone,* op. cit., 587, 588. Both G. Cingari (*Storia della Calabria,* op. cit., 61–62) and F. Spezzano (*La lotta politica,* op. cit.) mention the episode described by Padula in connection with the Sila question and the end of the Barraccos' hegemony in the Marquisate, but neither gives any additional details.

40. Between 1867 and 1877, over 100,000 hectares (about 247,000 acres) of former ecclesiastical properties had been sold in the southern provinces, almost a third of them in the province of Catanzaro (Ministry of Agriculture, Industry and Commerce, Department of Agriculture, *Notizie e Studi sull'Agricoltura, 1877* [Rome, 1879], 1025–31). By the end of 1877, in all three Calabrian provinces, only sixty-nine lots, totaling barely 50 hectares (124 acres), were still in the public domain (ibid., 1033).

41. As always, the authorities saw the protest against the flour tax in terms of brigandage and rebellion. According to court records, a band of brigands operated in Savelli and Verzina between November of 1868 and August of 1869, perpetrating acts of resistance and rebellion against the National Guard. Numerous trials were held between 1869 and 1871 for "insults and threats against the Royal Carabinieri" and for "speeches against the flour tax law and against civil marriage" (SACZ, Great Court of Lower Calabria II, Political Trials and Brigandage).

42. Besides the works cited in chapter 3, see E. Greco, *Le società operaie di mutuo soccorso* (Turin, 1922); and A. F. Parisi, "Per la storia delle società operaie ed artigiane in Calabria: La Società di mutuo soccoso di Maida," in *Brutium* (Reggio Calabria, 1953).

4. Autonomy from the Market

Social peace was clearly a sine qua non of the latifondo system's equilibrium, but it was not the only one. Equally important was its high degree of autonomy with respect to the market, assured by self-sufficiency, low cash wages, and flexibility in the allocation of capital and in production. We have already discussed all these factors; here we shall only reexamine their role in maintaining the latifondo system's economic and social equilibrium.

The enterprise's self-sufficiency depended on both its diversified production, which meant that very few process materials had to be purchased outside, and the nonmonetary nature of its resources. Self-sufficiency enabled a thriftless use of inputs that would have been wholly unviable had their cost been accounted for at market prices.[43] This had already been noted by Luigi Grimaldi.

> [E]xpenses per *moggio* of land sown with wheat are put at around 8 ducats, and for the crop to be profitable, the yield should be six times the amount of seed. However, these expenses are not considered heavy, because either the owner has the work done with his own oxen, or the peasants do it with their own arms . . .[44]

In this connection, let us look again at the two balance sheets for the Fallistro spinnery. The one drawn up according to methods valid for a capitalist enterprise—that is, valuing land, buildings, cocoons, firewood, transportation, and labor at market prices—shows the mill operating at a loss. But, when the account is taken of the fact that the land and buildings had been purchased for much less than their market value through a foreclosure on the Mollos, that the wood came from the Barraccos' own forests and the cocoons from their own silk barns, and that transportation was effected with Barracco mules and carts driven by muleteers on the Barracco payroll, the Fallistro balance sheet shows a high profit.

The discrepancy between theoretical monetary valuations and costs actually incurred was obviously most important with regard to labor. As will be recalled, the nominal wages paid by the Barraccos were in line with the going regional and national rates, but real wages, and even their monetary components, were rarely paid in cash. The value of commodities and services sup-

---

43. As Kula observes, "If we were to draw up a balance-sheet for any feudal 'enterprise' (large landed estate, group of demesnes, a single demesne, a manufactory) according to the methods of validating calculations for capitalist enterprises (i.e., assessing the price of all the elements which enter into production but which have not been purchased on the market) . . . the result would almost always be that that enterprise was operating at a loss" (W. Kula, *An Economic Theory,* op. cit., 35).

44. L. Grimaldi, *Studi statistici,* op. cit., 110.

plied to employees was computed at current market prices, but in reality they never went through a market, as they were provided out of the latifondo's own production, property, or structure. This meant that a monetary wage's actual cost to the latifondo was much lower than its nominal value,[45] and this was a fortiori true for the nonmonetary part of a wage, such as remuneration in kind or share in output. While the latifondista thus saved on the cost of labor, the worker—who made his own calculations by natural criteria—drew his subsistence, security, and authority from the marginal lands he was entitled to use as parasforo or cortaglia, plus any minor products in which he had a joint interest.

In turn, the latifondo's self-sufficiency and low real costs of production enabled the monetary sector to maintain a high degree of flexibility with respect to the market. There were two sides to this flexibility. On the one hand, the latifondo economy, being traditional, simple, and unencumbered by fixed investments, was able to follow the ups and downs of the markets, converting capital from one form to another without eroding its own structure.[46] On the other hand, the latifondo could increase its commercial output in response not only to positive market incentives (high commodity prices) but also to negative signals (low prices). The first aspect of flexibility allowed the enterprise to oscillate painlessly over the century between livestock and grain production, to tilt from grain to olive oil, to plant cotton, mulberry groves, and licorice root— in short to adjust to all the export market's fluctuations without forfeiting its multicrop character. Thus, for example, in the 1840s the enterprise cut back its cheese production and increased the output of licorice and raw silk; in the late 1850s it practically discontinued silk production (destroyed by worm atrophy) and increased grain output; and in the late 1860s it began to downscale grain production and increase that of olive oil.[47]

---

45. It might be objected that the land, goods, and services provided by the Barraccos to their employees were in fact removed from the market, where they might have been sold at current prices. But, as we have already demonstrated, the land, goods, and services the workers received were part of a different circuit from the commercial one; that is, there existed no regular, profitable market for such marginal lands and low-grade produce.

46. M. Rossi Doria, "Riforma agraria," op. cit., 8–9.

47. The estate's production was flexible only under favorable market conditions, however. Demand for the products of Calabria's rural industries—olive oil, raw and processed silk, wheat, licorice, madder, and hemp—by foreign trading partners, especially in France, Great Britain, and Austria, grew in the second half of the eighteenth century and continued strong, with various ups and downs for various products at different times, in the nineteenth. Napoleon's colonial system encouraged the production of grain, timber, and cotton for export, but it was followed by an extremely severe crisis. Exports of a wide range of products picked up after the return of Bourbon absolutism (1821) and especially after 1838. On the eighteenth century, see R. Romano, *Le commerce du Royaume de Naples avec la France et les pays de l'Adriatique au XVIII siècle* (Paris, 1951), passim; P. Chorley, *Oil, Silk, and Enlightenment: Economic Problems in 18th Century Naples* (Naples, 1965), passim (although Chorley gives a very positive picture of the kingdom's

The second aspect of flexibility, regarding price fluctuations, enabled the enterprise to weather periodic market depressions in the best of health and prosper during both the highs and the lows of the economic cycle. As we have seen, the latifondo was assembled in the wake of the late-eighteenth-century price boom and during the wartime burst of the Napoleonic period (up to 1816–17), but it continued to grow and prosper as the cycle bottomed out during the "thirty-years' peace" (1817–1849).[48] The correlations between price trends and latifondo output clearly demonstrate the enterprise's ability to respond positively to both positive and negative market trends. In some cases the latifondo reacted to market stimuli as any capitalist producer would; high grain prices were followed by increased grain output and, vice versa, a price decline was echoed by a decline in output.[49] Mounting oil prices in the mid-1840s prompted increased oil production, and a 50 percent rise in the price of licorice paste between 1852 and 1864 led to a doubling of output. In other cases, the latifondo reacted in the opposite way, increasing the output of a given product as prices declined. This happened with grain in the post-Napoleonic period,[50] with grain, oil, and cheese in 1834–35, and with the same

foreign trade, he thinks Romano's figures are excessive [32–33]); G. M. Galanti, *Nuova descrizione,* op. cit., 348ff.; and H. Swinburne, *Travels in Calabria,* op. cit., 24, 29–30. On the nineteenth century, see V. Giura, *Russia, Stati Uniti d'America e Regno di Napoli nell'età del Risorgimento* (Naples, 1967), passim; G. H. Hildebrand, *Growth and Structure in the Economy of Modern Italy* (Cambridge, Mass., 1965); A. Graziani, "Il commercio estero del Regno delle Due Sicilie dal 1832 al 1858," *Archivio Economico dell'Unificazione Italiana,* ser. 1, 10 (1960); *Giornale di Statistica,* ser. 1, 8 (1854), and ser. 2, 1 (1858); and L. Bianchini, *Della storia delle finanze,* op. cit. On oil, see F. Bracci, "L'olivo e l'olio in Italia," in his *L'Italia agricola alla fine del secolo XIX* (Rome, 1901); on silk, see F. Marincola di San Floro, *Statuti dell'arte della seta in Catanzaro,* op. cit.

48. See E. Labrousse, "Elément d'un bilan," op. cit., 473–97; E. Tarlé, *Le blocus continental et le Royaume d'Italie* (Paris, 1931); F. Crouzet, "Wars, Blockade, and Economic Change in Europe, 1792–1815," *Journal of Economic History* 24 (1964): 567–88; F. Crouzet et al., *Essays in European Economic History, 1789–1914* (New York, 1969); J. Lescure, *Des crises générales et périodiques de surproduction,* 5th ed., 2 vols. (Paris, 1938) 2ff.; F. Mauro, *L'expansion euro-péenne, 1600–1870,* (Paris, 1964); N. F. Faraglia, *Storia dei prezzi in Napoli dal 1131 al 1860* (Naples, 1878), 297ff.; and H. Martineau, *History of the Peace* (Boston, 1865) on the "price-making market" during the "thirty years' peace," 1815–45.

49. Grain production does seem to respond positively to market stimuli. After remaining high throughout the 1870s, prices began to slip in 1881; the decline became strong and steady starting in 1883, and in reality continued until 1896, though with brief and illusory upswings in 1891–92 (despite the protectionist laws of 1887, which we shall discuss later). The estate's grain output followed a parallel curve: after maintaining a yearly average of over 26,000 tomoli (1,170 tons) between 1871 and 1883, it fell to an average of 14,000 tomoli (630 tons) in the years from 1887 to 1899. That is, the landowners reduced output when its profitability declined. In fact, this was the most frequent explanation for the so-called agrarian crisis of those years.

50. The wartime boom during the Napoleonic period, for example, was followed by a dramatic and prolonged decline in prices, actually much sharper than the one that prompted cries of "agrarian crisis" sixty years later. Grain prices fell more than 50 percent between 1816 and 1817

three products during the so-called mid-century crisis (1849–51).[51] Indeed, the Barraccos embarked on the modernization of their licorice works precisely during the years when prices for paste were low, and they modernized the Rivioti oil press (with a net increase in productivity) during a period (1872–75) when oil prices stayed very low. The latifondo thus increased its output, sometimes even at considerable capital cost, in response to either positive or negative market incentives, aiming in the first case to augment its profit margin and in the second to offset losses.[52]

On the whole, autonomy from the dictates of the market enabled the latifondista to be at once a modern capitalist producer and an old-style lord of the manor and to manage the enterprise "more for luxury than for profit," as Guglielmo Barracco put it, without upsetting its overall equilibrium.

Flexibility with respect to the market obviously had its limits—a physical limit determined by the amount of available land, a social limit imposed by the constraints of the guarantee system, and a technological limit represented by the threshold of modern labor-saving methods that could be introduced without causing the system to crash.[53] These three limits in turn determined the maximum volume of production. But within these limits the latifondo economy operated at maximum capacity with full use of the land and other production factors. Equilibrium conditions—maintenance of the guarantee system and of collective forms of land use, relative self-sufficiency, and retention of traditional methods of production and control—made this economy highly competitive even (or especially) when prices were low. Scale economies, the use of

---

and in the ensuing two years, while the drop between 1879 and 1880 and the next period was less than 30 percent. These were the years, however, when the Barraccos were engaged most aggressively and intensely in accumulating land and when their grain output consequently grew fastest.

51. In 1849–51, the very low prices for olive oil and grain were offset by a 25 percent increase in output. In 1834 and 1835, when the price of wheat hit the century's record low and the prices of oil, cheese, and wool had also declined, an agricultural boom exploded throughout Calabria, with double the acreage planted in grain and a 40 percent increase in cattle herds. See the 1834 statistics compiled for Upper Calabria by Provincial Intendent Gennaro Petitti and for Lower Calabria II by Intendent Giuseppe De Liguori. Luigi Grimaldi calculated that yearly grain output averaged 650,000 tomoli (29,250 tons) during the decade from 1820 to 1830 and 860,000 tomoli (38,700 tons) during the next decade—an increase of over 30 percent.

52. Investments "to preserve one's standard of living and social position" are typical of feudal-type "entrepreneurs." As Kula writes, "The investments decided upon by the nobility usually did not depend at all, or only to a minimal degree, on market phenomena; at times, they actually depended on them in a reverse sense." The difference between entrepreneurs like the Barraccos and the feudal lords lies in the fact that the latter invested only when their way of life was threatened, whereas the former also reacted to positive market stimuli (W. Kula, *An Economic Theory,* op. cit., 53).

53. As we shall see, technological innovation was by no means incompatible with the estate economy, but it could not be given absolute priority without rapidly modifying the system's whole socioeconomic structure.

TABLE 20.   Revenues of Barracco Latifondo Administrations (in ducats)

	1849–50	1853–54	1857–58	1860–61	1865–66	1869–70	1874–75	1877–78
Altilia	18,125	21,190	26,011	18,046	15,000	13,416	11,527	13,389
Isola	24,696	42,918	48,297	56,872	48,649	48,920	26,974	34,357
Concio di Neto	15,267	28,092	23,445	34,104	30,343	15,855	15,178	16,907
Concio S. Pietro	1,817	19,229	22,272	33,451	25,403	17,710	16,376	18,105
Cotrone	7,665	1,675	3,887	1,450	1,430	2,330	3,179	1,548
Spezzano P.	3,502	10,551	8,524	5,429	6,406	5,714	6,511	7,055
Napoli		179,437	199,096	247,970		149,680	126,090	64,747
Camigliati	5,869	2,979	3,422	4,884	5,066	5,895	2,837	41,180
Caccuri		1,870	4,110	4,000	4,000	5,053	5,287	
Petrizia							9,009	5,135
Total excluding Naples	105,086	129,504	139,968	158,236	136,297	112,893	96,878	104,676

traditional techniques, social peace, self-sufficiency, labor paid in low-cost goods and services with high subjective value—all these factors helped keep down the cost of fixed assets, raw materials, depreciation, surveillance, and wages. As long as equilibrium conditions were maintained, the latifondo enterprise remained profitable and stable. As table 20 shows, notwithstanding fluctuations due to general economic trends, political events, family circumstances, and the ups and downs of specific products, the various administrations always closed their yearly accounts with a profit.[54]

5. Equilibrium in Jeopardy and the Modernizing Mentality

It was the Barraccos themselves who modified the equilibrium conditions and debased the medium that had permitted their development. The changes were prompted by the family's need for a larger income, but the way they came about was the result of a modernizing mentality.

Luigi Barrocco was an only son and heir, and he and his wife, Chiara, continued to live as his father had: a rather spartan existence, devoted to managing the family's affairs, with few interludes in Naples and few luxuries. The couple produced twelve children, however, for whom they had to create a social position at a time when younger sons were no longer being channeled into traditional careers. In fact, none of the Barracco boys became a soldier,

---

54. Fluctuations could be sharp, depending on a variety of causes such as harvest size, livestock epidemics, peasant uprisings (as in fiscal year 1849–50), or the reorganization effected in the years after the family's property was partitioned. But they also were affected by improved administration, for instance, the greater profits from Caccuri that resulted from Guglielmo's presence there.

priest, or government official, and none of the girls was compelled to take the veil. Providing for the children's support and future thus required considerable amounts of capital; we have already seen Baron Luigi laying out half a million ducats for his daughters' dowries. Moreover, the family not only became more numerous, but it altered its lifestyle; in moving to Naples in 1849, it opted for a very high, *more nobilium* standard of living.

The latifondo's natural sector continued to provide for the family's subsistence needs. Their bread was baked with home-grown flour, Altilia's best wines were sent to their table in Naples, and so were the latifondo's olive oil and cheese, lambs and kids, suckling pigs, figs, oranges, and lemons. But subsistence was now merely a drop in the bucket compared with the family's ever-growing need for goods and services that had to be bought with money. Rental and upkeep of the luxurious palace in Via Monte di Dio came over and above the Barraccos' expenses for their numerous mansions in Calabria, and they were now immersed in the life of high society, with carriages and gigs, imported crystal, porcelain and silverware, trained butlers and servants, chefs from Brescia, a stable with "top-rated horses," fashions by Berthez and Allis for the young ladies, and outfits by Peirée, Lennon, Taylor, and Mackenzie for the gentlemen. Maurizio Barracco was the high-society's oracle in male fashion, Giovanni was the soul of the racing set.[55] There were trips and long stays in Paris, and balls and private theatricals (quite frequent in the years of tightest censorship); there was Giovanni's precious collection of antique marble statues. In short, the Barraccos were rated the wealthiest family in the kingdom[56] and led a life that matched that image. After 1861, the costs of their conspicuous consumption were augmented by the campaign costs of seating at least one Barracco in the Chamber and the Senate in every legislature.

The family was thus faced with the problem of how to increase its income. The method that had worked so well in the early days of the latifondo's formation was to increase the absolute value of revenues by extending the area under cultivation. This was an easy, well-known, and time-tested way to increase profit,[57] and the Barraccos continued to apply it until the death of Baron Luigi in 1849. The property grew by 136 percent in the decade from 1822 to 1831 and by another 14 percent from 1831 to 1844, with a proportional increase in output. But over the next twenty years acreage grew by only 2 percent, signaling that the old method had been abandoned. This happened for two reasons, one physical and contingent, the other intellectual. In the first

---

55. R. De Cesare, *La fine di un Regno,* op. cit., 362.

56. Ibid., 255.

57. According to Ascanio Branca, himself a great landowner, it was absurd to expect owners to invest "their capital in new crops rather than in buying new land, which is more profitable and much easier to do" (*Atti della Giunta per la Inchiesta Agraria,* Branca Report, op. cit., xlii).

place, land was not as easy and cheap to come by in Calabria as it had been in the past; available reserves had been depleted during the period when the state-owned properties, former feudal lands, and peasant allotments were sold off, while encroachment had been made much more difficult by the existence of the Civil Commission for the Sila and by the stiffer opposition of the municipalities, now emboldened by government support. After unity, the government unsealed the cornucopia of church properties once more—the Barraccos' only purchases during the 1860s were from this source[58]—but this time it depleted all the reserves. By 1877, the state owned barely fifty hectares of former church lands in all of Calabria.

The second reason was the modernist and modernizing mentality of these landowners, representative members of an elite within their class. It was a city-bred elite, well-educated, informed, and active, that emerged into a position of hegemony during the French decade and remained, after Restoration, constitutionalist, antifeudal, liberal, and consciously modern. Culturally, it had been shaped by the reformist literature produced by the Neapolitan Enlightenment, Genovesi, Filangieri, and Galiani. Though essentially adhering to physiocratic and laissez-faire ideas, it had supported statist reformers from Tanucci, through Murat, to Luigi De Medici. Naturally, this part of the landowning class took issue with Ferdinand II's policies—short-sighted, hostile to innovation, repressive, protectionist, and populist. Dissent turned into open opposition in 1848 when members of this elite formed, province by province, liberal and pro-Savoia committees, which gave way to short-lived provisional governments. This was the mental landscape in which Baron Luigi Barrocco's children grew up, most of them still young at the time of his death in 1849: Alfonso, the eldest, was thirty-nine, Giovanni was twenty, and the youngest were still minors. In 1848, they supported the committees in Calabria, and they were attuned to modernist ideas—Giovanni's library contained several constitutional histories and works by socialist authors. Upon moving to Naples, they entered the liberal milieu of patricians and upper bourgeoisie, where anglophile and pro-Savoia modernism was in fashion (it centered around the king's own brother, Leopoldo Borbone, who had married a Savoia and made no secret of his liberal views). In economic matters, the tenets held in this milieu were laissez-faire and favored free trade. Stanislao Barracco, along with some of the most illustrious names in the progressive segment of high society, served on the Oversight Board that controled the privately owned railroad construction

---

58. The Barraccos bought government land in Isola, Rocca di Neto, Rocca Bernarda, San Mauro Marchesato, Celico, Caccuri, and Polligrone, with a nominal value of 116,700 lire and payment extended to 1874. Guglielmo Barracco estimated that the property was really worth over 100 thousand ducats, four times as much. However, as they were heavily taxed these purchases were much less advantageous than those made during the French decade. See BA: A69, 141–42 (Tax assessments for purchases of ecclesiastical properties).

company.[59] In 1862, the newly elected Giovanni Barracco endorsed the program put forward by "Industria Italiana," which was promoting a match between free-trade policy and southern industrial interests (Barracco's support came *after* the shutdown of Mongiana and other southern industrial establishments).[60]

This class, sincerely concerned as it was over the country's economic backwardness, was possessed by a true "agromania," which, in that era of the (second) agricultural revolution, it shared with all the progressive landowners in Europe. Societies for the promotion of agriculture, training schools and farmers' associations, periodicals, fairs, exhibitions, and experimental farms were springing up everywhere.[61] The Economic Societies of the Kingdom of Naples, founded in 1810 (originally as Agricultural Societies, then, in 1812, transformed by Murat into Economic Societies so that "they would concern themselves with manufacturing and commerce as well"), continued to devote themselves principally to agriculture and were very active in technical instruction and incentivation; in research and the testing of new methods, machinery, and crops; and in decrying the ignorance of the farming class. In an 1853 survey of "the progress of manufacturing, farming, animal husbandry, and industries in the continental provinces of the kingdom," promoted by the Naples Royal Institute for Encouragement to Natural Sciences, nine of the thirteen questions related to agriculture. Numerous schools of agriculture were opened over the years, culminating, in 1871, with the establishment of the University Level School of Agriculture at Portici (the second in Italy after the one founded in Pisa by the enlightened Grand Duke Leopold of Tuscany).[62]

---

59. Besides Giovanni and Maurizio Barracco, the circle included the prince of Ottajano (nephew of Luigi De Medici), Camillo Caracciolo, Cesare and Alfonso Casanova, Carlo and Luigi Giordano, Arenolfi, D'Afflitto, Gallotti, Antonacci, the Pandola brothers, and Antonio Capecelatro. See R. De Cesare, *La fine di un Regno,* op. cit., 128. The various private railroad construction projects did not attract capital from Naples, however. See J. A. Davis, *Merchants,* op. cit. 150.

60. This circle maintained its antifeudal attitude even at court. Alfonso Barracco, for example, relinquished the title of knight of the Order of Saint Gennaro due him by aristocratic tradition and Bourbon grant. At his father's death, "Alfonso, the eldest son, a man of liberal sentiments like all his family," returned his parent's insignia of knight of the Order of Saint Gennaro to the king, as tradition dictated, but did not then pray the king, also according to tradition, to confer the honor on him. See R. De Cesare, *La fine di un Regno,* op. cit., 254, 291.

61. See J. Blum, *Noble Landowners,* op. cit., 130ff.; D. Spring, *The English Landed Estate,* op. cit.; J. D. Chambers and G. E. Mingay, *The Agricultural Revolution, 1750–1880* (London, 1966); and F. M. L. Thompson, *The Second Agricultural Revolution,* op. cit.

62. R. Villari, *Problemi dell'economia napoletana alla vigilia dell'Unificazione* (Naples, 1958), 22ff.; T. Pedio, "Le condizioni economiche della Calabria Citeriore dopo la restaurazione borbonica in una relazione di Andrea Lombardi," *Calabria Nobilissima* 44 (1962): 187–202; M. Rossi Doria, "La Facoltà di Agraria di Portici nello sviluppo dell'agricoltura meridionale," *Quaderni Storici* 36 (1977): 836–53; B. Tommasi (director of the School of Agriculture after 1874),

Agrophile landowners saw backward agriculture as the crux of the southern problem, and they ascribed it to apathy and lack of individual initiative. These factors, though engendered and encouraged by the Bourbons' economic and general policies, would in any case inevitably have resulted from the heterogeneous land-tenure system. The heterogeneous system, comprising collective and semicollective ownership, common and open lands, was seen as the defining characteristic of Neapolitan "feudalism" and the major enemy of "progress." If southern agriculture was ever to break out of the vicious circle of backwardness, the old ownership system would have to be eliminated (this is why the progressive elite had supported the program of the "Partenopei" and the work of Giuseppe Zurlo),[63] definitively releasing property from the old easements and completing the partitioning of municipal and other public lands. The heterogeneous system—"economically unjustified for the state and a serious obstacle to agrarian improvement and private property"—necessarily made southern agriculture backward and its products inferior to those of other nations.[64] The provincial nobility and government officials shared this view. In 1836, Giuseppe De Liguori, intendent of Lower Calabria II, wrote in his report:

> The division of state lands formerly held by feudal lords and the termination of heterogeneous tenure of municipal and church lands are matters of great weight . . . for the improvement of those lands, because when a legitimate owner is determined, he has a greater interest in making them prosper, they are better tended and safeguarded, and agriculture progresses on them, as is generally the case with land owned by individuals.

Only with legally well-defined private ownership of land could agriculture partake of the three requisites of modernity: a market, technical progress, and direct management.

An optimistic faith in the free market was widespread among the great

---

Scuola Pratica di Agricoltura. Cosenza (Cosenza, 1904); A. Allocati, "Le società economiche di Calabria," in *Atti del Secondo Congresso Storico Calabrese* [Proceedings of the second Conference on Calabrian History[(Naples, 1961); R. Ciasca, "Le trasformazioni agrarie in Calabria dopo l'Unità," in *Archivio Storico per la Calabria e la Lucania* (Cosenza, 1954); D. Demarco, *Il crollo del Regno delle Due Sicilie* (Naples, 1960), 13–37; D. Demarco, "La borghesia fondiaria del Regno di Napoli nel secolo XIX: Le origini, i problemi," in *Rassegna Storica del Risorgimento,* (1951), esp. 359–62; L. Cafagna, "The Industrial Revolution in Italy, 1830–1914," in *The Fontana Economic History of Europe* (London, 1973), 279–328.

63. The need to break with the old landholding system was fundamental in Zurlo's thought and work. See P. Villani, "Giuseppe Zurlo: La crisi dell'antico regime e la ricostruzione dello Stato," in his *Mezzogiorno tra riforme e rivoluzione* (Bari, 1973), 213–330.

64. Carlo De Cesare expressed an opinion widely held among the liberals in his *Il mondo civile e industriale nel secolo XIX* (1857). See R. Villari, *Il Sud nella storia,* op. cit., 62–63.

landowners who produced for export and felt no threat from foreign competition. Moreover, the antiprotectionist position identified itself with the more general need for renovating the kingdom and with opposition not only to the Bourbons' fiscal and customs policy but to their whole conservative policy. These people also sincerely and more concretely believed that free enterprise—a boon to agriculture above all—would ultimately benefit the whole economy even if industry might be hurt at the start.[65] This optimism was justified by the persistence of a strong world market for the South's products.[66]

Just as deeply felt, in this era of the second agricultural revolution, was the need to bring technical progress to agriculture, prodding it out of its habitual inertia ("a great hindrance to agriculture is people's obstinacy in sticking to methods handed down by their forebears," complained Luigi Grimaldi).[67] If the yields of Neapolitan agriculture (that many saw to be particularly favored by nature), though markedly increased during that period, remained lower than those of English and Dutch farms, the fault lay in southerners' ignorance of farm machinery, new crop strains, rotation systems, and improved methods, which Luigi Grimaldi, with a well-chosen metaphor, called "the propelling power of the whole farming machine."[68]

Direct owner management was another enthusiasm shared by all of Europe's "improving landlords."[69] Land relegated by absentee landlords to the care of poor, unmotivated, and ignorant peasants was badly tilled; partnerships and sharecropping were unprofitable for owners and detrimental for the land itself; split management was incompatible with the needs of a modern farming enterprise, which required a large amount of working capital and management expertise; and, lastly, partnership arrangements made it impossible "to raise up

---

65. This is precisely what did happen when the Piedmont tariff was introduced on October 30, 1860, and the Mongiana works near Catanzaro and other Bourbon industries were forced to close.

66. Not everyone thought that the South's produce was inferior to foreign produce. Ferdinando Lucchesi, for example, believed that Naples wheat need not fear competition from Ukrainian wheat (the problem of American wheat had not yet arisen), "since it is a better grade and heavier than the Black Sea wheat."

67. L. Grimaldi, *Studi statistici,* op. cit., 125.

68. L. Granata, "Le campagne nell'Ottocento," in A. Lepre and P. Villani, *Il Mezzogiorno nell'età moderna e contemporanea* (Naples, 1974), 348. Various solutions were proposed to finance technical improvements: monti frumentari, perpetual leases granted by townships with improvement clauses, and government loans. The myth of a South bountifully endowed by nature but wasteful and backward survived until after unification (see F. S. Nitti, *Scritti politici,* op. cit., 147–52).

69. J. Blum, *The European Peasantry from the 15th to the 19th Century* (Washington, D.C., 1960). Paul Bairoch speaks of the "reorganization of the systems of land ownership, in particular the disappearance . . . general throughout Europe, of certain quasi-collective forms of property and labour . . ." ("Agriculture and the Industrial Revolution," in *The Fontana Economic History,* op. cit., 463).

the rural class," keeping it in "poverty, ignorance, and brutishness."[70] Only direct involvement by the owners, preceded and accompanied by agrarian instruction,[71] could thwart these evils.

These liberal and modernizing attitudes, already widespread among the landowning nobility and the bourgeoisie,[72] became more pronounced as a result of the political closed-mindedness that set in after 1848. An essay by Antonio Scialoja decrying the conservative orientation of the Bourbons' economic policy and comparing it unfavorably with Piedmont's—aimed, conversely, at wide mobilization of productive energies—became famous.[73] In a mental climate like this, it was only natural that agrarian operators like the Barraccos should see in modernization a way to meet their need for greater income.

6. Modernization

The modernization that the Barraccos gradually introduced on the latifondo naturally comprised technical innovations but also, and still more importantly, radical changes in its management. As regards technical progress, the Barracco latifondo had always been an advanced enterprise, one often praised for its use of modern technology and machinery,[74] which in many cases had been imported at considerable expense. A twelve-horsepower Guppy "locomobile," or steam engine, was promptly bought and installed at the Fallistro spinnery; the licorice works was equipped as early as the 1840s with a very costly "cast-iron press," (the largest in the kingdom) and later with a high-powered steam engine, mechanical rollers, and a tannin-extracting machine; the slow, heavy, and inefficient old olive press was replaced around 1840 with a much more efficient model possessing a "Genoa-type neck," and later by Mure presses; and steam threshers appeared on the Isola and San Leonardo farms as early as 1865, followed by Bodin and Bodin-Cantoni seeders, Alen plow-harrowers,

---

70. This was the "feudalism of money," as Conforti wrote in an 1848 circular, and at that time no one wanted to be "feudal." These writers were generally opposed to excessively large landholdings because, like M. De Augustinis (*Della condizione economica del Regno di Napoli* [Naples, 1833]), they favored the growth of a peaceful and practical bourgeoisie. Like Grimaldi, they also disapproved it for technical and scientific reasons: "a small but properly run farm is more profitable than one that is large and badly run" (*Studi statistici,* op. cit., 125).

71. Grimaldi had suggested that all university faculties should require students to pass an examination in agronomy before graduation.

72. Luigi Blanch maintained that by 1830, when the Carboneria had practically disappeared, its ideas had already become universal (*Scritti storici,* ed. B. Croce [Bari, 1945], 2:308–16).

73. Antonio Scialoja, *I bilanci del Regno di Napoli e degli Stati Sardi* (Turin, 1857).

74. Luigi Barracco was the only one of Lower Calabria's landowners to be repeatedly praised in Luigi Grimaldi's 1846 report.

and even a McCormick combine (the combine was unsuitable for the terrain, however, and had little success).[75]

Likewise, the Barraccos were attentive to farming methods and prompt to innovate them. Grain yields obtained on the masserie often amounted to twelve or eighteen times the amount of seed, ratios comparable to those obtained on experimental farms.[76] Olive oil quality was carefully supervised: the deposit was separated from the yellow oil, expert pruners and gangs of "pressmen" were brought in from Apulia, and trials were made of the hot-extraction method.[77] In 1894, Barracco oils were exhibited at the olive oil trade fair in Milan, and, although they won no prizes, they earned plaudits from the magazine *Agricoltura Meridionale*. But the latifondo's greatest boast was its livestock operations. When Luigi Barracco, in his 1848 appeal to the minister of internal affairs, mentioned the

> finest breeds of horses, cattle and merinos introduced into Calabria through the petitioner's ceaseless efforts over many years and at huge expense to buy Arabian and English stallions and mares, Saxon merinos . . .

his claims were not exaggerated. The Barracco breed of horses, described in the Murat statistics as strong but of middling quality,[78] had become over the ensuing decades one of the best in the kingdom thanks to imported studs and attention to genealogy. Swiss sheep and Rambouillets from France, prized for their soft wool, were added to the merino flocks in 1859, and in 1863 high-yield Swiss dairy cattle were introduced. Efforts were make to improve silk throwing; Greek licorice root, a better variety than the Calabrian or Sicilian, was

---

75. The harvester-baler "left too many ears of wheat uncut, sheared them off too close to the ground, and took longer to separate the wheat from the straw than it would take with sickles." The Barraccos also saw to the traditional types of tools. In engaging a team of ten hoemen in October of 1874, the agent specified to the foreman Franzi that "the hoes are to be provided by us in good condition" and that he would have to keep them in good repair (BA: A69, 157). Each livestock operation and each territorial administration kept inventories of every piece of equipment, down to the last shears, hoe, and pail. Cart chassis and beds were bought in the Serre from renowned craftsmen; numerous plows had iron shares, later replaced with steel shares.

76. These were higher than the average yields Grimaldi found for the whole province (*Relazione,* op. cit., 114) and the same as those obtained on the most advanced farms in the North as well as the South (see G. Porosini, *Produttività,* op. cit., "Statistical Appendix," 1–5, 354–67).

77. Sometimes all that was needed to increase oil output and improve its quality was to fertilize and hoe the olive groves, separate the deposit from the oil, and store it in clean containers. "Baron Barracco," Grimaldi approvingly observed, "had expert workers brought in from Apulia" to prune the trees.

78. In 1812, Intendent Galdi described the Barracco breed of horses as strong but, like all those in the province, "lacking studs." "Overly thin, ungainly, good only as draft animals and for breeding mules" (U. Caldora, *La Statistica murattiana,* op. cit., 104–5).

imported to improve paste quality; and cotton production and export were resumed during the the the American Civil War.

Lastly, although the Barraccos, like other landownwers, contributed heavily to the destruction of Calabria's forests, they used this natural resource in a rational and flexible manner. If they burned wood from their forests in the furnaces at their licorice works, spinneries, and other workshops when there was no other way to use it,[79] and cleared woodland to make way for grain cropping during the boom years, they also planted "northern pine" in the Sila nurseries and kept an eye out for alternative uses. In fact, when Calabrian Railways began, in 1862, to look around for tie-wood suppliers, the Barraccos lost no time in getting in touch with the Royal Engineers.[80]

But, as mentioned above, the Barraccos' most significant modernization effort was in the area of management. The incentive to modernize livestock operations was the discrepancy between the strong market for livestock and the higher-value products of animal husbandry, on the one hand, and the low productivity of partnership arrangements on the other.

The year 1844 was one of famine and poverty. In Calabria, "indigence appeared everywhere,"[81] and, "due to the penurious year," the Barraccos, too, took their losses (the "Bitonti partnership," for instance, "yielded 20 ducats apiece, at the master's loss") but so begrudged them that they took the occasion to begin to terminate the latifondo's partnership arrangements. Between 1846 and 1851, all partnerships with shepherds were terminated and in 1853 those with landowners followed (the Morelli brothers, the Macrys, "Gregorella," and De Lucro). The flocks, minus the third owned by the partners, were brought under direct management on a wage basis, and the shepherds became provisionees; they still had the benefit of cortaglie and minatici, though in smaller measure, but no longer a share in the yield. The new arrangement naturally meant a larger cash outlay for the Barraccos, as they were now alone in defraying costs and the wage expense was significantly higher. But the commercial output also increased, easily offsetting the greater expense, and the yield now went entirely to the Barraccos. In 1862, for instance, the flock of 10,000 sheep yielded 5,500 lambs, whereas twenty years earlier, when it numbered 15,000 head, the Barraccos's share was only 4,000 lambs. Net wool

---

79. "[I]t is necessary to examine whether, in that place and that period, there existed other possibilities for making use of those forests. . . . If no other possibilities existed, 'burning the woods' in the furnaces of foundries or glassworks was, indeed, the only justifiable and profitable way to use them for economic purposes" (W. Kula, *Economic Theory,* op. cit., 37).

80. The Barraccos rightly saw that great profits could be made here. Railway ties were then being paid "11 and even 13 lire apiece," and the "Neapolitan and Calabrian railways will be needing no less than 3 million ties." "In Piedmont, ties first sold for 6.5 lire . . . ; as the need for oak timber grew immensely, they went up to 11 lire apiece . . ." (BA: E20[2]).

81. Intendents' reports quoted by A. Lepre, *Storia del Mezzogiorno nel Risorgimento* (Rome, 1974), 175–76.

output grew from 100 quintals in 1839, to 181 in 1847, and 316 in 1855, and the net caciocavallo cheese output doubled. Product quality also improved, especially as the result of care in breeding; by separating the coarse-wooled sheep from the fine-wooled and by importing merinos, the Barraccos lay the foundations for the development of their own hybrid. Over the same period— the first half of the 1850s—the Barraccos also increased wheat output (to over 46,000 tomoli in 1855) and improved its quality. These were the years when wheat prices were climbing to one of the century's highest peaks,[82] wool fetched consistently high prices, and stock raisers' demand for choice lambs held strong. In that period, the modernizing solution seemed the right answer. As table 20 shows, the administrations' revenues grew from year to year. In 1853–54 they were up 23 percent from 1849–50, by 1857–58 they had risen another 8 percent, and a further 13 percent increase was achieved over the next four years. Overall, latifondo revenues grew by 50 percent over the twelve years prior to 1861, and the owners reaped praise for their exemplary modern and cost-efficient management.

It was only logical, then, for the Barraccos to stick with modernization when times turned hard. Italian unity extended the Piedmont's schedule of customs duties to the former Kingdom of Naples, reducing protective tariffs by 80 percent and creating difficulties for southern landowners, including free traders like the Barraccos, whose income fell 7 percent in the first five years. In light of the strong world market for wheat, the Barraccos sought to make up the shortfall with a larger wheat output obtained through a reorganization of production, that is, by bringing more acreage under direct management.[83] To do so, they resumed possession of land previously granted as paraspori and cortaglie. This solution seemed the best available: it responded to market opportunities and it was socially cheap because the rights acquired by users were weak. Moreover, it appeared in keeping with the idea of progress, considering that one reason the so-called Calabrian sharecropping system had been under fire for so long was that by granting use of a holding for only one or a few crops, rather than in its entirety, the system split property into two parts, with smaller aggregate earnings as the inevitable result.[84] Accordingly, the Bar-

---

82. The price on the "Italian market" was 34.55 lire per quintal in 1854, exceeded only in 1815–17 and 1873–74. Local prices were lower.

83. The Barraccos tried to react in the traditional manner as well, namely, by enlarging the property by purchases of government lands, but this operation encountered the difficulties mentioned earlier.

84. Many decades later Ernesto Marenghi, disagreeing with Taruffi, De Nobili, and Lori, remained critical of "Calabrian sharecropping." See E. Marenghi, "Calabrie," in *Inchiesta Parlamentare,* op. cit., vol. 5, pt. 2, 391. The agronomist Flavio Mario Calizza wrote in 1914 that the absence of "true sharecropping" in Calabria was the cause of its failure to increase farm output because the peasant, "compelled to work as a simple day laborer," had no interest in cultivating the land properly (*L'Agricoltura calabrese nel passato e nel presente* [Castrovillari, 1914], 12).

raccos drastically reduced the number of tenants in Rocca di Neto, Altilia, and Isola, attached the relevant land to the large masserie, and put it entirely into wheat. The same fate befell the Sila uplands, which had traditionally been granted to massari as paraspori and to shepherds as cortaglie.[85] The positive effect on production was not long in coming: by 1863, wheat output was up by half to 36,000 tomoli, and it remained high throughout the next decade.[86]

However, the modernization solution had adverse social effects. In the first place, by shifting the traditional intersector balance toward grain production, it increased the weight of hired laborers as against provisionees. In the second place, the provisionees lost access to the three tomolate on which they had grown their daily (rye) bread and enjoyed some jussi (*pascendi, arandi*). In other words, they saw their peasant status and their very subsistence threatened.[87] These effects produced almost immediate repercussions on the latifondo, which now had to cope for the first time with two new problems—the recruitment and cost of labor. In fact, the latifondo had never before been faced with a scarcity of labor, though the phenomenon was fairly general throughout the nineteenth century, especially in Lower Calabria.[88] On the contrary, the latifondo used to replace sick or absent workers the very same day, often with their own relatives. But now that the provisionees were forced to seek hired work to augment their wages they had fewer reasons to seek it with the Barraccos, especially since seasonal work was much better paid in nearby Apulia, where far-reaching changes were under way in agriculture.[89] The latifondo's hiring bosses began to be hard put to assemble gangs for periods of

---

85. As a first step, the Barroccos drastically reduced the number of sharecroppers. Lands that tenants had farmed for grain were incorporated in the large masserie along with grazing lands now turned over to wheat. Immediately afterward, the same lot fell to the higher lands in the Sila, which had traditionally been granted as parasporo to the massari and as manured cortaglie to the herdsmen, who farmed them for rye and flax.

86. This was the decade of the steam thresher, of the attempt to use the harvester, and of the effort to destroy grasshoppers. "[H]onorable mention must be made," reported the Croton Agrarian Committee in 1870, "of Mr. De Angelis, the subprefect of Croton, of Mayor Morelli and of the Barracco brothers, who worked to effect this destruction" (Ministry of Agriculture, Industry, and Commerce, Department of Agriculture, *Relazione intorno alle condizioni dell'agricoltura in Italia, 1870–1874* [Rome, 1876], 817).

87. The massari lost access to their three tomolate of parasforo and the half-tomolata used to grow broad beans. The herdsmen retained their right to part of the manure, but no longer to the use of two tomolate of manured land, and the chief massari and herdsmen retained their lots of six to eight tomolate planted in rye and flax.

88. "Both the herdsmen and the farmers," wrote Grimaldi (*Studi statistici,* op. cit., 122), "are insufficient for the needs of the province." See also the discussion of the seasonal migrations from northern to southeastern Calabria in G. Arrighi and F. Piselli, "Capitalist Development," op. cit.

89. See, for example, F. Snowden's study, *Violence and Great Estates in the South of Italy* (Cambridge, 1986).

intense labor and were forced to seek them "outside the region."[90] The second problem was created by the monetization of wages. With the disappearance of partnerships, paraspori, cortaglie, and jussi, average cash wages increased by 20 to 50 percent, with a proportional increase in the enterprise's operating costs.[91]

The problems of labor recruitment and cost called into question, also for the first time, the dimensions of the latifondo enterprise. The property was too big to be managed properly, wrote Guglielmo to Alfonso, the eldest brother. A very large property was a fine form of organization and management as long as the latifondo embraced a variegated universe, with an extensive grain-and-livestock cycle, large masserie next to tiny peasant holdings, and land status varying with the seasons. But with the breakdown of harmony among the various land uses that form was beginning to become outdated. According to Guglielmo, the property was not kept in adequate repair. For instance, the Camigliati buildings damaged in July of 1848 had never been properly repaired, and the Petrizia olive groves, destroyed by brigands in 1863, had not been replanted. Moreover, the burden of liabilities and bad credits was growing steadily (Guglielmo even advised selling off several holdings, for instance, in the San Leonardo district, to cover them).

Again, the remedies applied by the Barraccos conformed to the precepts of modernization: direct owner involvement, downsizing (and intensification) of operations, reduction of the workforce, and specialization in choice crops. In this context, the 1868 decision to waive the principle of majorat and split up Baron Luigi's estate not only had great symbolic significance, but it also seems to have been an attempt to solve the problems posed by the latifondo's size. As will be remembered, the Calabrian assets were divided among the four elder sons, of whom three—Stanislao, Francesco, and the energetic Guglielmo—moved their homes to Calabria. As owners of their individual shares of the estate, and also as their brother's agents, they maintained unity and cooperation in all operations, even consolidating part of the accounts, but at the same time they brought the property down to a more manageable size and put the owners back on the scene.[92] In a way, this was a throwback to the old pioneering days. Don Checco and Don Guglielmo were the ones who actually paid grazing fees

90. In 1862, for instance, the overseer Luigi Mancini could not manage to find twenty laborers for the harvest at the Isola holding, and in 1864 the Petrizia administrator was forced to seek youngsters for harvesting "outside the region."

91. The administrators' pay increased from 5 to 8 ducats a month to 12 or 13, chief herdsmen's from 3 to 5 or 6, chief cowherds' to 10 or 12, and guards from 3 or 4 to 7. Even the wages of the lowliest women servants rose from 1.5 to 2 ducats.

92. They shared rights of way, the use of storehouses and of houses on their trips, pack trains and transport services, and the labor force. As to the accounting system, the Barracco brothers kept "portable books" whose entries were periodically posted to the master ledgers of the General Administration.

and rent to the town governments, they were the ones who collected the large rents in Santo Janni, and they concluded major sales.

Activities were scaled down as well. Although the Barraccos could never bring themselves to sell any land, Guglielmo's advice notwithstanding, almost all the leases were dropped, San Leonardo was leased out to a tenant and the cultivation of marginal lands was abandoned.[93] Stock raising was sharply cut back. The number of goats fell from 2,900 to 300, and in 1870 goat raising ceased to be a separate operation. The five flocks of sheep were merged in 1871; the number of sheep was reduced by one-third, and the remainder were divided into two flocks, one coarse-wooled and the other fine-wooled.

These steps made it possible to cut the total number of provisionees by 20 percent, from 573 in 1859 to 463 in 1879 (see table 9), and in some sectors, such as stock raising, by more than 40 percent (from 332 in 1859 to 189 in 1879). The makeup of the workforce also changed. In the same period, the number of overseers grew from 162 to 188, though the number of workers they were overseeing had fallen. Overseers now comprised 40 percent of the fixed workforce, while they accounted for only 9 percent at the beginning of the century, and less than 30 percent in the 1850s (table 10). In other words, the latifondo reduced its use of fixed employees—bearers of autonomous skills and members of the guarantee system—and increased the proportion of braccianti, workers hired by the season for specific jobs, guided and closely supervised by the overseers. The new workforce was a better fit for the new turn of production because innovative methods and new machinery required both new skills and greater protection from theft, error, and sabotage.

The latifondo, like other great European landed properties, was beginning to specialize in the production of choice commodities for distant markets, selecting seeds, and breeding livestock.[94] Its grain output was dominated by prime wheat and "French wheat";[95] steam harvesters and threshers were introduced, with attendant mechanics and stokers. The olive groves, pruned and tended by skilled workers from Apulia, and the new presses, also run by Apulian experts, yielded more and better quality oil; the top-grade output from

---

93. For instance, the Barraccos ceased to rent Gambia—a large, fenced, irrigated farm they had kept for twenty years—and the Sila township lands adjacent to their enclosures at Derroiti, Macchiasacra, Accerina, Pizzirillo, and Manche. They also gave up farming marginal lands in the Sila.

94. P. Bairoch, *Agriculture,* op. cit., 464ff.

95. I have not been able to discover what was meant by "French wheat." The *Enciclopedia agraria italiana* of that day (ed. G. Cantoni [Torino, 1880]) makes no mention of it. The contemporary English literature on farming, which I looked into on Joan Thirsk's kind suggestion, identifies "French wheat" or "French barley" as buckwheat. See Rev. J. M. Wilson, *Rural Cyclopedia or a General Dictionary of Agriculture* (Edinburgh, n.d. [late eighteenth century]); and J. Banister, *A Synopsis of Husbandry* (London, 1799). However, there is no evidence that buckwheat was grown in Calabria.

the Rivioti press, for instance, multiplied ten times in ten years. The commercial production of oranges and lemons in the Rocca and Isola groves increased as well. The coarse-wool flock was converted almost entirely to the production of cheese, while the fine-wool flock (merinos, Swiss, Rambouillets, and hybrids) was kept for breeding and fleeces. The cattle administration gradually came to specialize in Swiss dairy stock, mainly raising calves and heifers that it shipped to the Naples and Rome markets by rail; the old caporali were now "administrators" and knew how to read, write, and use the telegraph. Specialization in choice products naturally reduced the output of "poor" products (rye, corn, beans, sheep's-milk cheese, and coarse wool), thereby decreasing the latifondo's self-sufficiency; it was still able to provide subsistence to the baronial family but no longer to the workers (white wheat, yellow oil, and Rambouillet wool were not for the lower classes). All this resulted in a further monetization of wages; with the disappearance of the part paid in kind, of minatici, benefits, "baskets," and comestibles, new workers were hired at a flat cash wage.

Modernization seemed to work even in the decades after Italian unity. The prices of oil, wheat, wool, licorice, and caciocavallo cheese remained at satisfactory levels; revenues began to rise again (fiscal year 1877–78 showed an 8 percent increase over 1874–75); the Barracco brothers who resided in Calabria were praised by the agrarian committees; and people sat up when Giovanni Barracco spoke in the Chamber on agricultural affairs.[96] But the changes that transformed the latifondo enterprise made it generally more vulnerable to market fluctuations, social tension, the scarcity of labor, and political upheavals.

This brings us to the ninth decade, which in Calabria as elsewhere was marked by the so-called Great Depression. After a decade of activism, the Barraccos's presence in the region was rarified once again. Francesco died in 1878 and Stanislao in 1881; Guglielmo and his wife, the only Barraccos still residing in Calabria, came to spend more time in Sorrento and Sant'Agata than in the castle of Caccuri. With the Left's accession to power, Alfonso, Giovanni, Roberto, and young Luigi and Alberto shifted their attention to Rome where the grand political battle over protectionism was in full swing.

---

96. See, for example, the proceedings of the Senate for 1886–87 (*Atti Parlamentari,* Senate of the Kingdom, 16th Legislature).

CHAPTER 8

The Mechanisms of the Crisis

1. The Decline of the Latifondo Economy

In the last two decades of the nineteenth century, the commercial production of the Barracco latifondo,[1] traditionally destined for distant markets, began to show signs of a decline. It affected, in varying degrees and time frames, all of the quality commodities: grain, cheese, fine wool, olive oil, and licorice. As table 7 shows, the volume of wheat and rye outputs fell off steadily after the 1860s boom and by the turn of the century had reached levels that were not only four times less than in the years just after Italian unity but two times less than in the first two decades. Moreover, this was not due to a shift of capital into stock raising because we see the same pattern repeated there, too. By 1887, the number of sheep had dwindled to 70 percent of the figures for 1862 and 1867 (after the operation was reorganized), and over the next decade it continued downward to less than half; the number of goats was all of seven times less.[2] The output of livestock operations plummeted: between 1887 and 1903, the latifondo's average production of sheep's-milk cheese was three to four times less than in the 1850s and 1860s (and ten times less than in 1835–43); and its production of caciocavallo cheese and fine wool was halved. The same trend appears in the production of olive oil and licorice, typical Mediterranean products thought to be insensitive to world market fluctuations. Oil output remained steadily high up to 1887—the portentious year of bumper harvests and protective tariffs—then began to fall, reaching an all-century low in 1899.

---

1. In this chapter we shall be mainly concerned with the specialized products of the latifondo, which were destined for sale in distant markets from the time its "two-track" economy began and were subject to the price fluctuations and the general economic mechanisms of the world market. As we shall see, the decline also involved the "poorer" commodities produced for the local markets.

2. Only the ox-raising operation, which in fact served the needs of the enterprise and was not for export, remained at the same level of about a thousand head—the level to which it had dropped in 1854 after the livestock partnerships were terminated.

In the last five years of the century, licorice output plummeted, too, after an upswing between 1867 and 1891.[3]

Chronologically, this trend of the latifondo economy occurred during the so-called European agricultural crisis.[4] The United States, where Reconstruction was in full swing, flooded the European markets with fine wheat from the virgin lands of the Midwest, grown and transported at costs so low as to cause an unprecedented drop in prices, which fell by more than half between 1873 and 1895.[5] In Italy, protected partly by its isolation and partly by artificial pegging of the lira, the full brunt of the crisis was not felt until 1881 when the artificial exchange rate was abolished. The manifestations of crisis became omnipresent: small-farm failures,[6] lower wages, greater unemployment, and abandonment of property improvements and of the marginal lands that had

---

3. Of the various industrial plants, licorice is one of the best indicators of the trend of agriculture because, as the plant grows wild in the Mediterranean, it was little affected by competition from foreign growers. In that period, for example, the cultivation of madder—formerly an important item in the South's exports—began to decline due to the development of artificial dyes. Flax acreage contracted because of competition from Russia and cotton because of the return of American production after the Civil War. See V. Peglion, *Le nostre piante industriali* (Bologna, 1919).

4. On the crisis in Italy, see E. Sereni, *Capitalismo e mercato nazionale in Italia* (Rome, 1966); E. Corbino, *Annali dell'economia italiana* (Città di Castello, 1933); A. De Bernardi, ed., *Questione agraria e protezionismo nella crisi economica di fine secolo* (Milan, 1977); P. D'Angelini, "L'Italia al termine della crisi agraria della fine del secolo XIX," *Nuova Rivista Storica* 3, no. 4 (1969): 323–65; and C. Supino, *Le crisi economiche* (Milan, 1907). On the crisis in Calabria, see G. Cingari, *Storia della Calabria,* op. cit., 57ff.; L. Izzo, *Agricoltura e classi rurali in Calabria* (Geneva, 1974); I. Giglioli, *Malessere agrario ed alimentare in Italia* (Portici, 1903); M. Bandini, *Agricoltura e crisi* (Florence, 1937); and R. Soldi, "La crisi economica in Italia dal 1882 al 1896," *Rivista di Politica Economica* 23 (1933): 1002–16, 1124–34. On the crisis in Europe, see M. Tracy, "Agriculture in Western Europe: The Great Depression, 1880–1900," in *Agrarian Conditions in Modern European History,* ed. C. K. Warner (New York, 1966), 98–111; T. W. Fletcher, "The Great Depression of English Agriculture, 1873–1896," *Economic History Review* (1961); A. R. Eckler, "A Measure of the Severity of Depression, 1873–1932," *Review of Economic Statistics* 15 (1933): 75–81; R. Fels, "Long Wave Depression, 1873–1897," *Review of Economic Statistics* 31 (February 1949): 69–73; N. D. Kondratieff, "The Dynamics of Industrial and Agricultural Prices," *Voprosy Konjunktury* 4 (1928): 5–85; J. W. T. Newbold, "The Beginnings of the World Crisis, 1873–96," *Economic History* 2 (1930–33): 425–41; and F. Simiand, *Les fluctuations économiques à longue période et la crise mondiale* (Paris, 1932). For critiques of traditonal interpretations of the crisis, see, as to England, S. B. Saul, *The Myth of the Great Depression, 1873–1896* (London, 1969); and, as to Germany and Central Europe, H. Rosenberg, "Political and Social Consequences of the Great Depression of 1873–1896," *Economic History Review* 13 (1943): 58–73.

5. W. Malenbaum, *The World Wheat Economy, 1885–1939* (Cambridge, Mass., 1953).

6. There was an extraordinary increase in the number of forced sales for nonpayment of taxes during this period. See G. Luzzatto, *L'economia italiana dal 1861 al 1914* (Milan, 1963), 1:222; and E. Corbino, *Annali,* op. cit., 3:58–59 (tables). We may infer that many farmers opted for this unusual form of abandoning the land. It is certain that many tenants left their land before their leases were up.

been brought into cultivation during the wheat-boom years. Farmers with sufficient strength and capital tried to pull through by converting from wheat to grapes, citrus fruit, olives, and livestock, thereby augmenting the general confusion.[7] In Calabria, too, the first wave of the crisis brought the small peasant proprietors to ruin (according to Napoleone Colajanni, every one of them was selling wheat or other grain). This was followed, especially in the Cosenza region, by an advance flow of emigration. Here, too, the depression squeezed tenant farmers who had signed high-rent leases in better days; here, too, it triggered a frantic race to plant citrus groves and vineyards.[8]

If the chronological correlation between the latifondo's decreasing output and the onset of the so-called agricultural crisis was not merely a coincidence, then we must explain the mechanisms whereby the European crisis affected the latifondo economy. According to one current explanation, the crisis of latifondo property was simply a belated repercussion of the so-called tenants' crisis: when leases came up for renewal, absentee landlords, who relied on rents collected by their agents, found themselves squeezed by the tenants' financial straits and were forced to lower lease prices.[9] However, this explanation, which measures the whole South by a Sicilian yardstick, does not apply to continental latifondism. The latter, unlike the Sicilian brand, was characterized by landlords who stayed on hand and preferably managed their property them-

---

7. Conversion from wheat to "fruit, early vegetables, dairy products, meat, silk, flax, hemp, wine, olive oil, tobacco, citrus fruit, chestnuts, almonds, figs, raisins, eggs, and poultry" was recommended by S. Jacini in 1884 at the end of his famous investigation. See the final report in *Atti della Giunta,* op. cit., 39.

Many authoritative historians, including R. Romeo (see especially his *Risorgimento e capitalismo* [Bari, 1959], particularly 194), explain the standstill in agriculture during this period by a lack of capital, as investors were turning elsewhere. But this thesis does not explain the difficulties encountered by both great landowners like the Barraccos, who did not need capital to convert their production (the balance between grain and livestock had always been quite flexible) and the small freehold farmers who had often pioneered agricultural transformation (as M. Minghetti frequently repeated in the Chamber of Deputies).

8. Between 1879 and 1887, Italy more than tripled its wine exports. Overproduction of wine and citrus fruit cost Italy dearly after 1887 when France imposed high tariffs on Italian wine and Russia curtailed citrus imports by means of a 300 percent tariff; again, after 1894, when French wine production, having overcome the effects of the phyloxera epidemic, topped Italian production; and yet again after the terrible 1897 citrus crisis in Sicily, combined with one of the worst crop failures of the century, led to the revolutionary uprisings of 1898. See Ministry of Agriculture, Industry, and Commerce, Department of Agriculture, *Notizie e Studi sull'Agricoltura, Produzione e Commercio del Vino in Italia e all'estero* (Rome, 1892), 161.

9. "[T]he great landowners," runs this argument, "were mostly absentee landlords. Especially in the South, they leased out vast lands in which they invested but little capital and little labor; extensive farming of grain, which needs the least tending—despite its low profitability, traditionally assured the easiest and safest revenues." See P. D'Angelini's otherwise fine article, "L'Italia al termine," op. cit., 344. Many scholars share this conception.

selves, making extensive use of hired labor;[10] Their rent income was of secondary importance and, being paid mainly in kind, was not subject to inflation.
If the continental latifondo economy was shaken to its roots, it could not have
been as a belated consequence of the tenants' crisis but must have been due to
mechanisms of some other kind. To understand how the crisis came on, its
long-term effects, and the adjustments made to weather it, we must examine
the mechanisms whereby the general crisis affected the Barracco latifondo's
production and analyze the forms and rationality of the owners' response at the
level of the enterprise and at the level of national politics.

2. Traditional Reaction Mechanisms

These mechanisms are less self-evident than one might think. It is customary,
when dealing with a business enterprise, to identify them through price analysis; this is especially appropriate in our case because the latifondo's "rich"
products were highly commercial, entered the commercial circuit (as was true
to some extent for all latifondo products), and were traditionally destined for
distant markets. Moreover, as we have seen, the prices at which the Barraccos
sold their commodities were determined by, and followed the fluctuations of,
the national and/or international markets rather than any calculation of production costs.[11] In fact, if we compare the prices that the latifondo's commercial
products (olive oil, sheep's-milk cheese, wheat, licorice, fine wool, and
caciocavallo cheese) brought in the local, Naples, and Italian markets (table 8),
we find, whatever the absolute value differences, the same pattern in each
trend: local prices echo the fluctuations in Naples prices and average Italian
prices. All this means that the latifondo's commercial products were vulnerable
to changes in the wider market; any weakness (the "crisis") in the latter was
immediately transmitted to the producer (whether latifondista or capitalist
operator) through falling prices and evoked a response in the form of adjustments in production.

   At this point, the analysis becomes more complicated. How would a true
capitalist enterprise have reacted to market fluctuations? It would have reacted
by turning production capacity toward the product that sold best and cutting
back on the less successful ones. And, since other producers would have been
doing the same thing, the market's equilibrium would have been upset, a glut of
more successful commodities would have ensued, and prices would have been

---

   10. A case in Apulia similar to ours in Calabria has recently been studied by F. Snowden
(*Violence,* op. cit). Though Snowden analyzes the Pavoncelli latifondo in a later period than ours,
in outlining the history of the property in the ninteenth century he notes that "Pavoncelli . . .
continued to manage every aspect of the family concerns personally" (13).
   11. In a perceptive reflection on the changes that competition underwent during the nineteenth century, C. Supino noted that trade had become a game (*La concorrenza e le sue più recenti
manifestazioni* [Bologna, 1893], 32 and passim).

driven still farther down, ruining farmers who had signed expensive leases or brought marginal lands into cultivation in the boom years. An adjustment of this kind would also have upset the production balance of individual enterprises and of agriculture in general, making the less successful commodities scarce, impoverishing the soil through lack of manure, and possibly creating dependence on imports of commodities normally produced domestically. This was the classic mechanism whereby the market governed farm production.[12] Such mechanism assumes, however, the existence of a true market economy, characterized by unlimited flexibility in the placement of production factors, with reserves that can be mobilized or demobilized at the right time, and in which the maximization of profit is the ultimate goal of production activities.

But we cannot infer the existence of an economy of this kind from the existence or predominance of market-oriented production and correlations among price trends. In reality, the latifondo economy was not a market economy but simply an economy whose profits were realized in the market: an economy in which straight selling was more important than calculating competitive edges, low production costs assured a gain on sales at whatever price, and the goal of production was to assure consumption not to maximize profit. The latifondista, however committed to rational modernization, was still something of a gentleman farmer; he was not, that is, an "economizer." In fact, he did not react to market incentives in the same way that a capitalist would; for him, as for the Polish nobleman studied by Witold Kula, decisions about production "depended in no way, or only minimally, on market phenomena; indeed, that dependence was sometimes inverse."[13]

In the first place, the value of the latifondo's output was not market-dependent. A comparison of price and output trends (see tables 7 and 8) shows that their correlations were sometimes positive and sometimes negative. In the period from 1887 to 1899, wheat output declined to a yearly average of 14,000 tomoli, down from 26,000 in the prior period, in agreement with the marked downswing in prices; wool prices in the 1880s were low and output decreased; and olive oil production fell off after 1888 when prices, which had been slipping since 1879, fell still further.[14] On the other hand, output volume decreased between 1835 and 1839, when prices were rising, and between 1855 and 1859, when their level was very high. Moreover, we have seen the Barraccos making their most aggressive and intense efforts at land accumulation (with consequent growth in wheat output) in the post-Napoleonic years and

---

12. Alternatively, the growers, who enjoyed a certain degree of political power, could have tried to oppose the fair workings of the market and keep prices artificially high through political action, which usually means imposing protective tariffs.

13. W. Kula, *Economic Theory*, op. cit., 55–56.

14. See A. Necco, *La curva dei prezzi delle merci in Italia negli anni 1881–1909* (Turin, 1910).

again during the so-called midcentury crisis, that is, in periods of market depression.

Hence, the latifondo's output volume did not reflect price trends; quite the contrary. Given the operation's low production costs and the permanent gap between local and world prices, the owner's interest lay in selling in distant markets at the going price, whatever it might be. Indeed, world prices (paid in the Naples or Italian markets) were always higher, in absolute terms, than local prices. First-pressed oil, for instance, sold for at least 13 percent more in Naples than at local fairs in Calabria and often as twice as much on the national market; the same was generally true for sheep's-milk cheese and wool, although the gap for these products narrowed toward the end of the century.[15] However low the Italian or Naples price, the local price would always be lower; conversely, however high the local price, the national price would be higher still, and the landowner always had an advantage selling in distant markets (some products, such as licorice and caciocavallo cheese, were virtually never traded in local markets). Moreover, he could realize a profit, and thus had an interest in producing, even when prices were low. Of course, there was such a thing as a nonremunerative price, but, thanks to the latifondo's low operating costs, this threshold, too, was quite low; the amount of profit might vary according to the general economic situation and price trends, but there was always some gain to be made (in fact, as we have seen, the latifondo administrations always closed their yearly accounts with a net profit.)[16]

Lastly, it was their very mentality that led the latifondisti to react to market fluctuations differently than a capitalist would, that is, to increase production not so much when prices were high as when they were so low as to threaten income. Witold Kula has analyzed the mechanisms whereby the price decline in seventeenth-century Europe stimulated Poland's feudal lords to increase their wheat-growing efforts and output; in fact, their goal was not to maximize profit but to maintain their levels of consumption: they wanted, not money, but what money could (or was supposed to) buy. Mutatis mutandis, the great nineteenth-century landowners, especially those located in the world

---

15. Wheat was a somewhat special case because, while the national price was always higher than the local price, the price in Naples was sometimes lower. But in reality local demand for wheat was so inelastic that price fluctuations did not affect supply.

16. Here we need recall only the most important factors that made the latifondo economy so profitable. Land was an extremely low-cost factor (because it was acquired at a low price, or inherited, or "usurped") not subject to calculations of comparative advantage. Labor, another low-cost factor, was available in practically "unlimited supply." Wages were computed in pecuniary terms but in reality were largely paid in goods and services that never entered the cash economy. The great landowners' realty was substantially unencumbered by mortgages, which weighed heavily on land revenues in northern Italy. At the regional level, mortgage debt amounted to 34 percent of land revenues in Piedmont and Liguria but only 14 percent in the Neapolitan provinces. See L. Musella, *Proprietà e politica agraria in Italia* (Naples, 1984).

market's peripheral regions, such as Calabria, were operating in just the same mental landscape. It was not prices that they were interested in but the *terms of trade* between the commodities they could sell and those they had to buy. As long as revenues from their property sufficed to meet their needs for social ascent and standing, if possible thanks to high prices, then the barons felt no need to act. Only incontrovertible evidence that market terms had worsened and that, if they hoped to maintain their standard of living and social standing, losses would have to be made up by increasing aggregate output, could prompt them to take action.[17]

> If in this case we can speak of "market incentives to investment," for the most part, unlike the case in capitalism, they were negative incentives; if market terms worsened, they set off a stimulus to compensate for losses by producing more.[18]

A Calabria baron threatened with a reduction in his income due to lower prices would therefore have reacted by seeking to increase output, either by "investing" in the old way—avoiding cash outlays and using socially and economically cheaper methods to extend the scale of production in absolute terms—or by modernizing and mechanizing his operations, the practice in more recent decades. At any rate, he would seek to augment output to offset the price decline. By contrast, what we see in the 1880s—a simultaneous decline in prices and in latifondo output—was, qualitatively, a new fact. If the agricultural crisis was indeed what caused the latifondo's output to diminish, the process was a totally new one in that world.

3. The Agricultural Crisis and Italian Trade Policy

Our question—why the decline?—is still unanswered. Why did the traditional responses to market incentives, which landowners indeed tried, prove inadequate in the last twenty years of the century? The explanation lies in a combination of internal and external causes: the latifondo's greater market dependence plus the closure of commercial outlets. The modernizing changes discussed in the last chapter had made the latifondo more dependent on the market, hence more sensitive to its changes. As will be recalled, the latifondo had gradually

---

17. See W. Kula, *An Economic Theory,* op. cit., 55. J. Topolski amplified this same argument to explain the birth of capitalism in Europe, maintaining that it was precisely the nobility in various European countries who were forced to undertake economic activities because the adverse economic trends of the seventeenth century jeopardized their standard of living (*La nascita del capitalismo in Europa* [Turin, 1979]). A. Hirschman, in *Passions and Interests* (Princeton, 1977), uses a similar argument as regards the political reaction of the aristocrats (or "gatekeepers").

18. W. Kula, *An Economic Theory,* op. cit., 54–55. See also A. Placanica, *Alle origini,* op. cit., 407–28.

eliminated the "natural" sector, shifting instead to an exclusively monetary basis, and it had specialized in "rich" products destined for distant markets, neglecting alternative local outlets almost entirely. These changes had made the latifondo vulnerable to market fluctuations, mainly in terms of demand, but also, for the first time, in terms of price. Although the no-profit threshold was now higher, the latifondo could still sell cheap. But, if market outlets closed, increasing output—the traditional response to a weak market—would be an obsolete and unviable strategy. It would be pointless to produce more in the face of insufficient demand, and in the end the enterprise would have no choice but to reduce output.

This was how things stood in the last two decades of the nineteenth century: the Barracco latifondo began to be hard put to find outlets for its products, and an ever larger proportion no longer found its way to Naples. A comparison between outputs and quantities shipped to Naples—the commercialization rate (table 21)—evidences this pattern of increasing difficulty: sales of sheep's-milk cheese, of which the latifondo used to sell 100 percent or more (if the supply in any one year did not meet demand, an advance sale of the next's year's output would be "bespoken"), fell to an average of 80 percent; the commercialization rate for licorice, which had no alternative outlet, fell from 90 or 100 percent to less than 30 percent. The situation with regard to wheat and oil was still more dramatic. In the past, around 35 to 40 percent of the latifondo's wheat output was sold directly in Naples, and most of the remaining 60 to 65 percent was taken up by large local traders who then channeled it into distant markets. But, beginning in the mid-1870s, the Naples market absorbed no more than a meager fraction (3 to 5 percent) of the wheat output, while the large Calabrian traders either bought less (Domenico Ingarozza, for instance, cut his purchases from a yearly average of 1,500 tomoli to 200) or ceased to buy at all (Santo Ranieri of Reggio Calabria was one of these). Likewise oil; for decades it had followed a set pattern—75 percent shipped to Naples, the remainder distributed by way of minatici, gifts, and palace consumption (the occasional surpluses were sold locally)—but saturation in the Naples market reduced the commercialization rate by a quarter, and the large local traders began to demand oranges instead. Unsold stocks on hand in the Naples warehouse now amounted to around 50 percent of the quantity shipped, creating serious problems for Don Macry, the scrupulous administrator, who sent the baron a written report on the matter in 1890 (see table 22).

During the same period, the latifondo also received more and more complaints from buyers about the quality of its products: the oil was rancid, there was more deposit than good oil, the quality of the wheat was poor.[19] This was a

---

19. For example, at Gioia Tauro oil was kept in huge stinking containers (L. Izzo, *Agricoltura e classi rurali, op. cit.*, p. 82.

TABLE 21. Commercialization of Barracco Latifondo Products

Year	Olive Oil (hectoliters) Output	Na	Sheep's-milk cheese (rounds) Output	Na	Grain (*tomoli*) Output	Na	Licorice (quintals) Output	Na-Me	Wool (quintals) Output	Na	Caciocavallo cheese (pairs) Output	Na
1827											3,592	
1831											4,364	
1835	2,163	1,626	95,031	98,000	25,202	15,664	1,273	1,097	27	27	4,300	3,670
1839	3,041	2,281	111,500	111,000	17,185	4,970	1,558	4,412	103	102	9,078	22,000
1843	1,934	1,451	86,614	667,800	29,367	10,900	1,267	5,036	78	77	9,650	4,200
1847	4,259	3,194	56,741	57,750	27,977	26,384	7,516	3,093	2,578	125	4,908	1,714
1851	6,449	4,837	52,979	47,770	32,264	12,560	2,278	2,469	219	176		
1855	3,537	2,653	33,904	45,556	46,446	14,420	1,915	1,694	316	169	5,735	2,504
1859	2,781	1,403	35,333	30,354	24,449	8,550	1,658	1,662	200	182	8,036	2,376
1863	3,042	1,214	26,873	21,175	36,029	7,650	3,093	25,778	125	119	10,166	2,688
1867	3,101	1,471	34,746	29,941	32,567	8,200	4,313	1,750	162	146	11,259	2,560
1871	4,999	2,544	12,047	9,000	30,220		3,333	3,250	110	97	8,133	1,940
1875	4,265	2,584	14,071	11,428	29,268	820	2,645	2,500	110	97	6,093	2,050
1879	4,805	2,979	14,487	12,310	21,732	1,152	1,991	1,828	126	106	4,890	2,550
1883	4,776	2,600	10,181	7,973	25,874		4,167	1,259	99	90	5,163	3,973
1887	8,249	5,517	9,604	8,037	15,285	4,963	4,204	1,167	68	63	3,378	1,496
1891	3,992	2,274	11,762		13,911	8,997	4,287	1,259		6,195		
1895	2,101	1,576	9,128		18,169	9,217	2,877	770	52	6,204		
1899	1,313	175	7,565		8,799	7,416	1,559	1,500	55	4,506		
1903	1,081	811	6,010		10,037		1,506	1,400		2,430		

* Na = shipped to Naples; Na-Me = shipped to Naples and Messina

TABLE 22.   Commercialization of the Latifondo's Olive Oil Output

Year	(1) Output	(2) Na	(3) % 2÷1	(4) Unsold	(5) % 4÷2
1835	2,163	162	75		
1839	3,041	2,281	75		
1843	1,934	1,451	75		
1847	4,259	3,194	75		
1851	6,449	4,837	75		
1855	3,537	2,653	75		
1859	2,781	4,103	50	485	34
1863	3,042	1,214	40	683	53
1867	3,101	1,471	47	814	55
1871	4,999	2,544	51	1,607	63
1875	4,265	2,584	60	820	32
1879	4,805	2,979	62	833	28
1883	4,776	2,600	54	1,309	50
1887	8,249	5,517	67	896	16
1891	3,992	2,274	57		
1895	2,101	1,576	75		
1899	1,313				
1903	1,081	811	75		

Na = shipped to Naples

sign that the technical progress we described earlier was coming to a halt. The Barraccos, though still willing to sell at any price, found fewer and fewer buyers. The large traders in Naples—the Forquets, the Rouths, the Klentzes— once used to buy everything that reached Naples or Castellammare,[20] but now the Wolf Stolts, the Klunzes (Klentzes), the Langrafàs, the Gervasis, the Savas, and the D'Amores were buying one commodity only, or only a certain quantity, and the Calabrian market was too rigid to absorb the difference. There was nothing for it but to reduce, change, or transform production. The traditional systems for responding to a weak market no longer worked; the problem lay not in the terms of trade but in the unavailability of markets.

It was precisely here, in the matter of market outlets, that the latifondo took the full force of the European agricultural situation and of the so-called crisis. The impact was not direct; to the contrary, since the southern latifondisti were not directly influenced by price trends, the fact that American wheat imports had driven Italian prices down might actually have played in their favor if falling prices had led to greater per-capita consumption, with a conse-

---

20. J. A. Davis, *Merchants,* op. cit., 65ff.

quent increase in aggregate demand.[21] At any rate, in the early years of the crisis the latifondo's output continued to find its way to one market niche or another, the wheat stopping in Naples, the oil, licorice, and bergamot proceeding, with the aid of foreign traders, to Marseilles' soap, perfume and pharmaceutical factories. Italy's exports of typical southern products remained at satisfactory levels: annual olive oil exports fluctuated around 700,000 quintals, citrus exports climbed swiftly until 1887, virtually all the licorice output was exported, and imports were negligible (in 1875, for instance, Italy exported 11,000 quintals and imported 388), while imports of competitive products were judged "reasonable." Up to 1884, Italy imported an average of 200,000 tons of wheat per year and exported 70,000. Hence, despite the price depression and some problems with grain, the latifondo economy did well as long as Italy maintained a free-trade policy and continued to keep its doors open to trade. That situation changed with the introduction of tariffs in 1887.[22]

It is now a well-established fact that the impact of protectionist legislation on Italy's trade in farm products was especially damaging to commodities typically produced in the South. The wheat trade—apparent cause of the legislation—was affected to little or no degree; Italy's wheat exports were negligible even before 1887, and decreased still further thereafter (table 23),[23] while imports, which appear dramatically smaller if we compare 1888 with the abnormal prior year, actually increased from a yearly average of 400,000 tons in 1880–86 to almost 700,000 in 1888–94.

The commodities that did suffer strongly from the introduction of tariffs were wine, olive oil, licorice, and citrus fruit, whose previously upward export trends turned sharply downward. This was not due to price mechanisms, however, but to the predictable retaliations taken by the importing countries, whose boycotts and embargoes targeted southern products in particular. It is common knowledge that France—Italy's major trading partner, especially as regards southern farm commodities—responded to Italy's protectionist measures with a tariff war that struck mainly at wine, oil and licorice, while Russia imposed a

---

21. This increase does not seem to have actually occurred. Per-capita wheat consumption in Italy was .5 liters a day in 1870–74 and dropped to .27 liters in 1897–98 (see A. De Bernardi, ed., *Questione agraria,* op. cit., 41). Although the 1897–98 figure is not statistically significant, as this was a year of terrible dearth, there seems to be no question that popular consumption failed to grow over this period. See also I. Giglioli, *Malessere agrario ed alimentare in Italia* (Portici, 1903).

22. "La concurrence des céréales américaines, en déclenchant la baisse des prix, allait inciter à une plus grande productivité . . . mais le progrès technique s'interrompt après le relèvement . . . des droits d'entrée sur les produits agricoles. . . . Il en va de même en Italie, où le tarif douanier de 1888 bloque une évolution progressiste . . ." (G. Garrier, "La domination du capitalisme, 1840–1914: Les nouvelles agricultures," in P. Léon, *Histoire économique,* op. cit., 4:409).

23. *Annuario statistico italiano* (Rome, 1892), 566–75.

TABLE 23. Imports/Exports of Farm Commodities in Italy (1871–94)

Year	Oil (hectoliters)		Grain (quintals)		Citrus fruit (quintals)		Wool (quintals)	
	Imp.	Exp.	Imp.	Exp.	Imp.	Exp.	Imp.	Exp.
1871	33,157	841,106			29,340	877,943	43,696	15,938
1872	26,645	673,593	329,528	79,280	37,829	37,829	59,742	13,897
1873	48,608	602,605	268,778	106,114	33,622	836,226	52,498	5,464
1874	31,822	476,832	364,360	40,115	41,117	717,495	63,065	9,096
1875	81,195	926,673	311,126	60,351	38,454	960,066	68,020	8,499
1876	19,629	812,897	328,896	74,747	47,308	932,847	84,160	6,285
1877	44,757	602,301	209,567	72,606	48,638	1,007,585	82,437	7,138
1878	11,643	514,127	346,229	59,174	29,941	977,986	65,386	9,090
1879	50,044	886,555	488,399	22,722	19,351	994,918	85,389	11,025
1880	14,223	576,598	229,958	80,857	12,962	931,592	73,285	17,538
1881	89,727	677,990	147,358	94,790	12,302	1,286,575	95,357	8,991
1882	19,302	813,805	164,600	96,212	20,084	1,916,721	75,084	17,471
1883	110,232	806,269	232,405	80,207	20,835	1,587,118	97,398	14,490
1884	93,446	538,774	355,146	37,953	17,412	1,733,710	100,714	7,588
1885	181,521	358,549	723,586	13,015	18,881	1,522,729	111,112	23,232
1886	53,955	648,011	936,233	7,702	31,266	1,248,791	121,434	13,073
1887	45,327	640,730	1,015,860	4,755	20,144	2,298,089	111,284	13,879
1888	31,425	523,952	669,789	2,635	7,965	1,652,669	93,788	17,820
1889	58,075	552,680	872,743	570	13,068	1,942,524	97,589	13,305
1890	25,178	378,318	644,986	418	25,457	1,905,711	82,230	12,795
1891	22,412	568,378	464,367	696	13,605	1,351,690	89,919	22,751
1892	5,531	574,076	697,143	500	17,845	1,704,628	97,828	
1893	33,268	430,759	861,418	674		1,973,249	88,983	17,906
1894	75,825	605,297	486,846	374		2,143,473	94,017	30,854

300 percent tariff on Italian citrus fruit.[24] Thus, the South's farm production, including the latifondo's, was in trouble not because of changes in the world market but because of Italy's trade policy, which, in response to those changes, provoked the closing of the South's traditional market outlets.

Nor was the tariffs' impact on Italian commodity prices good for the latifondo economy. As we have seen, they did not slow the inflow of foreign wheat but simply prevented a further fall in its price. This effect was indeed stimulating for capitalist farmers in northern Italy, but for the latifondo economy it spelled loss of its main competitive advantage. While latifondisti had been the only ones in Italy able to hold their own against American wheat, because they were the only ones able to produce at such low cost and sell at competitive prices (for reasons similar to the ones that made Russian wheat competitive, and different from the ones that gave American farmers their edge), they were less able than capitalist farmers to take advantage of protection and upgrade wheat production. The new tariff policy thus created de facto protection for northern Italy's farm commodities at the expense of the South's peasant and latifondo producers. Northern commodities began to saturate the domestic market, driving out the South's. In fact, the South's wheat output— already falling off in the 1880s due to the difficulties discussed earlier[25]— plummeted after 1887 (see table 24).

But, if tariff protection artificially deprived the latifondo economy of its competitiveness and its markets, the owners' simple, obvious, and fundamental interest would have been to oppose the wheat tariff, the more so since the reprisals taken by Italy's trading partners and their effects were all perfectly predictable. In this perspective, the role the great southern landowners are supposed to have played in enacting the 1887 legislation appears illogical and self-defeating. Was it really, as Giustino Fortunato suggested, a simple case of shortsightedness?

---

24. L. Izzo, *Storia delle relazioni commerciali tra l'Italia e la Francia dal 1860 al 1875* (Naples, 1965); F. Chabod, *Storia della politica estera italiana dal 1870 al 1896* vol. 1 (Bari, 1971); F. Braudel, ed., *Histoire économique et sociale de la France* (Paris, 1976), 3:105ff., 323ff.; J. Bouvier, "Les interventions françaises dans quelques affaires financières de l'Unité italienne, 1863–1870," *Annali dell'Istituto G. G. Feltrinelli* (1961); B. Gille, "Les investissements français en Italie, 1815–1914," *Archivio Economico dell'Unificazione Italiana,* ser. 2, 16 (1968); A. Lepre, "Sui rapporti fra Mezzogiorno ed Europa nel Risorgimento," *Studi Storici* 10, no. 3 (1969): 548– 86. It is interesting to note that, contrary to what is commonly thought, the Bourbons' trade policy supported typical exports, to the point where in 1845 it ceased favoring the kingdom's own merchant marine in order to induce the English to continue importing olive oil. See E. Pontieri, *Il riformismo borbonico nella Sicilia del Sette e dell'Ottocento, Saggi Storici* (Naples, 1961).

25. This decline was a source of some worry to contemporaries. See B. Tommasi, *Come si possa riparare alla diminuita produzione del grano* (Cosenza, 1885); and P. Saraceno, *La mancata unificazione economica italiana a cento anni dall'unificazione politica* (Rome, 1961).

TABLE 24.   Grain Output in Selected Regions (thousands of hectoliters)

	1885	1898	%
Piedmont	1,634	3,600	+120
Lombardy	2,441	3,380	+ 38
Emilia	4,795	6,130	+ 28
South	9,937	5,780	− 42

We southerners, seduced by the mirage of a wheat tariff, allowed our-
selves to be persuaded by the exaggerated claims of the Po Valley
factories.[26]

It appears, however, that the southern latifondisti were much more aware of the
dangers of protection than Fortunato says. They opposed it as long as they
possibly could, ultimately surrendering only to the logic (shortsighted indeed!)
of political alliances. Let us try briefly to reconstruct this episode.

4. Political Alliances and the Historic Bloc

Even today, many historians believe that the so-called historic bloc originated
in the tariff deal of 1887, seen as an agreement of interests between northern
industrialists and southern agrarians.[27] In this view, the agrarian party (oddly
but significantly headed by a northern industrialist, Alessandro Rossi), supported by the southern "feudalists," supposedly forced this economic, political,
and cultural about-face on the governing classes and the traditionally free-trade
Parliament. There is no doubt as to the role played by the representatives of
northern industry on this issue; moreover, their position was perfectly
understandable—they wanted the government to protect infant industries—
and it was eventually justified by the policy's success.[28] What appears more
ambiguous is the role played by the so-called agrarian party, especially its
southern supporters, considering that the unfortunate alliance was to wreak
havoc on their enterprises and throughout southern agriculture. Were the latifondisti aware that they were sacrificing themselves? If so, what were their

---

26. G. Fortunato, *Il Mezzogiorno,* op. cit., 1:277.

27. See, for example, A. Caracciolo, *L'Inchiesta Jacini* (Turin, 1958); S. Pozzani, *L'economia italiana: Situazioni e problemi* (Milan, 1961); and L. Villari, "Per la storia del protezionismo
in Italia," *Studi Storici* 6 (1965) 651–63.

28. The question of whether protectionism was truly effective in determining the takeoff of
industrialization continues to be debated. A. Gerschenkron's well-known thesis is that no real
modernization occurred in Italy until the end of the 1890s. (*Economic Backwardness in Historical
Perspective* [Cambridge, Mass., 1962]).

reasons? Why did they vote with Rossi's party? Why didn't they oppose the deal?

The generous and somewhat sentimental reading offered by Epicarmo Corbino:

> the sacrifice of the South was not made deliberately, but almost unwittingly. Even when immediate and direct economic interests of a private or only regional nature were at stake, decisions were usually dictated by the desire to safeguard the general interest of the Nation . . .[29]

may credit the southern representatives with too much altruism. During the same period, the South—or, rather, the deputies it sent to Parliament—was perfectly capable of staunchly opposing other measures introduced by the government under the same banner of the "general interest of the nation" (meaning the disastrous financial situation and the difficulties encountered during the country's first exercises in imperialism); one need but think of the resolute antigovernment position taken by southern lawmakers on the issues of property tax equalization, railroad construction, and war taxes. Moreover, the southern deputies—almost all landowners themselves—were hardly unaware of the risks to which protectionism would subject their own interests. Traditionally free traders—not only because "the fortunes of agriculture in general and the South's in particular were tied to free trade"[30] but also because they were perennially opposed to government intervention in their affairs—they had already fought customs reform in 1878, worrying that in an economically weak country like Italy,

> a tariff war would actually benefit only a few industrialists, who would levy a tax on the entire nation, and this would create purely artificial interests.[31]

In 1887, they were demanding the same or even more laissez-faire policies as in 1878. Toward the end of the year, when a breakoff of trade with

---

29. E. Corbino, *Annali,* op. cit., 3:23.

30. G. Carocci, *Agostino Depretis e la politica interna italiana dal 1876 al 1887* (Turin, 1956), 442. Carocci acknowledges that over this whole period, protectionist pressure encountered substantial opposition from southern and agrarian interests. He maintains, however, that during Depretis's last government "wide sectors of the southern bourgeoisie were being converted to protectionism" (442). Curiously enough, this part of his otherwise precise and reliable discussion is rather vague. He makes no distinction between those of the southern parliamentarians who spoke for the new bourgeoisie of midscale landowners and professionals and those who represented the great latifondisti, just as he does not distinguish between Sicilians and mainlanders.

31. Quoted from a speech by Ascanio Branca, landowner and deputy from Lucania, in the Chamber of Deputies on June 17, 1878. See G. Carocci, *Agostino Depretis,* op. cit., 442n.

France was in the offing—the treaty, denounced by Italy, was to expire on December 31, and the Paris negotiations were deadlocked—the Association of Landowners and Farmers of the Provinces of Naples (of which Roberto Barracco had been a founder in 1866)[32] addressed a resolution to the prime minister and the ministers of agriculture and foreign affairs, calling on the government to "guarantee Italian agricultural production to the greatest extent possible in the future trade treaties." The document argued explicitly that "*the great annual availability of products*" required finding "regular and convenient foreign outlets" and that a trade war would have caused "irreparable discouragement to the already shaky agricultural economy."[33] No mention was made of prices.

Moreover, of the thirty petitions the Chamber received in 1885 in favor of a higher tariff on wheat, not one came from Calabria. In reality, the "combativeness and aggressiveness" of the southern agrarians' lobbying for protectionism in 1885–87, which Carocci takes as evidence of a turnaround in their position,[34] came mainly from the compact group of Sicilian landowners led by Camporeale. Only one Calabrian landowner, Antonio Cefaly, spoke in favor of grain protection, and he was a member of the opposition; not one of the latifondisti—a conspicuous group in Parliament if we count the two Barraccos, Compagna, Chimirri, De Blasii, and Quintieri—did so. *L'Agricultura Meridionale,* the organ of the Landowners and Farmers Association and a bastion of technologically "progressive" latifondism, stuck to its guns: "to weather the crisis, a remedy should have been sought not in import tariffs but in a transformation of the system of cultivation . . ."[35]

The latifondisti's coolness toward protectionist ideas did not escape Rossi, who demagogically stressed it at an Agrarian Defense rally held in Verona in 1887.

> I say the feudalists are against import duties, and I could name quite a few who are also deputies in Parliament and, though large landowners, are not calling for tariffs.[36]

The southern barons and latifondisti remained free traders in 1887 and thereafter. A rather isolated voice, Napoleone Colajanni's, patently irritated by

---

32. In connection with the landowners' associations, see C. Dragoni, "Il movimento di organizzazione di classe fra i proprietari e i conduttori di fondi in Italia," in *L'iniziativa del Re d'Italia e l'Istituto internazionale di agricoltura* (Rome, 1905).

33. Emphasis added. The text of the petition was published in *L'Agricoltura Meridionale,* January 1, 1888, 4–5, and is quoted in L. Izzo, *Agricoltura e classi rurali,* op. cit., 48.

34. G. Carocci, *Agostino Depretis,* op. cit., 450 and note.

35. R. Arcuri, "Aiutiamo l'agricoltura," January 1885, 122. See L. Izzo, *Agricoltura e classi rurali,* op. cit., 63.

36. *L'Agricoltura Veronese* (1887), 4, quoted by L. Musella, in *Proprietà e politica,* op. cit., 36.

the generalizations circulating with regard to the alliance of 1887, made it clear that this group (in which he included also the Sicilian barons) had not contributed at all to the protectionist turn. He cited the names of Quintieri, Barracco, Compagna, Piedimonte d'Alife, Farina, Fortunato, Pavoncelli, De Rudinì, Giusso, Guarnieri, and Maiorana Calatabiano—all latifondisti and deputies from the South and all still resolute free traders (partly, he added, because they had no ideas and no programs).[37] The tariffs, according to Colajanni, were the result of a strictly northern campaign.

> The whole great movement in favor of a protectionist reform of customs duties was exclusively northern: politicians, industrialists and chambers of commerce—organizations that in the Mezzgiorno had barely begun to show signs of life—promoted it in the North, and there was no initiative or contribution from the South.[38]

But, while it is true that the continental latifondisti made no contribution to the enactment of protectionist legislation (unlike the landowning deputies from Sicily, who lobbied strongly for it between 1885 and 1887),[39] they certainly put up no great opposition. When the tariff bill came to a vote in the Senate in April of 1887, and in the Chamber in June, most of the latifondisti lawmakers were absent. Although the "sacrifice of the South" was not made on the initiative of the southern latifondisti, they did provide at least passive support. Why?

First of all, the interests of the so-called agrarian party were far from homogeneous:[40] landlords' interests were different from and often diametrically opposed to tenants', absentee landlords' interests were opposed to those of owner-operators, and northern farmers' interests conflicted with those of their southern counterparts. Moreover, the onset of the crisis was perceived at different times by different groups: At first the downswing in prices mainly hurt tenants whose leases dated from the boom years (this is known as the

---

37. N. Colajanni, *Per l'economia nazionale e pel dazio sul grano* (Rome, 1901), 24–27.

38. Ibid., 26.

39. In 1885, Paolo Acton Beccadelli Di Camporeale moved a resolution in the Chamber of Deputies to set "a temporary, fair import duty on foreign grain." The motion was supported by other Sicilian landowners: Astolfone Filì, Simone Cuccia, Vincenzo Pugliese Giannone, Salvatore Gangitano, Simone Corleo, Biagio Licata di Baucina, Ottavio Nicolacci di Villadorata, Emanuele Antoci, Vincenzo Saporito, Benedetto Emanuele di San Giuseppe, Valentino Caminneci, Ferdinando Firmaturi, Raffaele Palizzolo, Girolamo Coffari, and Francesco Giardina. See Camporeale's speech in the Chamber, February 15, 1885, reprinted in A. De Bernardi, ed., *Questione Agraria,* op. cit., 91.

40. Carocci himself acknowledges this in mentioning the self-serving use both Depretis and Crispi made of these conflicts (*Agostino Depretis,* op. cit., 438ff.), though he partly contradicts himself by affirming that the southern agrarian interests had the power to amalgamate the national bourgeoisie.

"tenants' crisis";[41] only later did it affect absentee landlords whose tenants paid cash rents, along with landlords paid in wheat and, obviously, the small farmers. The high salt tax weighed most heavily on tenants and small farmers, as did the movable property tax, from which landowners were exempt.

The initial impact of falling prices differed from group to group. As we have seen, the large, directly managed, southern estates, where farming investments were low, had a notable capacity to weather hard times, whereas landed property in the North, heavily burdened by mortgages,[42] could not make a profit if prices fell below a certain level. Cash wages weighed much more heavily on the accounts of smaller properties than on large ones and on northern farms more than on southern. There were significant differences even within the southern farmers' group, in which latifondo owner-operators were by no means a majority; in fact, the Sicilian latifondisti were rentiers who, as we have seen, opted for protectionism. Entrepreneurs like the Barraccos in Calabria and the Pavoncellis in Apulia were a minority—a rich, powerful, and politically overrepresented minority but a minority all the same.

To defend its vital and immediate interests, this minority was now forced to seek alliances and compromise. What were those interests? Doubtless the whole conservative group had a common political and ideological interest in forming a solid "rural bloc" to isolate the farm workers' movement: an interest that, in a rhetorical climate that had, as Caporeale put it, "the stink of socialism," made it practically impossible for members to vote in company with the far Left (we shall return to this matter). But in the immediate contingency it was their fundamental economic class interest that prompted the farmers to form a united front.

Four major political issues directly affected the interests of the farming class, including the latifondisti: property tax equalization, the three-tenths war surtax on property, the revised railroad construction plan, and tariffs. The stakes were not the same for everyone. Tax equalization would benefit northern farmers at the expense of their southern counterparts; repeal of the war tax would benefit all farmers; the revised railroad construction plan would hurt all regions south of Rome; and the new tariffs would benefit northern industry and farming, as well as some southern landowners, but it would hurt southern agriculture as a whole and specifically the latifondisti. If, notwithstanding all its internal differences, "the agrarian party . . . had continued and still continued to lobby for its goals with perseverance and skill" and managed to

---

41. On this distinction, and more generally on the various phases of the depression, see P. D'Angelini, "L'Italia al termine," op. cit., 323–65.

42. Mortgage debt encumbered 34 percent of land revenues in Piedmont, 21 percent in Lombardy, 14 percent in the Neapolitan provinces, and 10 percent in Sicily. See L. Musella, *Proprietà e politica,* op. cit., 16.

obtain a majority in key parliamentary committees,[43] it was precisely because political alliances were formed by compromises in which the South's general interests, and some of the latifondisti's immediate interests, were gradually sacrificed.

Land tax equalization for the sake of fiscal justice (according to Carocci, a climax of Depretis's entire political life and philosophy) had been the subject of parliamentary debate ever since Italian unity. The implicit and explicit target of several bills was the tax privilege allegedly enjoyed by southern landowners. Compared to their counterparts in other regions,

> the large southern landowners paid less than their fair share of property tax not only, and not so much, because the property registers of their regions were less accurate and less onerous, but above all because they possessed large quantities of unregistered property, such as the state lands they had misappropriated.[44]

The mishaps that had befallen equalization ever since the days of the governments of the Right are well known. The southern deputies staunchly opposed it, not so much by contesting the principle of a fairly distributed tax burden—that principle, dressed in Risorgimento rhetoric, could hardly be refuted—as by arguing, not without reason, that the tax burden as a whole weighed disproportionately on the South. Accordingly, they demanded a lower property tax, and more specifically repeal of the three-tenths war surtax, as a precondition for equalization. However, the proposed repeal met strong opposition, too, because many lawmakers argued that it would bring little relief to agriculture in general, favoring only the large landowners, and would considerably worsen the nation's already disastrous finances. In a politically astute move, Depretis (and finance minister Magliani in his behalf) succeeded in linking the two measures.[45] In an omnibus law decree submitted in November 1885, the government committed itself to repealing one of the war-tax tenths as of January 1, 1886, but it made repeal of the other two-tenths conditional upon enactment of the equalization law. During the ensuing debate at the beginning of 1886, the government sought to gain the southerners' consent to equaliza-

---

43. A. Plebano, *Storia della finanza italiana nei primi quarant'anni dell'Unificazione* (Turin, 1900; rpt. Padova, 1960), 2:336, 338. But Plebano, like Carocci later, saw "the vigilant party of the agrarians, connected with the Southern delegation," as a homogeneous and compact political force.

44. G. Carocci, *Agostino Depretis,* op. cit., 429 and note. But, according to S. F. Romano, taxes on southern properties amounted to 16 percent. (*Momenti del Risorgimento in Sicilia* [Messina and Florence, 1952]).

45. Magliani made the linkage explicit in a speech he delivered in the Chamber on behalf of the government: "what is most important to note is that abatement of the tenths cannot be decreed in the present situation of unequal taxation" (A. Plebano, *Storia della finanza,* op. cit., 250.

tion by offering to repeal the second tenth as of July 1, 1887, and the third as of July 1, 1888. In short, if the agrarians hoped to obtain tax relief, they would have to present a united front against the opposition, and if they wanted the government's support, they would have to accept its terms: no tax reduction without equalization. The southerners capitulated.

> And certainly no one could complain that granting faster and greater relief to overtaxed property would help remove a serious and dangerous cause of possible squabbling among the Italian regions. And the trick worked: the equalization law . . . was put through on February 5, 1886, with the landowners' vote.[46]

Another contingent reason for the southerners' submission was their need of support from other agrarians on the railroad issue. In view of the tight financial situation, the government proposed to cut back and slow down its ambitious railroad construction plan. But such a retrenchment, at a time when the railroad system south of Rome—already inferior to that of the rest of Italy at unity—was allocated only half the amount of public investment as were the northern railroads, would have constituted direct and explicit discrimination against the South and would have hurt the interests of export farming in general, and the interests of the latifondisti in particular.[47] The southern land-owners, who needed allies to defend the interests of their region and their class, were forced to compromise.

This was the setting—with the railroad issue still pending, and the threat of a reinstated war tax (or suspension of the repeal) in the air—in which the issue of tariffs, especially the wheat tariff, must be seen. In April of 1887, with the news of the massacre of Italian troops at Dogali still fresh, and in the midst of general concern about the worsening of public finances, the government (represented by Finance Minister Magliani) argued that the pressing and imperative need for revenue called for new and effective resources. Appealing to

---

46. Ibid., 280. At any rate, Plebano expressed a very poor opinion of the government's handling of taxation (and not only taxation). He saw in it "the antithesis between proposals logically deduced from the principles of healthy public finance and those imposed by politics . . ." (Ibid., 251).

47. Rocco De Zerbi, a complex character who often made common cause with Calabrian latifondism, conducted a fierce battle against the bill in Parliament, denouncing its discriminatory character and citing incontrovertible data (see ibid., 308):

	Expected Expense for the Lines Authorized by the Law	Appropriated in the Budget	Spent or Committed
North of Rome	408,875,000	203,047,227	540,932,007
South of Rome	578,674,000	158,562,254	247,822,548

the spirit of sacrifice, he introduced an emergency bill, which included two measures: suspension of the repeal of the second and third tenths of the war tax on property, and the modification in import duties, that is the introduction of the grain tariff.[48] The wheat tariff was presented simultaneously as compensation to agrarians for reimposition of the war tax and—somewhat contrariwise—as a purely fiscal measure. In the midst of a widely shared "comeback spirit" skillfully exploited by Crispi, the latifondisti found themselves caught in a pollitical squeeze. Firmly opposed to both the war taxes and the tariffs, they could not fight a whole tangle of interlocking interests at once: those of the government in its attempt to cope with the budget, those of the northern industrialists who were demanding maximum protection even for the weakest industries (cf. the minister Ellena's report), and those of the segment of the agrarian party that was demanding tariffs as "a matter of justice for the agricultural industry, which, in a country where all industries are protected, also has a right to protection."[49] Unable to stand against everything at once, the latifondisti opted once more to defend their immediate interests and cooperated to recompose the unity of the agrarian party, making it possible for them to defeat the government's war-tax bill on a committee vote. In exchange for the southerners' passive support on tariffs, expressed by their absence during the vote, the northerners gave theirs on the railroad issue. Thus it was that in June of 1887 the wheat tariff passed by a large majority in the Chamber.[50]

This complicated battle of interests was played out, as we mentioned, in a flood of rhetoric on the feared social and political repercussions of the crisis. Alessandro Rossi insisted, in his speeches, on the general advantage the political establishment would gain by protecting agriculture; according to the small landowners, protection would shield them from socialist influences. In other words, the agrarians were being asked to bear some little sacrifice in order to isolate the farm workers' movement. The government, it was said, was counting on the loyalty of the landowners, "on whom it now had to rely in view of the spread of socialism among the masses."[51] Use of this rhetoric tied the

---

48. According to Corbino, the government linked the proposal for restoring the two-tenths to the proposal on import duties "in order to mask the measure's protective character" (E. Corbino, *Annali dell'Economia Italiana,* op. cit., 94).

49. The words are Ascanio Branca's (see A. Plebano, *Storia della finanza,* op. cit., 337). A free trader in 1885, he became spokesman for the protectionist agrarian interests in 1887 but with the idea of coping with the faits accomplis. While he recognized the need for new tax revenues, Branca preferred the import duty to the flour tax (or, rather, he thought it "a tax that will let you put back the flour tax in some other form").

50. I. Pauli, *Leggi e lotte elettorali, 1848–1948* (Rome, 1953); A. Caracciolo, *Il Parlamento* (Milan, 1960); N. Rodolico, *Storia del Parlamento Italiano* (Palermo, 1903); D. Capecelatro Gaudio, *Reazione a Napoli dopo l'Unità* (Naples, 1974); T. Pedio, *Vita politica in Italia Meridionale* (Potenza, 1966).

51. E. Corbino, *Annali,* op. cit., 3:96.

hands of the traditionally conservative latifondisti; though fairly indifferent to this issue (farm workers' organizations had not yet appeared in Calabria, and the "farming class," Cefaly assured the Chamber, "was an element of order and conservation") and embittered by the government's ploy, they could hardly vote against it in company with the opposition.[52] In reality, both sides—free traders and protectionists—used the stalking horse of socialism in the debate on the agricultural crisis. Free trader Tommaso Galanti argued that free access to American wheat "was saving Europe from famine and also helped slow the spread of socialist ideas,"[53] while Camporeale sniffed "a certain stink of socialism" in such theories, and Egisto Rossi (Alexander Rossi's secretary) affirmed that the tariff was a measure capable of "preventing a revolution that might drag the country into a social catastrophe."[54] The agrarians may also have been allured by the "Prussian way" (in one speech, Camporeale referred explicitly to Bismarck's protectionism), but in the end they adhered to a simpler political calculation: when in doubt, vote with the government and against the opposition. In fact, this was latifondism's most "governophile" period, on the one hand because of the growing importance of formal political institutions and on the other because they needed government support on local matters, from patronage to railroads and public works. As the prefect of Catanzaro noted in 1885,

> [T]he constitutional party . . . is divided into two parts, which take the name of government side and opposition side.[55]

As Gramsci rightly remarked, this political climate provided an ideal humus for Crispi, who, exploiting the general fear of social disorder,

> teamed up with the Sicilian latifondisti . . . at the same time that his general policy was tending to strengthen northern industrialists with the tariff war against France and protection against imports; he did not hesti-

52. Quoted in G. Cingari, *Storia della Calabria,* op. cit., p. 110. Thirty years later, the Nitti investigation confirmed Cefaly's statement: "Calabria is the region where no one ever goes on strike." The first congress of Calabrian workers—the Congress of Mutual Aid Societies—was held only in 1896, and even here the presence of peasants and farm laborers was nil. The first time any explicitly socialist speeches were delivered was at the Nicastro Convention, in 1908, by Enrico Mastracchi's group. See G. Mastroianni, "Il movimento operaio," op. cit., 793–807.

53. "Agricoltura americana ed agricoltura italiana," in A. De Bernardi, ed., *Questione agraria,* op. cit., 45.

54. *Stati Uniti e concorrenza americana* (Florence, 1884), quoted in ibid., 56ff.

55. He went on to list the members of the two parties in the Chamber and Senate; in both, the latifondisti formed a compact progovernment group. See G. Cingari, *Storia della Calabria,* op. cit., 122.

tate to throw the South and the islands into a fearsome commercial crisis . . .[56]

These were the trade-offs that made the latifondisti accomplices to the "sacrifice of the South" rendered with the introduction of the grain tariff—the plundering of the rural South by Italy's politicians, as Jacini bitterly observed. In the last analysis, "this sovereign remedy" (in Supino's ironic phrase) benefitted only northern farmers[57] and the treasury. The former were able to boost wheat production 23 percent over the 1870–74 output (the South's fell 43 percent in the same period; cf. table 24), the latter took in 365 million lire extra in one decade (customs revenues rose from 16 million lire in 1886–87 to 64 million in 1895–96).

Nonetheless, the latifondisti were far from being the major victims of the protectionist policy. On the contrary, latifondism alone in the plundered South managed to adapt to the new situation in a new way by making radical changes throughout its productive and social organization—in other words, by reacting with a structural response to the challenge of the European "crisis."[58]

5. From the Guarantist Latifondo to the Capitalist Latifondo

The major problem facing the latifondisti during the period of the so-called crisis was once again that of declining income. The Barraccos were hardly in real financial straits, but by the end of the century, liabilities on their Calabrian properties had climbed to 1,816,000 lire (equal to almost a third of their equity), palaces and properties were run down, and Guglielmo Barracco—still the family member most involved in administering its affairs—was demanding strong remedial action. But, if the problem was the same as before, the remedies could not be. The latifondisti could no longer respond to falling revenues by increasing output; on the one hand, the traditional way of achieving such an increase, by acquiring cheap new land, was no longer feasible (due to the unavailability of church lands and the new property tax), and on the other hand that response was not viable in a saturated market. New ways would have to be found for the latifondo to function within the post-1887 Italian economy. Not all latifondisti succeeded in this; the Mollos and the Ferrari d'Epaminondas (to take two examples from among the most powerful families) saw their fortunes wane. But the more aggressive ones—the Barraccos, the Berlingieris, and the Compagnas—set out to seek new solutions.

---

56. *Quaderni dal Carcere,* ed. V. Gerratana (Turin, 1975), 3:2018 (*Quaderno* 19).

57. In his gloss on an article by Salvatore Valitutti, Gramsci wrote that "agrarian protectionism benefitted the North more than the South, because it protected grain, of which the North was a great producer (relatively more than the South)" Ibid., 1804–5 [*Quaderno* 15]).

58. See B. Chimirri, *La Calabria e gli interessi del Mezzogiorno,* 2 vols. (Milan, 1915–19).

In the emblematic case of the Barraccos, the new solution was to make qualitative and quantitative transformations in the latifondo's production and in its social organization—transformations that in the long run gave rise to a completely new structure. The changes were essentially three: a scaling down of production, an upgrading of product quality and "modernization" of production processes, and a transformation of labor relations and control. To the extent that changes of this kind had already been successfully implemented in the precrisis years, the solution was not altogether new, but now, becoming predominant, these changes defined the very character of the new latifondo.

In the 1880s and 1890s, the Barraccos downsized every single line of production on the latifondo. Logically enough, the first victim was grain production, which was reduced by altering the same factor—planted acreage—used to increase it in the past. The Barraccos sold no land—that would have been contrary to the gentleman-latifondista tradition—but they stopped cultivating marginal land (poor in quality or inconveniently located) and reduced it to pasture, yielded in decades-old lawsuits over public lands,[59] and reduced the number of masserie, closing the one in San Leonardo and drastically downsizing the one in Castella. The energies released from grain raising were not applied to other sectors that were likewise being cut back. The reorganization and downsizing of sheep raising that had begun in the previous decade continued in the latter part of the century; the Campolongo flock of coarse-wooled sheep was sold en bloc in 1898, leaving the latifondo with only one of the five flocks it had owned in the past. The old licorice works in Neto, which the Barraccos had operated since 1812, was shut down in 1891, and the Amantea works, which had been in service for only a score of years, had been closed some time before, so that at the end of the century only the San Pietro works was still operating and licorice output was down by half. In 1888, the Barraccos began to shut down their oil presses, too—the huge old works in Polligrone and the smaller ones in Trigani, Cupo, Cardinale, and Lupia—and the output of the Pidocchiella and Altilia presses was halved. By the end of the century, the aggregate output of the remaining presses—at Altilia, Rivioti, Forestella, Pidocchiella, and Petrizia—had fallen to around 30 percent of the 1870s average (or one-sixth of the figure for 1887, a bumper year).

---

59. This was the period in which the family lost or abandoned many lawsuits involving public property (though some would drag on for another hundred years): against the township of Rocca di Neto in 1882 (another suit against this town was settled only in 1961), against Rocca Bernarda in 1879, against Taverna in 1877, and against Cutro in 1896. This fact can also be seen as indicating an ebbing of the family's fiery spirit described in chapter 1. Probably both explanations are valid: part of the reason the family was now defending the common rights it had usurped less energetically was that it needed them less, considering the reductions in crop and livestock production.

The reduction of output proceeded hand in hand with further specialization and "modernization." More and more of the smaller acreage was planted in prime white wheat and, starting in 1890, only in "French wheat." The remaining masserie were equipped with Bodin and Bodin-Cantoni seeders, steel plows, Alen plow-harrowers, and steam threshers. The Marina flock—the only one left—consisted solely of merino, Swiss, and Rambouillet sheep. The cattle administration took pains with its public image, showing prize stock at local fairs and at the national fair held in Palermo in 1892. Contraction of the olive oil market after the 1887 tariff law, as well as growing competition from seed and mineral oils, forced the Barraccos to upgrade their oil production as well; they installed new Mure presses at the remaining works, tried extraction from heated olives, and showed their products at the 1894 oil exhibition in Milan. The one licorice works still in operation was equipped with mechanical rollers and tannin extractors, and greater attention was paid to product quality.

Lastly—and this was the real unspoken dimension of the whole process of modernization—the latifondo enterprise radically transformed the old labor contracts, with repercussions the extent of which the owners themselves may not have fully realized.[60] As we have seen, the elimination of multiuse leases for the sake of productivity and rational management had already deprived the workers of access to land, while crop specialization led to a gradual monetization of wages and the disappearance of remuneration in kind. These new features, which had first appeared in the previous decades, became more marked as a result of the crisis, when the Barraccos, like all European landowners, opted for labor efficiency, thereby causing far-reaching changes in labor relations.[61] Numerically speaking, the regular workforce decreased by a further 27 percent over the decade from 1880 to 1889 (see table 9), and, as table 25 shows, hiring was drastically reduced as well (152 people hired in the 1880s, as against 311 in the 1850s). And, qualitatively speaking, three new aspects came to characterize relations with the remaining workers: monetization, the demise of the guarantee system, and anonymity.

As will be recalled, the monetization of nominal wages began in the 1860s, but now even real wages were monetary. Employees were paid a flat

---

60. G. Galasso takes the opposite view: "in the hands of the dominant rural classes, the practice of increasing land rent by perpetuating and sometimes warping the ancient contractual forms that centuries of feudalism had spread throughout the South continued to be one of the main tools for consolidating their position" (*Mezzogiorno medievale e moderno* [Turin, 1975], 35).

61. "The main incentive to change," writes Eric Hobsbawm, "came from the well-known tendency of profit-margin to decline in the Great Depression. . . . Whether pressure from competition or from labour was more important in turning employers' thoughts towards labour efficiency is uncertain" (*Labouring Men,* op. cit., 421). The same change in labor relations was taking place at the same time on the great estates of Mexico (J. Bazant, *Cinco haciendas mexicanas* [Mexico City, 1975]) and Russia (S. Bensidoun, "L'évolution des grands domaines en Russie de 1861 à 1902," *Revue du Nord* 54 [1972]: 173–84).

TABLE 25. First-time Hirings on the Barracco Latifondo (by decades)

Decade	No. Hired
1801–19	178
1820–29	182
1830–39	321
1840–49	297
1850–59	311
1860–69	286
1870–79	231
1880–89	152
1890–99	67

cash wage with no supply of commodities (no more pork distribution at Carnival time, no more ricotta cheese for shepherds, no shoes, and no wool). In consequence, wage payment became a more formal process; advances against future earnings and aid (in cash and commodities) during the off-season were a thing of the past. Now a worker was paid only for and by the months he actually put in at a job, with an "earnest" at hiring time and a "balance" at month's-end. Moreover, debt was no longer tolerated. A flat cash wage, though higher than before (as is commonly known, farm wages were rising throughout Italy during this period), was all a man could expect from the latifondo.[62]

Clearly, the monetization of wage relations further vitiated the guarantee system, already suffering from the reorganization of land use and the elimination of heterogeneous tenures, which had wiped out its ability to produce subsistence and perpetuate peasant status. But the knockout blow came from the reduction in the scale of operations, which destroyed the system's keystone: job security.

It will be remembered that very few people were ever dismissed on the old Barracco latifondo: all told, only 32—an average of 6 per decade—during the first half-century of its existence, up to 1860 (table 26). This rule changed radically after 1860; from that time to 1889, the number soared to 215, or 70 per decade, a more than tenfold increase. Moreover, dismissals were now definitive. In the past, 3 out of every 4 men fired eventually returned to work on the latifondo, but now returnees were as scarce as hen's teeth (see table 13). Considering the now high frequency of dismissals, the administrators felt less obliged to state the reasons, something they had always done before. The offenses—disobedience, drunkenness, brawling, bearing weapons without a

62. See S. F. Romano, "Lo sviluppo dell'agricoltura meridionale e i contratti agrari," *Cronache meridionali* (September 1955): 566–69, 571–73; and P. M. Arcari, "Le variazioni dei salari agricoli in Italia dalla fondazione del Regno al 1933," in *Annali di Statistica,* ser. 4, 36 (1936).

TABLE 26.   Reasons for Definitive Severance

Reason	1811–19	1820–29	1830–39	1840–49	1850–59	1860–69	1870–79	1880–89	1890– →	Total
Change in qualifications	0	2	23	21	12	14	25	3	1	101
Emigration	0	0	0	0	0	1	4	8	8	21
Conscription	0	0	0	0	0	1	3	8	4	16
Prison	0	0	0	0	1	3	2	1	0	7
Sickness	0	1	0	0	0	0	0	4	0	5
Death	1	2	6	8	22	31	25	23	27	145
Dismissal for other reasons	1	0	1	11	19	69	98	48	40	287
Resignation	1	3	40	80	152	132	65	36	29	538
Total	3	8	70	120	216	251	222	131	108	1130

permit, theft, or carelessness on the job—were the same as before, revealing not so much a change in workers' behavior as the management's exercise of greater control and discipline. Moreover, workers could now be fired for reasons that had nothing to do with their jobs. For instance, having been found guilty of a crime not involving the business of the latifondo led to dismissal in 7 cases after 1860, whereas only 1 case of the kind had occurred in the previous half-century. Furthermore, it became harder for a man to get his job back after military service; 12 draftees lost theirs after 1870, as against only 1 in the six previous decades. Lastly, after 1880 the latifondo began laying off sick and injured workers who in earlier days would have simply been assigned less strenuous work. During the same period in which it was breaking the tradition of job security, the latifondo also ceased to act as mediator and provider of services. A worker could no longer go to the latifondo's own lawyer, notary, or doctor, procure a gun permit, or buy medicine with the master contributing his customary "third."

All this could hardly fail to affect the way the workers perceived their jobs on the latifondo, characterized as they now were by an unprecedented anonymity. A worker hired at a flat wage entered the Barraccos' employ solely as a seller of working time, while his whole social existence, formerly so tightly bound up with the latifondo structure, was now outside the sphere of labor relations. In addition, the new employment relationship was strictly individual; there was no longer any hope of getting one's children and/or relatives onto the payroll.[63] The kinship networks that had played so important a part in assuring

---

63. Alexandr Chayanov emphasized the fact that peasant families frequently found themselves with temporary surpluses of labor and the importance of their satisfying the need to employ these extra members: "since the subjective significance of its satisfaction is valued higher than the burden of labor necessary for such satisfaction, the peasant family will work for a smaller re-

peace on the latifondo began to break down; in the decade from 1850 to 1859, there were eighty-four "family groups" of two or more relatives (father and sons, brothers and brothers-in-law), but the number dwindled to thirty-three from 1870 to 1879, to seven in the 1880s, and to barely three in the last decade of the century (see table 16). This meant the total disappearance from the latifondo of the lineages of cattle and hog drivers, massari, overseers, shepherds, and agents who for generations had handed down their jobs and their know-how, and also their loyalty, to the Barraccos. In consequence, the new latifondo, no longer able to rely on the traditional patriarcal sources of authority and control, had to increase surveillance. As part of the growing anonymity of social relationships, the Barraccos' place in their social territory changed, too, becoming an absence more than a presence; for instance, they ceased to attend the great fairs and no longer contributed to local charities.[64] In short, the new latifondo took on a harsher, more repressive, and threatening aspect.

Yet the transformations made by the Barraccos were representative of a new dynamism then appearing in a segment of the latifondo class in many parts of the continental South. From the Apulian plain to the hinterland of Naples and Croton, they had accomplished the modernization of many great wheat-and-stock-raising enterprises.[65] The Barraccos, like the Pavoncellis and the Berlingieris, took actions rationally aimed at preserving their own fortunes and class privileges. From the standpoint of economic performance, their activism was crowned with success. The new management, which now employed college graduates in economics, was energetic and able; specialized products found outlets (admittedly limited) in the domestic market; and technical progress continued.[66]

But in making these transformations the latifondisti unwittingly set in motion a process of capitalist transformation of the latifondo system itself, and

---

muneration that would be definitely unprofitable in a capitalist economy" ("Socio-Economic Nature," op. cit., 144–45).

64. In 1878, the Barraccos informed the abbess of the Croton Orphan Asylum that "they no longer wish to contribute" the fifty ducats a year they had been giving for decades to support two orphan girls, though they would continue to use orphan labor for spinning flax and weaving sacks, bedsheets, and tablecloths. While they had "aided" the widows and orphans of their own employees during the great cholera epidemic of 1866–67, during the "fucina" epidemic of 1886–88 they were neither seen nor heard.

65. See the discussions of the "laborious" emergence of this core of new productive forces in A. Cormio, "La crisi agraria e la svolta del 1887," in *Problemi di storia delle campagne meridionali,* ed. A. Massafra (Bari, 1981), 539–67; and P. Bevilacqua, "Uomini, terre, economie," in *La Calabria,* op. cit., esp. 249–65. From this standpoint, one exemplary estate was the Pavoncellis' in Apulia. See G. Pavoncelli, "La vigna in Puglia," in *La Puglia* (quoted in A. Cormio, "La crisi agraria," op. cit., 549n, 550, 554); F. De Felice, *L'agricoltura in Terra di Bari dal 1880 al 1914* (Milan, 1971); and F. Snowden, *Violence and Great Estates,* op. cit. (Snowden mistakenly treats the Pavoncelli estate as an exception in the South).

66. On this point, see M. Rossi Doria, "L'evoluzione delle campagne meridionali," *Nord e Sud* 5 (April 1955).

of its social territory, engendering contradictions in the political and social sphere that were to prove insurmountable a few decades later and led to the system's demise. In fact, in the long run the transformations made the latifondo extremely vulnerable socially, politically, and even economically. By sweeping away the traditional contracts and partnerships, and all the elements of the guarantee system, they simplified social relations within the latifondo structure. The only bond remaining between the masters and the mass of employees was the objective and impersonal one between buyers and sellers of working time. And, since there was now nothing else to tie a worker to the latifondo and emigration flows were swelling, the owner encountered growing difficulty in recruiting hands. Moreover, the new relationship was by definition antagonistic and, given the right occasion, could become explosive.

In the second place, the transformations further increased the market dependence of both the latifondo and its workers. As the enterprise came to operate on a strictly monetary basis, its economy not only depended more and more on the availability of outlets for its products, but it had to take much greater account of market prices. Moreover, since the workers' subsistence now depended solely on the buying power of their wages, they were emboldened to voice protest and fight for better pay. Even back in the 1870s, protests against the flour tax (the notorious "hunger tax") had been directed not, as one might expect, against government agents but, significantly, against the Barraccos and their gristmills. In fact, the old minatico of rye "to be ground at the master's expense" was replaced by a cash wage that had to cover both grain purchases and the tax payable at the mill.[67] In short, the new latifondo, like any other capitalist enterprise, was vulnerable both economically and socially. The race to modernize and its liberal-unitarian confidence had stripped it of all protection not only against market fluctuations but against the adverse effects of national commercial and fiscal policies.

Thus it was that the latifondo system—not the latifondo per se but the economic and social structure that, guided by laws of its own making, had ruled parts of the South throughout the nineteenth century[68]—waned at the end of the century amid "warnings, and portents and evils imminent": phylloxera, which destroyed the vineyards; oil flies, which decimated the olive groves; and the earthquake of 1894. The downfall of the old system released and speeded

---

67. G. Fioretti, *Pane, governo e tasse in Italia* (Naples, 1898). For the earlier centuries, see S. Di Bella, *Grano, mulini, baroni nella Calabria moderna e contemporanea* (Cosenza, 1979). In 1880, women were demanding 1.25 lire a day to work in the Barraccos' spinning mills in the Sila, though the pay in Cosenza was only eighty-five centimes; in fact, the wages paid in the Sila had to cover everything from food to lodging.

68. M. Rossi Doria, too, sees in the classic latifondo a true system in the sense of its interweaving a social structure and an economic system into a fabric in which "each element is inseparable from all the others and from the mechanism governing their interaction, which preserves and constantly reproduces the overall arrangement according to what might be called its own laws" ("Strutture e problemi dell'agricoltura meridionale," in *Riforma agraria*, op. cit., 9).

the transformations under way in its once tradition-bound and compact social territory, as evidenced on the one hand by the extremely rapid increase of emigration[69] and on the other by the development of mutual assistance associations, the foundation of a Chamber of Labor in Catanzaro (the only branch in the South outside Naples), and the short-lived but intense struggles of 1898.[70]

The traditional latifondo system was not an immediate economic victim of the so-called agricultural crisis. Rather, it declined because the "crisis," by making it harder to market the latifondo's products, spurred the owners into an economic dynamism that completed the process of capitalist transformation touched off by the legal reforms of the French decade.[71] In its eighty years of existence, the latifondo system had successfully blended the traditional and the modern with great and autonomous rationality; when it cast the modernist lot, it dug its own grave. The system expired without heirs; the capitalist latifondo that took its place never possessed or attempted to develop the cohesive mechanisms of a true and proper socioeconomic system. The system's demise rent the social fabric of old Calabria; like any other laceration, it was painful, and, like any other laceration, it opened the way to hidden or suppressed forces and tissues.

---

69. A hundred and five people emigrated from the province of Catanzaro in 1876, 142 in 1880, 1,581 in 1885, 5,092 in 1888, 8,733 in 1893, and 10,420 in 1900: an increase of 10,000 percent over twenty years! See Ministry of Agriculture, Industry, and Commerce, Division of Statistics, *Statistica della Emigrazione all'estero* (Rome), yearly volumes. See also P. Sitta, *Emigrazione e popolazione rurale in Italia* (Rome, 1900); G. Scalise, *L'emigrazione dalla Calabria: Saggio di demografia sociale* (Naples, 1905); G. Rosoli, ed., *Un secolo di emigrazione italiana, 1876–1976* (Rome, 1978); Z. Ciuffoletti and M. degl'Innocenti, *L'emigrazione nella storia d'Italia,* 2 vols. (Florence, 1978); R. Gonnard, *L'émigration européenne au XIXième siècle* (Paris, 1906); F. Coletti, "Dell'emigrazione italiana," in *Cinquant'anni di storia italiana* (Rome, 1911), 3:216ff.; and I. Glazier and L. De Rosa, eds., *Migration Across Time and Nations* (Boston, 1986).

70. On the limits of the original mutual-aid movement inspired by "social concord," on its radicalization, and on the peasant question, see G. Mastroianni, "Il movimento operaio," op. cit. See also F. Renda, *Il movimento contadino in Sicilia e la fine del blocco agrario nel Mezzogiorno* (Bari, 1976); and A. L. Denitto, F. Grassi, and C. Pasimeni, *Mezzogiorno e crisi di fine secolo (capitalismo e movimento contadino)* (Lecce, 1978), on similar phenomena in Apulia. For another point of view, see L. Zinzi, *Proprietari e contadini in Calabria* (Rome, 1919). In 1883, Leopoldo Franchetti was already denouncing that spoliation of the peasantry of which the Italian government, together with all the political parties, including the far Left, was both author and accomplice (*Sulle condizioni dei lavoratori agricoli, interpellanza parlamentare, 1883* [Rome, 1883]).

71. In his study of the Borghese properties, G. Pescosolido observes similar mechanisms: in response to the crisis of the 1880s, the princes—traditionally innovators—had significantly improved their latifondo, thereby digging their own graves.

Index